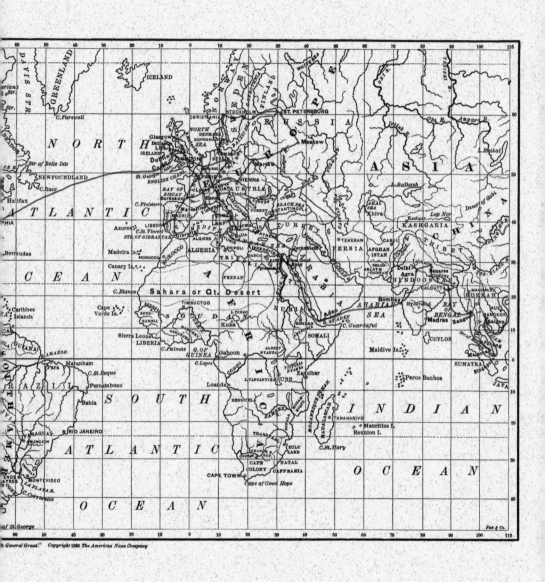

Around the World with General Grant

DESIGNED & ENGRAVED BY WM. E. MARSHALL.
FOR
"AROUND THE WORLD WITH GENERAL GRANT".

JOHN RUSSELL YOUNG

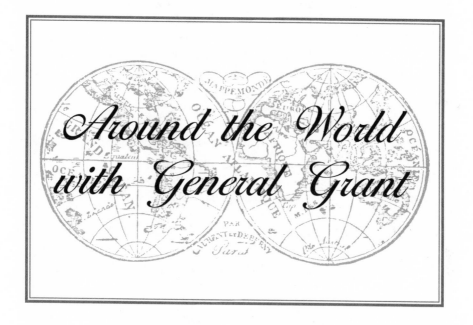

Around the World with General Grant

Abridged, Edited, and Introduced by

MICHAEL FELLMAN

THE JOHNS HOPKINS UNIVERSITY PRESS

Baltimore and London

Originally published by the American News Company,
Subscription Book Department, New York, 1879.

© 2002 The Johns Hopkins University Press
All rights reserved. Published 2002
Printed in the United States of America on acid-free paper

2 4 6 8 9 7 5 3 1

The Johns Hopkins University Press
2715 North Charles Street
Baltimore, Maryland 21218-4363
www.press.jhu.edu

Library of Congress Cataloging-in-Publication Data
Young, John Russell, 1841–1899.
Around the world with General Grant / by John Russell Young ; abridged,
edited, and introduced by Michael Fellman.
p. cm.
ISBN 0-8018-6950-1 (hardcover : alk. paper)
1. Voyages around the world.   2. Grant, Ulysses S. (Ulysses Simpson),
1822–1885—Journeys.   3. Young, John Russell, 1841–1899—Journeys.
I. Fellman, Michael.   II. Title.
G440.G7 .Y7   2002
910.4'1—DC21   2001006619

A catalog record for this book is available from the British Library.

Frontispiece: Gen. Ulysses S. Grant

In memory of Robert H. Wiebe, mentor and friend

CONTENTS

ACKNOWLEDGMENTS

Material support for this project was provided by the Social Science and Humanities Research Council of Canada. Lynn Gorchov, my able research assistant, also compiled the index. From beginning to end, Bob Brugger of Johns Hopkins University Press has been a prince among editors.

This book is dedicated to the memory of Bob Wiebe, my once and always mentor. Unhappily, this is the first book of mine that he will not have a chance to read, but his spirit of independence and tough-minded affirmation will always light my path.

INTRODUCTION

W hat was the departing president to do? He was still a vigorous fifty-five, and, despite all the scandals of his administration, he remained vastly admired by the American public. He wanted to stay out of the hair of his successor, a man he heartily disliked, yet he wished to remain in the public eye in some politically unthreatening but highly visible manner. Also, he was restless in his unsated, if only partly conscious, desire to live life to the full. And so, much as Teddy Roosevelt would do thirty-two years later when confronted with a similar problem, on May 17, 1877, less than three months after he completed his second term in the White House, Ulysses S. Grant sailed out of Philadelphia on the warship "Indiana" for a long voyage abroad.

In Grant's party were his wife, Julia, whom he adored, his youngest son, Jesse, and several old friends, including James Russell Young of the *New York Herald*. They intended to do Europe up right, but they had no clear plans beyond that, nor did they know how long they would be gone. What transpired was a trip around the world that lasted more than two and one-half years—all done in the height of style. The American navy laid on the best and biggest warships much of the time; foreign governments, foreign peoples, and Americans abroad greeted Grant with never-ending acclaim and ceaseless banquets. If anything, Grant, the victorious military guardian of American liberty, proved to be even more popular abroad than he was at home. And so his voyage was a public event more than a private excursion, well covered in the press abroad and at home, particularly in the *New York Herald*. Although nothing he said or did on his trip was remarkable, he was out in the world being adulated, and this made for good political capital back home. Americans have always been eager to be admired, keen to believe that everyone in their secret hearts wants to be just like Americans, even if they cannot bring themselves to immigrate to the Promised

Land. Grant was their avatar, not the superior personality but the successful Everyman.

And a solid fellow he was, too, packing 184 pounds on his five-foot seven-inch frame, 50 more pounds than he had carried during the war. When we learn about the eating customs of well-bred Victorians, as we do at length in this book, it is no wonder that all those late-nineteenth-century presidents were so stout. John Russell Young, at thirty-seven, was built just like Grant, and he also wore a closely cropped beard. And both men shared a sense of the superiority of the United States that travel, of course, only confirmed. When they finally got home in 1879, Young cobbled together his newspaper pieces with his journals and spun off a two-volume account, abridged here, that sold very well indeed. Young entertained his American readers with accounts of court life and street life in the European nations from which their ancestors—and often their parents and they themselves—had come, as well as immersing them, through pen sketches, in even more distant and exotic lands.

Young's book is well worth reading, in part because of the considerable liveliness of his prose and the strikingly high quality of the engravings that accompany the text. Young's powers of description were impressive. Of even greater importance is that he reflected the values carried through life by self-made men of the broad American middle class, including Young and Grant. In a sense, these were semi-educated and rather uncultivated innocents abroad (and thus it is somewhat ironic that Grant read Mark Twain's book of that title while on the oceans wide). Decadence, whether of European royalty or Indian dancing girls, both titillated and alarmed them, and when they found themselves luxuriating in the sensuality of tropical evenings, they grew somewhat nervous with their own sense of release from common sense, hard work, and duty. Both the attraction and the withdrawal color this text with a fascinating and revealing ambivalence.

However tentative they may have remained concerning cultural alternatives to their down-to-earth Americanism, Young and Grant commented quite fully, and sometimes incisively, on the political structures and processes of the lands they were visiting. As rough and tumble as their own Grand Old Party was becoming, European power politics seemed even more ruthless—always on the brink of revolution or war—and European aristocrats seemed both alluring in their charm and sophistication and repellent in their haughty class consciousness. Then, when they traveled through the Middle East and Asia, the Grant party also confronted European imperialism (particularly, of course, of the British variety) in its full force. Again, the Yankee reactions were a mixture of repulsion and at-traction: repulsion from the nakedly grasping brutality of European dom-ination and attraction for the sheer energy and power of it all. They be-lieved that Americans could relate to the world in a far more open and gentle manner, creating ties through trade rather than conquest. And yet, even if they could not fully acknowledge it and despite their considerable outrage over the oppression they observed, they shared an irreducible and often unstated sense of cultural and racial superiority with their fellow Westerners far more than they felt solidarity with the conquered peoples of the world. This tension is one of the most significant themes of this book. After all, the imperialistic conquest of the Philippines was only two decades away, and that experience would only reinforce American am-bivalence, verging on hypocrisy, about entering the race for empire.

In addition to a vivid travelogue and a long commentary on the state of European power politics and Western imperialism, Young's book also con-tains the most sustained and candid reflections Grant ever made about himself and the men and events of his life and times. While crossing vast oceans, Grant and Young had lots of time on their hands, and so the jour-nalist got the famously taciturn man to ramble in a highly gossipy way that revealed far more of his beliefs, fears, and hopes than anything he later ex-pressed in his famously close-to-the-vest memoirs. These "conversations"—highly interesting for historians and readers of history alike—are reprinted in full in this volume.

Writing his own memoirs, many years after Grant's death, Young con-cluded that Grant's reputedly silent nature was in fact the product of a pro-found shyness that "surrounded Grant as with a mist, so that it was hard to make him out. It was the basis of many of the misconceptions of his char-acter,—that he was a dull man . . . stolid, indifferent, commonplace." Grant could be silent for hours on end, Young conceded, and yet at other times his conversation could be "incessant, brilliant, penetrating." Although Grant's musings in this book may lack the brilliance Young attributed to them, they are quite cool, candid, and revealing in their observations of the other actors in Grant's life. Although Grant remained essentially kind in his chats, Young was not off the mark when he concluded that "no one who ever deceived him ever regained his confidence." There is a hard steel of judgment underlying the bonhomie of Grant's assessments of others. At the same time, Grant frequently betrayed a lack of self-confidence, de-spite all his success and fame. It was as if the prewar failure could never quite believe the enormous good fortune that had come to him through his generalship. And so at times Grant appeared to be sleepwalking through the world, doggedly doing all he was expected to do, duty bound even in recreation, but with a curiously aloof, never fully engaged persona.

Grant's lack of self-certainty was a cultural as well as a personal phenomenon. Americans abroad, even elite Americans, were prickly about their reception in Europe, where aristocrats had admitted some bourgeois men and women to their ranks and yet still dominated high society. Often with good reason, Americans abroad feared that those self-defined noblemen and their ladies of ancient families looked down on plain, born-yesterday Americans. This awareness and the constant edginess it induced runs like a steady stream of wariness and anticipated resentment beneath this jolly travel account, beginning when the "Indiana" first discharged its famous visitor in Britain.

In his 1887 book concerning Grant's last years, Adam Badeau—who was Grant's aide during the war and his official biographer afterward and who, as a member of the American legation in England during Grant's visit, was usually at his side—commented more explicitly and bitterly about Grant's initial reception among the blue bloods of England than Young revealed in this book. At a reception given by the Prince of Wales, Young observed an absolutely classic act of snobbery: "The Prince presented General Grant to the Earl of Dudley, one of the worst-bred men in any company in any country; and his lordship . . . put his hands behind him and simply acknowledged his Prince's introduction with a slight bow . . . said not a word and left the group. It was by far the most marked impertinence General Grant had received in sixteen years." The prince himself had been "perfectly affable and genial," Badeau recalled, but ever insistent on maintaining "etiquette . . . General Grant was not royal, and the Prince was determined not to treat him as if he were." Although he had not gone on the continuation of the voyage to Egypt, India, and the Far East, Badeau wrote that others—including Grant himself—told him that English colonial officers "must have received instructions from home not to pay too much deference to the ex-president. He believed that the British Government was unwilling to admit that any Western Power was important, or that any authority deserved recognition except their own."

Young glossed over the slights and the injured feelings, but he indicates by inference, as would Badeau, that Grant was far better than his hosts, that he was a natural gentleman, morally superior to the pretentious Europeans who cut him or treated him with condescending reserve. He could walk out in the world with a heart open to everyone, regardless of rank. "Always he was the same simple, impassive man, the genuine democrat," Badeau insisted. "The adulation offered by whole populations did not elate him unduly, . . . and he was quite as much at home . . . with his Jewish friends . . . the Seligmans as if they had been princes. He liked people more than scenery, and the common people the best." In turn, genuine people responded to him, particularly in the north of England, where enormous throngs of workingmen roared their approval when he addressed them as his fellows in hard toil. Back home, Grant had fallen in with the hustling nouveaux riches despite his identification with ordinary folks, but Europe elicited this simpler and more genuine side.

And plain Grant was, in presence and in tastes. Grant barely glanced at all the pictures in all the galleries he passed through, and while Julia went off shopping for gowns and gewgaws, he would stroll or sit and smoke a cigar or read a paper (or ever so rarely a book). Adam Badeau concluded charitably that the general was "practical" rather than "sentimental." While in Italy, for example, Grant "was more curious about geography than mythology. The coasts and channels he inspected closely, but cared nothing for the fables of Homeric origin." Nearing the island of Calypso, a young naval officer warned Julia Grant to remember the fate of the ancient Ulysses and to plug her husband's ears with cotton lest the Sirens lure him to destruction. "Oh," she replied, "my Ulysses has no music in his soul. And am I not with him? Do you suppose that I, after such a lesson from dear old Penelope, would remain at home? No indeed! I defy all outside enchantments." Once, while in India, a beautifully sensual young woman took her Ulysses' hand and held it. Julia later wrote that she "decided I did not like the custom of this country where young ladies came out . . . in such an effective costume to meet my Ulysses, even if I were with him."

But she need not have worried, because her Ulysses, as she herself realized, was as blind to beauty and the seductiveness of luxury as he was deaf to music. Julia herself was somewhat less immune. She bought trunkfuls of Parisian frocks, later describing them in sensuous detail. When she visited Napoleon's tomb, her romantic soul "was seized with a violent shivering which was most alarming to me," while Young could not persuade Grant to enter Les Invalides because he considered Napoleon to have been a great general but an absolute monster. While in Egypt, Julia Grant liked to watch the runners dashing ahead of their carriage, "in their flowing white sleeves, velvet jackets, and full Greek skirts with silver helmets and silver wands held high in the air, flying . . . like Mercury before my phaeton." Ulysses fired them, insisting that such a custom was inhuman.

Yet there was no doubt that, however entrancing she found the old worlds, America was superior as far as Julia Grant was concerned. Asked over dinner by the wife of the Turkish foreign minister to compare the United States to the Continent, Julia glanced up at "a beautiful crystal chandelier that shed its soft light over the large and rather gloomy room," turned to her Turkish hostess and declaimed in best spread-eagle patriotism that, "as that chandelier is to this room, so is America to other countries, very good, very good." Asked to elaborate, she added that "our country is a great garden producing everything." And furthermore, "in America we are all equal. Our school system is the most liberal; the humblest and poorest woman or man has the same facilities for education as the wealthy. The factory girls are not so badly off." The young men were more independent, and so any pretty, modest, amiable, chaste girl could marry up. Love, not property, defined the American marital choice, the most crucial of social moments.

The general, of course, shared such opinions. In a letter to an old friend back home, Grant asserted that America was different, more simple than Europe. "We are the only first class power that is not compelled to grind the laborers to the last degree to pay the interest on [military] debts and to support large armies and navies." Travel only confirmed that America was better. "I have seen nothing that would make me want to live outside the United States." The productive classes everywhere viewed America the same way. "I love to see our country honoured and respected . . . and I am proud to believe that it is by most all nations, and by some even loved."

And so, armed with the democratic privilege of being born a free, independent, and self-actualizing American, Ulysses S. Grant observed and ate, and talked and ate, and talked and marched determinately through the wide world, his Boswell by his side, immune to flattery (or at least apparently so), sizing up the chances for American trade and American influence, and enjoying himself enormously in his rather detached and modest fashion.

Grant seemed to relish most the bohemian suspension of everyday life that travel induced. As he was preparing to sail home from Japan, he wrote a friend that, at the end of the first year abroad, he had been "quite homesick, but determined to remain to see every country in Europe at least. Now at the end of twenty-six months I dread going back."

Once home, as he clearly understood, Grant would have to decide how deeply to plunge back into the old political maelstrom. Part of him had wanted a third term in 1876, though he had never come out and seized the day, and now that same part welcomed the possibility of another term to start in 1880, something his political friends in the Stalwart, hyperconservative end of the Republican Party were urging on him. About this prospect he remained utterly enigmatic, however. He did not confide even to his closest companion, John Russell Young, telling him during the voyage only that "some [newspapers] speculate on my designs. They may know them, but if they do, I do not." Grant almost certainly did not know his own mind; indeed, he never explicitly sought the nomination, nor did he ever clearly withdraw, an ambivalence that drove his backers to distraction.

After landing in San Francisco on September 20, 1879, the Grants continued their indefatigable wandering. Even though he might be missing some big stories, Young was worn down, and so he soon left the Grants to go back to New York and his normal journalist's life. The Grants whirled through the West Coast, the Midwest, and the border states, arriving for Christmas in Philadelphia, the city from which they had embarked so long before. There they were welcomed by an enormous parade and yet more banquets. Then it was on to the South for the winter before returning home to Galena, Illinois, in the spring.

However long they had been away, the Grants' return was politically premature. Several more months remained until the Republican Convention would be held in Chicago in June 1880, and the longer Grant was at home, the more he appeared to be the cat's-paw of Senator Roscoe Conkling of New York, abetted by the *New York Herald*, among other journals, political forces who used Grant to batter Conkling's great enemy, James G. Blaine of Maine, the leading candidate of the so-called Half Breed faction of the party. Despite an overexposure that reminded American voters of the corrupt machinations of his supporters, Grant still might have been able to capture the nomination had he appeared in Chicago to rally his troops. But he did not, remaining passively open to accepting a draft if it were handed to him without any demeaning expenditure of energy on his part. He would not hustle for the prize he may or may not have wanted. Deadlocked between Grant and Blaine, the convention finally turned to the dark horse James A. Garfield, senator-elect of Ohio, another bearded, stout ex-general, but one with fewer skeletons in and out of the closet than Grant.

The remainder of Grant's life proved enormously painful. Restless and financially strapped in the sleepy town of Galena, the Grants soon went off to New York and pursuit of the main chance. Given a beautiful mansion on East Sixty-sixth Street near Central Park by some of his old industrial-ist backers, Grant entered merchant banking with Ferdinand Ward, who proved to be another of Grant's company of crooks. Ward milked the firm dry and cheated Grant out of his bottom dollar. Barely escaping bank-ruptcy, living in despair and in increasing physical pain from throat can-cer, Grant desperately sought to rebuild an inheritance to provide for his family by writing his memoirs, which he heroically completed just before his death on July 23, 1885.

When they were published in 1885 and 1886, Grant's two volumes rap-idly eclipsed *Around the World with General Grant,* which had appeared in 1879, as well as Adam Badeau's three-volume military biography published in 1882. But by then, Young's two sturdy, lavender-bound volumes already had sold very well. They long rested on the reading tables in many par-lors of the northern middle class, where they could be perused for the fine engravings, even if readers glided over Young's sprightly prose.

In truth, it had not been easy for Young to find a publisher. During the voyage, he had tried to peddle the European portion of the trip to the noted publisher, J. W. Harper, who responded to Young with wicked can-dor about the central actor of the voyage. "Entre nous, the general saw nothing, said nothing, and did nothing in Europe worthy of record be-yond the newspapers. He may, however, furnish a dry stick as a nucleus for a brilliant volume, and if anybody can make sunbeams out of cucumbers you are the man. But . . . I question [any] permanent success in book form." After this rejection, Young thought to induce the long conversa-tions that stirred the cucumber into greater animation, thus making a more salable product. On his return to New York, encouraged by Henry George, no mean journalist himself, Young contacted the American Book Company, who took the book and sold it by subscription at fifty cents per week for twenty weeks. Purchasers received two fat 7½″ by 10¾″ octavo-for-matted books with heavy, rich paper and more than eight hundred illus-trations.

Persistent loyalty to Grant paid Young well, and not merely in book sales. In 1882, responding to Grant's active patronage, President Chester A. Arthur, the old Stalwart Grant man who had succeeded the assassinated Garfield, named Young U.S. minister to China, where he remained for three years. It had been on the voyage, of course, that Young had made contact, through Grant, with the most powerful men in China, the same voyage during which Young had demonstrated to the general his considerable political acumen. In 1885, Young returned to the *New York Herald*, serving much of his time as a foreign correspondent in Paris and London. Finally, in 1897, President William McKinley appointed Young librarian of Congress, where he superintended the move of the library from the Capitol to the magnificent new congressional library building that remains the core of the library to this day. On January 17, 1899, at age fifty-nine, Young died of Bright's disease.

J. W. Harper had not been not altogether wrong in his assessment of Grant the traveler. Grant's speeches were amazingly platitudinous, his presentation of self profoundly guarded. Therefore, Young was compelled to build his narrative on other grounds—the scenery and the people, the politics and the banquets. And yet, in the conversations Grant did come alive in a way he *never* did elsewhere, in speech or in print. If these conversations were all that were present in this volume, it would still be a fascinating read. But Young was a talented journalist, and so his observations are also well worth reading, not because they were exceptional but because they revealed so much about the values of the people doing the traveling while also portraying the lands traversed. All good travel writing does that, of course, and this is very good travel writing indeed. In addition, this book further illuminates Ulysses S. Grant, a man who has forever eluded his biographers. Something quite fresh comes through here, even for those who think they already have Grant's number.

Bibliographical Note

Of the many single-volume biographies, William S. McFeeley's Pulitzer Prize–winning *Grant: A Biography* (New York: W. W. Norton, 1981) is the most engaging and the most critical. Also very useful is Geoffrey Paret, *Ulysses S. Grant: Soldier and Statesman* (New York: Random House, 1997).

Several studies illuminate the voyage around the world, frequently in amusing manner. They include John Y. Simon, ed., *The Personal Memoirs of Julia Dent Grant* (New York: G. P. Putnam's Sons, 1975); John Russell Young, *Men and Memories: Personal Reminiscences,* ed. Mary D. Russell Young (New York: F. T. Neeley, 1901); and Adam Badeau, *Grant in Peace: From Appomatox to Mount McGregor, a Personal Memoir* (Hartford, Conn.; S. S. Scranton, 1887). And, of course, *The Personal Memoirs of U. S. Grant,* first published in two volumes in 1885 and 1886, are widely available in many reprinted editions.

As for primary sources, the John Russell Young papers in the Library of Congress provide information about both the author and the history of this book. John Y. Simon's printed edition of the papers of Ulysses S. Grant have reached only to 1873 thus far.

The editor has silently supplied first names and ranks throughout where missing from the original text.

Around the World with General Grant

Philadelphia to England

His political reputation besmirched, but his public popularity apparently undimmed, just over two months after leaving office on March 4, 1877, ex-President Ulysses S. Grant entrained for Philadelphia to set sail on his voyage round the world. If he had harbored some thoughts that this would be a private journey, the huge crowds that sent him on his way soon disabused him of that belief: about twenty-five hundred people per hour streamed past him in Independence Hall. At a great public reception, William T. Sherman reminded the throng that it was Grant the war hero—not the mere politician—who all wished to honor, a military figure Sherman ensconced next to George Washington in the American pantheon (in part because Sherman was so disturbed by the rising reputation of Robert E. Lee and the Lost Cause and the parallel denigration of Grant—and Sherman).

The two cutters it took to ferry the Grant party to the "Indiana" had to dodge a squadron of small private boats that cluttered Philadelphia's harbor. During the ten-day voyage across the Atlantic, the Grants were subjected to formal dinners every night, following two daily lunches. Because of the steady eating, Grant later wrote: "I thought I was a good subject for seasickness [as was experienced by his wife, Julia], and expected the motion of the ship to turn me inside out. As a matter of fact, I was disappointed." Throughout his voyage Grant would prove an ironclad traveler, never growing ill or weary despite a frequently grinding schedule. Of course, the military campaigns of the Civil War had been far harsher, and Grant had never wanted for stamina back then.

Enormous crowds greeted Grant when he landed in Liverpool. Particularly in the industrial cities of the north of England, Grant was as much a hero as he was in the United States, although there was less clamor and more propriety among the upper classes, many of whom, during the Civil War, had supported to a greater or lesser extent their fellow aristocrats in the South, who opposed the emerging industrial North, by then rapidly surpassing England in economic might.

At his first receptions in Liverpool and Manchester, listeners got earfuls of Grant's wooden formality when in public, his relentless dependence on platitudes in public utterance. As John Russell Young is keen to point out, in his more private moments Grant could unwind and become a pleasant and rather garrulous conversationalist. This private/public split in character was heightened by the semi-official quality of his travels, where he was always the American-hero-on-display (suppressing the possible re-emergence of the bewildered, failed merchant of Galena, Illinois). Despite the fact that Grant would always protest that he was no orator and was just another American citizen, there is no doubt that he thrived on the adulation he received.

Down in London, the banquets and private parties escalated in social standing and glitter. Grant freely acknowledged England as the mother country of his fellow Anglo-Saxon Americans, while sometimes reminding the English that the more vigorous children were surpassing their mother. Thus was it ever for nineteenth-century Americans, who still felt a cultural inferiority to the English, whose praise they very much wanted, all the while resenting them for their arrogant presumption of superiority.

Such tension, which did not often reach the pages of the Young book, climaxed when Queen Victoria, noting the huge public fuss being made of Grant, condescended to ask him to Windsor for dinner. As Grant was not a current head of state, Victoria did not greet him at the palace door when he arrived—she was off riding. And she had planned not a state but a private banquet for sixteen (actually a greater honor, but how was an American to know that). The fuss came when the queen proposed to seat son Jesse Grant and the American diplomat, Adam Badeau, with the servants rather than at the head table, which almost stopped the dinner cold before it started. However, the queen relented and placed her children as well as Jesse (whom she found an ill-bred young Yankee) with the grownups. The chitchat went well enough, but the Grants were glad to escape the castle, their republican dignity somewhat strained.

In the month of May, 1877, the Department of State issued to its representatives in foreign countries the following official note:

"DEPARTMENT OF STATE, WASHINGTON,
May 23d, 1877.

"*To the Diplomatic and Consular Officers of the United States.*
"GENTLEMEN: General Ulysses S. Grant, the late President of the United States, sailed from Philadelphia on the 17th inst., for Liverpool.

"The route and extent of his travels, as well as the duration of his sojourn abroad, were alike undetermined at the time of his departure, the object of his journey being to secure a few months of rest and recreation after sixteen years of unremitting and devoted labor in the military and civil service of his country.

"The enthusiastic manifestations of popular regard and esteem for General Grant shown by the people in all parts of the country that he has visited since his retirement from official life, and attending his every appearance in public from the day of that retirement up to the moment of his departure for Europe, indicate beyond question the high place he holds in the grateful affections of his countrymen.

"Sharing in the largest measure this general public sentiment, and at the same time expressing the wishes of the President, I desire to invite the aid of the Diplomatic and Consular Officers of the Government to make his journey a pleasant one should he visit their posts. I feel already assured that you will find patriotic pleasure in anticipating the wishes of the Department by showing him that attention and consideration which is due from every officer of the Government to a citizen of the Republic so signally distinguished both in official service and personal renown.

"I am, Gentlemen,
"Your obedient servant,
"WM. M. EVARTS."

This action on the part of the Government was a fitting manifestation of its esteem and regard for one among the most illustrious of its citizens. These sentiments had been still further emphasized by the people of one of our chief cities, this homage serving to introduce General Grant to the nations of the Old World. General Grant had been from the hour of his retirement on March 4th, 1877, the recipient of more flattering testimonials of respect and admiration than had perhaps ever before fallen to the lot of any American. The successful conducting and victorious termination of the late war between the opposing sections of the country; the judicious direction of the Executive branch of the Government for eight years; the re-establishment of peace and harmony with a great foreign power, when these relations had been seriously threatened; these acts had secured for General Grant a hold upon the heart of the nation which could hardly be too strongly manifested.

Having, as President of the United States, extended to the representatives of foreign states the welcome of America to its Centennial Anniversary Celebration, General Grant was now, in the capacity of a private citizen, about to visit those countries to obtain needed rest, and to inform himself concerning the characteristics and customs of the people of the

Old World. It will be generally conceded that no more appropriate occasion could occur for a special recognition of great public services.

General Grant selected as a medium for the transportation of his party to Liverpool the "Indiana," one of the only American line of steamships crossing the Atlantic Ocean.

Having thus chosen this particular steamship line, it was natural that the Philadelphians should take pride and pleasure in extending their hospitality to General Grant; and accordingly, from the hour of his arrival in Philadelphia, its citizens vied with each other in doing him honor.

During the week which elapsed before his departure, the General was the guest of George W. Childs, Esq.*

On May 10th, the day following his arrival in Philadelphia, General Grant visited the "Permanent Exhibition" Building, on the occasion of its opening.† The 11th, 12th, and 13th were passed in the enjoyment of the hospitalities of prominent Philadelphians, and on the 14th a reception took place at the Union League Club, the reception closing with a review of the First Regiment Infantry of the National Guard of Pennsylvania. On the 16th a very pretty ceremony took place, when the soldiers' orphans—wards of the State—marched in procession past Mr. Childs' residence. Generals Grant and Sherman stood on the steps of the house, extending to each little one, as they passed, a pleasant word. On the same day General Grant received the veteran soldiers and sailors, to the number of twelve hundred, in Independence Hall, after which he lunched with Governor Hartranft at Mr. Childs', where in the evening he was serenaded, the house being brilliantly illuminated.

On the 17th, the day appointed for the departure of the "Indiana," Mr. Childs entertained at breakfast, to meet his distinguished guest, the late Secretary of State, Hon. Hamilton Fish, Governor Hartranft, General Sherman, and Hon. Simon Cameron. After the breakfast the party proceeded on board a small steamer and visited the Russian corvette "Cravasser." After a brief stay the steamer proceeded down the river. The party on board now included Mayor Stokley, Henry C. Carey, Esq., General Stewart Van Vleet, Colonel Fred. D. Grant, Major Alexander Thorpe, Hon. Isaac H. Bailey, of New York; U. S. Grant, jr., General Horace Porter,

---

* George W. Childs was a wealthy publisher and one of Grant's most devoted political and material backers.

† Grant was cheered wildly when he opened the Centennial Exposition, which showed the world lots of folklore and arts but featured American technological and industrial might, most notably the mighty Corliss steam engine—seven hundred tons of steel and forty feet in height.

The Reception at the House of George W. Childs, Philadelphia

the members of the City Council of Philadelphia, and others. Mrs. Grant and a party of friends were taken down the river to the "Indiana" by the United States revenue cutter "Hamilton," on board of which were Admiral Turner, George W. Childs, Esq., and Mrs. Childs, Hon. A. E. Borie, and Mrs. Borie, A. J. Drexel, Esq., and Mrs. Drexel, Mrs. Sharp—Mrs. Grant's sister—Hon. Morton McMichael, A. Bierstadt, the artist, Hon. John W. Forney, and others.

The wharves on the Delaware were lined with people, who made the air resound with their cheers. Steamers and small craft filled the stream, all decorated with bunting and crowded with enthusiastic people.

A brief stoppage was made at Girard Point, and the following telegraphic dispatches were received by General Grant:

"NEW YORK, May 17th, 1877.
"GENERAL GRANT, *Philadelphia:*
"Mrs. Hayes joins me in heartiest wishes that you and Mrs. Grant may have a prosperous voyage and, after a happy visit abroad, a safe return to your friends and country.

R. B. HAYES."

To this General Grant replied:

"STEAMER 'MAGENTA,'

"DELAWARE RIVER, May 17th, 11 o'clock A.M.

"PRESIDENT HAYES, *Executive Mansion, Washington:*

"DEAR SIR: Mrs. Grant joins me in thanks to you and Mrs. Hayes for your kind wishes and your message received on board this boat just as we are pushing out from the wharf. We unite in returning our cordial greetings, and in expressing our best wishes for your health, happiness, and success in your most responsible position. Hoping to return to my country to find it prosperous in business, and with cordial feelings renewed between all sections,

"I am, dear sir, truly yours,

"U. S. GRANT."

On board the "Magenta" luncheon was served, General Grant occupying the head of the table. The first toast of the occasion, offered by Mayor Stokley, was, "God-speed to our honored guest, Ulysses S. Grant." The General responded briefly, being evidently affected by the warmth of the greeting and the compliments which were being showered upon him.

The health of General Sherman was next toasted, and he replied:

"MR. MAYOR AND GENTLEMEN: This proud welcome along the shores of the Delaware demands a response. General Grant leaves here to-day with the highest rewards of his fellow-citizens, and on his arrival on the other side there is no doubt he will be welcomed by friends with as willing hands and warm hearts as those he leaves behind. Ex-President Grant—General Grant—while you, his fellow-citizens, speak of him and regard him as Ex-President Grant, I cannot but think of the times of the war, of General Grant, President of the United States for eight years, yet I cannot but think of him as the General Grant of Fort Donelson. I think of him as the man who, when the country was in the hour of its peril, restored its hopes when he marched triumphant into Fort Donelson. After that none of us felt the least doubt as to the future of our country, and therefore, if the name of Washington is allied with the birth of our country, that of Grant is forever identified with its preservation, its perpetuation. It is not here alone on the shores of the Delaware, that the people love and respect you, but in Chicago and St. Paul, and in far-off San Francisco, the prayers go up today that your voyage may be prosperous and pleasant, and that you may have a safe and happy return. General Grant" (extending his hand), "God bless you, God bless you, and grant you a pleasant journey and a safe return to your native land."

Mayor Stokley then said:

The Departure of the "Magenta" from Delaware Bay, May 1877

"GENERAL GRANT: As I now feel that it is necessary to draw these festivities to a close, I must speak for the City of Philadelphia. I am sure that I express the feelings of Philadelphia as I extend to you my hand, that I give to you the hands and the hearts of all Philadelphia" (cheers), "and as we part with you now, it is the hope of Philadelphia that God will bless you with a safe voyage and a happy return; and with these few words I say God bless you, and God direct and care for you in your voyage across the ocean."

General Grant, who was visibly affected, replied:

"MR. MAYOR AND GENTLEMEN: I feel much overcome with what I have heard. When the first toast was offered I supposed the last words here for me had been spoken, and I feel overcome by the sentiments to which I have listened, and which I feel I am altogether inadequate to respond to. I don't think that the compliments ought all be paid to me or any one man in either of the positions which I was called upon to fill.

"That which I accomplished—which I was able to accomplish—I owe to the assistance of able lieutenants. I was so fortunate as to be called to the first position in the army of the nation, and I had the good fortune to select lieutenants who could have filled" (turning toward Sherman)—"had it been necessary I believe some of these lieutenants could have filled my place may be better than I did." (Cries of "No.") "I do not, therefore, regard myself as entitled to all the praise.

"I believe that my friend Sherman could have taken my place as a soldier as well as I could, and the same will apply to Sheridan." (Cheers.) "And I believe, finally, that if our country ever comes into trial again, young men will spring up equal to the occasion, and if one fails, there will be another to take his place." (Great cheers.) "Just as there was if I had failed. I thank you again and again, gentlemen, for the hearty and generous reception I have had in your great city." (Prolonged cheers.)

Complimentary speeches were also made by Ex-Secretaries Fish, Chandler, Robeson, Senator Cameron, and Governor Hartranft.

The steamer "Indiana," having on board the officers of the American Line of Steamship Company and a number of invited guests, was reached at 2.40 P.M. by the "Magenta" and "Hamilton." This was off Newcastle, and about thirty-five miles below Philadelphia. Here Mrs. Grant and her son Jesse were transferred from the "Hamilton" to the "Indiana;" after which General Grant, Governor Hartranft, and a few friends passed on board from the "Magenta." A salute of twenty-one guns was now fired from the "Hamilton;" deafening cheers from the crowded steamers were mingled with the shrill noise of the steam whistles; and presently the "Indiana" steamed out from the midst of the fleet.

The "Indiana" made the passage to Liverpool in eleven days, arriving on May 28th.

During the voyage the only occurrence calculated to mar its pleasurable features was the death and burial of the child of a steerage passenger.

That reticence which had characterized the manner of the Ex-President during the many years of his onerous and toilsome employment in the service of his country, dropped from him as though it were a mask; now that he was free from official care and permitted to display that geniality and sympathetic nature which more justly belonged to him. It was established by the universal testimony of those on board the "Indiana," that no more agreeable companion on a sea voyage could be chosen than the General. He smoked and chatted in the smoking room; entered with interest into the diverse games which were proposed; conversed freely on all subjects except politics; and charmed every one by his urbanity and good fellowship. It is even on record that he succeeded in winning the friendship of some persons on board who had been for years politically and personally opposed to him.

General Grant appreciated highly the enthusiasm which had greeted him on his departure from his native land. Such a scene as had accompanied him on his way down the river had never before been witnessed in this country, and it made on its recipient a vivid impression. He could hardly refer to this scene without emotion, and it certainly repaid him, in

Discussions at Sea

his own modest estimation, for all his services to his countrymen. General Grant enjoyed the best of health during the entire voyage, never missing a meal. Mrs. Grant suffered slightly from *mal de mer.* According to Captain Sargent, the excellent officer of the ship, General Grant was the most interesting and entertaining talker he had ever met. "In fact," said Captain Sargent, "there is no one who can make himself more entertaining or agreeable in his conversation—when nobody has an 'ax to grind.'" This rough speech gives a better insight into the true reason of General Grant's distaste for talking while in office than could be otherwise expressed in a whole chapter. The fact was that in his official capacity he had always to be "on guard," as few ever approached him without a selfish purpose, or "an ax to grind."

On the first morning at sea, General Grant said "that he felt better than he had for sixteen years, from the fact that he had no letters to read, and no telegraphic dispatches to attend to." Indeed, this sense of freedom from the strain of such unremitting devotion to severe application was not unnatural in the beginning of General Grant's journey, and was the predominant impression which his manners conveyed to those around him. General Grant smoked incessantly during the voyage, a test, as every ocean traveler is aware, of any one's capacity to resist the effects of the motion of the sea. The voyage was a rough one, and the weather did not improve as the ship neared port. Off Fastnet Light she had to lay to for eight hours in a fog; when this lifted, the Irish coast was in sight. On the day before

The Grants' Debarkation at Liverpool

arriving at Queenstown, the cabin passengers of the "Indiana" presented to Captain Sargent, her estimable commander, a letter of compliment and thanks for his courtesy as a gentleman, and skill as a seaman, General Grant being the spokesman.

At about seven o'clock on the evening of May 27th, the "Indiana" entered Queenstown harbor. Here a tug boarded the steamship, bringing to meet General Grant, Mr. J. Russell Young, and a number of prominent citizens, who welcomed the General to Ireland, and cordially invited him to remain for a time among them. This deputation was received in the captain's cabin, where General Grant heard their kindly expressions of welcome with evident satisfaction. He responded to these briefly, regretting that arrangements already made for the route of his journey would prevent his acceptance of the invitation until a later period, when he should certainly avail himself of their hospitality. Letters and dispatches which had been awaiting were delivered, and the "Indiana" again pushed out to sea, followed by hearty cheers from the kindly Irishmen on the tug. Among the General's letters received at this point, were a large number from the leading statesmen of England, conveying invitations to a round of receptions and dinners—a foretaste of the friendly hospitality which was to characterize his visit.

The "Indiana" arrived at Liverpool on May 28th. Here a bright and pleasant day welcomed the travelers; the ships in the Mersey displayed the

American and other flags, and at the dock where the passengers from the steamships landed, the Mayor of Liverpool, Mr. A. R. Walker, was in readiness to receive General Grant, and to extend to him the courtesies of the great commercial city. Here also was General Adam Badeau, the General's old-time aide-de-camp, now United States Consul at London. Friendly salutations having been offered and received, the Mayor of Liverpool addressed General Grant as follows:

> "GENERAL GRANT: I am proud that it has fallen to my lot, as Chief Magistrate of Liverpool, to welcome to the shores of England so distinguished a citizen of the United States. You have, sir, stamped your name on the history of the world by your brilliant career as a soldier, and still more as a statesman in the interests of peace. In the name of Liverpool, whose interests are so closely allied with your great country, I bid you heartily welcome, and I hope Mrs. Grant and yourself will enjoy your visit to old England."

General Grant thanked the Mayor for his reception. The Mayor presented to the General several prominent citizens of Liverpool, and then the whole party drove off to the Adelphi Hotel. On the following day the General, accompanied by the Mayor and a deputation of citizens, visited the docks. The party embarked on the tender "Vigilant." The boat proceeded as far as the extreme north end of the river wall, and the party minutely inspected the new dock works in progress. On their return they visited the Town Hall, where they were entertained by the Mayor and a company numbering some sixty or seventy gentlemen and ladies, after which they passed some time in inspecting the Liverpool Free Library. The reception in Liverpool was closed by a banquet tendered to General Grant and his party by the Mayor.

On Wednesday morning, May 30th, General Grant left Liverpool for Manchester, where he was the guest of Mayor Heywood, and publicly received by that official in the Town Hall, being accompanied thither by a deputation of the City Council which met him at the station. He was then escorted on a round of visits among the celebrated manufactories of Manchester to the warehouse of Sir James Watts, to the Assize Courts, and the Royal Exchange. At the latter building a large assemblage of merchants were gathered who received the General enthusiastically. The party was met by the members of Parliament for Manchester—Mr. Birley and Mr. Jacob Bright, and by the Dean of Manchester. The Mayor presented an address, preceding it by recalling the circumstance that when he previously held the office of Mayor, fourteen years before, it had been his duty to welcome the captain of the "George Griswold" relief ship, which came from America laden with provisions for Lancashire during the cotton famine. The address was then read by the Town Clerk.

In his reply the General said:

"MR. MAYOR, MEMBERS OF THE COUNCIL OF MANCHESTER, LADIES AND GENTLEMEN: It is scarcely possible for me to give utterance to the feelings called forth by the receptions which have been accorded me since my arrival in England. In Liverpool, where I spent a couple of days, I witnessed continuously the same interest that has been exhibited in the streets and in the public buildings of your city. It would be impossible for any person to have so much attention paid to him without feeling it, and it is impossible for me to give expression to the sentiments which have been evoked by it. I had intended upon my arrival in Liverpool to have hastened through to London, and from that city to visit the various points of interest in your country, Manchester being one of the most important among them. I am, and have been for many years, fully aware of the great amount of manufactures of Manchester, many of which find a market in my own country. I was very well aware, during the war, of the sentiments of the great mass of the people of Manchester toward the country to which I have the honor to belong, and also of the sentiments with regard to the struggle in which it fell to my lot to take a humble part. It was a great trial for us. For your expressions of sympathy at that time there exists a feeling of friendship toward Manchester distinct and separate from that which my countrymen also feel, and I trust always will feel, toward every part of England. I therefore accept on the part of my country, the compliments which have been paid to me as its representative, and thank you for them heartily."

Jacob Bright, Esq., M.P. for Manchester, proposed the health of the Mayor, referring to the fact that in the great American conflict General Grant had not fought for conquest or for fame, but to give freedom to the people, and preserve the union of his native land. A wonderful magnanimity had been shown in all his conduct, and it was truly said that, when the conflict was over, he employed all his great influence to obtain generous terms for the vanquished. He trusted that wherever General Grant went in England, he would receive the honor that was his due.

A deputation of American merchants resident in Manchester waited upon the General at the close of the reception, and offered him a welcome.

On Thursday, the 31st May, General Grant took luncheon with the Mayor and Corporation of Salford. During this entertainment the General, in proposing the health of the Mayor and Mayoress, said:

"My reception since my arrival in England has been to me very expressive, and one for which I have to return thanks on behalf of my country. I cannot help feeling that it is my country that is honored through me. It is the affection which the people of this island have for their children on the other side of the Atlantic, which they express to me as an humble representative of their offspring."

At Leicester an address was presented in behalf of the Mayor, Magistrates, Aldermen and Council of the Borough. In acknowledging this address General Grant said:

"Allow me, in behalf of my country and myself, to return you thanks for this honor, and for your kind reception as well as for the other kind receptions which I have had since the time that I first landed on the soil of Great Britain. As children of this great commonwealth, we feel that you must have some reason to be proud of our advancement since our separation from the mother country. I can assure you of our heartfelt good will, and express to you our thanks on behalf of the American people."

The General was accompanied to London by General Badeau, Mr. Ellis, the chairman of the Midland Railway, and Mr. Allport, the general manager. At Bedford the train was met by the Mayor of the city, who presented him with an address, terming him the Hannibal of the American armies, and praying that he might be spared to enjoy the honors and rewards which would continue to be heaped upon him. The General thanked the Mayor for his courtesy, and regretted that he could not make a speech that would compare with the eloquence of his British friends.

If the reception which had thus far attended General Grant's appearance in England was a surprise to him—and he frequently gave expression to such a sentiment regarding it—to his fellow-citizens at home it was a revelation.

This chapter may not inappropriately be closed by General Grant's letter after his arrival in England, to his friend George W. Childs.

"LONDON, JUNE 19th, 1877.

"MY DEAR MR. CHILDS:

"After an unusually stormy passage for any season of the year, and continuous sea-sickness generally among the passengers after the second day out, we reached Liverpool Monday afternoon, the 28th of May. Jesse and I proved to be among the few good sailors. Neither of us felt a moment's uneasiness during the voyage. I had proposed to leave Liverpool immediately on arrival and proceed to London, where I knew our Minister had made arrangements for the formal reception, and had

London, 1877

accepted for me a few invitations of courtesy. But what was my surprise to find nearly all the shipping in port at Liverpool decorated with flags of all nations, and from the mainmast of each the flag of the Union most conspicuous. The docks were lined with as many of the population as could find standing-room, and the streets to the hotel where it was understood my party would stop were packed. The demonstration was, to all appearances, as hearty and as enthusiastic as in Philadelphia on our departure. The Mayor was present with his state carriage, to convey us to the hotel; and after that he took us to his beautiful country residence, some six miles out, where we were entertained with a small party of gentlemen, and remained over night. The following day a large party was given at the official residence of the Mayor in the city, at which there were some one hundred and fifty of the distinguished citizens and officials of the corporation present. Pressing invitations were sent from most of the cities in the kingdom to have me visit them. I accepted for a day at Manchester, and stopped a few moments at Leicester and at one other place. The same hearty welcome was shown at each place, as you have no doubt seen. . . . I appreciate the fact, and am proud of it, that the attentions I am receiving are intended more for our country than for me personally. I love to see our country honored and respected abroad, and I am proud that it is respected by most all nations, and by some even loved. It has always been my desire to see all jealousies between England and the United States abated, and every sore healed. Together, they are more powerful for the spread of commerce and civi-

Meeting the Prince of Wales

lization than all others combined, and can do more to remove causes of war by creating mutual interests that would be so much endangered by war. . . .

"U. S. GRANT." . . .

The narrative of General Grant's visit to London must be confined to a record of the honors paid him by various English public men, by the people, by municipal bodies like that of the City of London, and by the Queen. To print in detail all that was said and written on the occasion of the General's month's stay in London, would be to print a volume. I shall therefore confine myself to the General's movements, and those ceremonies incident to the stay which attracted attention at the time, and which are worthy of remembrance as part of the history of the two countries.

The morning after arriving in London, General Grant went to the Oaks at Epsom, where he met for the first time the Prince of Wales.

On the evening of the 2d of June the General dined with the Duke of Wellington at Apsley House.* On Sunday, the 3d, he visited Westminster

---

* This noble Englishman, the son of the Iron Duke, pleased Grant by comparing him to the hero of Waterloo.

Abbey, Dean Stanley in the course of his sermon making a graceful allusion to the presence in England of the Ex-President of the United States, and the desire of the English people to honor America by honoring its illustrious representative.

On the evening of the 5th, Mr. Pierrepont, the American Minister, gave the General a reception at his house in Cavendish Square. Cavendish Square is the center of what may be called the Faubourg Centralain of London. The American Embassy is a fine old English mansion, with a capacious interior, but with a dark, somber exterior. It adjoins a grim castellated edifice which is the residence of the Duke of Portland, from which Thackeray is said to have drawn his description of the House of the Marquis of Stein in "Vanity Fair." Cavendish Square is the center of the homes of the Bentincks and other great noblemen, and was the refuge for the aristocracy when driven from their houses in Soho Square, by the mob of 1730. It is traversed by "the long unlovely street" where Hallam lived, of which Tennyson writes in "In Memoriam." The Pierrepont reception was attended by leading representatives of both parties. Lord Beaconsfield sent his regrets that he could not attend on account of illness. The royal family were absent because the court was in mourning for the recently deceased Queen of the Netherlands. Among those who crowded the capacious saloons of the embassy were the Lord Chancellor, the Duke of Leeds and the Duke of Beaufort, the Marquis of Salisbury, the Marquis of Hertford, Earl Derby, Earl Shaftesbury, John Bright, Mr. Gladstone, Lord Houghton, the Marquis of Ripon, the Marquis of Lorne, and representatives of every phase of English society. On the 6th of June, the General dined with Lord Carnarvon. On the 7th he was presented at court. On the 8th he made a hurried visit to Bath, where an address was presented by the Mayor. On the evening of the 8th there was a dinner at the Duke of Devonshire's and a reception by Consul-General Badeau. The latter was a brilliant affair, and was attended by large numbers of the nobility and many notable persons of English society. On the 9th, there was a dinner with Lord Granville. On the 10th, General Grant dined with Sir Charles Dilke.

Two or three days were given by the General to a visit to Southampton, where his daughter, Mrs. Sartoris, resides. This was a pleasant episode in the routine of dinners, receptions, and excitement. The General and family enjoyed exceedingly their drives round the southern coast to Netley Abbey and other places of historic interest about Southampton, which never looked so beautiful as in this calm summer weather.

On the 15th of June took place one of the most important incidents connected with the General's visit to Europe—the conferring upon him of the freedom of the City of London. This is the highest honor that can be paid by this ancient and renowned corporation. The freedom of the city was presented in a gold casket. The obverse central panel contains a view of the Capitol at Washington, and on the right and left are the General's monogram and the arms of the Lord Mayor. On the reverse side is a view of the entrance to the Guildhall and an inscription. At the end are two figures, also in gold, representing the City of London and the Republic of the United States. These figures bear enameled shields. At the corners are double columns, laurel-wreathed, with corn and cotton, and on the cover a cornucopia, as a compliment to the fertility and prosperity of the United States. The cover is surmounted by the arms of the City of London, and in the decorations are interwoven the rose, the shamrock, and the thistle. The casket is supported by American eagles in gold, standing on a velvet plinth decorated with stars and stripes.

The ceremonies attending the presentation of the freedom of the City of London are stately and unique. Guildhall, one of the most ancient and picturesque buildings in the city, was specially prepared for the occasion, and eight hundred guests were invited to the banquet, a considerable proportion of them being ladies. There were the members of the Corporation, the American Minister, the Chancellor of the Exchequer, members of Parliament, and representatives of the American colony resident in London. On arriving at the Guildhall the General was received by a deputation of four aldermen, with the chairman and four members of the City Lands Committee, including the mover and seconder of the resolution presenting the freedom. This deputation conducted the General to his place in the Common Council on the left hand of the Lord Mayor. The Lord Mayor, Sir Thomas White, came in state from the Mansion House. The passage leading to the library was guarded by a detachment of the London Rifle Brigade.

At one o'clock the Common Council was opened in ordinary form for the transaction of business. The Council never deviates from its established routine, not even for ceremonies. A resolution was passed with reference to some ordinary matter of municipal interest, and the Town Clerk read the minutes of the past meeting. This over, the Chamberlain, Mr. B. Scott, addressed General Grant and said:

"The unprecedented facilities of modern travel, and the running to and fro of all classes in our day, have brought to our shores unwonted visitors from

Asia, as well as from Europe—rulers of empires both ancient and of recent creation; but amongst them all we have not as yet received a President of the United States of America—a power great, flourishing, and free, but so youthful that it celebrated only last year its first centennial. A visit of the ruling President of those States is scarcely to be looked for, so highly valued are his services at home during his limited term of office; you must bear with us, therefore, General, if we make much of an Ex-President of the great Republic of the New World visiting the old home of his fathers. It is true that those first fathers—Pilgrim Fathers we now call them—chafed under the straitness of the parental rule, and sought in distant climes the liberty then denied them at home; it is true, likewise, that their children subsequently resented the interference, well intended if unwise, of their venerated parent, and manifested a spirit of independence of parental restraint not unbecoming in grown-up sons of the Anglo-Saxon stock. Yet, for all this, there is furnished from time to time, abundant evidence that both children and parent have forgotten old differences and forgiven old wrongs; that the children continue to revere the mother country, while she is not wanting in maternal pride at witnessing so numerous, so thriving, and so freedom-loving a race of descendants. If other indications were wanting of mutual feelings of regard, we should find them, on the one hand, in the very hospitable and enthusiastic reception accorded to the Heir Apparent to the British throne, and subsequently to H. R. H. Prince Arthur, when, during your presidency, he visited your country; and on the other hand, in the cordial reception which, we are gratified to observe, you have received from the hour when you set foot on the shores of Old England. In this spirit, and with these convictions, the Corporation of London receives you today with all kindliness of welcome, desiring to compliment you and your country in your person by conferring upon you the honorary freedom of their ancient city—a freedom which had existence more than eight centuries before your first ancestors set foot on Plymouth Rock; a freedom confirmed to the citizens, but not originated, by the Norman conqueror, which has not yet lost its significance or its value, although the liberty which it symbolizes has been extended to other British subjects, and has become the inheritance of the great Anglo-American family across the Atlantic. But we not only recognize in you a citizen of the United States, but one who has made a distinguished mark in American history—a soldier whose military capabilities brought him to the front in the hour of his country's sorest trial, and enabled him to strike the blow which terminated fratricidal war and reunited his distracted country; who also manifested magnanimity in the hour of triumph, and amidst the national indignation created by the assassination of the great and good Abraham Lincoln, by obtaining for vanquished adversaries the rights of capitulated brethren in arms, when some would have treated them as traitors to their country. We further recognize in you a President upon whom was laid the honor, and with it the responsibility, during two terms of office, of a greater and more difficult task than that which devolved upon you as a general in the field—that of binding up the bleeding frame of society which had been rent asunder when the demon of slavery was cast out. That the constitution of the country over which you were thus called to preside survived so fearful a shock, that we saw it proud and progressive, celebrating its centennial during the last year of your official rule, evinces that the task which your countrymen had committed to you did not miscarry in your hands. That such results have been possible must, in fairness, be attributed in no inconsiderable degree to the firm but conciliatory policy of your administration at home and abroad, which is affirmed of you by the resolution of this honorable Court whose exponent and mouthpiece I am this day. May you greatly enjoy your visit to our country at this favored season of the year, and may your life be long spared to witness in your country, and in our own—the two great branches of the Anglo-Saxon family—a career of increasing amity, mutual respect, and honest, if spirited rivalry—rivalry in trade, commerce, agriculture, and manufacture; in the arts, science, and literature; rivalry in the highest of all arts, how best to promote the well-being and to develop the industry of nations, how to govern them for the largest good to the greatest number, and for the advancement of peace, liberty, morality, and the consequent happiness of mankind. Nothing now remains, General, but that I should present to you an illuminated copy of the resolutions of this honorable Court, for the reception of which an appropriate casket is in course of preparation; and, in conclusion, offer you, in the name of this honorable Court, the right hand of fellowship as a citizen of London." (Cheers.)

General Grant replied:

"It is a matter of some regret to me that I have never cultivated that art of public speaking which might have enabled me to express in suitable terms my gratitude for the compliment which has been paid to my countrymen and myself on this occasion. Were I in the habit of speaking in public, I should claim the right to express my opinion, and what I believe will be the opinion of my countrymen when the proceedings of this day shall have been telegraphed to them. For myself, I have been very much surprised at my reception at all places since the day I landed at Liverpool up to my appearance in this the greatest city in the world. It was entirely unexpected, and it is particularly gratifying to me. I believe that this honor is intended quite as much for the country which I have had the opportunity of serving in different capacities, as for myself, and I am glad that this is so, because I want to see the happiest relations existing, not only between the United States and Great Britain, but also between the United States and all other nations. Although a soldier by education and profession, I have never felt any sort of fondness for war, and I have never advocated it except as a means of peace. I hope that we shall always settle our differences in all future negotiations as amicably as we did in a recent instance. I believe that settlement has had a happy effect on both countries, and that from month to month, and year to year, the tie of common civilization and common blood is getting stronger between the two countries. My Lord Mayor, ladies, and gentlemen, I again thank you for the honor you have done me and my country to-day."

At the conclusion of this speech, which was received with hearty cheering, General Grant subscribed his name to the roll of honorary freemen, and after that attended a luncheon. This was served on twenty tables. After drinking the health of the Queen, the Lord Mayor proposed the health of General Grant. Perhaps I can give no better description of the General's speech and of the impression it made upon those present, than by quoting the account from the pen of George W. Smalley, the distinguished correspondent of the New York *Tribune,* who was among the guests present. I did not have the opportunity of attending the festivities at the Guildhall, and therefore borrow Mr. Smalley's pen as that of an accomplished eyewitness. Speaking of General Grant as an orator, a character in which he had never before appeared, Mr. Smalley said that he had heard three speeches in one day. "The first," said Mr. Smalley, "was a somewhat elaborate address in the library of the Guildhall, in response to the still more elaborate address of the Chamberlain in offering him the freedom of the City of London. It was thoroughly well done in manner and matter. The second was at lunch in the Guildhall, and was simply a gem. It is so clumsily reported in this morning's papers that I insert here the true version. The Lord Mayor having proposed, and the guests having drunk General Grant's health, the General replied in these words: 'My Lord Mayor, Ladies and Gentlemen: Habits formed in early life and early education press upon us as we grow older. I was brought up a soldier—not to talking. I am not aware that I ever fought two battles on the same day in the same place, and that I should be called upon to make two speeches on the same day under the same roof is beyond my understanding. What I do understand is, that I am much indebted to all of you for the compliment you have paid me. All I can do is to thank the Lord Mayor for his kind words, and to thank the citizens of Great Britain here present in the name of my country and for myself.'

"I never heard," continues Mr. Smalley, "a more perfect speech of its kind than that. There is a charm, a felicity in the turn of one or two of its

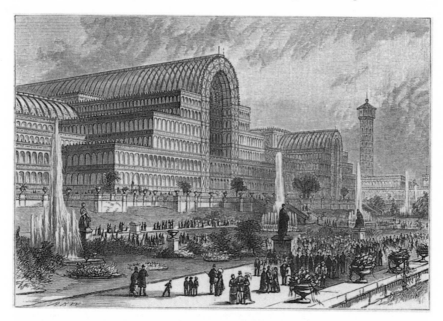

The Crystal Palace

phrases that would do credit to the best artists in words—to Mr. Kinglake or to Mr. Matthew Arnold themselves. Later in the day, at the quiet and almost private dinner at the Crystal Palace, Mr. Thomas Hughes asked the company, in a few words full of grace and feeling, to drink the health of General Grant. Mr. Hughes took pains to say that the occasion was not formal, and that he did not mean to impose upon his guest the burden of a reply. General Grant sat looking up into Mr. Hughes' face; there was a moment's pause, and then the General, screwing himself slowly up out of his chair till he stood erect on his feet, said: 'Mr. Hughes, I must none the less tell you what gratification it gives me to hear my health proposed in such hearty words by Tom Brown of Rugby.' I do not know what could be better than that. Still later in the evening, during the exhibition of fireworks, General Grant sat silent while his own portrait—a capital likeness—was drawn in lines of changing flame against the dark background of Beckenham Hills. Not a muscle moved; there was not a sign of pleasure at the splendid compliment paid him; not a movement of recognition for the cheers with which the great crowd below hailed the portrait. But when this had burnt out, and the next piece—a sketch of the building which crowns the heights above the Potomac—was blazing, a slight smile parted the General's lips as he remarked to Lady Ripon, who sat next to him: 'They have burnt me in effigy, and now they are burning the Capitol!'"

The entertainment at the Crystal Palace to which Mr. Smalley refers, was specially arranged for General Grant. The American and English national airs were played. "Hearts of Oak" was sung by Signor Toli, and was followed by "Hail Columbia" on the whole band. There was an anniversary overture with a chorus, written by S. G. Pratt, of Chicago, dedicated to General Grant, and performed for the first time in England on the occasion of his visit to the Crystal Palace.

Signor Campobello sang Longfellow's "Village Blacksmiths," and Mrs. Osgood, with a chorus, "The Star-spangled Banner."

On the 16th of June, the General and family dined with the Princess Louise and the Marquis of Lorne, at the Kensington Palace, and on the 17th with Mr. Morgan, the banker. On the 18th, Mr. Smalley, the correspondent of the New York *Tribune,* entertained the General at breakfast at his beautiful house in Hyde Park Square. This was a famous gathering in some respects. Among those present were Matthew Arnold, Robert Browning, A. W. Kinglake, Anthony Trollope, Professor Huxley, Thomas Hughes, F. H. Hill, editor of the *Daily News,* the Rt. Hon. Jas. Stansfeld, and others. John Bright sent a regret at his inability to be present. In the evening there was a dinner at the Reform Club, Lord Granville, wearing his ribbon and star of the Garter, presiding. This dinner was given in the House Room of the club, and those present were mostly representative of the Liberal party in England. Mr. Pierrepont, the Minister, had some scruples about attending, not wishing, in his representative capacity, to be present at a political demonstration. Among those present were Mr. Geo. H. Boker, the American Minister to Russia, Mr. Mundella, W. E. Forster, Mr. Bagston, Frederick Harrison, and others. After the toast of the Queen had been proposed, Mr. Forster made a speech welcoming General Grant, and paying a compliment to President Hayes for his reunion policy, which, he thought, would end by making the United States what they were before the war, really one country, and what they were not before the war, one country and free at the same time. To this Mr. Boker made response, dwelling upon the importance of sustaining friendly relations between England and America, and recalling the anxiety that all Americans felt for English friendship during our war with the South. Lord Granville then proposed the health of General Grant, in the course of which he alluded to the beneficent results accruing to both nations from the amicable settlement of the Alabama Claims. The General in his response said: "I am overwhelmed by the kindness shown to me in England, and not only to me, but to my country. I regret that I am unable adequately to express—

even with the aid in doing so of the omnipresent enterprise of the New York *Herald*—express my thanks for the courtesy I have received. I hope the opportunity may be afforded me, in calmer and more deliberate moments, to put on record my hearty recognition of the fraternal sentiments of the English people and the desire of America to render an adequate return. The speech of Lord Granville has inspired thoughts which it is impossible for me adequately to present. Never have I lamented so much as now my poverty in phrases—my inability to give due expression of my affection for the mother country." He trusted that his life would have no higher aim than to contribute as much as possible to the union of the English-speaking peoples throughout the world.

On the evening of the 19th of June, the General dined at the Prince of Wales's, at Marlborough House, where he met the Emperor of Brazil. After dinner, he drove to the office of the London *Times,* and was received by J. C. Macdonald, the manager of that paper, and was shown over all the departments of that ancient and interesting institution. On the 20th, there was a dinner at Lord Ripon's. On the 21st he dined with Minister Pierrepont to meet the Prince of Wales. On the 22d, Mrs. Hicks, an American lady resident in London, gave a reception, at which he was present, while in the evening, he attended the opera at Covent Garden, witnessing the performance of "Martha." The General was accompanied by Mrs. Grant and General Badeau. The curtain rose upon their entrance, disclosing Mlle. Albani and the full chorus of the company, the rear of the stage being grouped with American flags. The General wore his uniform as general. Mlle. Albani sang the "Star-spangled Banner" with full chorus and orchestral accompaniment, while the whole audience and the General remained standing. On the evening of the 22d there was a banquet given by the Trinity Corporation in their hall on Tower Hill, the Prince of Wales presiding. The company was a distinguished and brilliant one. Among others were Prince Leopold, Prince Christian of Schleswig-Holstein, the Prince of Leiningen, Prince Edward of Saxe-Weimar, the Duke of Wellington, the Earl of Derby, and others. The Prince of Wales in his speech said: "It is a matter of peculiar gratification to us as Englishmen to receive as our guest General Grant. I can assure him for myself and for all loyal subjects of the Queen, that it has given me the greatest pleasure to see him as a guest in this country." This reference to the General was received with cheers. Lord Carnarvon, who was then Secretary for Home Affairs, proposed General Grant's health. Speaking of the relations between America and England, Lord Carnarvon said he believed the two countries were

Queen Victoria's Reception at Windsor Castle

entering upon a new era of mutual trust, mutual sympathy, and mutual support and strength. "I have had, perhaps," said Lord Carnarvon, "special opportunities of observing this in the office I have the honor of holding. It has been my duty to be connected with the great Dominion of Canada, stretching as it does several thousand miles along the frontier of the United States, and during the last three or four years I can truthfully say that nothing impressed me more, or gave me more lively satisfaction, than the interchange of friendship and good offices which took place between the two countries under the auspices of General Grant." The General thanked the Prince of Wales and the gentlemen present for the compliment paid to him, and the dinner came to an end.

The next morning General Grant drove to Richmond Park to pay a visit to the late Earl Russell. This distinguished nobleman was living in retirement, at an advanced age, having quitted public life, spending his few remaining years at Pembroke Lodge, a house given to him by the Queen. The General found Lord Russell extremely well considering his years, and they had an interesting conversation on the relations between America and England, arising out of the war, and about the part Lord Russell played during the war. On Monday there was an entertainment at Mr. McHenry's house, Holland Park, and a dinner with Lord Derby at St. James's Square.

The Queen of England showed a desire to pay a compliment to General Grant and the United States by an invitation to the General and his family to visit Windsor Castle. The invitation was as follows: "The Lord Steward of Her Majesty's household is commanded by the Queen to invite Mr. and Mrs. Grant to dinner at Windsor Castle, on Wednesday, the 27th inst., and to remain until the following day, the 28th of June, 1877." Invitations were also extended to Mr. Pierrepont and his wife, J. R. Grant and General Badeau. On the 26th of June the party left for Windsor by the afternoon train. At half-past eight, the Queen, surrounded by her court, received General Grant in the magnificent corridor leading to her private apartments in the Quadrangle. The Quadrangle is formed by the state apartments on the north, the historical Round Tower on the west, and the private apartments of the Queen and the royal household on the south and east. This corridor is 520 feet long, and extends round the south and east sides of the Quadrangle. The ceiling, which is lofty, is divided into large squares, the centers of which bear a number of ornamental devices, typical of ancient, modern, and ecclesiastical history. The dinner was served in the Oak Room. Among those present were Prince Leopold,

Prince Christian, Princess Beatrice, Lord and Lady Derby, the Duchess of Wellington, General Badeau, and others. The ladies were dressed in black with white trimmings, owing to the recent decease of the Queen of Holland. During the dinner a dispatch was received from Governor Hartranft, of Pennsylvania, as follows:

"PROVIDENCE, RHODE ISLAND.

"*From* GENERAL HARTRANFT, *Commander-in-Chief,*

"*To* GENERAL U. S. GRANT, *care of* H. M. THE QUEEN:

"Your comrades, in national encampment assembled, in Rhode Island, send heartiest greetings to their old commander, and desire, through England's Queen, to thank England for Grant's reception."

To this the General responded:

"Grateful for telegram. Conveyed message to the Queen. Thank my old comrades."

The dispatch came just as the party were assembling for dinner, and was given by the General to her majesty, who expressed much pleasure at the kind greeting from America. During the dinner the band of the Grenadier Guards played in the Quadrangle. After dinner the Queen entered into conversation with the party, and about ten took her leave, followed by her suite. The evening was given to conversation and whist, with members of the royal household, and at half-past eleven they retired. The next morning the General and party took their leave of Windsor and returned to London.

When the General landed in Liverpool, he promised to return to that city and accept a dinner from the Mayor and corporation. This promise he was unable to fulfill until the 28th. On the evening of that day he arrived at Liverpool, accompanied by his son and General Badeau, and at once drove to the house of the Mayor, Mr. Walker. About two hundred and fifty guests attended the banquet, mainly citizens of the flourishing and prosperous town of Liverpool. In proposing a toast to General Grant, the Mayor congratulated himself on the fact that Liverpool was the first place in which the General set foot on British soil. The band played "Hail Columbia," and General Grant in response said:

"MR. MAYOR AND GENTLEMEN: You have alluded to the hearty reception given to me on my first landing on the soil of Great Britain, and the expectations of the Mayor that this reception would be equaled throughout the island have been more than realized. It has been far beyond anything I could have expected." (Cheers.) "I am a soldier, and the gentlemen here beside me know that a soldier must die. I have been a President but we know that the term of the presidency expires, and when it has expired he is no more than a dead soldier." (Laughter and cheers.) "But, gentlemen, I have met with a reception that would have done honor to any living person." (Cheers.) "I feel, however, that the compliment has been paid, not to me, but to my country. I cannot help but at this moment being highly pleased at the good feeling and good sentiment which now exist between the two peoples who of all others should be good friends. We are of one kindred, of one blood, of one language, and of one civilization, though in some respects we believe that we, being younger, surpass the mother country." (Laughter.) "You have made improvements on the soil and the surface of the earth which we have not yet done, but which we do not believe will take us as long as it took you." (Laughter and applause.) "I heard some military remarks which impressed me a little at the time—I am not quite sure whether they were in favor of the volunteers or against them. I can only say from my own observation that you have as many troops at Aldershott as we have in the whole of our regular army, notwithstanding we have many thousands of miles of frontier to guard and hostile Indians to control. But if it became necessary to raise a volunteer force, I do not think we could do better than follow your example. General Fairchild and myself are examples of volunteers who came forward when their assistance was necessary, and I have no doubt that if you ever needed such services you would have support from your reserve forces and volunteers, far more effective than you can conceive." (Cheers.) . . .

CHAPTER TWO

After a Run to the Continent, Scotland and the North Country

On July 5, the Grant entourage set off for a quick first spin to the Continent, where they were feted in private and in public, by royalty, by businessmen anxious for a piece of the rapidly expanding American trade, and by what Young characterized as an adoring European public. Stately climbs in the Alps burned off some of the calories consumed at endless state and semi-state banquets.

While in Belgium, Grant found King Leopold (notorious in history as the butcher of the Congo) to be a "man of more than ordinary gifts," and the two exchanged grand dinners. Leopold was especially keen on starting a shipping line from Antwerp to the American ports.

Thence the party went to the cathedral of Cologne, on the usual boat ride down the Rhine, and then to Frankfurt, where the American community had arranged a dinner for 150 people at the famous Palmer Garten restaurant. After the dinner, Grant could barely negotiate the gardens, clogged as they were by ten thousand admirers come to see him.

After Germany came Switzerland, where the Americans in Geneva persuaded Grant to lay the cornerstone of the American Episcopalian Church. At dinner that night, Grant professed himself to be very happy "among this assembly of fellow republicans of America and Switzerland [no King Leopold here]. I have long had a desire to visit the city where the Alabama Claims were settled without the effusion of blood, and where the principle of international arbitration was established, which I hope will be resorted to by other nations and be the means of continuing peace to all mankind." Grant referred to the 1871 settlement of American war claims against the British and British against the Americans, a thorny set of problems that had led Senator Charles Sumner, among others, to rattle the sabers of war against the British for having played too comfortably with the Confederates during the late conflict. (This settlement made Grant's stay in Britain far more comfortable than it otherwise would have been.)

After more Alps and a spin through Alsace-Lorraine, the Prussian-French flash point, Grant returned to Edinburgh on August 31. Because the Scots claimed the Grants as a Highlander family (of which the general apparently knew nothing), this part of the far-reaching journey had special sentimental value.

Leaving Edinburgh, it was off for a tour of the Highlands, replete with visits to the castles of the local lairds, and thence to Glasgow, where Grant was given the freedom of another city—honorary citizenship. In his response to that honor, Grant made a jest about corrupt immigrant voters in American elections—from whom he insisted that his Democratic enemies reaped the greater benefit. Grant relished his trip down through the industrial midlands of Britain. In Newcastle, on September 22, 1877, thousands of workingmen improvised a huge parade in Grant's honor, together with later speeches demonstrating their sense that America was the democratic model for many European workers, the place where upward mobility and the dignity of working people were most advanced and where the destruction of slavery had served as a beacon of universal liberty. Later, during the official municipal banquet, the local MP honestly noted the considerable support the Confederacy had received for her political leaders, while lauding the Americans as the noble, liberty-loving younger brothers of the English stock. Grant, the Representative American, the humble, self-made hero, replied to all such addresses with platitudes, no doubt heartfelt, about peaceful relations between the English-speaking peoples and the solidarity of all workingmen everywhere.

After a similar stop in Sheffield, it was back down to the south of England, to Stratford, already a Shakespearean tourist trap, where the Grant party made the obligatory visits. In Birmingham, Grant made a special point of praising John Bright, perhaps the leading middle-class English politician, repaying him for Bright's staunch pro-Unionism during the war. In other speeches, Grant defended American trade protectionism—essentially anti-British measures—as temporary necessities designed to give American factories a leg up, promising that the United States soon would re-engage in free trade. He also praised volunteer armies (as opposed to professional ones) as the backbone of Anglo-Saxon martial defenses, which needed to be based on well-educated ordinary citizens, not on mercenaries or unwilling, ignorant, and poor social outcasts.

On the General's return from the Continent, he made his promised visit to Scotland. On Thursday, the 31st of August, he arrived in Edinburgh, where he was received by the Lord Provost, whose guest he was during his stay in Scotland. The freedom of the city was presented in the Free Assembly Hall. There were upward of two thousand persons present. In reply to the Lord Provost's speech, General Grant said:

> "I am so filled with emotion, that I hardly know how to thank you for the honor conferred upon me by making me a burgess of this ancient city of Edinburgh. I feel that it is a great compliment to me and to my country. Had I eloquence I might dwell somewhat on the history of the great men you have produced, or the numerous citizens of this city and Scotland that have gone to America, and the record they have made. We are proud of Scotchmen as citizens of America. They make good citizens of our country, and they find it profitable to themselves." (Laughter.) "I again thank you for the honor you have conferred upon me." . . .

On the 13th of September, General Grant visited Glasgow. At three o'clock in the afternoon of that day he was presented with the freedom of the city. The City Hall, one of the largest public buildings in Glasgow, was filled with spectators. The bailiffs attended in their cocked hats and furred gowns. Exactly at three o'clock the Lord Provost stepped on to the platform and said that Grant had proved himself the Wellington of America. "The great and good Lincoln," said the Provost, "struck down the upas tree of slavery; but Grant tore it up by the roots, so that it should never live in his country to suck nutriment from its soil. I think the example shown by the American people in the forgiveness of injuries, and in their desire to live amicably with those who had been their enemies, presents the greatest triumph of Christian principle and practice the world has ever seen. In other countries, what crimes of vengeance have followed on revolutionary wars! The scaffold, the galleys, the fetid swamps of Cayenne, or the frozen deserts of Siberia, have been the fate of misguided patriots; but no such thing happened in America when the war closed. Not a drop of blood was spilled in vengeance. North and South shook hands, agreed to decorate together the graves of their dead, and to go on as one nation—a united and a free people." After this the address was read. In it the Common Council "admitted and received, and hereby admit and receive, General Ulysses Simpson Grant, Ex-President of the United States of America, to be a burgess and guild brother of the city and royal burgh of Glasgow, in recognition of his distinguished abilities as a statesman and administrator, his successful efforts in the noble work of emancipating his country from the horrors of slavery, and of his great services in promoting commerce and amity between the United States and Great Britain."

Cowgate, Edinburgh

This address was received with enthusiasm. In replying, General Grant said:

> "I rise to thank you for the great honor that has been conferred upon me this day by making me a free burgess of this great city of Glasgow. The honor is one that I shall cherish, and I shall always remember this day. When I am back in my own country, I will be able to refer with pride not only to my visit to Glasgow, but to all the different towns in this kingdom that I have had the pleasure and the honor of visiting." (Applause.) "I find that I am being made so much a citizen of Scotland, it will become a serious question where I shall go to vote." (Laughter and applause.) "You have railroads and other facilities for getting from one place to another, and I might vote frequently in Scotland by starting early. I do not know how you punish that crime over here; it is a crime that is very often practiced by people who come to our country and become citizens there by adoption. In fact, I think they give the majority of the votes. I do not refer to Scotchmen particularly, but to naturalized citizens. But to speak more seriously, ladies and gentlemen, I feel the honor of this occasion, and I beg to thank you, ladies and gentlemen of this city of Glasgow, for the kind words of your Lord Provost, and for the kind expression of this audience."

There was a visit to Ayr on the 14th of September, the land and home of Burns. This was followed by a tour in the region of Loch Lomond, and a visit to Inverary, where General Grant was the guest of the Duke of Argyle. No part of the Ex-President's tour in Scotland pleased him more than his visit to this illustrious nobleman. The part taken by the Duke of Argyle during our war, his unswerving adhesion to the cause of the North, and his efforts to secure for America in her struggle with the South the consideration and support of the English people, had excited in the General a high feeling of gratitude. This feeling grew to one of sincere friendship, and frequently during our journeys in Europe the General, in adverting to his Scotch trip, spoke of his visit to Inverary Castle as an experience he would never forget, and of the Duke of Argyle as a nobleman for whom he entertained the highest respect and esteem.

Perhaps no part of General Grant's reception in England was so striking as the short tour he made on his return from Scotland through the manufacturing districts of England. This journey embraced Newcastle, Sunderland, Sheffield, Birmingham, with excursions to Leamington, Stratford-on-Avon, Warwick, and places of historic interest. It was here that the General met the working classes of England, and the enthusiasm which his visit inspired makes it impossible almost to bring it within the limits of a sober narrative. I will, however, confine myself, as far as possible, to a brief recital of the incidents of the trip, and the demonstrations of welcome.

On Wednesday, the 19th of September, General Grant left Edinburgh and arrived in Newcastle on Thursday. The streets in the neighborhood of the central station were filled with thousands of people. A detachment of the Newcastle Rifle Volunteers were on duty to preserve order. The General, on appearing on the platform, was greeted with hearty cheering, and was received by the Mayor, Sir William Armstrong, and other representatives of the citizens of the town. The houses and shops had flags waving from the windows and roofs, and the bells of St. Nicholas rang out merrily. General and Mrs. Grant drove to the Mansion House, and in response to loud cheers, appeared on the balcony. In the evening there was a dinner with Sir William Armstrong, two hundred guests present. On Friday morning, the 21st inst., came sight-seeing. There was a visit to the old castle, to the ancient church of St. Nicholas, and the Exchange. An address was delivered to General Grant by the vice-president, council, and members of the Newcastle and Gateshead Incorporated Chamber of Commerce, which referred to the natural riches and industries of the Tyne district—iron in all its branches, chemicals, lead, copper, earthenware, fire-bricks, colors, and coals. "The various branches of the iron trade," said the address, "include melting the ore into pig iron, the manufacture of all kinds of wrought iron, rails, machines, ordnance, and the building of iron vessels, for which our river is famous. The shipment of coal from the town exceeds 7,109,000 tons per annum, and the number of vessels annually leaving the river, engaged in the coal trade, or loaded with the produce of our man-

ufactories, is larger than the number leaving any other port in the world."
The address alluded to this rapid increase as the result of free trade, and
expressed a regret that this policy had not been more generally followed
by other nations. The General in his response said:

> "The president in his remarks has alluded to the personal friendship exist-
> ing between the two nations—I will not say the two peoples, because we are
> one people" (applause); "but we are two nations having a common destiny,
> and that destiny will be brilliant in proportion to the friendship and coop-
> eration of the brethren on the two sides of the water." (Applause.) "During
> my eight years of Presidency, it was my study to heal up all the sores that were
> existing between us." (Applause.) "That healing was accomplished in a man-
> ner honorable to the nations. " (Applause.) "From that day to this feelings
> of amity have been constantly growing, as I think; I know it has been so on
> our side, and I believe never to be disturbed again. These are two nations
> which ought to be at peace with each other. We ought to strive to keep at
> peace with all the world besides" (applause), "and by our example stop those
> wars which have devastated our own countries, and are now devastating
> some countries in Europe."

After the reception by the Chamber of Commerce the party drove to
the new Tyne Swing Bridge, which was opened for inspection. The company then embarked on board the steamer "Commodore." This was accompanied by another steamer called the "Lord Collingwood," and which
carried from one to two hundred of the leading inhabitants of the borough. The band of the 1st Northumberland Volunteer Artillery were stationed on the boat. Shortly after one o'clock the boats left the new quay,
amid the cheers of thousands of spectators, and ran to Wallsend. The
weather was cold but fine, and the river banks were crowded with workmen, who gave a noisy, hearty welcome to the Ex-President. The shipping
was decorated with streamers, bunting, and flags. There was a firing of
guns, mortars, fog signals, and every species of instrument that could be
induced to make a noise. The General stood in the bow of the boat, bowing his acknowledgments. At the "Wellesley" training-ship there was a short
pause to witness the discipline. On reaching the bar the Tyne pier was examined, and at Tynemouth the General disembarked. An address was here
presented to the General, complimenting him on his sagacity and valor in
battle, and his clemency in victory. The General said that he had seen that
day on the banks of the Tyne no fewer than one hundred and fifty thousand people, mostly workmen, who had left their occupations and homes
to manifest, as he felt it, their friendship for their grandchildren—he

would not call them their cousins—on the other side of the Atlantic. He did not agree with the Mayor or member of Parliament who had spoken, in referring to the river as an insignificant one. It was true in America they had some large streams, but their greatest industries were carried on on the small streams. They had not one stream in America as yet that could show the number of industrial pursuits that the Tyne showed between Newcastle and the point at which they were now standing.

After this address there was a trial of the Life Brigade—a force maintained at Tyneside to save life. Two or three lifeboats were manned by the crews and floated among the waves, which were dashing heavily against the pier. Under the direction of their captain they executed the motions necessary to rescue a disabled ship. A rocket was fired, various lines were made fast, and a thick hawser was fixed from the battery to the west end of the pier with commendable celerity. The whole operation occupied about fifteen minutes.

On the 22d of September, a demonstration of workingmen took place in Newcastle. The importance of this ceremony may be comprehended from the fact that the local paper, the Newcastle *Chronicle,* the next morning, devoted twenty columns to a report. "Not since the great demonstration of 1873," says *The Chronicle,* "has the grass of the town moor been covered by so vast an assembly around a platform, as that to receive General Grant. It was estimated that no less than eighty thousand people were around the platform while Mr. Burt, M.P., read the address." It was dry, the air cold and bracing, and every way favorable for an outdoor demonstration. The proposal that the laboring men should do honor to General Grant came from Mr. Burt, in a letter suggesting that the Trades' Councils of Newcastle should take up the matter and secure the General a fitting reception. From an early hour Newcastle assumed a holiday aspect. Crowds came in by railway and other conveyances, from all parts of the northern country. Every spot where a view could be obtained was crowded. Stephenson's Monument was a cluster of human beings. Walls, cabs, windows, balconies, were full. The fronts of the town buildings and other edifices were covered with American and British flags intertwined. The flags of other nations were displayed from their respective consulates. Trophies of Venetian masts, crossed with bannerets, illuminated with the word "Welcome," were shown in different parts of the town. Thousands of pitmen from the mines of Northumberland, their wives and sweethearts, came to join the demonstration. . . .

"A golden era bursts upon the world:
The principle of right shall soon prevail:
Meek truth and justice soon shall lift their heads,
And wrong shall sink to everlasting night."

Then came the Hammermen's Society, the Plumbers, the Household Furnishers, and the Tanners of Elswick. The latter carried a banner bearing these words: "Welcome back, General Grant, from Arms to Arts," "Let us have Peace," "Nothing like Leather." The Masons, the Independent Order of Mechanics, the Newcastle Brass Moulders and Finishers, the Tyne District Carpenters and Joiners, and the Mill Sawyers and Machinists followed. The Sawyers carried a banner with these words: "Welcome, General Grant, to Newcastle. Tyneside rejoices to see thee. Welcome, Hero of Freedom." The United Chainmakers' Association finished the procession. These workmen marched in good order like battalions of soldiers. There was no disturbance of the peace, and a few policemen only kept the line. It was a moving stream of red and blue banners, and badges, and insignia.

The General rode in the procession to the town moor, rapturous cheering attending him until he reached the platform, at half-past three o'clock. As the General advanced to the front of the platform, "the cheers of the crowd," says the *Newcastle Chronicle,* "could be heard at St. Thomas's Church, nearly a mile distant. The Mayor opened the proceedings by asking the crowd to keep good order. Mr. Burt, M.P.,* then advanced and presented the address. In doing this he said that the prolonged civil war which raged in America excited the greatest anxiety and interest among the workpeople of the North. "Never," he said, "was there a war in which English armies were not employed that went so directly to the popular feeling. This was not merely because their kinsmen were in mortal combat; but because it was a battle for great principles. It was not a war for conquest, for selfish aggrandizement, or for the propping up of a tottering throne; but it involved the great questions of freedom, of the rights of man, and the dignity and honor of labor." Mr. Burt then congratulated America on the abolition of slavery, upon the pacific tenor of General Grant's administration, and upon the settlement of the Alabama Claims as one of the grandest moral victories ever achieved by statesmanship. . . .

"And now, General, in our final words we greet you as a sincere friend of labor. Having attested again and again your deep solicitude for the indus-

* Thomas Burt, the great Liberal working-class leader, had turned out this magnificent popular parade.

trial classes, and having also nobly proclaimed the dignity of labor by breaking the chains of the slave, you are entitled to our sincere and unalloyed gratitude; and our parting wish is, that the general applause which you have received in your own country, and are now receiving in this, for the many triumphs which you have so gloriously achieved, may be succeeded by a peaceful repose, and that the sunset of your life may be attended with all the blessings that this earth can afford.

"General! we beg your acceptance of this address as a testimony of the high regard and admiration in which you are held among the working people of Northumberland and Durham."

General Grant, who was received with the most enthusiastic cheering, then replied as follows:

"MR. BURT AND WORKINGMEN: Through you, I will return thanks to the workingmen of Tyneside for the very acceptable welcome address which you have just read. I accept from that class of people the reception which they have accorded me, as among the most honorable. We all know that but for labor we would have very little that is worth fighting for, and when wars do come, they fall upon the many, the producing class, who are the sufferers. They not only have to furnish the means largely, but they have, by their labor and industry, to produce the means for those who are engaged in destroying and not in producing. I was always a man of peace, and I have always advocated peace, although educated a soldier. I never willingly, although I have gone through two wars, of my own accord advocated war." (Loud cheers.) "I advocated what I believed to be right, and I have fought for it to the best of my ability in order that an honorable peace might be secured. You have been pleased to allude to the friendly relations existing between the two great nations on both sides of the Atlantic. They are now most friendly, and the friendship has been increasing. Our interests are so identified, we are so much related to each other, that it is my sincere hope, and it has been the sincere hope of my life, and especially of my official life, to maintain that friendship. I entertain views of the progress to be made in the future by the union and friendship of the great English-speaking people, for I believe that it will result in the spread of our language, our civilization, and our industry, and be for the benefit of mankind generally." (Cheers.) "I do not know, Mr. Burt, that there is anything more for me to say, except that I would like to communicate to the people whom I see assembled before me here this day how greatly I feel the honor which they have conferred upon me." (Cheers.) . . .

[Newcastle was the next stop.] In the evening there was a banquet at the Assembly Rooms, the Mayor of Newcastle occupying the chair. In response to the toast of the evening the General said:

The Address at Newcastle

"MR. MAYOR AND CORPORATION OF NEWCASTLE: I scarcely know how to respond to what has been said by the Mayor. I have a very vivid recollection that immediately upon my arrival upon these shores the Mayor invited me up here, and we have been carrying on a correspondence, directly and indirectly, ever since as to the time when I should be here. But as to my saying anything after I came, such a thing never occurred to me." (Laughter.) "I will say that the entertainment by your worthy Mayor has exceeded my expectations. I have had no better reception in any place, nor do I think it possible to have a better." (Cheers.) "All I have seen since I have been on the Tyne has been to me most gratifying as an individual, and I think when I go back to my own country I will find that it has been very gratifying to my countrymen to hear of it. It has been gratifying all along the Tyne to Tynemouth. It has been gratifying ever since my landing upon English soil. It has been gratifying because I have seen that which is extremely pleasant, namely the good relationship existing, that should always exist, between English-speaking people." (Applause.) "I think that is a matter of the vastest importance, because I believe that we have the blessing of civilization to extend. I do not want to detract from other civilizations; but I believe that we possess the highest civilization. There is the strongest bond of union between the English-speaking people, and that bond should and will serve to extend the greatest good to the greatest number. That will always be my delight."

Mr. Cowen, M.P., responded to the toast of the House of Commons, and in the course of his speech he said "that Newcastle honored General Grant as a man, and welcomed him as representing that great, free, and friendly nation, that Younger Britain on the other side of the broad Atlantic." (Applause.) "In the days of his country's dangers and trials he nobly did his duty. His highest honor was, that during the darkest hour he did not despair of the Republic. General Grant's achievements would fill a large and glowing page in the history of his native land, and no inconsiderable one in the history of our times. His position as a soldier and a statesman was fixed, and there was not now time, and this was not the occasion, to dilate on it. He had won the confidence of his contemporaries and secured the encomiums of posterity. The world had often spoken with admiration of his valor and his resolution—of his courage and ability. He had no wish to underrate or overlook these virtues; but to-night he would speak of his modesty and magnanimity. He knew of nothing more touching than the gentleness with which General Grant conveyed a necessary, but at the same time a hasty and unpleasant command, from the American War Minister to his brave companion-in-arms, General Sherman, nor more generous than his dignified treatment of the vanquished Confederate captain—a foeman worthy of his steel. These actions reminded us of the fabled days of chivalry. . . . We all followed his career with interest and with admiration—many of us, most of us in this district, with sympathy. The different views existing in English society found memorable expression on two occasions in Newcastle. In the midst of the war, at a banquet in our town hall, Earl John Russell [then British Foreign Secretary] gave it as his opinion that the North was fighting for empire and the South for independence. Mr. Gladstone, the year after, in the same place and on a like occasion, declared that the South had made an army, were making a navy, and would make a nation. He referred to these statements not for the purpose of reviving a long-forgotten and exhausted controversy, nor with the object of pointing out that the 'common people,' when great principles were at stake, were often right when statesmen, who took a technical view of the struggle, were in error." . . .

Lord Russell, with characteristic courage and candor, not long after he made his speech in Newcastle, declared that he had misapprehended the objects of the American war, and acknowledged he had been wrong in the views he had entertained. Mr. Gladstone was scarcely so ready and frank with his recantation, but he also ultimately confessed that he had not understood the purposes of the Republican leaders. He trusted that General Grant's visit to this country would prevent a repetition of such misconceptions, would help to draw still closer the bonds of unity between America and England, and tend to prevent the bellicose spirits in both nations plunging us into suffering and confusion for the gratification of unworthy and antagonistic passions. Our common interests were peace. We were streams from the same fountain—branches from the same tree. We sprang from the same race, spoke the same language, were moved by the same prejudices animated by the same hopes; we sang the same songs, cherished the same liberal political principles, and we were imbued with the conviction that we had a common destiny to fulfill among the children of men. We were bound by the treble ties of interest, duty, and affection to live together in concord. A war between America and England would be a war of brothers. It would be a household martyrdom only less disastrous than war between Northumberland and Middlesex. The pioneers of the Republic—the Pilgrim Fathers—were pre-eminently English. It was because they were so that they emigrated. They left us because England in that day had ceased to be England to them. They went in the assertion of the individual right of private judgment and the national right of liberty and conscience. They carved out for themselves a new home in the wilderness, into which they carried all the industrial characteristics and intellectual energies of the mother land. They did not leave us when England was in her infancy. Our national character was consolidated before they went, and Shakespeare and Milton and Bacon, and all the great men of the Elizabethan era, were not only figuratively but literally as much their countrymen as ours. They repudiated the rule of the English king, but, as they themselves declared, they never closed their partnership in the English Parnassus. They would not own the authority of our corrupt court, but they bowed before the majesty of our literary chiefs. They emigrated from Stuart tyranny, but not from the intellectual and moral glories of our philosophers and poets, any more than from the sunshine and dews of heaven. These literary ties had been extended and strengthened by years. The names of Longfellow and Lowell, Bryant and Whittier, were as much household words with us as those of Campbell and Coleridge, Byron and Burns, Dickens and Thackeray. Bulwer and Jerrold wrote as much for America as for England. The works of Hawthorne and Cooper, Emerson and Irving, came to us across the sea bathed in the fragrance of their boundless prairies, redolent of the freshness of their primeval pine forests, and were read and admired as warmly on the banks of the Tyne and the Thames as on the shores of the Potomac and the Mississippi. But in addition to the intellectual, there were strong material ties intertwining the two nations. When the United States ceased to be part of the English dominions, an increased commercial intercourse sprang up between us. Coincident with the close of the American War of Independence, the ingenuity and skill of our countrymen led to the discovery of those great mechanical inventions which produced the cotton trade. While the spindles of the Lancashire mill-owners had been weaving wealth for themselves and power for their country, they had bound in a web of interest and good-will the American planter and merchant and their English manufacturer and workman. They trusted that when their distinguished guest returned home, he would assure his fellow countrymen that there was, amongst men of all classes, sects, and parties in England, only one feeling toward America, and that was one of friendship—that we had only one rivalry with her, and that was to excel in the arts of peace and the works of civilization." I print this part of Mr. Cowen's speech because it gives a fair idea of the feeling of the people of Newcastle toward the United States. At the close of this reception, General Grant drove to Hesley Side, and spent the Sunday with W. H. Charlton, Esq. . . .

. . . Arriving in Stratford at eleven o'clock by special train, the General was met by the Mayor, Mr. J. J. Mason, and was driven to New Place Gardens, where he strolled about. Afterward the party visited the Church of the Holy Cross and the Grammar School, where they were shown the corner which Shakespeare as a boy occupied, where he learned his "little Latin and less Greek." The General before leaving the school asked a holiday for the boys; which kindness was recognized by three times three cheers, and one for Mrs. Grant. The Shakespeare Memorial, now in process of erection on the Avon bank, was inspected, and afterward a visit made to the Church of the Holy Trinity, where repose the ashes of Shakespeare, and where the vicar, the Rev. F. Smith, received the party and showed them the various memorials of the poet. On quitting the church

London and once in Newcastle-on-Tyne. In my response, on both occasions, I expressed what I thought was due to the workingmen, not only of my country and of Great Britain, but to the workingmen all over the world. I said that we in our country strove to make labor respectable. There is no class of labor that disqualifies a man from any position, either in society or in official life. Labor disgraces no man; unfortunately you occasionally find men disgrace labor. Your Mayor has alluded to the fact that the population of Birmingham had tripled itself in fifty years. I would ask the Mayor whether, if Birmingham had been deprived of its handicraft laborers, it would have seen any such increase? It is due to the labor and to the manufacture of articles which are turned out by the means of labor, that you have grown in population and in wealth. In response to the kindly feelings which exist between the workingmen of Birmingham and those of the United States, and the compliments you have paid to me for the efforts I have made in the cause of freedom and the North, I thank you most heartily."

Then came an address read by Mr. A. O'Neill, on behalf of the International Arbitration Union. Mr. O'Neill recalled the fact that when General Grant became President, he frankly declared his motto to be "Let us have peace." No event, said Mr. O'Neill, in the history of the American Government could surpass in importance the great experiment of adjusting disputes by arbitration. Allusion was made to General Grant's efforts as President to ameliorate the condition of the Indians by the appointment of commissioners from the Society of Friends. "Our hearts," continued Mr. O'Neill, "have been also deeply touched by your just and beneficent treatment of the colored freedmen. You guided them in their faltering steps as they marched out of bondage; you defended them from their enemies; you cared for them in their distresses; you aided them in obtaining education; and you claimed for them their rights as citizens; and now 'the blessing of him that was ready to perish shall come upon you, for you delivered the poor that cried, and the fatherless, and him that had none to help him.'" . . .

CHAPTER THREE

Paris

In 1870, France had experienced military and political catastrophe when the Prussians had conquered and destroyed the Second Empire of Napoleon III. Out of humiliation and conflict among monarchist factions, who taken together composed the majority of French voters, the Third Republic had been born. During the subsequent seven years, republicanism had overtaken monarchism in public opinion and in the French Chamber of Deputies, while the president since 1873 had been Marshal Patrice de MacMahon, a staunch monarchist. On May 17, 1877, MacMahon had sought to end this deadlock by provoking the resignation of the republican government and forcing a new election. The Grant party arrived in Paris just after a smashing and apparently conclusive republican victory. In fact, all was not yet settled, as many on the right then urged MacMahon to stage a military coup d'état. In the event, he would refuse to do so, and, after more electoral victories for republicanism, he resigned in 1879. At the time of the Grant visit, the outcome was not altogether clear; though republicanism was apparently triumphant, MacMahon—the man on the white horse—might yet seize power.

Clearly, Grant was uncomfortable in the political climate into which he was swept despite himself. He was blamed as harboring militarist sentiments, rather unfairly, and for having tilted to the Prussians during the war of 1870, which he in fact had done in a public pronouncement. And this attention came in a most public manner, in a blazing poem damning Grant on his arrival by the eminent old republican, Victor Hugo. In this embarrassing climate, Grant lay low, confining himself almost entirely to dinners with the extensive American colony in Paris, to shopping and sightseeing, and to sitting alone watching the passing parade on the Champs Élysées.

Grant barely appears in this chapter—Young's clearest snapshot is of him sitting reading the morning papers in the *New York Herald* offices—a convenient bit of promotion for Young's paper. Leaving Grant sitting and reading, Young goes off on a brilliant sociological exposition of the lives of Americans in Paris, then, as now, rather more romantic a place than Albany or Peoria.

General Grant's visit to Paris had been somewhat postponed. Originally the idea had been entertained of visiting Paris in midsummer, on the way to Italy. A reception had even been proposed for the General, which was to have taken place in Paris on the 4th of July. Certain changes in France, however, were transpiring, which, in the opinion of the American representatives in Paris, might give General Grant's visit in July somewhat of a political character. The struggle between the President of the Republic, General MacMahon, and the Jules Simon cabinet had set in, and it was thought that the presence of General Grant would be taken by the monarchical and imperial parties in France as savoring of a political character, in favor of the republicans. General Grant could not come to France without becoming the guest of General MacMahon, and a false interpretation of the visit might have been entertained. It was then determined that the journey to Paris should be postponed until October.

In France political feeling was at fever heat. Though Paris, the great city, was apparently as peaceful as on the eve of the Lenten feast, as quiet as before that *coup d'état* which Victor Hugo has described in his "Histoire d'un Crime," every one knew that the crisis had come. The boulevards might throng with eager bustling throngs; all the currents of life, society, business, and pleasure might be rushing on; still in an instant there might come revolution and anarchy. The writer strolled under the shadow of the Madelaine, and turned into a street leading to the Place de la Concorde. It was here the guillotine once stood; and where the fountains were now gushing, oceans of blood had been shed, which those waters would never cleanse. On toward the Bastile swept a broad avenue of light. There were masses of illumination clustered around the obelisk of Luxor, and the moon shed its beams on the gilded dome of the Invalides. All around was the murmur and hum of a great city, the many voices of the night rising and falling like the cadence of the sea. Paris never looked more beautiful, more self-composed, but never was more anxious. Walls were covered with parti-colored appeals. Prominent were the proclamations of Marshal MacMahon, calling on the patriotism of the people, with official white-paper posters. The wild enthusiasm of a New York election was wanting, with its flashing torches and multitudes of marching men. Such a thing would have been impossible in France. Attempt a political demonstration and squadrons of cavalry would inclose the street, or otherwise there might be tumult and massacre.

It was the coming election which was to settle the fate of France. If honest republicanism could gain the day, it would show the highest allegiance to the law. It would demonstrate this fact, that France had grown greater, through all her sore trials—that the France of the days of Messidor, which Barbier in his famous poem had compared to a wild, untrainable colt, had at last been broken, and had become disciplined and obedient; not coerced by the iron grip of a Bonaparte, but by the kinder hand of enlightened public opinion.

Never was republic encompassed with greater difficulties. Pretenders to the throne were striving to mount its slippery steps, policemen were trammeling and tethering the press, spies were dogging every leader, and the clergy were praying for republican discomfiture. As to the army, it was marching and counter-marching, a threatening reminder of its power. Worse than all, the fearful shadow of the Commune rose like a dark cloud casting its gloom over Paris. When, in spite of all this, republicanism triumphed, this was the first step toward true conservative republicanism.

It was when France was all aglow with excitement caused by a true republican victory that General Grant arrived in Paris. On the morning of the 24th of October, 1877, the General, accompanied by his wife, his son, and the writer, left London in a special train from Charing Cross. A crowd of Americans assembled at the station bid the General God-speed. Folkestone was soon reached, the express train speeding rapidly through the pleasant Kentish county. At Folkestone the Mayor and many of the prominent citizens were assembled, who expressed their well-wishes, and with hearty cheers the party took the steamer and crossed the channel. The trip was calm and pleasant. As the white cliffs of England disappeared in the seas, the green fields of France loomed up on the horizon. On landing at Boulogne, the prefect of the department welcomed the General, in the name of the Marshal President of France. As there were not the excuses of seasickness to delay the party at Boulogne, after but a very short rest the General proceeded to Paris. Time enough was spent in Boulogne to understand why it is so appreciated by the English. Lying but a few hours from London, it is both the summer and winter resort of many an impecunious Englishman, pleasant climate and cheapness of living being the great desiderata.

Just before reaching the depot at Paris, General Noyes, the American

Minister, General Torbert, the Consul-General, and an aide-de-camp of Marshal MacMahon entered the car. In the name of the President of the French Republic the Ex-President of the Republic of the United States was welcomed to France. On arriving, a large crowd, comprising the leading members of the American colony in Paris, received the General. After greetings had been exchanged, the General drove to the Hôtel Bristol, through a heavy rain. It would be impossible to give in detail an account of the many receptions and dinners given to General Grant in Paris. His stay in Paris was a pleasant one. It is not worth while to detail such minor incidents of a disagreeable character which arose because French political feeling would not regard General Grant's visit to France in the exact light he intended it to be, a purely unofficial one. Because Mr. Elihu B. Washburne, our Minister to France during the Franco-Prussian war,* had at the same time the rights of the German residents in Paris intrusted to his care, and because he had acted with justice and humanity, it suited monarchists, imperialists, and some few of the republican party, to think that General Grant during his Presidency, in accepting the acts of his foreign minister had rather inclined toward the Prussians than to France. Victor Hugo did much to intensify this feeling. Poetic license sometimes becomes quite indifferent as to facts. It is a matter of regret that this feeling should have existed, but as it belongs to the history of General Grant's visit to France as such I am forced to write it. Although this feeling existed, the French were too polite a people to show the least discourtesy to a guest. It must be mentioned that the Bonapartists and their reactionary papers went out of their way to excite anti-German feelings against the General. It was alleged by them that the General's visit was a demonstration in favor of republicanism. As a matter of fact the feelings of General Grant toward France were of the friendliest character. It is true, however, that one of his few aversions was directed toward the Bonapartist family. He looked upon the war between France and Germany as a causeless war, made by an ambitious and selfish despot to save his dynasty. In regard to Napoleonism, though General Grant had never written a poem on the same subject, he entirely agreed with Victor Hugo.

Although during the first few days the weather was bad, this did not pre-

---

* Elihu B. Washburne was one of Grant's oldest supporters, having helped him to obtain his first military command in 1861, when Washburne was in the House of Representatives from Illinois and Grant was a nobody. Grant's first secretary of state in 1868–69, Washburne was hastily packed off to be minister in Paris when he embarrassed Grant with his rather crude country manners in the sole cabinet post that required a gentleman.

Parading the Champs Élysées

vent the General's visiting all the places and public buildings worthy of attention in Paris. There is no enjoyment in Paris so complete as that of threading its streets. The party scaled the heights of Montmartre. Montmartre is an elevated quarter of Paris from whence a full view of the immense city can be had. The Quartier Latin was frequently visited. Here are the universities, the schools of medicine, the far-famed Sorbonne; it is the old heart of Paris, where for eight hundred years and more, students from all parts of the world have come; here all the great libraries are concentrated. It is a world in itself, a center of study and amusement, with its famous theater, the Odeon. There is a well-known street in the Quartier Latin, the Rue de l'Ancienne Comédie, which tells of its former character. Paris is indeed the elysium of loungers. Save when entangled in the very center of the old *cité*, go as you will, after a while you must emerge to some large and open place, which acts as a frame to a fine public building. Here are the Champs Élysées with their broad carriage-ways, where all the dashing equipages of Europe are assembled. The sidewalks are thronged by elegantly dressed people. Walk its length until you stand at the Rond Point midway, and look up and down. Far beyond you stands in its lofty magnificence L'Arc de l'Étoile. This triumphal arch, which is the grandest in Europe, conceived by the Emperor Napoleon I. in 1806, was finished thirty years afterward. Noble in form, it is ornamented with famous bas-reliefs, due to the greatest artists in France. Cast your eye farther beyond this arch, and the buildings of Neuilly and the green woods of the Bois de Boulogne, the famous riding and driving park of the Parisian, is seen. Now, standing as you are, face to the left, and see looming in the sky the lofty dome of the Invalides, the last refuge of France's brave soldiers. Many a veteran lives there and talks of his eventful life, while in his midst there reposes in his porphyry tomb all that remains of Napoleon Bonaparte. Now turning directly around, on your rear look down the broad Champs Élysées until your eye lights on the obelisk of Luxor, the Place de la Concorde, and the Tuileries. If we had been in Paris before the Commune you would have seen the palace of the Tuileries. Now they only show their ruins; but the eye goes beyond them. The massive buildings of the Louvre are seen, and away beyond that looms up Notre Dame de Paris, and many a massive church and spire. Still the picture is not concluded yet. On your right spreads out the busiest portion of the great city. The line of the boulevard is distinguished with the Madelaine—and following it on—there is the column of the Bastile. Perhaps, if not from the Rond Point, at least from the Place Concorde, the finest architectural *aperçu* the world knows is seen. Nothing is wanting—for a river with many bridges, flanked with stately buildings, gives variety to the scene.

"How I long," said Mr. Greeley, "for the time when I can leave this desk and lose myself in the wilderness of London." If London is a wilderness, and I have often thought the loveliest spot I ever saw was Cheapside at noon, Paris has its especial charms.

A formal visit was paid to the Élysées, and there was a presentation to Marshal MacMahon. The Marshal was extremely cordial, and greeted General Grant as a comrade and fellow soldier, and wanted to show him the army and some military shows. But here came something which often perplexed the General's hosts while in Europe, and that was his aversion to military displays. He never seemed to want to see a review nor hear a drum beat, nor visit any military pageant. There were many meetings between General Grant and Marshal MacMahon, and the General was impressed with the sincere straightforwardness of the President, who was devoted to France, and who seemed animated only by the purposes of both preserving and strengthening his country.

Before the courtesies which were to be extended to General Grant by the Americans in Paris were rendered, the series of visits to various parts of Paris were continued and afforded much amusement to the party. The

Palais Royal, with its covered squares of shops, where the most brilliant, the most tempting merchandise is offered, was visited. For the major part of the day the interior gardens of the Palais Royal are thronged. Here are many leading restaurants; and from a dinner there, the party could go to one of the two theaters which are in the immediate proximity. Across the river, skirting again the Latin Quarter, was the Luxembourg Palace, with its noble gallery, containing the works of contemporaneous artists; the garden, with the observatory. An especial object of interest to General Grant was the church of Notre Dame, which, after St. Peter's, is the grandest ecclesiastical building in the world. Before its columns, in dusky crypt, has been enacted the whole history of France. Royal marriages, baptisms, and funerals have taken place here. The Revolution set up within its precincts the Goddess of Reason upsetting religion, to be followed by the coronation of Napoleon and a return to the faith. To contrast ancient church edifices with more modern work, the church of La Trinité, erected in 1860, was visited. The commercial aspect of Paris interesting General Grant, the Tribunal de Commerce on the Quai Desaix, and its method of working, had the particular attention of the American party.

It was to the Louvre that numerous visits were paid. If a man with endless time and leisure could visit this most remarkable of galleries, its numerous treasures could hardly be exhausted in a life of study. Gallery follows on gallery. Here are all the great masters of the world, the Leonardo da Vincis, the Raphaels, the Correggios, Guidos, Van Dycks, Murillos, Metsus, and Ostades. It is a progression of art, from the earliest times up to today. Pictures, statues, stretch out in endless view. There are single rooms devoted to the works of a particular country, and there is no style or method of art which is not represented. As we passed through the many galleries, perched on high scaffolds were artists from all countries copying and studying the glorious masters of the past.

Skirting the Rue de Rivoli, emerging from the Louvre, passing the demolished Tuileries, the Column Vendôme rears its height. Built by the Emperor Napoleon I. in 1810, it perpetuates the victories achieved at Ulm and Austerlitz. It is made of bronze, coming from the cannons captured by the French, and the metal bears carvings commemorative of the French campaigns. All know how Courbet, the realistic artist, as a revolutionist, with savage iconoclasm tore down this column, and how after peace was restored to France and the Commune was crushed, this trophy of French victory was again put in its former position.

Sight-seeing was interrupted from time to time by the numerous attentions and civilities showered on General Grant. On the 29th of October, General Edward F. Noyes, the American Minister, gave the Ex-President a reception at his house on the Avenue Josephine. This reception was of the most brilliant character, and was attended by all the leading Americans in Paris. None of the republican leaders were, however, present. Subsequently, Mr. Healey, the artist, arranged a meeting at which General Grant met M. Gambetta. From this and other meetings, a high feeling of esteem arose for the French republican leader, who impressed the General as one of the foremost minds in Europe. It was on the 6th of November that the members of the American colony, numbering some three hundred, gave a public dinner to General Grant at the Grand Hotel. With but few exceptions, every American in Paris was present. General Noyes presided, and among the guests were MM. Rochambeau and Lafayette, the latter descended from the Revolutionary hero of that name. The veteran journalist Emile Girardin was there, whom Horace Greeley called the greatest journalist in the world. Edmond About and Laboulaye were present. This dinner proceeded without special incident, the General being received with the greatest enthusiasm, and making a brief speech. These two dinners, with one at the Élyseés, were the special events of the General's visit. General Torbert entertained the Ex-President at his apartment. On the 20th of November, Madame Mackey of California gave a reception at her house near the Arch of Triumph, which from its splendor recalled scenes in the "Arabian Nights." The Marquis Talleyrand-Perigord, descended from the great Talleyrand, one of the few noblemen in France who cheerfully accepted the Republic, gave a princely dinner to the Ex-President, which was attended by over a hundred guests. M. Laugal gave a dinner, when the Count of Paris was presented to General Grant. Mrs. Sickles, wife of General Sickles, Madame Bakmitoff, formerly Miss Bates of Washington, Dr. T. W. Evans, I. H. Harjes, of the firm of Drexel, Harjes & Co., R. R. Scott, the Secretary of Legation, and R. M. Hooper, Vice-Consul of the United States in Paris, were among those who gave dinners and entertainments in honor of General Grant and his family.

The American colony, of which General Grant was for the next few weeks the honored guest, is an institution in Paris. In this city of many nationalities, the American plays a prominent part. Several causes contribute to this. American society is composite; and citizens of the older nationalities desire to return to the memories and scenes of the older world. There are exiles, idlers, and students; business exiles, driven away in the bankruptcy revolution; political exiles, suffering from the fall of Tammany and the Southern Confederacy; social exiles, who seek oblivion in absence. There is so much in Paris to attract, that, when cultivated citizens gain wealth, they come to enjoy the art-life of the metropolis which is surpassed in no other city. There is a permanent colony, and a floating colony. The permanent colony numbers in winter as many as three thousand. The floating colony is at its height in the summer, and reaches in average years ten thousand. In years of war, like 1870, it falls below the average. In years of the Exhibition, it exceeds the average. I remember reading in the statistics of travel, during the Exhibition, that the American was next to the English in number. Every year adds, because persons who once visit Paris are pretty certain to come again; and the means of travel grow so much more easy and attractive each year, that the coming is less and less difficult. There is a section called the American Quarter. I am afraid it is the gaudiest and most expensive in Paris. In this quarter you find newspapers addressed to the American taste; drinking shops with the latest American contrivance in beverages; bazaars, where American fashions are taught in apparel. The hotels cultivate American custom, and pander to a supposed American appetite for fishballs and buckwheat cakes. The American section includes the Champs Élysées, the Boulevard Haussmann, the Grand Hotel, and Grand Opera Quarter, and the radius of wide, magnificent avenues which sweep around the Arch of Triumph. It is noted that in this quarter the tradesmen paint American coats of arms on their windows, and charge twenty-five per cent. more for their wares than their neighbors over the river. There are American clergymen who minister to your spiritual comfort; and the American dentist becomes an institution almost royal in its relations and appliances. There is a Fourth of July which, in ancient days, was wont to be the season for patriotic refreshment of soul. But since the jar which the war gave to our patriotism, Americans do not come together as much as in the past, and the eagle-worship, which in other days was a characteristic of our people, has faded away. There was something of a revival on the occasion of the coming of General Grant, which, let us hope, may be the beginning of a better and kinder era.

The center and head of the colony is the American Minister. Washburne reigned for many years, and Noyes reigns in his stead. Washburne is remembered as a sturdy, prompt, brave, kindly man, who won renown by remaining at his post during the siege and the Commune, when the other diplomatists ran away. Washburne, as I have shown, is not much liked by the French because of his supposed German sympathies; but I presume it was the fact that he was assigned to the care of the German residents in

Paris that led to the impression that he took sides in the war. It was a severe bit of work, and no American can read the story of our Minister's devotion without increased respect for his character. The old relations between Washburne and General Grant would have made it pleasant for the Minister to welcome the President. But this was not to be. When General Grant came Washburne had gone, and General Noyes reigned in his stead. General Edward F. Noyes is a young man, who came to Paris with an honorable record—the record of a man who had risen from poverty to the highest office in his State, who by the processes of self-education had become a famous member of the Ohio Bar, and who when the war broke out went into our volunteer army. One of his legs was left in Georgia, and he shows traces of suffering in his keen, handsome face. His is an honorable record in peace and in war, and it was pleasant to see in so important a post as the mission to France one who had given his blood for the Union. The Consul General, General Alfred T. Torbert,* had commanded a division under Sheridan, and succeeded the amiable, accomplished, and everkindly Meredith Read. After Torbert, Lucien Fairchild was to come.† Of him too it may be said that his record was an honorable one. In his boyhood days he crossed the plains, and was among the Argonauts of California. He returned home, and became Governor of Wisconsin. He lost an arm in the war, and his dangling sleeve, like the shorn limb of the Minister, is an eloquent suggestion of what our citizens did for the Union. Although it was a disappointment to General Grant not to meet his old friend Washburne, it was pleasant to have in official places men who had served under him in the war, and whose records had been so creditable as those of Noyes, Torbert, and Fairchild.

Around the legation and the consulate the colony revolves. General Noyes holds his court on the Rue du Chaillot, the old hill of Chaillot that you find in the early maps of Paris. If one place was not as near as another in Paris this might be called out of the way, but I can well understand how a legation might be too near for comfort. The tendency of the American mind to seek his minister upon all occasions when he is overcharged for candles, when he has lost his baggage, when he is homesick and lacks in themes of conversation, when the mails are irregular, when the right gloves

---

* Torbert was a West Pointer and a division commander during the later stages of the war in Grant's Army of the Potomac. He served as counsel-general in Paris, 1873–78.

† Fairchild, a Wisconsin colonel who was severely wounded at Gettysburg, later served as governor of Wisconsin (1866–72) and as counsel-general in Paris (1880–82). He was also very active in the Grand Army of the Republic.

have not come home from the bazaar, would make the legation a burden if it were too convenient of access. The fact of an American being a tax-payer gives him a sense of possession in dealing with ministers and consuls which it is inconvenient to question. There are other centers, however, in Paris, besides the legation: the newspaper offices in the Rue Scribe, the banking houses, the leading hotels. In journalism there is *The American Register*, the property of Dr. Evans, and under the control of Dr. Crane. *The Register* is the oldest of American journals on the continent, and its real advantage is as a bulletin which tells every American in Europe where every other American resides. Through its columns the members of our colony can touch elbows, and feel themselves at home. There is another journal called *The Gazette*, under the direction of Mr. Kremer, who was formerly the publisher of *The Register*, and which shows the energy of new and ambitious undertakings. Monroe has a banking house on the Rue Scribe, while the famous house of Drexel will lend you money or sell you bonds on the Boulevard Haussmann. On the Avenue de l'Opera is the office of the New York *Herald*. This avenue is too beautiful to be called a vandalism, but those who loved old Paris, who remember the curious streets and by-ways, every street a remembrance of the past and every corner tinted by some historical association; those who remember what a pleasure it was, for instance, to leave the boulevard at Rue Neuve Saint Augustin and lose yourself in its devious winding ways, feeling that around you was the Paris of Henry IV. and Louis XIV., until you came into the sylvan inclosures of the Palais Royal; those who remember what a pleasing stroll it was and what a comfort to plunge out of the fresh and modern Paris, and revel in the quaint and dying past, will resent the Avenue de l'Opera. But it had to be. In new Paris it was necessary to have a shorter road from the Grand Opera House to the palace of the Louvre. So this avenue came into being, like the Boulevard Haussmann, the Boulevard St. Germain, the Street of the Fourth September, and other pretentious avenues. The map was taken, and a line was drawn direct from the steps of the Grand Opera House to the gates of the Louvre. The Republic did this, and it was commended at the time as an illustration of the fact that Republic and Empire were alike animated by a desire to improve and beautify Paris. The Avenue of the Opera is a beautiful street with beauty of a pretentious kind. As you turn from the boulevard, from the Rue de la Paix, along which falls the shadow of the Vendôme Column, you come to one of the centers of the American colony, the office of the New York *Herald*. This office is among the shrines of the American abroad. He can hear all the news. He can write

General Grant at the Herald
Office, Paris

his name on the register, and know that it will be called next morning to
New York, and his presence in Paris spread to an envious or admiring
world at home. He can read all about home, for here is the best reading-
room in Europe. Whether he comes from Pennsylvania or Oregon, Maine
or Texas, he will find his home paper, and read all about the church and
the county fair, the latest murder or the pending canvass—deaths and marriages. Perchance he will find some wandering brother, and there will
ensue comforting chat about America, and how much cheaper it is than
Paris, and what scoundrels these Frenchmen are, especially in the matter
of candles. If he has any news to bestow, Mr. Ryan, who is in charge of the
office, and is one of the oldest and most distinguished members of *The
Herald* staff, will listen with an eager and discerning ear.

The Herald office was one of the favorite haunts of General Grant in
Paris. He would slip in of a morning and seek out a quiet corner, and
brood over the newspapers for an hour or two. There are other haunts patronized by the colony. There is the clubhouse, the Washington Club, over
which Colonel Evelyn presides, where members may discuss baccarat for
twenty thousand dollars, or the Athanasian creed, just as they please, for

the deliberations of this club are secret. The colony breaks up into little zones or worlds, in which there is not always the harmony that you could wish. There is a Congress or a Jacobin Club, which holds sessions in the Grand Hotel. You can obtain admittance to this assembly by the franchise of a cigar or a glass of wine. The colony has class distinctions and draws lines. There is the old resident and the new resident, the American in trade; the idle American; the American who speaks French; the one who does not, but always buys a French newspaper and pretends to read it in public in a dazed condition. There is the colonist who has family relationships—the colonist who never obtrudes his domestic life upon friends; the American who wears the red ribbon of the Legion of Honor; the democrat, who despises all such aristocratic nonsense, but who would give a good slice of his income to be able to wear it without danger from the police. These are the phases of colonial life which are apparent to the looker-on in Paris; but under all is another phase which you must know Paris well to know it at all—the real life in Paris, the life of those who come for the enjoyment of the higher phases of Paris society.

There are those who belong to what might be called the *virtuoso* colony. The members form that uneasy class of people who collect things. There are many phases in this class: the *virtuoso* who is a kind of pawnbroker or Chatham-street dealer of the Original Jacobs tendency, and who runs from one *bric-à-brac* and curiosity shop to another, buying all that is curious and odd, to be resold to American customers in the summer. There are some in the colony who follow the trade, who will sell you anything from a china jug of Louis XIV.'s time to a stolen fragment of the Column Vendôme, and failing to make five hundred per cent. profit, will take five. There is one collector whose hobby is the French Revolution. A picture, print, or book on the French Revolution is to him a source of joy. He is a bit crazed on the subject, and will spend an afternoon on the quays among the old-book stores, and if he can find a print of Mirabeau, a colored caricature of Robespierre, or an edition of Père Duchesne, goes home in triumph. If he has one rare print and sees another of the same, he will buy it, not because he needs it, but to prevent some one else from possessing it. I know another, a most respected member of the colony, whose taste is for books and prints illustrating the American Revolution. There was a time when Paris was a mine for those who had fancies in this way. America and France were so closely connected during the Revolution that a great part of the literature of the country was tinted with events in the Jerseys and Virginia, and the achievements of the famous General Washington. Franklin, residing in Paris for several years, had French sympathies, and was honored by the French people. I do not know how many portraits of Franklin there are, but I have heard hundreds as the figure. To collect these Franklins, to have copies of the peculiar prints, those with a turn to the nose or an extra button to the garment, or rudely engraved and with no more resemblance to the philosopher than to any conspicuous figure in that history—any odd, quaint, or unusual Franklin—is a rare pleasure.

There was a collector who had an admiration for Napoleon the First. So he searched and inquired and purchased until he had "a collection." One day he was in the Latin Quarter discussing his fancy with a dealer in prints. "How many different prints of Napoleon are there?" "Three thousand," was the answer. There is another of the colony whose specialty is the Commune. This came and flourished and fell in 1871. One would think that it would be an easy matter to gather the records of that brief and recent time. But there are necessary documents and copies of proclamations and newspapers of the Commune as difficult to buy as those of the French Revolution. Another of my *virtuoso* friends has a fancy for Horace. Let it come in any shape, any translation or style, and the day that brings it is calendared among the red-letter annals. Another finds life only supportable through the painter Velasquez. My friend spends his time in going from place to place, wherever there is a reputed work of Velasquez, to look at it, and dwell upon the color and the movement, and the clear life and light that come from the marvelous canvas. Others collect old china and porcelain. Of this I know little—my fancies in the cup and plate line being easily satisfied. But I am told that no fascination grows upon the collector with more power than this for china, and that some of our countrymen have been known to experience emotions of an agitating nature upon discovering a plate of the time of Louis XIV. There are collectors, too, whose designs in the collecting line are neither quaint nor high nor patriotic, but who have grossly diseased fancies for things forbidden to men. Of such one writes with pain and anger.

There are types not classes of an original character. There is the stout old dowager, who has three daughters she wants to marry, and she trails them from Paris to the Springs, and from the Springs to Paris, and to Italy and the Pyrenees. You always encounter her just when you don't want to be bothered; and she informs you how that horrid beast in yellow whiskers came so near marrying Matilda; but he was not a count or a Prussian officer—only an adventurer from Wiesbaden. Then comes your friend the British officer, once in the Guards, who plays billiards, and likes Americans

Americans at the Grand Hotel

so much that he will not consort with Englishmen. He says he is a relative of the Duke of Bethnal Green, and wears his colors. Our British friend has troubles with his family, and they limit his allowance; when he becomes thirty he will have his money, and a little loan until that time would be so jolly—and if you would like to know the Duke, be at Chantilly on Sunday. Then we have our friend the Count, who speaks English with such a clear accent, and has been all over America, and will become a director in your company and place shares with his noble family for £5,000. Then you have your Irish friend, whose French—barring the Tipperary accent—is fluent, who is a graduate of Trinity College, and was punished for his devotion to the true cause, and found times bad enough even in New York, and would like to travel with you, and pay his share of the expenses, if you could advance him a little until he hears from his bankers. Then you have your friend who chews tobacco and sees nothing in Paris to compare with America, and he has an invention, and wants to ascertain how he can in-vite the whole Paris press to a *déjeuner;* never mind the expense—a bottle of champagne on each side of each plate, if necessary. Then you have your friend who belongs to the Church, and has a cough, and travels on a purse made up by his congregation, and means when he reaches Rome to de-liver a lecture against the Catholics; who wants to dispute with the Pope in person, who eats an early breakfast, is always on the run from one palace to another, and carries a carpetbag with him, which holds his clothes. Then comes your sharp young man, who crosses the ocean six times a year —as purchaser of goods for wholesale houses in New York, and knows the best *tables d'hôte,* and tells English travelers of the horrors of American life, and how no prudent man would walk up Broadway without carrying a loaded pistol, and how Americans are dying for a monarchy, and would like to be ruled over by one of the Queen's sons. Then you have your friend who is always in trouble, whom no one treats well, who suffers from a succession of unappeasable wrongs; and you lend him a hundred francs to pay the landlady who is actually in possession, and have your own thoughts when you see him beaming with smiles, riding in the Bois de Boulogne in the afternoon with—well, we need not be too particular.

There are colonists that one does not meet at the Grand Hotel or on the boulevards. One who knows told me that during the siege Americans came to light of whose existence the legation was not aware. Some come for study and rest—literary people and artists—who slip down to Fontainebleau during the summer, and in the winter do their work in quiet out-of-the-way studios, over near the Luxembourg. When Mr. Lowell came to Paris he took an apartment in the Latin Quarter, near the libraries, and was never seen in hotel or banking house. Here he entertained Mr. Emerson, and I question if one colonist out of twenty knew that two of the most famous Americans of the day were dwelling with them. As an art center Paris is not as pretentious as Florence or Rome. There is no such gallery as in Madrid or Dresden. But good work has a perpetual market, and around Paris there are endless opportunities for study and observation. In Paris it is so easy to burrow into the deep earth and hide away, with no care for society or kid gloves. Paris is a charming place for true literary work. Writing people—who suffer from the damp, depressing fogs of London and the roar and fever of New York life, say that Paris has a tranquillity and sunshine that they do not find elsewhere. When the mind becomes jaded and will not obey the spur, there are the outlying forests and long walks in the Bois, and little runs to Sceaux to dine under the chestnut trees, or a day at Versailles to see the fountains play.

If the colonist is literary and historical in his tastes, he will find inspiration in the associations of the wonderful city. You may walk miles and miles along the Paris streets and almost at every step you have palaces and palace ruins, from the wall of the baths where the Roman emperor Julian bathed, down to the charred wall of the Tuileries. But under this is a history. Here, for instance, lived Robespierre. It is a plain, dingy house, on the Rue St. Honoré—a house of his time, as the architecture shows, but now occupied by a tradesman. Duplay, the carpenter, and the daughter, and Robespierre, with his dog, have vanished like shadows; and this narrow gateway, which looks so dark now, and through which passed and repassed the first men of France in the anxious days of terror, is given over to workmen who plod in and out, and tradesmen who chaffer with you over a bargain. And you have only to take a short walk along the route paced daily in those days by Robespierre himself, and you come to the site of the Jacobin Club, where brother Jacobin ruled until Thermidor came. But club and club house, and all the men and women who were wont to gather there, have gone into the realms of silence, and now you see a commodious market-house, and burly women cry fish on the spot where Danton once thundered. Nor is it far to the old Church of St. Roch, which has this memory—that one Napoleon Bonaparte found the beginning of his career here—for St. Roch is the church which was held by the insurrectionists when he, as general of the Convention, opened upon them with real powder and ball, and so ended the French Revolution. Cross the river and see the top garret-room which Napoleon and Junot occupied at five francs a month—the darkest shadows ahead—nothing to do but to sit brooding and looking out at the Tuileries, sweeping so majestically before them and mocking their fate with the irony of its grandeur. You may return and cross the boulevard and walk a little way toward Montmartre, and see the house where Napoleon lived when he returned from Egypt. It is on the Rue de la Victoire. When he went to live there with Josephine it was called Rue Chautereine, but in his honor it was named the Street of Victory, and is so named until this day; and you may see his home, where was planned the Eighteenth of Brumaire, with its open court-yard, which has a general appearance of dinginess and looks like the court-yard of a livery stable. While in this vicinity you may see where Mirabeau lived and died, and in the room underneath you may now suit yourself with hats and caps; or you may continue your inquiries and discover the house where John Paul Marat, "the friend of the people," was taking his bath one day when Charlotte Corday stabbed him.

Two institutions around which our colony centers harmoniously are the circus and the Bon Marché. Saturday is the evening given to fashion; and upon every Saturday evening you will find the high benches and uncomfortable seats crammed with the American colony. Here all distinctions are lost. Here the lords of the Washington Club and the commoners of the Congress, in the Grand Hotel, assemble in strength. Next to the circus, as an institution, is "Au Bon Marché." If there are fond husbands who, having visited Paris, read these words, I know what memories they recall. O fellow countrymen, who love and honor and have vowed to protect and cherish, when you come to Paris avoid "Au Bon Marché"! Who enters here with a full purse, and wife and daughter in train, must leave all hope behind, at least while the money holds out. "Au Bon Marché" is a magazine for the sale of everything that woman can crave. When you compass what is meant by this definition, you will know its dangers and temptations. I mention it as one of a class—a vast class. You run against stores of this character all over Paris. They are named like the cafés and the taverns, but with a wider sweep of fancy. "The Scottish Mountains," "The Carnival of Venice," "The Spring," "The Great House of Peace," "The Good Devil," "The Infant Jesus," "Old England," "A Thousand and One Nights." These are some of the names given to the dry-goods stores, or rather shops, containing all that woman can need or crave, and where Americans are expected to come and squander their fortunes.

Our countryman when he comes to Europe not as a colonist, but as a sojourner, finds a fascination in Paris. He plans his continental trip, and you bid him farewell at the railway station, and see him disappear with hat-box, cane, shawl, umbrella, soft felt hat, and guide books, and say again "Good-by," as though you would not see him for a season. In a week or two you run against him on the boulevards, most probably wearing a new style of hat, and learn that he has "done" the Continent, and means to have another "go" at Paris.

During the midsummer months the self-constituted Congress in the Grand Hotel is well attended, and the home-sick American will have his heart gladdened by the sharp cockatoo accent in which he hears the English language spoken, reminding him so noisily of home. This Congress is easy of access. Social distinctions are overlooked. I have seen the Congress in full session, attended by a gambler, a doctor of divinity, two or three bankers, a general officer of the army, and one or two fraudulent bankrupts. The members were harmonious and discoursed in company, they drank out of the same wine-bottle, and talked at the top of their voices, and almost quarreled as to who should pay for the wine. But as the summer dies away the Congress thins out. Some hurry home; others go to the south; and whoever enters the high and stately room toward November will see a painful spectacle. The last American of the season, deserted by his companions, sits over his third bottle of wine, vainly looking for a familiar face, smoking a mammoth cigar, his feet spread over a chair, his eye looking dismally at the carving and the decorations and the equipages that come and go. The familiar faces have fled. There is no one to whom he can express his contempt for the French nation—no one to whom he can impart his information as to what Bismarck ought to have done. He is stranded and alone. On mail days he has his American paper as a comfort, and the eagerness with which he reads that journal would delight its editors. Down to the last, the very last items, marriages and deaths and ship news and advertisements, beginning with the personal column, he ruminates and reads again and again, until nature summons him to his champagne.

If we asked this belated American what he thought of Frenchmen, he would state his opinion that they were vastly overrated in the accomplishments which all the world assigns to them. No Frenchman, strange to say, can cook. He may make a little salad, or some inefficient sauce, but for a "square meal" give our American friend a good old-fashioned Virginia negro grandmamma, who understands hoe-cake. There are no oysters in France, and the few that may be had for their weight in hard money are a poor consolation for the body accustomed to saddle-rocks and blue-points. Our friend will confound you on this cookery question by showing that there is not an oyster stew in all this great city. There is champagne, to be sure, so dear to the heart of the American abroad as well as at home; but champagne, according to his theory, is made by Germans and German capital. Cheese is a grievance to him. How any human being can eat French cheese, and why every French waiter will insist upon offering our compatriot cheese at various stations of the meal, is something he cannot understand, unless there be some hidden insult to all the world in the composition of the cheese—a circumstance he is disposed to believe.

This same countryman believes that, as a general thing, French ladies are in the habit of dancing at the Jardin Mabille. Have I described Mabille? I am half afraid of that shrine. Well, Mabille is a garden just off the Champs Élysées, where you pay a moderately large fee for entrance. There are one or two small fountains, wooded walks, a shooting gallery, little alcoves, where you may sip coffee or what not, and a profusion of colored lanterns blaze everywhere, on painted canvas, that looks like endless forests, and innumerable mirrors flash the light to and fro. In the center is a band of musicians and a boarded dancing floor. This is the Jardin Mabille. Mabille is himself at the door, with his keen, Oriental face, taking the money. It is a summer garden, and the music and dancing are under the stars. Well, Mabille has in his employ several young women, with hard, leering faces, and several young men, with shiny hats, who mingle around in the crowd as though they had paid to come in. When the music commences (generally the music of the harmonious Offenbach) these young men and women rush upon the boarded floor and dance peculiar dances—the "Can-can," among others—not much worse than I have seen it on the New York stage. Our Paris-American Congress, assembled in a circle, believes that it sees the ladies of Paris at a common evening entertainment. I could never see the Jardin Mabille except to be disgusted with it, and why our American friends should visit it I cannot imagine, except that Mabille is said to be a very bad place, and they attend expecting that something outrageous will certainly happen. I do not imagine that it occurs to one out of ten of our observing countrymen that Mabille is simply an institution kept by a Frenchman for English and Americans to visit. During the first season the American frequents Mabille. If he prolongs his stay, and becomes a colonist, he takes this garden at its value and never visits it at all.

An instructive exhibition to those of our countrymen who are curious about the manners and customs of the nation will be found over in the Latin Quarter, in the dancing hall near the Luxembourg. There is a low entrance, guarded by gensdarmes. A circular sun of blazing red light points the way. If you are curious and pause a moment, you will see in the light the figure of a soldier in bronze on a pedestal, in the attitude of command his hand pointing to some imaginary foe. This bronze figure represents the famous Marshal Ney, and on this spot, where you may stand and hear the fiddling and the dancing, Marshal Ney was shot by French soldiers under Louis XVIII. for having commanded French soldiers under Napoleon. This dancing hall on Sunday evening, when the clerks are in abundance, or on Thursday evening, when the students come in numbers, is not without its attractions to the observing American mind. The romp and noise and clatter, the buzz and hum of loud conversation, song and repartee, smoking and drinking, continue until the music strikes up and the multitude dissolves into a mass of dancing humanity. As to the dancing, I cannot say more than that it is very wild and clumsy, and I have heard my American brethren condemn it in strong terms. There are other dancing halls in outside sections, and one especially on the Rue St. Honoré, much frequented by our countrymen, almost opposite where Robespierre lived.

You can understand, perhaps, how the average American abroad, his observations limited to the Luxembourg and Mabille, will have original notions as to the morals of France. The French are like the Chinese. They do not accept the foreigner. They have made Paris the most beautiful city

Luxembourg Palace

in the world, because they are artists by nature, and could not have made an ugly city had they tried. Whether you see Paris in detail as you go roaming along the boulevards, or see it by day from the top of the Arch of Triumph, or by night from the heights of Montmartre, you are impressed with its marvelous beauty. This Paris was made by Frenchmen for Frenchmen. But there is no excess of welcome. A Frenchman will never ask how you like his city. Of course you like it, and know and feel and are glad to admit that for beauty and taste and all the resources of civilization there is nothing in the world like Paris. But that American instinct for commendation which leads the Yankee to call every post village a "city" and every alderman a "celebrated" man is not found among the French. There is no welcome in the French character toward the foreigner, none of the going into society which greets the foreigner in America. The American colony is regarded very much by Paris in general as New York would regard a German colony in Hoboken or a colony of Poles near the Bowery. The average Frenchman when he thinks of America is apt to confound the United States with Brazil and Paraguay—to think of it all as one country, inhabited by an extravagant, expensive, and in some respects, a wild people, who, strange to say, are white. Nor is this surprising when one considers the character of the representatives of our country who come to Paris. There is, of course, the class accustomed to foreign life; studious men, who seek the Latin Quarter; business men, who keep in trading circles; the

American gentleman, with his "European habit" upon him, who knows Paris and avoids his fellow countrymen, and lives down in the narrow streets toward the Palais Royal. But every summer there comes the shoal of sight-seers from England and America. The English traveler is a type in himself. You see him in the comedies, in the satirical papers; the children play with a toy made like an Englishman. He is described as a man with one eyeglass, a small billycock hat, a plaided coat and striped trousers, a brown hanging beard, an opera glass swung over his shoulder, and the inseparable umbrella. This is the Englishman as French fancy paints him. So he was to our fathers. But the typical American changes with every season.

There was the hegira of "war Americans" during the Rebellion, when there were a Southern and a Northern colony, who used to frown on each other as they passed along the boulevards. The French police had their hands full to prevent these Montagus and Capulets from doing more than bite their thumbs at one another. I remember a comic print of the time entitled "North and South Americans Discuss Politics." The scene was an omnibus on a boulevard, filled with passengers. Seated on the top at one end was a Northerner with a pistol drawn, firing at a Southerner at the other end, who had a pistol drawn also, the alarmed passengers striving, in every attitude, to avoid the shots. French feeling was much with the South, upon whose supporters the Emperor was wont to smile his gloomy, inscrutable smile. After the cotton loan was sold and money ran short, our erring countrymen found Paris a hard place, and were reduced to many shifts. But with the war came the shoddy lords. During the closing years of the war this class ran over Paris, and amazed the frugal French mind by extravagance and want of culture. This was the harvest time of the cooks, and the *concierges,* and waiters, and more especially the dealers in pictures and imitation jewelry. The shoddy lords were followed by the petroleum aristocracy—an astonishing class, who generally came in groups, under a competent courier, who spoke all languages and robbed his clients. Then came the Tammany hegira. First we had Mr. Sweeny and some of the chiefs, who came to study Paris, so that they might gain hints for beautifying New York. The example became contagious, and all the Americus boys, wearing diamond pins and gaudy scarfs, drove around in carriages and drank champagne before breakfast, and smoked amazing cigars, and gave the waiters a napoleon for drink-money, and spent their time in riot and folly. As most of these astonishing young men were known as colonels, or generals, or judges, or senators in Albany, and as in their interviews with Frenchmen they took no pains to diminish their importance at home, Frenchmen began to have their own ideas as to the ruling classes of our dear native land. But this happy hegira came to an end. The men with their diamonds are gone. They no longer boast of their consequence in New York.

To those having artistic or literary tastes, Paris has immense attractions. If you come here a stranger and under auspicious stars, and gain entrance into the art zone or the literary zone, you are blessed among wayfarers, and Paris comes to you as you would never see it were you to tramp the boulevards twenty years. The American colonist, thoroughly seasoned in Paris, with his European habit full upon him, is in the main a pleasant person. He has acquired the best qualities of the French. He does not hold you at arm's length and give you his views. His home animosities about politics and so on are deadened, and in their stead you see a genuine, full-grown patriotism—a love of the whole country, democratic and republican. The finished American colonist has acquired a thorough knowledge of the side streets—he is the discoverer of the oddest out-of-the-way places for dishes, or queer prints, or books, or odds and ends. You see in time what underlies the French varnish of Paris life—that French varnish which foreign eyes so frequently see and nothing else. You have glimpses of the true life in France and learn what it is that has made this people, with all their faults and misadventures, the richest and thriftiest in the world. This edge of colonial life is full of interest; but has it no drawback? I have spoken of what is called the European habit, and of the advantage that one finds in foreign travel when he has it upon him. "Ah, my friend," said a wise man that I know, who has lived many years here, to one who spoke with him in a hopeful bright way about coming to live in Paris and making it a home, "Ah, my friend, don't; you will never have any true home elsewhere should this Paris fever come upon you. It will not come at first. Madame your wife will see many things to annoy her. If she is religious and has our Puritan notions, as most women have, whether Catholic or Protestant, she will not understand the theaters being open on Sunday and races at Longchamps on the same day. Then there are social and personal freedoms permitted to men and women which fall rudely upon eyes that have always looked at such things behind a veil. This never-ending panorama of life and brightness and activity—these boulevards, the passage Choiseul, the Palais Royal, the Champs Élysées—where do you find a counterpart? If you are poor you can dine at Duval's for two francs; if you are rich you can pay a hundred at Bignon's. You can live in the Rue du Bac at fifty francs a month, or in the Avenue Gabriel at a thousand, and you will neither lose nor gain in respectability. You select your café. You give John a few sous now and then, and the café is your home. So in time the habit grows upon you. Life is so smooth! The Government being of the paternal kind, does so many things for you that you lapse into easy ways. Then the people are so pleasant. But this is not surprising. A Frenchman is always pleasant, but it is only courtesy. You know him twenty years, and he is as agreeable in the end as in the beginning—no more! It never is home. You like the city, you grow attached to certain ways and places. You form a sincere regard for your *concierge,* but it is not home. You never take root. But what are you going to do? You cannot go home. Who are you going to see? Then you have your European ways, which are not the ways of America. You want your coffee so, and so it never comes, and life begins to fret you. One home has gone, and you have not gained another. This ever running, rippling stream of life, many-tinted as the rainbow and as full of joy as a summer wind, this is not home! Then think of dying here, and of being buried in a hearse with plumes and coachmen with mourning garments—garments that have mourned over three generations, and will mourn over three more, perhaps. No, my friend, do not let this European habit come upon you, or you will one day be, in a dreary sense, a man without a country and a home."

These are the words of a colonist who knows France well—a satisfied colonist, no matter what his griefs may be, one who loves Paris well. But we come to the dissatisfied colonist—the American who sees in New York the consummate fullness of all civilization. He cannot leave Paris. He must educate his children or attend to certain business, or what not. He is always angry with the French people. He reads the American newspapers with hungry eagerness, and is in a state of constant excitement over events in New York. You meet him on the boulevard, and he flashes into speculations upon home news, and surprises you with his averments that the jury will never agree to convict that negro of arson down in Arundel County. His French is not of an illuminative, descriptive quality, and he supplements it by swearing at the coachmen, who take his speeches for compliments, and smile in answer. He has had a quarrel with his *concierge,* with his bootmaker, with a florist. It was a question of ten francs with the latter, and it was taken before one justice of the peace and another, and after paying five hundred francs in costs, he won his case. "Ah," he said to the writer, "you can never trust the French. Bismarck should have exterminated them. They are all cowards, all hypocrites—all—worse than that. I have lived here five years, and I tell you I never saw a Frenchman who would not steal. They are monkeys and barbers. I was at a French party the other night, and it shows just what they are. None of your square-up-and-down parties—champagne and cards in the back room, and boned turkey and terrapin, like civilized people—but ices and meringues and thin little cakes and liquors; and you rush out into the corridor and smoke a cigarette and hurry back, and then a young chap with a stubby mustache stands up and reads an original poem, and you cannot understand what he says except that it is about France and Germany, and Alsace and Lorraine; and it ends 'Revenge! Revenge!' and they all shout and cry, and the men rush up and kiss him on both cheeks—yes, on both cheeks, the fools. If I had my way—but let me tell you about a bill I got last month, and a charge for candles."

But is there any society abroad for the colony? Oh, yes; very charming circles—French, English, and American. The colonist who can speak French, to begin with, is an object of envy and reproach to those who cannot. I discover also that it is a great card to know a nobleman. I have heard of one family who entertain largely, especially floating Americans in summer, who, it is said, keep a marquis. This nobleman was in distress, and had a dismal home down in Montmartre. But an enterprising American found him out, and during the summer when he gives a dinner, the marquis, with a red ribbon in his lappel is present and presented. This gives dignity to the dinner, and has a majestic effect upon the American guests. Before he arrives it adds to the zest of the conversation to discuss whether the marquis will come, whether his engagements will allow him to come, whether the rumor is true that he was suddenly summoned to the Count de Chambord. After he goes (which is early, his highness not finding the average American conversation stimulating) comes the discussion of the marquis and his pedigree—Montmorency at least—grandfather guillotined by Robespierre. The circumstance of the marquis being actually under contract to wine and dine at so much a day, for the benefit of free and independent American travelers, I do not guarantee. It came to me as gossip from a satirical, slighted colonist, who had not been asked to meet the marquis and who, not being much in the society of French noblemen has the conviction that they are very poor and know nothing except to play on the violin and lie in wait for the daughters of wealthy American gentlemen, who, having garnered in their millions in the development of our petroleum industry, or in furnishing supplies to our brave boys in the field, crave a coronet for their family, if even only a French one.

But hold! for now I come upon enchanted ground, and before me

stretches a vista that would lead far beyond the patience of the most industrious reader. When I begin to speak of counts, I fear lest, in telling
tales that have been told to me, words would fall wounding where I have
no right to wound. So long as Americans are vain of title and rank and
have marriageable daughters, so long as our petroleum and bonanza
dowagers see in a coronet a glory exceeding the glory of the sun, or the
moon, or an army with banners, and to be prized even above true, genuine American manhood, so long will our maidens dear be bought and
sold in a strange sad way.

It was in this colony that General Grant lived for a month or so until the
winter days came, and early in December he left for the South of France.
The American Government had placed at his disposal the man-of-war
"Vandalia," which was cruising in the Mediterranean, and she had arrived
at Villefranche to await the General. On the 13th of December, 1877, at
five in the afternoon, General Grant, his wife, his son Jesse R. Grant, and
the writer of this narrative embarked on the "Vandalia," amid cheers from
the other American ships in the harbor, and kind wishes from the many
friends who came to see us off. We at once steamed out to sea toward Italy,
Egypt, and the Holy Land.

CHAPTER FOUR

Cities of Antiquity and the Western Mediterranean

As an expensive mark of esteem by a cheap national government, unusual as a gift to even an ex-president, Rutherford B. Hayes sent the battleship "Vandalia" to carry the Grant party on their Mediterranean cruise during the winter of 1877–78.

First came the western Mediterranean, with stops at Naples—and land excursions to Vesuvius and Pompeii—and then Palermo, Sicily (where the Grants celebrated Christmas, mainly on board "Vandalia," their portable little corner of the good old U.S.A.), and Malta. Young poked some gently condescending fun at the Neapolitan beggars—tanned, happy sprites, unlike the miserable beggars of England or America, where poverty was a badge of shame—and he used their travel guide, the multilingual Dutchman "Marquis" Jacques Hartog, as a sort of opera buffo caricature of the absurdly pretentious little European parvenu.

The "Vandalia" cast anchor in the beautiful Bay of Naples December 17th, about ten in the morning. We came hoping to find sunshine, but the Consul, B. Odell Duncan, Esq., who comes on board to welcome the General, tells us there has been no such weather known for many seasons. It would be even cold in our inclement New York. I rejoice in the possession of a capacious ulster, which I brought into the Mediterranean against many protests, but which has been a useful companion. Poor Naples looks especially cold. These poor Neapolitans need sunshine, and they are almost too cold to beg. So much has been written about Naples that I may be spared a catalogue of its attractions. On anchoring in the harbor the General and his wife landed, and made a tour of the city. There was the summer palace, in which royal persons live for a few weeks every year and whose grounds are open only by permission. There is the castle of San Martin, an old monastery, now turned into a museum and a barracks. We spent a good hour in looking at its curiosities, which did not impress us either as curious or startling. "This," said the guide, "is the picture of Mr. So-and-so, who generously gave this museum to Naples." "Well," said the General, aside, "if I had a museum like this I would give it to Naples or whoever would take it." There was a beautiful chapel, in which the Lord is no longer worshiped, but which was a gem of elaborate decoration. There was a burial ground of the monks, surrounded by marble pillars, upon which skulls were engraved. In the center was one larger skull, grinning, and over the temples a withering laurel wreath. Around this cemetery were the cloisters under whose arches our friends the monks used to walk and read and meditate, with such suggestions as the skulls would inspire. It was ghostly enough, and there was a comfort in turning from it to the balcony, a few steps off, which overlooked the brow of a hill, showing Naples beneath us and Vesuvius beyond, and the shining sea. We stood on the balcony and looked down from our dizzy height, and thought how much more in consonance with true religion it was to worship God as we saw him here in his majesty and glory, and not over stones and bones and sights of evil omen.

There, far above, was Vesuvius, and we were impatient for the ascent. It was too late when we arrived in Naples, but the General, with military promptness, gave orders for the march next morning. We stood on the deck and studied the stern old mountain, and picked out the various objects with a telescope, and did an immense amount of reading on the subject. The volcano was in a lazy mood, and not alive to the honor of a visit from the Ex-President of the United States, for all he deigned to give us was a lazy puff of smoke, not a spark, or a flame, or a cinder. I suppose the old monster is an aristocrat, and a conservative, and said, "What do I care for presidents or your new republics! I have scattered my ashes over a Roman republic. I have lighted Cæsar's triumphs, and thrown my clouds over the path of Brutus fresh from Cæsar's corpse. Why should I set my forces in motion to please a party of Yankee sight-seers, even if one of them should be a famous general and ex-ruler of a republic? I have looked upon Hannibal and Cæsar, Charlemagne and Bonaparte. I have seen the rise and fall of empires. I have admonished generations who worshiped Jupiter, as I have admonished generations who have worshiped the Cross. I am the home of the gods; and if thou would see my power, look at my base and

The Drive to Vesuvius

ask of the ashes that cumber Herculaneum and Pompeii." So the stubborn old monster never gave us a flash of welcome, only a smoky puff now and then to tell us that he was a monster all the time, if he only chose to manifest his awful will. We stood upon the deck in speculation, and some of us hoped that there would be an eruption or something worth describing. The General was bent on climbing to the very summit and looking into the crater, and with that purpose we started in the morning of Tuesday, December 18th.

We should have gone earlier, but many high people in uniforms, commanding one thing or another, had to come on board and pay their respects. It was ten before we were under way, the General and party in the advance, with our courier, whom we have called the Marquis, on the box, and Mrs. Grant's maid bringing up the rear. We drove all the way. You will understand our route when I remind you that the Bay of Naples is something like a horseshoe. On one side of the shoe is the city, on the other is Vesuvius. Therefore to reach the mountain we have to drive around the upper circle of the shoe. The shores of this bay are so populous that our route seemed to be one continuous town. We only knew that we were passing the city limits when the guard stopped our carriage to ask if there was anything on which we were anxious to pay duty. As there was nothing but a modest luncheon, we kept on, rattling through narrow, stony streets.

Beggars kept us company, although from some cause or another there were not as many as we supposed. Perhaps it was the new government, which we are told is dealing severely with beggars; or more likely it was the weather, which is very cold and seems to have taken all ambition out of the people. Still we were not without attentions, and from streets and by-roads a woman or a man, or sometimes a blind man led by a boy, would start up and follow us with appeals for money. They were starving or their children were starving, and lest we might not understand their distress, they would pat their mouths or breasts to show how empty they were. For starving persons they showed great courage and endurance in following our carriage. The General had an assortment of coins, and, although warned in the most judicious manner against encouraging pauperism, he did encourage it, and with so much success that before he was halfway up the mountain he was a pauper himself to the extent of borrowing pennies from some of his companions to keep up the demands upon his generosity.

What we observed in this long ride around the horseshoe was that Naples was a very dirty, a very happy, and a very picturesque town. We learned that the supply of rags was inexhaustible. I never knew what could be done with rags until I saw these lazzaroni. They seem to have grown rags, as a sheep grows his fleece, and yet there was no misery in their faces. Happy, dirty, idle, light-eyed, skipping, sunny—you looked in vain for those faces, those terrible faces of misery and woe, which one sees so often in London. I take it, therefore, that begging is an amusement, an industry, and not a necessity—that the Naples beggar goes out to his work like any other laborer. He is not driven to it by the gaunt wolves hunger and disease. One scamp—a gray-bearded scamp, too—who followed us, was a baker, who made and sold loaves. He was standing at his counter trading when our carriage hove in sight. At once he threw down his loaves and started after us in full chase, moaning and showing his tongue and beating his breast, and telling us he was starving. Well, when he received his coin he went to his store, and I presume began to haggle over his bread. That coin was clear gain. He was not a beggar, but a speculator. He went into the street and made a little raise, just as brokers and merchants at home go into the "street" and try an adventure in stocks. The Neapolitan speculator was a wiser man than his New York brother. He ran no risk. Even if he did not gain his coin the run did him good, and his zeal gave him the reputation of an active business man.

In the meantime our horses begin to moderate their pace and the streets to show an angle, and horsemen surround our carriage and tell us in a variety of tongues that they are guides, and, if we require it, will go to the summit. Women come to cabin doors, and hold up bottles of white wine—the wine called Lachrymæ Christi, by some horrible irreverence—and ask us to stop and drink. And already the houses begin to thin, and we have fields around us and glimpses of the sea; and although the lazy volcano, with its puffs of smoke, looks as far distant as when we were on the deck of the "Vandalia" miles away, we know that the ascent has begun, and that we are really climbing the sides of Vesuvius. . . .

. . . The horses go slower and slower. Some of us get out and help them by walking part of the way and taking short cuts. The few houses that we see on the roadside have evidently been built with a view to eruptions, for the roofs are made of heavy stone and cement. General Grant notes that where the lava and stones have been allowed to rest and to mingle with the soil good crops spring up, and here and there we note a flourishing bit of vineyard. Soon, however, vineyards disappear, and after the vineyards the houses, except an occasional house of shelter, into which we are all invited to enter and drink of the Tears of Christ. Our convoy of horsemen, who have been following us for a mile or two, begin to drop off. The Marquis has been preaching to them from the box in various languages upon their folly in wasting time, and they heed his warnings. There are no beggars. It is remarked that beggars always prefer a dead level. One bright-eyed boy keeps at our side, a lad with about as dirty a suit of clothes and as pretty a pair of eyes as you could see even in squalid, smiling Naples. Well, there is something in the eyes, or it may be in the boyishness of their possessor, which quite wins one of the party, for when the Marquis insists that he shall join his fellow mendicants in the valley below, a gracious protection is thrown over him, and he follows us up the road. I think the patronage must have pleased him, for he gathered a handful of wild flowers and presented them, and refused a coin which was offered in return; but the refusal of this coin did not prevent his acceptance of two or three others, and a good dinner included an hour or two later in the day.

Still we climb the hill, going steadily up. Those of us who thought we could make the way on foot repent, for the way is steep and the road is hard. All around us is an ocean of chaos and death. There in all forms and shapes lie the lava streams that did their work in other days, black and cold and forbidding. You can trace the path of each eruption as distinctly as the windings of the stream from the mountain top. We are now high up on the mountain, and beneath us is the valley and the Bay of Naples, with Ischia and Capri, and on the other horizon a range of mountains tinged and tipped with snow. In one direction we see the eruption of 1872; the black lava stream bordered with green. What forms and shapes! What fantastic, horrible shapes the fire assumed in the hours of its triumph! I can well see how Martial and Virgil and the early poets saw in these phenomena the strife and anger of the gods. Virgil describes Enceladus transfixed by Jove and the mountain thrown upon him, which shakes and trembles whenever he turns his weary sides. This is the scene, the very scene of his immortal agony. There are no two forms alike; all is black, cold, and pitiless. If we could only see one living thing in this mass of destruction; but all is death, all desolation. Here and there, where the rains have washed the clay, and the birds, perhaps, may have carried seed, the grass begins to grow; but the whole scene is desolation. I thought of the earlier ages, when the earth was black and void, and fancied that it was just such an earth as this when Divinity looked upon it and said, "Let there be light." I thought of the end of all things, of our earth, our fair, sweet and blooming earth, again a mass of lava, rock and ashes, all life gone out of it, rolling through space.

The presence of a phenomenon like this, and right above us the ever-seething crater, is in itself a solemn and beautiful sight. We all felt repaid with our journey; for by this time we had come to the journey's end, and our musings upon eternity and chaos did not forbid thoughts of luncheon. For the wind was cold and we were hungry. So when our illustrious captain intimated that we might seek a place of refuge and entertainment, a light gleamed in the eyes of the Marquis, and he reined us up at a hostelry called the Hermitage. This is the last resting-place before we reach the ascent of the crater. Here the roads stop, and the remainder of the journey must be made on foot. Just beyond the Hermitage is a Government institution known as the Observatory, a point where information for weather reports is gained. We thought when we came into these upper regions that we were in an atmosphere too pure for the beggars. We were congratulating ourselves upon this circumstance coming up the mountain side, but on descending we had a beggar or two to await us. I suppose they belonged to the hostelry, and were simply speculating upon us like our friend the baker, whom we had left haggling over his loaves far down in Naples. Some of us, the General certainly, had come this distance meaning to climb the crater. But it was very cold, and we had delayed our departure from the ship, so that the day was well on. So, instead of climbing the rocks and looking into a sulphurous crater, we organized a kind of picnic in the Hermitage. The house seemed to have been an inquisition or a dungeon—the rooms were so large, the walls were so thick, there were such

Dinner at the Hermitage

mysterious, narrow passages and chambers. But people who build houses under the rim of Vesuvius must build for fire and flame, and showers of ashes and stones, and the Hermitage could stand a severe eruption before it became untenable. A slight crackling fire of twigs was made on the hearth, and a brazier of burning coals was brought into the room. We were some time in comprehending the brazier, but when its uses became apparent, it was comforting enough. There, in quite a primitive fashion, we had our luncheon, helping ourselves and each other in good homely American fashion, for we were as far from the amenities of civilization as though we were in Montana.

After luncheon we walked about, looking at the crater, where fumes were quite apparent—at the world of desolation around us, some of it centuries old, but as fresh and terrible as when it burst from the world of fire beneath us. But there was still another picture—one of sublime and marvelous beauty. There beneath us, in the clear, sunny air—there was Naples, queen among cities, and her villages clustering about her. Beautiful, wondrously beautiful, that panorama of hill and field and sea, that rolled before us thousands of feet below! We could count twenty villages in the plain, their white roofs massed together and spangling the green plain like gems. There were Capri and Ischia—their rugged outlines softened by the purple-golden glow of the passing day—lying at the mouth of the bay as if to guard this rich valley. There was Naples, her rags and dirt quite veiled and only her beauty to be seen. There was Misenum, where Pliny saw the destruction of Pompeii. There was Nisita, where Brutus took refuge when he fled from the murder of Cæsar. There was Sorrento, where Tasso lived. Every village has its history and associations, for these plains and islands and promontories have been for ages the seats of a brilliant and glorious civilization—a civilization which even now only shows the beauty of decay. The splendor of a Roman imperial civilization has gone from Italy. Ages of darkness and superstition and despotism have rested upon her like the ashes which cover Pompeii. Let us hope that a new era is coming, which, based upon freedom and patriotism, will far excel even that of the Cæsars. These were our thoughts as we stood in the cold winds studying the magnificent scene. And thinking of the living, we thought of the dead—of the cities of the plains which perished one thousand seven hundred years ago. The romance that surrounds Naples only deepens the tragedy of Pompeii and Herculaneum, and we found our thoughts ever turning from the glory and majesty of all we saw to those buried cities of the plains, as we were hurried home again—home to our graceful vessel whose lights awaited us in the harbor.

On the 19th of December the General and his party visited Pompeii. We arrived at Pompeii early in the morning considering that we had a long ride. But the morning was cold enough to be grateful to our northern habits, and there was sunshine. Our coming had been expected, and we were welcomed by a handsome young guide, who talked a form of English in a rather high key, as though we were all a little hard of hearing. This guide informed us that he had waited on General Sheridan when he visited Pompeii. He was a soldier, and we learned that the guides are all soldiers, who receive duty here as a reward for meritorious service. There was some comfort in seeing Pompeii accompanied by a soldier, and a brave one. This especial guide was intelligent, bright, and well up in all concerning Pompeii. We entered the town at once through a gate leading through an embankment. Although Pompeii, so far as excavated, is as open to the air as New York, it is surrounded by an earthen mound resembling some of our railway embankments in America. Looking at it from the outside you might imagine it an embankment, and expect to see a train of cars whirling along the surface. It is only when you pass up a stone-paved slope a few paces that the truth comes upon you, and you see that you are in the City of Death. You see before you a long, narrow street running into other narrow streets. You see quaint, curious houses in ruins. You see fragments, statues, mounds, walls. You see curiously painted walls. You see where men and women lived and how they lived—all silent and all dead—and there comes over you that appalling story which has fascinated so many generations of men—the story of the destruction of Pompeii and Herculaneum. . . .

Our first visit was to the museum, a carefully arranged collection. Here you may see windows and doors as they came from the ruins. There are also casts of eight human bodies, the faces and forms expressing the agony of the last moment. One is that of a finely formed woman, her brow resting upon her arm, lying in an easy attitude of repose. Some had their clothing on, others scarcely a vestige of clothing. Some were in attitudes of despair and combat, as though they would resent Death when he came. There were skeletons of animals and skulls. There were vases as they came from the opened chambers, rainspouts in terra-cotta, helmets, bucklers, and swords that belonged to the gladiators. There was bread as found in the oven, and a dish in which the meat was roasting. There was a pot in which were the remnants of a sucking pig, the skeleton of the pig clearly traceable. There were barley and olives and various kinds of food. Almonds, pears and figs, pouches of coin, sandals, garments, rings and trinkets, amulets that were to keep off the evil eye. All was here arranged as found in the ashes of the buried city. And all was so real—so horribly real—I cannot express the impression which came over us as we passed from the gate into the very streets of the buried town—the very streets of this bright, gay, luxurious town. We could not realize the solemnity of Pompeii. It seemed so natural that we should come here—so natural that we should be at home, so natural that this should be a living and not a town that had been buried and risen again—that our visit seems a day's holiday in a charming country town, and not a mournful march through a town of ashes and death. . . .

. . . The value of these ruins is in the truthfulness of what we see around us. We tire of temples, and fauns, and shows. How did these people live?

We see that there was little or no poverty in Pompeii. If there was any Five Points or Seven Dials quarter it has not been excavated. This was a happy summer town, where people came to find their pleasures. There was the house of unspeakable shame, which the guide, with glistening eyes, pointed out to the General as the special object of interest to tourists. But our General had no interest in scenes of shame and vice, and declined to enter the house. We sauntered about from street to street, and looked at the house called the house of the Tragic Poet. It is here that Bulwer Lytton places the home of Glaucus, in his "Last Days of Pompeii." We pass a lake house where the mills are ready to grind corn, and our guide explains how it was done in the ancient days—"Pretty much," the General remarks, "as it is done in primitive settlements now." Here is an arcade which was supposed to be a market. Here is a subterranean passage leading to a dungeon. In the roof was a hole through which the judge announced to the prisoners their fate. We can fancy Christian martyrs clustering under these walls, and fearing not even the lions, in the blessed hope of that salvation whose gospel had only come from the shores of Galilee. We see ruined tombs and evidences of cremation, and house after house, streets and houses without end, until we become bewildered with the multitude and variety of sights. The impression made by the journey may be summed up in a remark of General Grant, that Pompeii was one of the few things which had not disappointed his expectations, that the truth was more striking than imagination had painted, and that it was worth a journey over the sea to see and study its stately, solemn ruins.

The Italian authorities did General Grant special honor on his visit to Pompeii by directing that a house should be excavated. It is one of the special compliments paid to visitors of renown. The guide will show houses that have been excavated in the presence of Murat and his queen, of General Championnet, and Joseph II., of Admiral Farragut and General Sherman, and General Sheridan. These houses are still known by the names of the illustrious persons who witnessed their exhumation, and the guide hastens to point out to you, if you are an American, where honor was paid to our countrymen. When Sherman and Sheridan were here large crowds attended, and the occasion was made quite a picnic. But General Grant's visit was known only to a few, and so when the director of excavations led the way to the proposed work, there were the General and his party and a group of our gallant and courteous friends from the "Vandalia." The quarter selected was near the Forum. Chairs were arranged for the General, Mrs. Grant, and some of us, and there quietly, in a room that had known

Observing an Excavation

Pompeiian life seventeen centuries ago, we awaited the signal that was to dig up the ashes that had fallen from Vesuvius that terrible night in August. Our group was composed of the General, his wife and son, Mr. Duncan, the American Consul in Naples, Commander Robeson, of the "Vandalia," Lieutenants Strong, Miller and Rush, and Engineer Baird, of the same ship. We formed a group about the General, while the director gave the workmen the signal. The spades dived into the ashes, while with eager eyes we looked on. What story would be revealed of that day of agony and death? Perhaps a mother, almost in the fruition of a proud mother's hopes, lying in the calm repose of centuries, like the figure we had seen only an hour ago dug from these very ruins. Perhaps a miser hurrying with his coin only to fall in his doorway, there to rest in peace while seventeen centuries of the mighty world rolled over him, and to end at last in a museum. Perhaps a soldier fallen at his post, or a reveller stricken at the feast. All these things have been given us from Pompeii, and we stood watching the nimble spades and the tumbling ashes, watching with the greedy eyes of gamblers to see what chance would send. Nothing came of any startling import. There were two or three bronze ornaments, a loaf of bread wrapped in cloth, the grain of the bread and the fiber of the cloth as clearly marked as when this probable remnant of a humble meal was put aside by the careful housewife's hands. Beyond this, and some fragments which we could not understand, this was all that came from the excavation of Pompeii. The director was evidently disappointed. He expected a skeleton at the very least to come out of the cruel ashes and welcome our renowned guest, who had come so many thousand miles to this Roman entertainment. He proposed to open another ruin, but one of our "Vandalia" friends, a very practical gentleman, remembered that it was cold, and that he had been walking a good deal and was hungry, and when he proposed that, instead of excavating another ruin, we should "excavate a beefsteak" at the restaurant near the gate of the sea, there was an approval. The General, who had been leisurely smoking his cigar and studying the scene with deep interest, quietly assented, and, thanking the director for his courtesy, said he would give him no more trouble. So the laborers shouldered their shovels and marched off to their dinner, and we formed in a straggling, slow procession, and marched down the street where Nero rode in triumph, and across the Forum, where Cicero may have thundered to listening thousands, and through the narrow streets, past the wine shops filled with jars which contain no wine—past the baker's, whose loaves are no longer in demand—past the thrifty merchant's, with his sign warning idlers away, a warning that has been well heeded by generations of men—past the house of the Tragic Poet, whose measures no longer burden the multitude, and down the smooth, slippery steps that once led through the gate opening to the sea—steps over which fishermen trailed their nets and soldiers marched in stern procession—into the doors of a very modern tavern. Pompeii was behind us, and a smiling Italian waiter welcomed us to wine and corn, meat and bread, olives and oranges. Around his wholesome board we gathered, and talked of the day and the many marvels we had seen. . . .

. . . The morning came with the ringing of multitudinous bells, whose peals came over the bay, telling us that the good people of Palermo were rejoicing in the Nativity. The effect of this bustle and tumult of sound—bells in every key and tone, ringing and pealing and chiming, their echoes coming back from the gray hills, under whose shadow we were anchored, was unique, and as every bell awakened a memory of home, the day brought a feeling of homesickness, visible on many faces, as they came into the wardroom, interchanging the compliments of the season. The General remained on board until noon to receive the visit of the prefect, who came in state, and was honored with a salute of fifteen guns. His Honor remained only a few minutes, in which he tendered the General all the hospitalities and courtesies of the town. But the General declined them, with thanks. After the departure of the city authorities, the General and Captain Robeson went on shore and sauntered about for two or three hours, looking on the holiday groups who made the day a merry one in their Sicilian fashion. There were spurts of rain coming from the hills, which dampened the enthusiasm of this lazy, happy, sun-loving people.

There was nothing in the rain to deter any one accustomed to our cold, gray northern skies, and the General continued his walk without even paying the weather the tribute of an umbrella. Some of the officers went to the pretty little Episcopalian church, and others busied themselves in preparing for the Christmas dinner. I never knew the capacities of a narrow wardroom until I saw what Lieutenant Miller and his assistants achieved on the "Vandalia." The hatchway became an arbor, the low ceiling bloomed with greenery, the mast seemed about to return to its original leafage. The table became a parterre of flowers and trailing vines, and although the limitations of the service were felt in the candles and candlesticks, the whole room was so green and fresh and smiling when we came down to dinner, that it seemed like a glimpse of far, dear America. The hour for dinner was half-past five, and we assembled in the wardroom with naval promptitude. I give you the names of the hosts: Chief-Engineer J. Trilley, Surgeon George H. Cooke, Lieutenant-Commander A. G. Caldwell, Lieutenant E. T. Strong, Past Assistant-Engineer G. W. Baird, Past Assistant-Engineer D. M. Fulmer, Lieutenant Jacob W. Miller, Paymaster J. P. Loomis, Lieutenant Richard Rush, Captain L. E. Fagan, commanding the marines; Lieutenant H. O. Handy, Lieutenant W. A. Hadden, and Master J. W. Dannenhower.

In this list you have the names of the wardroom officers of the "Vandalia," and if it were not so soon after the feast as to excite a suspicion of my disinterestedness, I would tell you what a gallant, chivalrous company they are. The guests of the evening were: General Grant and wife; Commander H. B. Robeson, commanding the ship; Jesse R. Grant, and the writer of these lines. The General looked unusually well as he took his seat

Christmas Dinner aboard the "Vandalia"

between Lieutenant-Commander Caldwell and Paymaster Loomis, his face a little tanned by the Mediterranean sun, but altogether much younger and brighter than I have seen him for many years. The abandon of ship life, the freedom from the toils of the Presidency, the absence of the clamor and scandal of Washington life have driven away that tired, weary, anxious look which marked the General during his later years as President. And, as he sat under the green boughs of the Christmas decoration, the center of our merry company, it seemed as if he were as young as any of the mess, a much younger man by far than our junior Dannenhower, who looks grave and serious enough to command all the fleets in the world. Mrs. Grant was in capital health and spirits, and quite enchanted the mess by telling them, in the earliest hour of the conversation, that she already felt when she came back to the "Vandalia" from some errand on shore as if she were coming home. I wish I could lift the veil far enough to show you how much the kind, considerate, ever-womanly and ever-cheerful nature of Mrs. Grant has won upon us all; but I must not invade the privacy of the domestic circle. She was the queen of the feast, and we gave her queenly honor.

This was the company, and I give you our *menu*, as an idea of what a ship's kitchen can do for a Christmas dinner:

Potage.

Tomate purée.

Bouchées à la reine.

Cabellon à la Hollandaise.

Purée de pommes.

Dindonneau aux huitres.

Haricots verts.

Filets aux champignons.

Petits pois.

Punch à la Romaine.

Salade.

Plum pudding.

Mince pies.

Dessert.

It was nearly six when the soup made its appearance, and it was half-past eight before the waiters, in their cunning white canvas jackets and black silk scarfs, brought in the coffee. The dinner went with the cadence of a well-rehearsed opera. There was no hurry—no long pauses. The chat went around the table, the General doing his share of talk. I wish I could tell you many of the things that were said; but here again the necessities of my position fall in the way. Suffice it to say that it was a merry, genial, home-like feast, and when Mrs. Grant suggested that we remember in our toast, "Loved ones at home," it was drunk with many an amen, and many a silent prayer for the loved ones over the seas. I mention this toast because it was the only one of the evening. There was a conspiracy, headed by Surgeon Cooke, to force Lieutenant-Commander Caldwell into proposing the General's health and compelling him to speak. But Caldwell, like the illustrious captain on his right, is an obstinate and a somewhat silent man, and there was no speech. But what was more welcome was the cigar, which ended our evening.

It was between nine and ten when we came out on deck. The ships in our neighborhood were blazing with fireworks, and vocal with songs and cheers from neighboring ships—cheers among other things for "General Grant." The men who gave these cheers were Germans and Englishmen who were in port on their way from Constantinople to England. They were honoring Christmas in their honest, homely way, and, knowing that the General was with us, they sent him their hearty welcome and congratulation. So we sauntered about and listened to the merriment on the ships and the ringing of the Christmas bells in Palermo, and watched the moon trailing through the clouds, and studied the outlines of the hills where the Carthaginians once held the power of Rome at bay. Our Christmas had been a merry and pleasant one—as merry and pleasant, I will add, as such a day can be thousands of miles from home.

The next morning there were calls to make—official calls on consuls and generals and prefects and great people. This is one of the duties—I was nearly writing penalties—of our trip. The incognito of General Grant is one that no one will respect. He declines all honors and attentions, so far as he can do so without rudeness, and is especially indifferent to the parade and etiquette by which his journey is surrounded. It is amusing, knowing General Grant's feelings on this subject, to read the articles in English and home papers about his craving for precedence and his fear lest he may not have the proper seat at table and the highest number of guns. General Grant has declined every attention of an official character thus far, except those whose non-acceptance would have been misconstrued. When he arrives at a port his habit is to go ashore with his wife and son, see what is to be seen, and drift about from palace to picture gallery like any other wandering, studious American doing Europe. Sometimes the officials are too prompt for him; but generally, unless they call by appointment, they find the General absent. This matter is almost too trivial to write about; but there is no better business for a chronicler than to correct wrong impressions before creating new ones. Here, for instance, is an editorial article from an American newspaper which has drifted into our wardroom over these Mediterranean seas. The journal is a responsible newspaper, with a wide circulation. It informs us that General Grant travels with a princely retinue; that he is enabled to do so because the men who fattened on the corruptions of his administration gave him a share of their plunder. He went to the Hôtel Bristol in Paris. He took the Prince of Wales's apartments. He never asks the cost of his rooms at hotels, but throws money about with a lavish hand. These are the statements which one reads here in the columns of an American journal. The truth is that General Grant travels not like a prince, but as a private citizen. He has one servant and a courier. He never was in the Prince of Wales's apartments in the Hôtel Bristol in his life. His courier arranges for his hotel accommodations, as couriers always do, and the one who does this office for the General takes pains to make as good bargains for his master as possible. So far from General Grant being a rich man, I think I am not breaking confidence when I say that the duration of his trip will depend altogether upon his income, and his income depends altogether upon the proceeds

Mrs. Grant

of his investment of the money presented to him at the close of the war. The Presidency yielded him nothing in the way of capital, and he has not now a dollar that came to him as an official. By this I mean that the money paid General Grant as a soldier and as a President was spent by him in supporting the dignity of his office. Everybody knows how much money was given him at the close of the war. As this was all well invested and has grown, you may estimate the fortune of the General and about how long that fortune would enable him to travel like a prince or a Tammany exile over Europe. There are many people at home who do not like General Grant, who quarrel with his politics and think his administration a calamity. That is a matter of opinion. But his fame as a soldier is dear to every patriotic American, and I am glad of the opportunity of brushing away one or two of the cobwebs of slander which I see growing over it.

But this is a digression. I was thinking of Palermo in her holiday finery; for the Christmas bells are in the air, and, as we walk from street to street, we see the South, the Catholic South, in every group. I can well imagine how this sunny, picturesque town might grow on one after a time. Yet, to our prim, well-ordered Northern eyes, it is hard to become accustomed to its dirt and squalor. This Sicily is the land of many civilizations. Here the Greek, the Carthaginian, the Roman, and the Saracen have made their mark. This is the land of the poetry of Homer, the genius of Archimedes, the philosophy and piety of Paul. These hills and bays and valleys have seen mighty armies striving for the mastery of the world. Certainly, if example, or precept, or the opportunity for great deeds could ennoble a nation, Sicily should be the land of heroes. But its heroism has fallen into rags, and the descendants of the men who destroyed the Athenian fleet in Syracuse, and who confronted the power of Carthage at Agrigentum, now spend their time sleeping in the sun, swarming around chapel doors to beg, and hiding in the hills to waylay travelers and rob them or keep them for a ransom. . . .

There were many temptations to remain in Malta. Hospitalities showered upon us. All the great ones of the place, beginning with his royal highness the Duke of Edinburgh, vied with one another in making our visit a pleasant one. I think if our mail had been ordered to Malta instead of Alexandria, we should have remained anyhow. At the last moment there was a disposition to stay, but the General had taken his leave and sent his cards, and he is not apt to change his mind. In the morning of the last day of the year he pushed ashore and roamed about an hour or two through the quaint streets of the strange old town. I have called the town Malta, but it is really named Valetta, after John de la Valette, who was Grand Master of the Order of St. John, and built the town in the middle part of the sixteenth century. The knights held Malta for nearly two hundred and fifty years, and remained until the French and then the English drove them out. The people have a peculiar dialect, based on the Arabic, with plenty of Italian, French, and English thrown in. The prevailing industry seems to be following officers and strangers around all day and begging. The town has many beautiful views, and I could see very easily how life might be tolerated here for the warm, genial air. It was the last day of the year when we pushed out into the bay and turned our prow toward the Mediterranean. There was quite a group of officers on deck surrounding the General and his party. As we neared the "Sultan" the band played our national airs, winding up with "Auld Lang Syne." We exchanged greetings with them, and with our compatriots of the "Gettysburg," who had gathered on the quarterdeck to say good-by. So our last remembrance of Malta is the music that came from the "Sultan," the hurra that came from the

Jesse Grant

"Gettysburg," and the lowering of one solitary flag, far up the cliff, which indicated that our consular agent was on the watch and was bidding us good speed.

I am writing these lines while our ship is speeding through the Mediterranean, in the region where St. Paul found the wind called Euroclydon. We left Malta in a soft summer breeze, and in the night the winds came, and this morning the sea is high and sweeps over bows, and the rain falls and oozes into your cot. As stumbling about a slippery deck is not the most entertaining proceeding to one whose life has been mainly spent on land, I came down stairs and sat down to write. It occurred to me that folks at home would like to have a sketch of our life at sea, how we live and what we do when we are under sail.

Our company is composed of General Grant, his wife, his son Jesse R. Grant, a maid, and a courier, Mr. Hartog, who has been with the General on his journey. The General occupies the cabin, which he shares with the captain. It is a commodious cabin, prettily decorated, with the exception of one appalling print of Wellington and Blucher meeting at Waterloo. This print rather overwhelms the cabin, and I can imagine nothing more conducive to sea-sickness than a calm study of this bewildering work of art. The General has a commodious little room in the bow of the ship; his son lies in a swinging cot and takes his rest like the clock pendulum. The steady routine goes on around us. On a man-of-war, life moves to the beat of the drum. The hours, the watches, the calls, the drill, the discipline, the cere-

Meeting with the Duke of Edinburgh, Malta

mony—the sense of command and the sense of obedience—all this is so new to us that it becomes interesting. Life on board of a man-of-war is like being a cog in a wheel—you go around and around and cannot help yourself. You rise by the beat of the drum; the drum beats when you go to sleep. Its alarm summons you to dinner. Everything is strict, steady, precise. Here is a company of young gentlemen—and, as far as one can know, gifted and accomplished gentlemen—who give up home, and a career at home, to live for years and years in a space about as large as a New York drawing room. Their whole life changes. They merge their individuality in a code of regulations. They listen for the drum tap that may call them at any moment—at midnight to fight the storm, at daybreak to fight an armed foe. Home and friends are given up, and a new life—an artificial life—is accepted. I can think of nothing more attractive than such a life in the beginning, when faces are new, and one feels the sea breeze freshening his brow. But after six months, after a year or two—how wearisome it must be! Yet here are gentlemen who are now in the second year of their cruise, and one sees no signs of strife or chafing. I suppose such things do exist, and that there are skeletons in the staterooms which stranger eyes cannot see; but I have not seen them, or any token of their existence. I should not ask better comrades in time of peace, or better defenders in time of war, than my good friends of the "Vandalia" mess.

Our General fell into his sea life quite readily. He seemed to welcome the sea with the rapture of a boy going home for a holiday. He is not an early riser, but keeps up the American custom of a breakfast at ten. After breakfast he takes up a newspaper, if he can find one, and a cigar. My friend Mark Twain will be glad to know that the General read with delight and appreciation his "Innocents Abroad." In Naples one of us discovered an English version of the "Nasby Papers," which was a boon. About noon, if the weather is calm, the General comes on deck, and converses or studies the sea and the scenery. Dinner comes at six o'clock, and after dinner there is talk. When the General is in the mood, or when some subject arises which interests him, he is not only a good, but a remarkably good talker. His manner is clear and terse. He narrates a story as clearly as he would demonstrate a problem in geometry. His mind is accurate and perspicacious. He has no resentments, and this was a surprising feature, remembering the battles, civil and military, in which he has been engaged. I have heard him refer to most of the men, civil and military, who have flourished with him, and there is only one about whom I have seen him show feeling. But it was feeling like that of the farmer in the school-book who saw the viper which he had warmed to life about to sting him. I had known General Grant fairly well before I became the companion of his travels, and had formed my own opinion of his services and character. A closer relation strengthens that opinion. The impression that the General makes upon you is that he has immense resources in reserve. He has in eminent decree that "two o'clock in the morning courage" which Napoleon said he alone possessed among his marshals and generals. You are also impressed with his good feeling and magnanimity in speaking of comrades and rivals in the war. In some cases—especially in the cases of Sherman and Sheridan, MacPherson and Lincoln—it becomes an enthusiasm quite beautiful to witness. Cadet days are a favorite theme of conversation, and after cadet life the events of the war.

Among our company is a gentleman who attends the General as a courier or secretary in foreign tongues. I call our friend "secretary" because the title is the one of his own choosing. His name is Jacques Hartog, native of Holland, educated in Paris, and citizen of the world. We call him the "Marquis." The title expresses Mr. Hartog's address and accomplishments, and I am proud to publish the renown that the "Vandalia" mess has conferred upon him. He has an aristocratic air, and it is almost like a breeze from land—a breeze from the Sicilian shores laden with the odor of the orange blossoms—to see the Marquis come to breakfast in the wardroom, with the sea rolling heavily, having passed a bad night. We are all fuzzy and ragged; we have taken refuge in flannels and old clothes; we have that uneasy feeling which verges on illness. The Marquis comes with the manner of a lord of the antechamber in the days of Louis Quatorze. Every hair is in its place, the curl is posed on the brow, the face is clean as a parchment, the full brown mustache has the faintest suspicion of brillantine, the scarf-pin is adjusted. There is not a crease in his garments. If the Marquis were a good sailor there would be no special merit in this, but our noble friend is a bad sailor and hates the sea, every motion of the ship being a misery to him. For a nobleman in the agonies of sea-sickness, of a constant sea-sickness, to array himself as though he were about to promenade the Champs Élysées, shows a power of self-control which is worthy of admiration. The Marquis wants to know the American people, and this trip he proposes to make the glory of his career. Although General Grant pays him liberally, no pay could induce him to travel on board a man-of-war. To have been the courier or secretary of General Grant will be a title of distinction in his profession. Consequently, he takes pride in his office, and especially in fighting the General's battles with hotel-keepers, hackmen, and beggars. Partly because of his renown, and partly because he will not allow a feather of the General to be plucked, he has aroused enmity in his profession. Other couriers, jealous of him, write anonymous letters, saying he is a scoundrel, and threatening to expose him. These communications he reads with unruffled composure, and lays them before his master, who disdains them and treats the Marquis with unabated confidence. The Marquis does not express positive opinions on many subjects, cultivation and travel having hardened his mind. His intellect swings from point to point, like my swinging cot, into which I mount with so much care for fear of vaulting out on the other side. But about hotel-keepers and couriers, as a class, he has pronounced opinions. A hotel-keeper is very good so long as you keep him well in hand and show him you know his character and resources. But once give way, and he will overwhelm you with charges for soap and candles and extras. As for couriers, the Marquis thinks badly of them as a class. "My aim," he said, "has been to elevate my calling to the dignity of a profession. But your other courier, why, all he wants is a commission and to make money. Now I like to make money, of course, but I want to make reputation first." Two other subjects upon which the Marquis has pronounced opinions are sea travel and the fickleness and inconstancy of woman. If he had his way he would either make the ship go forty-five knots an hour and burn more coal or run her ashore.

As for woman, he shares opinions like those of Rochefoucauld and Voltaire and Lord Byron. I observe, however, that the fair sex always suffer from the observations of gentlemen of rank who see much of the world. You will know from this that our noble friend is unmarried. I advised him in one of our conversations to form an alliance with some of our ladies of great fortune; but he does not have an exalted opinion of American ladies, as seen in Paris, and would require a large sum of money before he offered his hand and his title. Another subject which interests him is the political future of General Grant. He believes the American people should elect the General to the Presidency, and that they should do it next year. I explained to him that it would be difficult, very difficult, for us to have a canvass for the Presidency next year, or indeed before 1880. The Marquis would read-ily come to the United States in the event of the General's election, and I gave him all the information in my power as to the law and mode of nat-uralization. His immediate purpose is to write a guide-book for European travel. In this book he will recommend only such hotels as General Grant has patronized. So great is the esteem in which the General is held by all English and American travelers that they will rush to the General's hotels and avoid all others. I suggested that this would be destructive of the other houses, but the Marquis answered that his aim was to destroy the other houses. He proposed dealing with them as Napoleon did with the Repub-lic of Venice and the minor States of Italy. His guide-book will have ample space for advertisements, which he will insert at reasonable rates, and on the proceeds of this work—to be called "Hartog's Guide"—and upon his fame as General Grant's secretary, the Marquis will retire to his home in Paris, and there spend the remainder of his days in glory—in envied glory and content—unless political events should summon him to the United States. These are the views of the Marquis, expressed at various times on our trip. This dream of glory came to me vividly as I was passing through the steerage only a few moments ago. It was early in the afternoon and the sea was high. There, on the floor of the deck, with his greatcoat around him—there, pale and ghastly, was my noble friend. Some of the midship-men had been trying to console him with suggestions of beans and pork and molasses. Others had been telling him of fearful storms in the air com-ing from the coast of Africa. My noble friend had surrendered, and there, huddled up against the walls of the engine room, he lay in pain and grief and illness. "And this," I said as I climbed up the stairway to the deck, not quite sure whether I would keep my feet—"And this is only another in-stance of what men will do for glory." For glory my noble friend leaves

Paris, the boulevards, the opera bouffe, his evening stroll and his cigar, his *petit souper* at Velour's, his *bal masque,* and all the joys of French life, and tumbles about on this cold and cruel sea. All for the glory of being the secretary of General Grant, who, by the way, was quietly walking up and down the quarterdeck in a greatcoat, smoking his after-breakfast cigar, caring nothing for the sea and the storm.

An English nobleman is reported to have said that a man who would say he liked dry champagne would say anything. I thought to-night, as I felt my way along the deck from the General's cabin, that a man who would say he liked the sea would say anything. The night was cold. The rain was falling and bubbling about in pools. The wind was ahead, and the good old ship every moment wriggled and trembled as she thrust her head in the sea. Officers in weird costumes of oil-cloth and gutta-percha were moving about, looking at the sky and the rigging, and the barometer and the canvas. Hadden was walking the bridge with his trumpet, like an uneasy spirit, staring into the night. There was the night before us, around us, beneath us—not a star in the sky, only heavy, angry clouds. Every now and then the sea came with a tug and whirl, and sometimes forced its way over the bow. Far up on the yards were the lights to warn other ships of our coming. There, perched in the rigging, was a dripping Jack Tar, staring into the night. Now and then a call is heard—a call in some dialect unknown to me, which is answered from the bridge. But on the forecastle one of my fair, peach-faced young friends in the steerage, a midshipman, keeps his dripping watch, staring into the night. On the quarterdeck my old friend the quartermaster, with his gray head and grave face, holds watch and ward, staring into the night. Somehow I have great confidence in the quartermaster, and feel safe when I see him on deck. There is something so respectable and fatherly about this quartermaster that you instinctively depend upon him in a storm. In the wardroom some of the officers are writing, others are trying to read. As we come from the deck there is a run of comments and criticisms in that fresh Saxon sailor method of speech which breathes of the sea. The night is very dark, relieved only by the phosphorescent flashes of the waves and a burst of lightning which illumines the horizon toward Sicily and Crete. The captain comes out and looks into the night, and visits the chart room and the binnacle, and goes up to the bridge to talk with Hadden and stare into the night. I suppose the oracle has given him some response, for he returns to the cabin. The General is cheerful over his zeal and success as a sailor, and is disposed to vaunt his seamanship when one of us proposes to go to bed to prevent further uneasiness. The lady of our ship has been unable to leave her cabin on account of the storm, although all reports concur in saying that she proves to be an admirable sailor. The captain overrules one of her suggestions—that we should come to an anchor—by the statement that it would do no good; and the General vetoes another suggestion—that we should return to Malta—by the argument that we are as near to Alexandria as to Malta, and nothing would be gained by returning. The good ship strains and twists and keeps on in her course. . . .

Egypt and the Holy Land

And so to ancient Egypt, an almost entirely autonomous nation within the Ottoman Empire, governed by the modernizing khedive, Ismail the Magnificent, aided in part by eighty thousand European settlers, half of them Greek or Italian. Because of Egyptian debts, the French and the British had intervened in 1876 to impose and run a Public Debt Commission that collected taxes and managed the Egyptian economy. Britain also had control of 44 percent of the Suez Canal company—the canal having been completed by the French in 1869. In 1882, the British would bombard Alexandria, land troops, and make Egypt their outright protectorate.

Describing their excursion through Egypt, Young reflected the Anglo-American fascination with Orientalism—the mysterious East that was in their eyes so attractive, exotic, and backward. Young's account of the Grant party passing up and then down the Nile in a long, narrow steamer reflected both the condescension and the dreamy, often sensual qualities contained in then-standard Western travel accounts of trips through the ancient "Orient."

In this context the Americans rather admired British imperialism—and much of the remainder of Grant's voyage traversed the British Empire—a phenomenon they also detested as arrogant (and un-American) expansionism. For example, Grant and Young clearly admired the famous British celebrity explorer, Henry M. Stanley, the (white) man who had just "discovered" the source of the Nile during his trip into "darkest Africa," whom they met in Alexandria. For them Egypt was quaint and in certain sectors well ordered after the European fashion that Young and Grant accepted as normal and good.

But then it was on to the Holy Land, where they found that what they considered the utterly primitive rule of the Turks had utterly impoverished this magical place. Primed by re-reading the Bible to scout out sites sacred to Christianity, they pushed on, although they clearly were holding their breaths and their noses the whole time.

We arrived in Alexandria January 5th, 1878, coming only because we wanted an anchorage, our point being Cairo and the Nile. We remained there three days. Our reception was cordial. The "Vandalia" had hardly anchored when the governor of the district, the admiral and the generals, pachas and beys, the Consul General, Mr. Farman; the Vice Consul, Mr. Salvago; Judges Barringer and Morgan, and the missionaries, all came on board. The receptions lasted an hour, and as each officer was saluted according to his rank and the salutes were returned, there was smoke enough in the air for a naval engagement, and we could almost fancy another battle of the Nile like that fought only a step or two up the coast one eventful day, nearly eighty years ago.* The governor, in the name of the Khedive, welcomed General Grant to Egypt, and offered him a palace in Cairo and a special steamer up the Nile. It is Oriental etiquette to return calls as soon as possible, and accordingly in the afternoon the General, accompanied by his son, Commander Robeson, Chief-Engineer Trilley, and Lieutenant Handy, of the navy, landed in the official barge. As this was an official visit, the "Vandalia" manned the yards and fired twenty-one guns. These salutes were responded to by the Egyptian vessels. A guard of honor received the General at the palace, and the reception was after the manner of the Orientals. We enter a spacious chamber and are seated on a cushioned seat or divan, according to rank. The pacha—who has a Greek face, and I presume is a Greek—offers the company cigarettes. Then compliments are exchanged, the pacha saying how proud Egypt is to see the illustrious stranger, and the General answering that he anticipates great pleasure in visiting Egypt. The pacha gives a signal, and servants enter bearing little porcelain cups about as large as an egg, in filagree cases. This is the beverage—coffee—or, as was the case with this special pacha, a hot drink spiced with cinnamon. Then the conversation continues with judicious pauses, the Orientals being slow in speech and our General not apt to diffuse his opinions. In about five minutes, we arise and file down stairs in slow, solemn fashion, servants and guards saluting, and the visit is over.

---

* Young is referring to the British destruction of the French fleet in 1796 at Aboukir Bay, near Alexandria, which scuttled the young Napoleon's invasion of Egypt.

The General and Mrs. Grant went to dine, and in the evening we had a ball and a dinner at the house of our Vice Consul, Mr. Salvago. This was an exceedingly brilliant entertainment, and interesting in one respect especially, because it was here that the General met my renowned friend and colleague, Henry M. Stanley, just fresh from the African wilderness. The General had heard of Stanley being in town, and had charged me to seek him out and ask him to come on board and dine. My letter missed Stanley and we met at the consul's. Stanley sat on the right of the General, and they had a long conversation upon African matters and the practical results of the work done by our intrepid friend. The consul general proposed the health of General Grant, and Judge Barringer proposed that of Mrs. Grant, who, by the way, was prevented by fatigue from coming. Then a toast was proposed in honor of Stanley, who made a grateful response, saying it was one of the proudest moments in his life to find himself seated by our guest. Stanley looks quite gray and somewhat thinner than when I saw him in New York, just before his departure, three years ago. I gave him all the news I could remember about friends in New York and elsewhere. Next morning Mr. Farman, our Consul General, and myself saw him on board the Brindisi steamer, which was to carry him to Europe—to new honors and the enjoyment of a well-earned and enviable renown. The entertainment at Mr. Salvago's at an end, we returned on board. The next day was Sunday. The General, accompanied by the writer, landed, meaning to stroll about the town. Walking is one of the General's favorite occupations, and he never sees a town until he has gone ashore and lost himself. His eye for topography is remarkable; but that is a military quality after all, and in Alexandria, one of the most huddled-up and bewildering towns, he had a fine opportunity for the exercise of his skills. Then there was an informal luncheon, as became the Sabbath, with Mr. Gibbs, the director of the telegraph; Commander Robeson and Lieutenant-Commander Caldwell forming the other members of the party. The event of Monday, January 7th, was that we formed a group on the quarterdeck and had our photographs taken, the General and family in the center, and around them the wardroom, steerage, and warrant officers of the "Vandalia."

This event closed our life on the "Vandalia" for a month at least. It was only *au revoir* and not good-by, but there was just enough of the feeling of parting to give a tinge of sadness to the mass of trunks and bundles which the sailors, under the orders of the Marquis, were arranging on deck. We were to do Cairo and the Nile, we were to be gone three weeks, and we were to return. But the only one of the party who really wanted to leave was our noble friend, the Marquis, whose spirits have been steadily rising since he came to land and heard the rumor of the Khedive's hospitality. As he takes command of the baggage and directs the sailors in their handling of it, you see in his eye the enthusiasm of one born to command when in his own element. When he pushes off in the tug, trailing the luggage in a boat behind him, there is a disposition to fire a salute, but the regulations are not elastic, and the Marquis with his important command has only a silent adieu. We are not long in following him. We have a special train at our command, and the captain and a group of the officers are going up to attend the presentation to the Khedive. The governor of the province, with his retinue, met the General, and at eleven the train, a special one, started. Judge Barringer and wife were of the company, and the run to Cairo was made in four hours. The General studied the scenery closely, and noted the resemblance in some portions to prairie land in Illinois. Mrs. Grant was more impressed with the poetry of the scene—with the biblical associations that cluster about this strange land. The officers formed a merry company in their compartments, while the Marquis was in an advanced section, holding guard over a lunch basket. The Marquis is a great admirer of the Khedive, and expresses himself earnestly in favor of a government which welcomes its guests to a palace. He takes no interest in the ruins, believing Cairo to be more interesting because of the cafés, which remind him of Paris, than the Pyramids, which he regards as entirely useless. At three o'clock we come to Cairo. There is a guard, a carpet way, and a group of officers and civilians. The General, looking at the group, recognizes old friends. "Why," he says, "there's Loring, whom I have not seen for thirty years;" and "There's Stone, who must have been dyeing his hair to make it so white." The cars stop and General Charles P. Stone enters, presenting the representative of the Khedive. This officer extends the welcome of his highness, which General Grant accepts with thanks. General Charles G. Loring comes in, and receives a hearty greeting from his old friend in early days and his enemy during the war. General Stone and General Grant were at West Point, and are old friends, and their meeting is quite enthusiastic. The General asks General Loring to ride with him, while General Stone accompanies Mrs. Grant, and so we drive off to the Palace of Kassr-el-Noussa—the palace placed at General Grant's disposal by the Khedive. Commander Robeson and Lieutenant Rush accept the General's invitation to reside in the palace while they are in Cairo, and the remainder of the party find homes in the hotel.

The General dined quietly with his family, and next day called on the

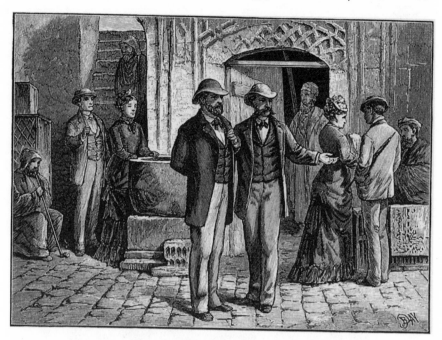

In Cairo

Khedive. The hour fixed for the reception was eleven, and a few minutes before that hour the state carriages called at the palace. The General wore plain evening dress, and was accompanied by the following officers: Commander H. B. Robeson, commanding the "Vandalia;" Joseph Trilley, chief engineer; George H. Cooke, surgeon; Lieutenant E. T. Strong, Lieutenant J. W. Miller, Paymaster J. P. Loomis; G. W. Baird, engineer; H. L. Hoskinson, ensign; B. F. Walling and E. S. Hotchkin, midshipmen; E. R. Freeman, engineer. Jesse R. Grant and Consul-General Farman accompanied the General. We reached the palace shortly after eleven. There was a guard of honor, and the officers of the household were ranged on the stairs. The General entered and was met by his highness the Khedive at the foot of the stairs. The General, his son, and Mr. Farman went into an inner room, where the ceremonies of the formal presentation took place. The officers then entered and were received by his highness, who expressed his gratification at seeing so many representatives of the navy. This reception lasted about half an hour, the Khedive showing the General the pictures on his walls painted in commemoration of the opening of the Suez Canal. We then returned to the palace. We had scarcely entered when the carriage of the Khedive was announced. The General received the Khedive, who

The Visit to the Khedive

was accompanied by his secretary for foreign affairs, and welcomed him in the grand saloon, where General Grant also received his highness. The officers of the "Vandalia" were present, and their striking uniforms, the picturesque costume of the Khedive and his attendants, and the splendid, stately decorations of the room in which they assembled made the group imposing. In the course of this conversation General Grant spoke of General Stone, now chief of staff to the Khedive. He said he had known General Stone from boyhood, and did not think he had his superior in our army; that he was a loyal and able man, and he was pleased to see him holding so important a command. The Khedive said he was very much pleased with General Stone, that he found him a most useful as well as a most able man, especially fitted to organize troops, and had made him a member of his privy council. At the close of the interview General Grant escorted the Khedive to his carriage. Official calls were then made upon the two sons of the Khedive, who at once returned the calls, and so ended our official duties.

Judge Batcheller, the American member of the International Tribunal, gave General and Mrs. Grant a reception and a dance, which was a most attractive affair. The Khedive intended to give the General a dinner and reception, but the death of the King of Italy threw his court into mourning, and this dinner will take place after our return from the Nile. The Consul General, E. E. Farman, gave a dinner at the New Hotel. The guests were General Grant, Mrs. Grant, Jesse R. Grant, Judge and Mrs. Barringer, Judge and Mrs. Batcheller, M. Comanos and Mme. Comanos, General Charles P. Stone, Mrs. Stone and Miss Stone, General Loring, Colonel Dye, Mme. Colestone, Colonel Graves, Colonel Mitchell, Rev. Dr. Lansing and Mrs. Lansing, M. and Mme. de Ortega Morejon, Judge and Mme. Hagens, Mr. Tower, Admiral Steadman, Mr. Van Dyke and Dr. George H. Cooke of the "Vandalia." The members of the Khedive's household and family who were invited could not come because of the mourning for the King of Italy. The dinner was worthy of the best kitchens in Paris, and gave the guests a good idea of the culinary resources of Egypt. At its close toasts were drunk to the Khedive and President. Mr. Farman then proposed the health of General Grant in a felicitous speech. He said we had with us a distinguished citizen of the United States, and made a graceful reference to the services of the General. During the darkest hours of our national life our guest had by his own merits risen from the modest position of colonel to command a million of men. After the war, which, under the leadership of this illustrious chieftain, had been brought to a successful close, a grateful people elected General Grant to the Presidency. They believed that a man who had done so much in war would be the proper ruler in peace. "They were not deceived," continued Mr. Farman, amid hearty cheering. "He administered the government so wisely that he was re-elected by an increased majority. He declined a third nomination, and comes to Europe, and now to Egypt, for rest and recreation. Coming as he does from one of the youngest of nations to a land abounding in monuments of antiquity, we can assure him of a hearty welcome." General Grant said in response that nothing in his trip thus far pleased him so much as his visit to Egypt, and he anticipated even more pleasure as he progressed in his journey. Speeches were made by General Stone and Judge Batcheller. Judge Hagens, in French, asked us to do honor to Mrs. Grant. This honor was paid most loyally. Dr. Lansing would not speak because he had to preach next

The Nile

day. After an hour or two of chat we went home, feeling that our entertainment by Mr. Farman had been of the most felicitous and successful
character—feeling also, as General Grant remarked to the writer, that
America had in Mr. Farman a most excellent representative, who could not
but do honor to our consular service.

On Wednesday, the 16th of January, we embarked on the Nile. As the
hour of noon passed the drawbridge opened, farewells were said to the
many kind friends who had gathered on the banks, and we shot away from
our moorings, and out into the dark waters of the mighty and mysterious
stream. One cannot resist the temptation of writing about the Nile, yet
what can a writer say in telling the old, old story of a journey through these
lands of romance and fable! The Khedive has placed at the disposal of the
General one of his steam vessels, and she swings out into the stream with
the American flag at the fore. We have all been in a bustle and a hurry to
get away. There was the leaving the palace, the massing of bundles, the
command of the impedimenta. We were alert for the trip, and we had
been feeding our imaginations with visions of Eastern life, with visions of
the faded but glorious remnants of the ancient civilization. Cairo was
French. The infidel had gilded and wall-papered the city of the faithful,
and it was hard to realize that you were in an Oriental land where everybody spoke Italian and French, and Vienna beer was among the principal
articles of merchandise. But now we were really to throw behind us the
tawdry French manners and customs which invaded us even in our palace,
and to go for days and days upon the waters of the Nile. We read about it

in guide-books, all except the writer of these lines, who resolved that whatever his impressions might be he would print them without incurring the mortification of seeing how well the work had been done before him. We bought each a Turkish fez, and some of us ventured upon the luxury of an Indian hat. Others went into colored spectacles, and the Marquis, a far-seeing man, who had been on the Nile and who was not in the best of spirits at leaving a palace to float for weeks between Arab villages, appeared with an astonishing umbrella. We had many friends to see us off—General Stone, Judge Batcheller, and Judge Barringer, with their wives, General Loring, and others. There were radiant mounds of flowers as remembrances to Mrs. Grant, and as much leave-taking as though we were bound from New York to Liverpool. Some one makes this suggestion, when the observation is made that we are about to undertake a journey as long as from New York to Liverpool and return. The General sits in a corner with Stone and Loring, talking about old days in the army, and making comments upon famed and illustrious names that the historian would welcome if I could only dare to gather up the crumbs of this interesting conversation. At noon the signal for our journey is given and farewells are spoken, and we head under full steam for the Equator. . . .

Our boat is called Zinet-el-Bohren, or as my omniscient friend translates it, the Light of Two Rivers. It is a long, narrow steamer, with two cabins, drawing only a few feet of water, with a flat-bottomed keel. The Nile is a river of sand and mud, and as the bottom is always changing, you must expect to run aground every little while and to run off again. This in fact we do, and the announcement that we are aground makes about as much impression upon us as if a passenger in a Broadway omnibus heard the wheel of his coach interlocking with another. The Nile boats seem arranged to meet any emergency in the way of land—for this river is sprawling, eccentric, comprehensive, without any special channel—running one way today, another next day. To know the river, therefore, must be something like knowing the temper of a whimsical woman—you must court and woo her and wait upon her humors. Navigation is a constant seeking after knowledge. We have a captain in a comely uniform, with a clear-cut Arab face, who stands in the middle of the boat and shouts. We have two men with poles, who lean over the prow and sink their poles in the water, and shout. Then at the wheel we have one, or perhaps two steersmen, generally fine, grave, swarthy fellows, who do not shout much, but knowing the river's coquettish ways, do as they please, unmindful of the shouting. For an hour, for two or three hours, we hunt along with an easy

General Grant and His Party in Egypt

trembling motion, the smooth, shining river lapping our sides, and the low, green banks falling behind us. Then we have a tremor, a sidling to one side, and the engines stop. This was so serious a business, especially to our seafaring friends, that for the first or second time they regarded it as a call to quarters or a fire alarm, but we soon became used to it, and running aground hardly interrupted the idlest conversation. When evening comes our captain picks out the best point that can be found after sunset and runs up to the land. The crew are sent ashore with torches and hammers, posts are driven into the soft clay, and we are tied to the shore. There, as if out of the earth they come, we have a group of Bedouins in their turbans, who gather on the river bank and make a bonfire of dried sugarcane or cornstalks, and keep watch over us during the night. The first night we tied up, Mr. Grant the younger and the writer went ashore, seeking out Hassan to keep us company. There was our group of crouching Arabs over the fire, their dark features lighting up into a strange but not unimpressive kind of beauty. We had been told—I believe all the books written by our English friends tell us—that the only way to extract courtesy from an Oriental is to beat him, trample him, or at least show him the hilt of your dagger or the muzzle of a pistol. The only daggers our party possess are the honest table-knives, which some one of the many Mohammed Alis in attendance on our party is at this moment most likely scouring. The only pistols I can trace are General Grant's and my own. The General, however, left his weapon in the bottom of one of his trunks in London, and mine is looked upon as a kind of infernal machine, dangerous to no one but the owner. However, we treat our Arabs with civility, and Hassan supplies them with cigarettes. They wish to stand in our honor, but we insist on their taking all the comfort possible out of their modest, crackling fire. They tell us their names, Mohammed one thing and Mohammed another. They have only one wife each, and live in the neighboring village. They have a sheik, and he sent them hither to watch over the hadji. Times are hard with them. The Nile has been bad, and when the Nile is bad calamity comes and the people go away to other villages. We did not like to talk politics with them because we feared that Hassan, who is an admirer and friend of the Khedive, might limit the tendencies of our inquiries and give only barren answers. They said, however, they would sit over us all night and keep us from harm. I have no doubt they were sound asleep, burrowed near the cinders, long before any one of our party had retired, except perhaps the Doctor, whose habits are exemplary, and who sets us an example of early hours.

There can be no more interesting, and, I am afraid, perilous experiment than to put ten human beings on a boat for three weeks and bid them enjoy themselves. I looked around the boat with a little curiosity as we came in and began to adjust ourselves to the conditions of our trip. There are two things that try friendship—getting married and traveling together. You have to dovetail, to make and receive compromises. Questions of coffee and tea and chocolate, of breakfast and luncheon, of amusement and conversation, enter into travel. There is the passenger who is never quite well, the passenger whose health is a reflection upon others, the passenger who worries about the engines and the mails, the passenger who cannot stand the sea cooking, and compares every dish with a famous dinner he once enjoyed at Delmonico's. Then there is the exasperating passenger, who contradicts everybody and is ready to wager. Our little party developed none of these eccentricities. So far as the daily and hourly rubbing together was concerned nothing came to mar our harmony. We adjusted ourselves to the General's modes of life; and as these were of the simplest and most considerate character, it involved no sacrifice. We live in a cluster of small rooms around the cabin. My own little room has a window within a few inches of the water. I have only to put out my hand to feel the cooling sense of the stream. It is a wonder how much you can do with a room not much larger than an ordinary sideboard. Clothing and books find rest in odd kinds of places. You sleep with your brushes and combs. In one corner is a little crate of Egyptian crockery which the Marquis induced me to purchase at Siout, and when I awake at night I wonder how I am ever to carry it over the seas. I do not think that the purchase was a useful one, but it did not cost much, and as everybody seems to be going mad on crockery, I may make a reputation as a connoisseur of Egyptian art at a small expense if only the crockery stands the seas. We breakfast whenever we please—in the French fashion. The General is an early or late riser, according as we have an engagement for the day. If there are ruins to be seen in the morning he is generally first on the deck with his Indian helmet swathed in silk, and as he never waits we are off on military time. If there are no sights to be seen the morning hours drift away. We lounge on the deck. We go among the Arabs and see them cooking. We lean over the prow and watch the sailors poke the Nile with long poles and call out the message from its bed. Sometimes a murderous feeling steals over some of the younger people, and they begin to shoot at a stray crane or pelican. I am afraid these shots do not diminish the resources of the Nile, and the General suggests that the sportsmen go ashore and fire at the poor, patient, drudging camel, who pulls his heavy-laden hump along the bank. There are long pauses of silence, in which the General maintains his long-conceded supremacy. Then come little ripples of real, useful conversation, when the General strikes some theme connected with the war or his administration. Then one wishes that he might gather up and bind these sheaves of history. Or perhaps our friend Brugsch opens upon some theme connected with Egypt. And we sit in grateful silence while he tells us of the giants who reigned in the old dynasties, of the gods they honored, of the tombs and temples, of their glory and their fall. I think that we will all say that the red-letter hours of our Nile journey were when General Grant told us how he met Lee at Appomattox, or how Sherman fought at Shiloh, or when Brugsch, in a burst of fine enthusiasm, tells us of the glories of the eighteenth dynasty, or what Karnak must have been in the days of its splendors and its pride. . . .

When the sun throws his shadow over the desert, and the white desert sands assume a browner hue, and the plodding camels pass like shadows over the horizon and pant with the long day's burden, our sailors begin to look out for the shore. The Arab mariner loves the shore and has no fancy for the night. It may be the evil eye, which has a singular influence in all Eastern deliberations. It may be that we are not in much of a hurry, and the river is not to be depended upon. By the time the twilight comes we have reached a convenient place, and our boat hugs up snugly beside the shore. Stakes are driven into the soft clay banks, rude steps are cut in the side if it is precipitous, and very soon we have the gray-headed sheik, with his followers, coming to watch over us. Then comes the clatter of cooking and supper, the crew sitting around a large dish and helping themselves with their fingers. We have two or three devout Moslems among our crew, who go ashore to pray. The steersman, who wears a turban and a white flowing robe, is the pattern of piety. He takes his woolen mantle about him. He steps down to the brink and washes his feet, his hands, and his forehead. Then he lays his mantle upon the ground and looks toward Mecca. He stands, and holding his hands in front, with the finger tips touching, makes a low bow, a stately, slow bow, his body bending almost into a right angle. He rises again, standing erect, murmuring his prayer— that there is no God but God, and Mohammed is his prophet. He prostrates himself on the earth, kisses it, and rising stands erect again. The prostration takes place two or three times; the prayer is over; the faithful Moslem gathers his garment over his shoulders and comes back to the boat and supper. When our dinner is over we have coffee on the deck, where we sit and talk. If we are near a village some of the younger ones go ashore. In a few minutes we know by the barking of the dogs that they have invaded the quiet homes of an Egyptian community. Hassan generally goes along on these expeditions; but the precaution has not been of any value thus far. The villages are sleepy enough and the villagers are quiet as possible. The children peer at you through the straw, the elder ones come clamoring for baksheesh, and there is sure to be a blind old soul to crave charity in the house of the most merciful God. You pass along through streets not more than a few feet wide, with dogs in the front and rear, and dogs barking from the roofs of the low mud huts thatched with straw. One or two of these expeditions generally satisfies even the most enterprising of our party; for Egyptian villages are, as far as I have seen, about the same. While some of us are ashore seeking adventure, and the others are clustered on the deck chatting about friends and home and the incidents of the day, our sailors gather in a circle and we have Arab music. I cannot claim any knowledge of music, although many of my most pleasant memories are associated with its influence. This music of the Arabs is a school of its own, which I would defy even the genius of Wagner to embody. I have often thought that the spirit of a people is expressed in its music as much as in its literature and laws. The music of our Northern nations always seemed to ring with the sense of strength and victory. I remember how the music of the Southern slaves was a strange contrast to the fiery strains of their masters. There was a low, plaintive key in it that spoke of sadness, despair, degradation; that was more a moan and cry than a harmony. I fancied I heard the same plaintive cry in the music of the Arabs. . . .

On the morning of the 19th of January, that being the third day of our journey, we came to the town of Siout, or Assiout, as some call it. We have a vice consul here, and tokens of our coming had been sent, as could be seen by the flags which decorated the bank and the crowd on the shore. Siout is the capital of Upper Egypt, and is a city of 25,000 inhabitants. The city is some distance back from the river, and grew into importance as the depot of much of the caravan trade from Darfour. Upon arriving the vice consul and his son came on board and were presented to the General. Congratulations were exchanged, and we offered our friends coffee and cigars in the true Oriental style. The name of our consul here is Wasif el Hayat. He is a Syrian and a landed proprietor. He is a grave elderly person, who speaks only Arabic, but his son had been educated in Beyrout, at the mission schools, and knew English. We all drove to the town. It was over parched fields, through a country that in more favorable years would

A Drive with the Khedive

bloom like a garden. But the Nile is bad this year, and a bad Nile is a calamity second only to a famine in Egypt. We rode into the town and through the bazaars. All the town seemed to know of our coming, for wherever we went crowds swarmed around us, and we had to force our donkeys through masses of Arabs and Egyptians of all ages and conditions, some almost naked—crowds crying for baksheesh or pressing articles of merchandise upon us. The bazaars are narrow covered ways, covered with matting or loose boards, enough to break the force of the sun. The stores are little cubbyholes of rooms, in front of which the trader sits and calls upon you to buy. As these avenues are not more than six feet wide at best, you can imagine what a time we had in making our progress. The town had some fine houses and mosques, but in the main it was like all towns in Upper Egypt, a collection of mud hovels. We rode beyond the town to the tombs built in the sand, and climbed the limestone rock on our donkeys. This was our first evidence of the manner of sepulture in the olden time. These desert rocks of limestone were tunneled and made into rooms, and here the mummied dead found rest. The chambers appointed for them were large and spacious, according to the means of the deceased. In some that we entered there was a chamber, an antechamber, and sometimes connecting chambers. There were inscriptions on the walls, but they had been defaced. The early Christians had deemed it their duty to obey the first commandment by removing the representatives of the gods that came in their way. The ceilings of the tombs had been once decorated, but modern Christians have deemed it their duty to deface them by firing pistol shots. When you visit a tomb and note the blue stars and astronomical forms that the ancients painted with so much care, it is so cunning to try the echo by firing your pistol. Consequently the roofs are spotted with bullet marks. Here also came the wanderers for shelter, and you see what the fires have done. What the tombs may have been in the past, when they came fresh from pious, loving hands, you can imagine. But what with ancient Christian iconoclasts, modern Christian wanderers, Bedouins, Arabs, selling the graves for ornaments, nothing remains but empty limestone rooms filling with sand and a few hieroglyphic memorials on the walls.

We were bidden to an entertainment at the home of Wasif el Hayat, and, seven being the hour, we set forth. We were all anxious about our first Arab entertainment, and after some deliberation our naval men concluded to wear their uniforms. The Doctor rode ahead in the carriage with General and Mrs. Grant and the consul general. As the Doctor wore his uniform and the others were in plain dress, he was welcomed by the awe-stricken Moslems as the King of America. Hadden and the rest of us rode behind on our trusty and well-beloved donkeys, Hadden in uniform, followed by wondering crowds. I suppose he was taken for a minor potentate, as in the Oriental eyes all that lace and gold could not be wasted on anything less than princely rank. But we all had more or less attention, although we could feel that the uniforms were the center of glory, and that we shone with borrowed splendor. As we came to the house of Wasif el Hayat we found a real transformation scene. Lanterns lined the street, servants stood on the road holding blazing torches, a transparency was over the gate with the words, "WELCOME GENERAL GRANT." The "N" was turned upside down, but that made no difference, for the welcome here in far Africa made the heart throb quicker. As we rode up torches blazed, rockets went up into the air, various colored lights were burned, and we passed into the courtyard glowing with light and color, passing into the house over carpets and rugs of heavy texture and gorgeous pattern. Our host met us at the gates of his house, and welcomed us in the stately Oriental way, kissing the General's hand as he clasped it in his two hands, and then touching his own heart, lips, and brow. Here we met the governor, and, more welcome still, the Rev. I. R. Alexander and his wife. Mr. Alexander is one of the professors in the missionary college, and is under the direction of the United Presbyterian Church. The dinner came, and it was regal in its profusion and splendor. I should say there were at least twenty courses, all well served. When it was concluded the son of the host arose, and in remarkably clear and correct English proposed the General's health. You will allow me, I am sure, to give you a fragment of this speech. "Long have we heard and wondered," said the speaker, "at the strange progress which America has made during this past century, by which she has taken the first position among the most widely civilized nations. She has so quickly improved in sciences, morals, and arts, that the world stands amazed at this extraordinary progress which surpasses the swiftness of lightning. It is to the hard work of her great and wise men that all this advance is imputed, those who have shown to the world what wise, courageous, patriotic men can do. Let all the world look to America and follow her example—that nation which has taken as the basis of her laws and the object of her undertakings to maintain freedom and equality among her own people and secure them for others, avoiding all ambitious schemes which would draw her into bloody and disastrous wars, and trying by all means to maintain peace internally and externally. The only two great wars upon which she has engaged were entered upon for pure and just purposes—the first for releasing herself from the English yoke and erecting her independence, and the other for stopping slavery and strengthening the union of the States; and well we know that it was mainly under God due to the talent, courage, and wisdom of his excellency General Grant that the latter of the two enterprises was brought to a successful issue." The speech closed by a tribute to the General and the Khedive. General Grant said in response that nothing in his whole trip had so impressed him as this unexpected, this generous welcome in the heart of Egypt. He had anticipated great pleasure in his visit to Egypt, and the anticipation had been more than realized. He thanked his host, and especially the young man who had spoken of him with so high praise, for their reception. The dinner dissolved into coffee, conversation and cigars. Mrs. Grant had a long talk with Mrs. Alexander about home—Mrs. Alexander being a fair young bride who had come out from America to cast her lot with her husband in the unpromising vineyard of Siout. And when the evening grew on we rode back to our boat, through the night and over the plain. Torch-bearers accompanied us through the town. Donkey-boys and townspeople followed us to the river bank. The moon was shining, and as we rode home—you see we already call the boat our home—we talked over the pleasant surprise we had found in Siout and of its many strange phases of Oriental life. . . .

[Then, it was away from the river on a long donkey-back ride, to the ruins of Abydos.] "Here," said Brugsch, as we dismounted from our donkeys and followed him into the ruins of the temple, "here we should all take off our hats, for here is the cradle, the fountain head of all the civilization of the world." This was a startling statement, but Brugsch is a serious gentleman and does not make extravagant speeches. Then he told us about Abydos, which lay around us in ruins. This was the oldest city in Egypt. It went back to Menes, the first of the Egyptian kings, who, according to Brugsch, reigned 4,500 years before Christ—centuries before Abraham came to Egypt. It is hard to dispute a fact like this, and one of the party ventured to ask whether the civilization of China and India did not antedate, or claim to antedate even Abydos. To be sure it did, but in China and India you have traditions; here are monuments. Here, under the sands that we are crunching with our feet, here first flowed forth that civilization which has streamed over the world. Hebrew, Indian, Etruscan, Persian, Roman, Greek, Christian—whatever form you give it, whatever shape it takes—this is the fountain of it all. Stanley had been telling me a few days ago, as we sat at breakfast at Alexandria, of the emotions he felt when he came to the sources of the Nile, where a trickling of water that you might arrest and imprison within the goblet's brim, set out on its mighty journey to the sea. I recalled the enthusiasm of my illustrious and intrepid friend as I thought that here was the source of another Nile that had been flowing for ages, that had enriched the world even as the river enriches these plains with all the arts and civilization and religion known to man, and that it was flowing and still flowing with growing volume and riches. You see I am a believer. I came to these lands with reverence and have faith in these stones. I shall never know much about Egypt; I am afraid I shall never care enough for it to enter into the controversies about time and men that adorn Egyptian literature. I believe in the stones, and here are the stones on which are written the names of the kings from Menes to Sethi I. Sethi built this temple somewhere about fourteen hundred years before Christ, and like a dutiful king he wrote the names of his predecessors, seventy-six in all, beginning with Menes. Here is the stone which Brugsch reads as though it were the morning lesson, reading as one who believes. Here is the very stone, beautifully engraved, and, thanks to the sand, kept all these centuries as fresh as when the sculptor laid down his chisel. It was only found in 1865, and is perhaps the most valuable of the monuments, because it knits up the unraveled threads of Egyptian history and gives you a continuous link from this day to a day beyond that of Moses. You pass your fingers over the stone and note how beautiful and clear are the lines.

And as you see it, you see the manifest honesty of the men who did the work, of the king who told all he knew, and of the truth of what was written. I believe in the stone and feel, as I said a moment ago, a little of the enthusiasm of Stanley when he stood at the trickling source of the Nile.

So we follow Brugsch out of the chamber and from ruined wall to wall. The ruins are on a grand scale. Abydos is a temple which the Khedive is rescuing from the sand. The city was in its time of considerable importance, but this was ages ago, ages and ages; so that its glory was dead even before Thebes began to reign. Thebes is an old city, and yet I suppose, compared with Thebes, Abydos is as much older as one of the buried Aztec towns in Central America is older than New York. When the temple is all dug out we shall find it to have been a stupendous affair; but there are other temples to be seen in better condition, and what interests us at Abydos is the city. Here, according to tradition—a tradition which Plutarch partly confirms—was buried the god Osiris. The discovery of that tomb will be an event as important in Egyptology as even the discovery of America by Columbus in his day. In the earliest times it was believed Osiris was buried here. To the ancient Egyptians the burial place of that god was as sacred as Mecca is to the Moslems or the Holy Sepulcher to the mediæval Christians. The Government has therefore been digging in all directions, and we started after Brugsch to see the work. Mrs. Grant rode along on her donkey, and the rest of us went in different directions on foot. There had been troubles in the neighborhood—riots arising out of the bad Nile and taxes. So we had a guard who hovered around us—one soldier whom we called, in obedience to the law of physical coincidences, Boss Tweed—keeping watch over the General. He was a fat and ragged fellow, with a jolly face. It was quite a walk to the ruins, and the walk was over hills and ridges of burning sand. So the Marquis went to the village to see if the camels had come bearing the luncheon—a subject that was of more value to his practical mind than the tomb of a dethroned deity. It was an interesting walk, to us especially, as it was our first real glimpse of the desert and of an ancient city. The General and the writer found themselves together climbing the highest of the mounds. It was rather an effort to keep our footing on the slippery sand. Beneath us was one excavation forty or fifty feet deep. You could see the remnants of an old house or old tomb; millions of fragments of broken pottery all around. You could see the strata that age after age had heaped upon the buried city. The desert had slowly been creeping over it, and in some of the strata were marks of the Nile. For years, for thousands of years, this mass, which the workmen had torn with their spades, had been gathering. The city was really a city of tombs. In the ancient days the devout Egyptian craved burial near the tomb of Osiris, and so for centuries I suppose their remains were brought to Abydos from all parts of Egypt. This fact gives special value to the excavations, as it gave a special solemnity to our view. As we stood on the elevation, talking about Egypt and the impressions made upon us by our journey, the scene was very striking. There was the ruined temple; here were the gaping excavations filled with bricks and pottery. Here were our party, some gathering beads and skulls and stones; others having a lark with Sami Bey; others following Mrs. Grant as a body guard as her donkey padded his way along the slopes. Beyond, just beyond, were rolling plains of shining sand—shining, burning sand—and as the shrinking eye followed the plain and searched the hills there was no sign of life; nothing except perhaps some careering hawk hurrying to the river. I have seen no scene in Egypt more striking than this view from the mounds of Abydos. . . .

[After Abydos came Karnak, then Luxor, then Thebes, through all of which the Grant party plodded with surprising interest.] We were to see the wonder of the world in Karnak. Karnak is only about forty minutes from Luxor, and does not involve crossing the river. I was grateful to the vice consul for sending us the same group of donkeys who had borne us to Memnon. And when I ascended the hill there was my friend Mohammed Ali jumping and calling and pushing his donkey toward me. A good donkey has much to do with the pleasure of your journey, and Mohammed Ali's was a patient, sure-footed little thing that it made me almost ashamed to ride. We set out early, because it was commanded by Sami Bey that we should return to the boat and breakfast, and while at breakfast steam up the river.

I cannot tell you when the Temple of Karnak was built. You see, in this matter of chronology, authorities as high as Wilkinson, Bunsen, and Mariette differ sometimes as much as a thousand years in a single date. But my own opinion is that Brugsch knows all about it, and he places the first building three thousand years before Christ. This seems to be a long time, but I wonder if we think how long ago it really was? You will remember reading how Abraham went down to Egypt because of the famine in the land, taking with him Sarah, his wife, who was fair, and whom he passed off as his sister. And Abraham, rich in cattle and silver and gold, went back from Egypt to become the founder and father of his race? When we recall the story of Abraham's visit to Egypt it seems as if we were going back to the beginning of things, for we go back to the time of Lot, Melchisedec,

Sodom and Gomorrah. Well, if Abraham on that visit had visited Thebes—and it is quite possible he did, especially after he became rich—he would have seen a part of this very temple of Karnak, and he could have read on its walls the very inscription which Brugsch translates today, and which would have told him, as it tells us, of the glory of a king who had reigned before him. It is, to the writer at least, this comparative chronology, this blending of the history you see on every temple and tomb with the history that came to us in childhood from the pious mother's knee, that gives Egypt its never-ceasing interest. You sit in the shadow of the column, sheltered from the imperious noonday sun—the same shade which, perhaps, sheltered Abraham as he sat and mused over his fortunes and yearned for his own land. The images are here; the legends are as legible as they were in his time. You sit in the shadow of the column, thinking about luncheon and home and your donkey, and hear the chattering of Arabs pressing relics upon you, or doing your part in merry, idle talk. It is hard to realize that in the infinite and awful past—in the days when the Lord came down to the earth and communed with men and gave his commandments—these columns and statues, these plinths and entablatures, these mighty bending walls, upon which chaos has put its seal, were the shrines of a nation's faith and sovereignty. Yet this is all told in stone. . . .

[After Karnak, the Grants' river boat took them as far as the rapids at Aswan, then turned around for the General's return voyage to Alexandria and the "Vandalia."] We left Port Said as the afternoon shadows were lengthening, and went out into the open seas with some misgivings. The weather had been stormy, and heavy dark clouds were banking up against the Syrian skies. A visit to Palestine depends altogether upon the weather, for there are no harbors on the coast, and Jaffa, where we were to land, is an open roadstead difficult to enter even in the best of weather. There was some anxiety during the night as to whether we could land at all, and unless Jaffa proved to be in a hospitable mood, we should have to abandon the Syrian coast and steam toward Smyrna. The idea of a visit to the East without setting our feet on the Holy Land was not to be endured, and when Strong, who was the officer of the ship especially in charge of the weather, reported in his quiet sententious way, late in the evening, that the clouds were vanishing, that we should see the Palestine shores shortly after dawn, and see them in a clear sea, there was a general feeling of satisfaction. We had been doing a good deal of Bible reading and revision of our Testaments, to be sure of our sacred ground, and when after breakfast we came on deck and saw the low brown shore of Palestine, we looked upon

Jaffa

it with reverence, and our gratitude was abundant when we also saw that the ocean beneath was as calm as a millpond, and knew that it was easy to land.

We steamed slowly toward the shore, watching every line and feature of the coast as it came into view. Jaffa welcomed us from her hilly seat. She seemed an overpacked town, thrown upon the seashore. But even Jaffa has now a noble place in the world's history, for her fame was green long before Europe felt the touch of civilization. At her wharves Solomon gathered his cedars from Lebanon. From her shores Simon Peter embarked when he went out to preach Christ and his crucifixion to the world. When we were told that the morning we arrived was the only morning for weeks that had known a calm sea, there was no disposition to murmur at the rain, which came in soft-flowing showers. Mr. Hardegg, our consul, came on board. Mr. Hardegg is an American citizen of German descent, who came to Palestine under the inspiration of a religious conviction that it was necessary for Christian people to occupy the Holy Land. This enterprise did not flourish, and Mr. Hardegg devoted himself to hotel keeping, and gave us welcome to one of the most pleasant hotels in the East. About eleven o'clock in the morning we landed. The Turkish Government for the cost of one of the Constantinople palaces could make a comfortable and safe harbor, but this is not Turkish policy, and among the theories which animate this strange people is that the surest way to protect a coast like that of Syria is to make access dangerous. The shore is marked by a series of jagged irregular rocks, against which the breakers dash, and it requires all the expertness of practiced boatmen to shoot between them. We were taken on the "Vandalia's" boat, the crew pulling their measured stately stroke. I would much rather, in a sea, trust myself to the Arab boatmen, who wabble about their huge clumsy boats with a skill which does not belong to man-of-war discipline. But we shot through the rocks, and came to the greasy stone steps, which were filled with howling Arabs. There was some difficulty in making our way through the greasy mob, and Mr. Hardegg was compelled to address them in tones of authority and menace; but in time we made our entrance, and walked into Jaffa through one of the dirtiest streets in the world. . . .

We made a pilgrimage through the mud and the narrow, dingy streets, to the house of Simon the Tanner. On our way we noticed that Jaffa had put on a little finery in the way of ribbons and flags and wreaths in honor of General Grant's coming. There was an archway, and an inscription over it, "Welcome General Grant." There was a large tent, called the headquarters of tourist expeditions through the Holy Land. The proprietor was at the door in a state of enthusiasm, and gave us three cheers all by himself as we passed along, and wanted us to come in and drink champagne. He informed us that he was the most celebrated dragoman in the East, and that if we did not wish to fall into the hands of Bedouins, we should patronize him and not the concern over the way. So you see how this commercial age has carried its spirit of emulation into the Holy Land. We passed through narrow streets and down slippery stone steps over a zigzag route, until we came to a low stone house. This we were told was the house of Simon the Tanner. . . .

. . . We had an escort of lepers as we took our places in our wagons, and were glad to hurry away. We kept our journey, our eyes bent toward Jerusalem, and looking with quickened interest as Mr. Hardegg told us that the blue mountains coming in view were the mountains of Judea. Our road is toward the southeast. The rain falls, but it is not an exacting shower. The General has found a horse, and when offered the affectation of an umbrella and urged to swathe his neck in silk, says it is only a mist, and gallops ahead. We are passing from the plain of Sharon into the country of Joshua and Samson. The road becomes rough and stony, and we who are in the carts go bumping, thumping along, over the very worst road perhaps in the world. But there is no one who, in the spare moments when he is not holding on to the sides of the cart lest there might be too precipitate an introduction to the Holy Land, does not feel, so strong are the memories of childhood, that it is one of the most agreeable and most comfortable trips ever made. We are coming into the foot-hills. We are passing into the country of rocks. The summits of the hills glisten with the white, shining stone, which afar off looks like snow. In some of the valleys we note clusters of olive trees. The fertility of Palestine lies in the plain below. Around and ahead is the beauty of Palestine—the beauty of nature in her desolation—no houses, no farms, no trace of civilization but the telegraph poles. Now and then a swinging line of camels comes shambling along, led by a Bedouin. If we were to stop and pause we might remember that until within a very recent period wild men dwelt in these fastnesses, and that we might have a visit from the Bedouins; but I don't think it ever occurred to any one. And if they came they would find no weapon more dangerous than a cigar case, or a New Testament, which some of us are reading with diligence, in order to get up our Jerusalem and know what we are really to see when we come within its sacred walls. The utter absence of all civilization, of all trace of human existence, is the fact that meets and oppresses you. The hills have been washed bare by centuries of neglect, and terraced slopes that were once rich with all the fruits of Palestine are sterile and abandoned. The valley over which we have ridden strikes the eye of the General as one of the richest he has ever seen, and he makes the observation that the plain of Sharon alone, under good government, and tilled by such labor as could be found in America, would raise wheat enough to feed all that portion of the Mediterranean. It is an abandoned land, with barrenness written on every hillside. For hath it not been written: "I will surely consume them saith the Lord: there shall be no grapes on the vine, nor figs on the fig tree, and the leaf shall fade: and the things that I have given them shall pass away from them." . . .

. . . We stop about eleven at the only place of entertainment on the way, and are shown into a gloomy, damp upper chamber. There we take luncheon on a pine table in primitive fashion, the Marquis unburdening the baskets and each one helping the others. Some of us walk over the hills for a short tramp while the horses munch their grain, and come back bearing anemones and buttercups and daisies, which we lay at the feet of the lady of our expedition as an offering from the Holy Land. We are off an hour ahead of time, thanks to our illustrious commander. It had been calculated by experts that we should reach Jerusalem about sundown; but the General had planned an earlier arrival and that we should enter the sacred city while the sun shone. So we went over hills that kept growing higher and over roads growing worse and worse. Some of us walked ahead and made short cuts to avoid the sinuous paths. We pass a village some way off, which in former years was the home of a bandit sheik. We are told that this is the village of Kirjath Jearim, about which you may read in the Bible, where, as Samuel informs us, the ark remained twenty years. If we stopped long enough we might see an interesting church, but we are just now running a limited express to Jerusalem, and the General means not to be behind time. We see beyond us Joshua's Valley of Ajalon, almost hidden in the mist, and remember how the Lord answered the warrior's prayer. We come to the scene of the great battle between David and Goliath. There were stones enough for the stripling's sling, as we can well see. The valley is deep and the brook still runs its swift course. We could easily imagine the armies of the Jews on one side of the valley and the armies of the Philistines on the other. It is the last ravine this side of the heights of Jerusalem, and one of the strongest natural defenses of the Holy City.

We have little time to meditate on these military achievements, for a horseman comes galloping toward us and says that at Koleniyeh—on the banks of the very brook where David found his pebbles for Goliath—a large company awaits us. In a few moments we come in view of the group. We see a troop of cavalry in line, representatives from all the consulates, a body of Americans, delegations from the Jews, the Greeks, the Armenians; the representative of the pacha—in fact quite a small army. The dragoman of our consulate carries an American flag. As we drive on, the consul, Mr. Wilson, and the pacha's lieutenant, ride toward us, and there is a cordial welcome to Jerusalem. We had expected to enter Jerusalem in our quiet, plain way, pilgrims really coming to see the Holy City, awed by its renowned memories. But, lo and behold! here is an army with banners, and we are commanded to enter as conquerors, in a triumphal manner! Well, I know of one in that company who looked with sorrow upon the pageant, and he it was for whom it was intended. The General had just been picturing to his companions what a pleasant thing it would be to reach Jerusalem about five, to go to our hotel and stroll around quietly and see the town. There would be no palaces, or soldiers, or ceremonies, such as had honored and oppressed us in Egypt. But the General had scarcely drawn this picture of what his fancy hoped would await him in the Holy City, when the horseman came galloping out of the rain and mist, and told us we were expected.

The Wailing Place of the Jews

Well, there was no help for it, for there were cavalry, and the music, and the dragomans of all nations, in picturesque costumes, and the American flag floating, and our consul the proudest man in Palestine. Mr. Wilson had a reverential feeling for the General. He was, he told us, the first American editor to name the General for the Presidency, and he had intended that the entrance of his favorite commander into the Holy City should not be a circus show or a one-horse affair, but a pageant. And he surveyed his line with pride, while the General looked on in dismay, feeling that there was no help for him. So we assembled and greeted our friends, and made the best appearance over it possible, and were presented to the various military and civil dignitaries, and partook of coffee and cigars in Turkish fashion. More than all, there were horses—for the General, the pacha's own white Arab steed in housings of gold. It was well that this courtesy had been prompted, for the bridge over the brook was gone and our carts would have made a sorry crossing. We set out, the General thinking no doubt that his campaign to enter Jerusalem at five had been frustrated by an enemy upon whom he had not counted. He had considered the weather, the roads, the endurance of the horses; but he had not considered that the pacha meant to honor him as though he were another Alexander coming into a conquered town. We trailed up the winding ways of the hill—the hill which sheltered Jerusalem from the Canaanite and Philistine. Jerusalem is two thousand five hundred feet above the sea, and even then it lies beyond a hill that must be passed. We wind around and around, patiently straining toward the summit. The mist and the clouds that had been hovering over our path finally enveloped us, and we could trace with difficulty the path over which we had come. The view on a clear day must be wonderful for breadth and beauty, and even now, with the gray clouds about us and the rain falling in a mist, we looked down the mountain's dizzy side and saw hill after hill sweeping like billows on toward the sea. As a glimpse of nature there was beauty in the scene to be remembered in many a dream. But we were thinking of the valley below, of events which have stirred the souls of Christian men for centuries, as the path of conquering armies—of Joshua and David—of Alexander and Vespasian—of Godfrey and Saladin. And here we were coming with banners and armed men, and at our head, riding side by side with the pacha's Turkish lieutenant, one whose name will live with that of the greatest commander who ever preceded him over this rocky way. The valley passes away. We ride about a mile through a suburb, the highway lined with people. The General passes on with bared head, for on both sides the assembled multitude do him honor. We see through the mist a mass of domes and towers, and the heart beats quickly, for we know they are the domes and towers of Jerusalem. There are ranks of soldiers drawn in line, the soldiers presenting arms, the band playing, the colors falling. We pass through a narrow gate, the gate that Tancred forced with his crusaders. We pass under the walls of the tower of David, and the flag that floats from the pole on the consulate tells us that our journey is at an end and that we are within the walls of Jerusalem.

We were taken to a small hotel—the only one of any value in the town. As I lean over the balcony I look out upon an open street or market place where Arabs are selling fruits and grain and heavy-laden peasants are bearing skins filled with water and wine. The market place swarms with Jews, Arabs, Moslems, Christians. Horsemen are prancing about, while the comely young officer in command sits waiting, calmly smoking his cigarette. A group of beggars with petitions in their hands crowd the door of the hotel, waiting the coming of the man who, having ruled forty millions of people, can, they believe, by a wave of the hand alleviate their woes. . . .

Free from our ceremonies, we set out to walk over the sacred places, our first walk being over the Via Dolorosa, the street consecrated to Christianity as the street over which Christ carried his cross. I am living within five minutes' walk of Calvary. I look at it in the morning from the terrace near my chamber door—a fair rounded dome, high in the air, covering the spot upon which our Saviour suffered. I do not enter into the question as to whether or not this was the real Calvary. Somehow one thinks it must have been one of the hills beyond the city, of which there are many; that the cross would have been more imposing on the top of the Mount of Olives, for instance, than here within the walls near the market places, under a dome. But executions, we must remember, are not pageants, and it would have been a weary road over the valley and up the hill for any careful centurion to send his soldiers. It is also known that in the time of Christ Calvary was without the city walls, that it was about sixty feet above the lower streets of the city, as high as Mount Moriah and Mount Zion. So that each historical condition of place and convenience is satisfied. We pass from our hotel on Mount Zion through a narrow, dingy street, paved with jagged cobblestones, rendered smooth by rain and mud. We make our way with difficulty. We stumble and slide rather than walk. We pass beggars who cry for alms, workmen at various industries, merchants selling their wares, camels, and asses, and beasts of burden. We turn into a covered way and are on the Via Dolorosa. The first place pointed out is the Coptic Monastery. Here Christ sank under the weight of the cross. We are going down the hill which he ascended. We come to the ruins of the Hospice of the Knights of St. John. Here is where Jesus addressed the women who followed him. We wind around the corner and follow the narrow, slippery way—beggars still crawling about us for alms—Alexander, of the legation, a fair young Syrian in Oriental costume, bearing a sword, leading the way. Alexander is in something of a hurry, the Via Dolorosa being of about as much interest to him as Broadway to a New York policeman. Here we are at the house where Jesus fell for the second time. We descend a slippery path, and at the corner is the house against which Christ leaned in his agony. The next house is that of Dives, the rich man. At this corner Simon of Cyrene took the cross and carried it a part of the way, for which pious office his soul found eternal bliss and his name has been made immortal by a grateful, sorrowing, Christian world. In front of the house of Dives is a stone, and over it a hovel. The hovel was the house of the beggar, the stone is where he sat in quest of alms; and under this archway where we now stand and look at the rich man's house, Jesus stood and pronounced the parable which you will find in the sixteenth chapter of Luke. We keep on until we come to a church, a bright new church, with an arch overhanging the street. This is the Church of Ecce Homo. It was here or hereabouts that the road to the cross began. There is a barracks on the site of

Pilate's judgment hall. We go into the church, a sweet-faced sister of some Catholic order opening the way. Behind the altar is an arch, and under this arch Pilate stood when he delivered over Jesus to the Jews. Here, in an inclosure, was the whipping, the crowning with thorns, the decoration with the purple robes, and here also Jesus took up the cross which he carried to Calvary. We can readily see as we retrace our way up the Via Dolorosa that it must have been a rough and weary road to one rent, and torn, and bleeding, and crushed under the cruel burden of the cross. Even to us— free as we are—wayfarers, in full possession of our faculties, it is a tedious task to climb the hill of Calvary. . . .

CHAPTER SIX

The Eastern Mediterranean and Return to Italy

After trekking to Bethlehem and Nazareth, the Grant party visited Damascus and Beirut and then returned to Jerusalem and Jaffa, reboarding the "Vandalia" for the short voyage to Constantinople. Expecting to chase the spring as they moved north from the Holy Land, in March 1878 the Grant party arrived somewhat prematurely in Constantinople. The chilly climate was matched by the rather distant reception from the Turkish sultan, preoccupied as he was by his recent military defeat at the hands of the Russians, which had compelled him to sign the Treaty of San Stefano on March 3, 1878. Young reflected what most Americans felt about the decaying Turkish Empire, expressing political pity while admiring the great mosques (and trying to feel tolerance for the Muslim religion) and enjoying the Oriental languor and the international flavor of Constantinople, rather like that of Alexandria and Beirut. This particular pleasure was heightened by their contact with the polyglot Ottoman officer caste, especially when many of them flattered General Grant with their knowledge of his military prowess.

In Athens, Young openly admired the Greeks for their go-ahead mercantile qualities (so unlike that of the Turks, he implied), and the Grant party once again enjoyed the banquets and public receptions that it had come to expect and, somewhat covertly, to relish. One signal honor was a private illumination of the Pantheon, though Young professed to have missed seeing this great monument by natural moonlight.

Young was professedly impressed by the military determination with which Grant viewed the sights, a habit that would continue in the next stop, Italy, where the general, no lover of art, nevertheless trudged past the Bernini's at Saint Peter's in Rome and through the endless rooms of religious paintings in the Ufizzi Gallery in Florence. Grant could unwind in Florence after the formal reception with the new pope, Leo XIII, arranged by Cardinal John McCloskey of New York (the first

American cardinal), and the state banquet with King Humbert, not so securely sitting on his new Italian throne. The party also admired the Arno River just a little, though it could not hold a match to the mighty Mississippi, which Grant had traveled fifteen years earlier on roaring Union gunboats. In Venice, although Young extolled travel by gondola, Grant is reputed to have remarked that this would be a fine city if only they drained it.

General Grant's arrival in Constantinople had been fairly well timed, as it occurred but a few days after the treaty of San Stefano. While in Palestine, notwithstanding our American capacity for obtaining news, we were for some time in doubt as to the course of events. Rumor flies rapidly in the East, and it was somewhat difficult to sift the false from the true. Of course our chief was thoroughly informed as to the nature of events, and we hoped that when the news of peace reached us, at least for a while there would be cessation of strife between Muscovite and Moslem. The journey from Asiatic to European Turkey was accomplished without any great fatigue by our party, and it was on the 5th of March when the General entered Stamboul. Immediately on arrival, General Grant was welcomed as usual by the diplomatic representatives of the United States, and all the Americans in Constantinople were eager in paying their respects to our distinguished chief. The usual round of visits of ceremony to our great good fortune were somewhat curtailed, owing possibly to the gravity of the events. The long and hard fight Turkey and the Sultan had made, perhaps tended toward diminishing the usual pomp and ceremony which belong to Oriental receptions. Of course though feeling peculiarly the position of his majesty the Sultan Abdul Hamid, General Grant, with his dislike of grand reviews and military displays, was rather pleased than otherwise that he escaped the usual rounds of warlike pageants. Among the most pleasant of the visits made to General Grant, was that of Sir Austen Henry Layard, the British Ambassador, and a grand soirée was given by this distinguished diplomatist, traveler, and archæologist to the Ex-President, which was attended by all the leading native and foreign officials.

I cannot say that sight-seeing in Constantinople in March was of an agreeable character, owing to the fact that March in this portion of Turkey is of the most disagreeable kind. Ice, snow, and rains prevail, and the warmest and stoutest clothing is necessary. A cold fog blows up from the Black Sea, which is of the most penetrating character. Some of the party felt the change from the warmer climate of Syria, but in our rapid tour of travel no one I am happy to say had the time to be invalided. Some cities have the great misfortune of being situated in those exact positions which seem to attract war and strife. From the time of Philip of Macedon until almost yesterday, when the Emperor Alexander with his hosts threatened its walls, Byzantium of the past or Constantinople of the present has always courted sieges. Here sooner or later will swords again be crossed and shots be fired, until the Bosphorus becomes the dividing line between two races of a different creed. But our party is so entirely unmilitary, from its chief down, that I must dismiss all warlike souvenirs, save to recall how in the fifteenth century Constantine XIII. reigned here, and losing his life in battling for his throne, the Moslem won Constantinople, and made it the great capital of the Turk.

Mingled together in its grandest mosque, St. Sophia shows the relics of Christianity in the midst of Mohammedanism. It is not even of ancient times this impress of European thought, for to keep it erect it was renovated only in 1847 by Fossati. Do what they may, save by leveling to the dust the proud dome of St. Sophia, the followers of the Prophet never can change the one great plan of the foundation, symbolic of Christ, which is in the plan of a cross. I do not think that the most ardent worshiper of that Christ ought to feel any degradation in the fact that so memorable a building should be devoted to a religion other than his own. Europeans and Americans rarely appreciate the devotion of a good Moslem. Traveling much in foreign lands ought to induce liberality of thought. Though St. Sophia from its immensity be not crowded, still it has its constant concourse of worshipers. Here are imaums, there sheiks reading their Koran, all imbued let us trust with pious thoughts. There is this peculiarity in Oriental adoration that it is indifferent as to the place or surroundings where God or the Prophet is to be worshiped. The Christian usually seeks the retirement of his closet to address there his Maker, while he who turns toward Mecca prays fervently whether he be alone or in the presence of thousands. Above the great mosque is the somewhat flattened dome, which in Justinian's time was all ablaze with gold and mosaics. St. Sophia spoke to many of us rather of the past than of the present. The Turk does not care for high decorative art in his mosques, and much that was beautiful with the miracles of Byzantine art have been covered over—perhaps defaced. Partly church, partly mosque, it still awes one with its grand story. Some day, when no man can say, those four six-winged seraphim, all in mosaic, Gabriel, Michael, Raphael, and Israel, will shine resplendent, and the names of Abu-beker, Omar, and Osman will certainly be translated to another sphere. But other mosques call our attention. The one of the Sultan Achmed is of a pure Oriental type, with its four airy domes and its six lofty minarets. The story goes that when Achmed conceived the design of this mosque, permission had to be asked of Mecca to build on it as many minarets as were over the tomb of the Prophet. This request was at last granted after innumerable delays, and not before a seventh minaret had been added to the shrine in Arabia. While one portion of the party visited the mosques, others, intent on collecting some souvenirs of their trip, sought the bazaars. Though the Russians were quite near, since peace had been declared business seemed to be reviving. Camels or the Turkish porters went briskly around, bent double under their heavy burdens, but were the only lively people on the scene. The Turkish merchant takes business in the most nonchalant way. He never is in a hurry. Prices we found were very exorbitant, that is if we chose to pay them. The act of chaffering or haggling seems to be expected, and one's time and patience are sorely tried. It is not because you are an infidel or a stranger that ten times what a thing is worth is asked you. It is simply the habit of the country. Here is a pipe shop, with the red-clay bowls, and cherry or jasmine stems; we buy pipes and saffron-yellow tobacco.

Some of us venture into a café; we find it to be of a mixed character. You might have all the civilization of the Boulevard des Italiens, Parisian coffee, a French waiter, your little glass of brandy or your Havana cigar, or you could indulge in the purest Orientalism with a native attendant. The waiter at a word of command will bring you an almond-stem pipe with its amber mouth-piece, will fill the bowl with the most delicate tobacco, and you can loll on a divan, propped up by cushions, and puff away by the hour, drinking from time to time your small cup of blackish, groundy coffee, in a filagree cup, or indulging in many of the peculiar sweet concoctions the Turk delights in. Some of us were bold enough to investigate the mysteries of a Turkish restaurant, one of the better kind, and found not only the service excellent, but the dishes quite palatable. All languages seemed to be spoken around us; one of our party, a polyglot, made out German, Hungarian, Italian, Polish, Armenian, and Greek. We had happened to enter an eating house frequented by military men, and the officers were apparently discussing the condition of affairs, which, though unfortunate they might have been, did not seem to have any depressing effects upon their appetites. Turkey, and especially the Turkish service, has been for the last forty years the refuge of so many foreigners, that one need not be sur-

A Street in Stamboul

prised at the varied character of the language spoken. With all her seeming exclusiveness, due to her religion, Turkey has been the home of many an exile, and among her bravest defenders have been soldiers of foreign birth. As known to be attached to General Grant, an acquaintance with our party was soon made by a group of superior officers, and the eulogium of our chief was pronounced. We were amazed at the thorough acquaintance many of the gentlemen present had with the leading events of our own civil war, and the conspicuous part played by General Grant. We found, what was not surprising, that the excellence of American arms was fully asserted by an ordnance officer present, and the important part our Yankee-made rifles had borne in the fight with Russia. They seemed grave and thoughtful men, and lauded the steady endurance, the frugality, the obedience and courage of their men. . . .

Our time is very fully engaged, and we make the most of our few days in Constantinople. We are told by American friends, who have resided for many years in Constantinople, that the City of the Golden Horn is not what it used to be. That the gloom of the terrible struggle, which has been looming like a dark cloud over the city, has not yet entirely disappeared, and that only within the last few days has something like former life returned to it. We are forced to decline many kind invitations proposed in the General's honor, but which cannot take place in consequence of the hurried visit he is making. Everywhere, notwithstanding the somewhat depressing character of Turkish events which absorb the people, the Ex-President is looked upon with honor, and the greatest interest is manifested in regard to his movements. Our stay though brief in Constantinople, notwithstanding bad weather, was of the most enjoyable character. We were due, however, in Greece, so after the usual warm leave-takings from all the Americans at Constantinople, following in the lead of our chief, we made straight for Athens.

The usual good weather which follows the General's movements accompanied him, and the journey to Athens was accomplished without fatigue. Through the Dardanelles we sailed, making before long the Gulf of Athens and the port of Piræus, some six miles from the chief city of old Greece. A short railroad trip took us to Athens.

The General is gradually getting over the idea that it is possible for him to travel as a private citizen, for here in Athens a most flattering reception met him. The United States minister at Athens, General John Meredith Read, with a large number of American citizens, were present to welcome him, and even the King and Queen vied with the citizens of Athens in doing him honor. More invitations, dinners, and receptions were offered than the General could have accepted in many months. It is out of my purpose to describe the political feeling, which was running high in Athens at the time of our arrival. The sympathy of Greece for Russia in the war against Turkey is well known, and perhaps great expectations of extension of territory had been hoped for by the modern Athenians. The dream of a great country, recalling the memories of thousands of years back, when Greece, with Athens as its center, gave art, politics, and literature to a world, had been thought once more as within their grasp. The suddenness of the peace of San Stefano had brought all ambitious thoughts to a standstill. Such topics were rife, however, and though the excitement was immense, it in no way tended to make our visit to Athens anything else than a most delightful one. A grand reception was offered to the General by the King and Queen of Greece, which was of the most agreeable character. This fête was attended by all the foreign ministers and the notables of the country. Here we saw, in all its elegance, the peculiar graceful costumes of the country. Nothing can exceed the distinction of the more aristocratic of the Greeks. If, however, the peculiar people of the Greek of Praxiteles have passed away, and another type has been presented, it is still a wonderfully handsome one.

Athens is a mine of ancient research, and not a day passes without some wonderful finds being made. Excavations are constantly being prosecuted, for not a spade is put on a foot of ground which does not enter classic soil. Dwelling as the Athenian does in the midst of history, he prides himself in being familiar with its past glories. With the Acropolis ever in view, capped by the grandest of all modern ruins, the Parthenon, the great deeds of his ancestors are ever present in the Athenian mind.

We defer for a day or so the visit to the Parthenon, as it is to be illuminated on the occasion of General Grant's visit, and as the city itself has claims on our attention. Life in Athens is mostly out of doors, and the cafés in the street are numerous. The coming prosperity of Greece is evident from the bustle and business we see. We try and study the peculiarities of the Greek temperament, and are amazed at its activity and business-like qualities. Proud of what their country has achieved in so short a time—for liberty acquired at Navarino is not half a century old—the Greeks are now the leading commercial people in the Levant. We know in the United States how assiduous and clever in business are the Greek merchants. Of course it is not in Athens that can be seen the commerce of this country; but still its effects were plainly visible by the elegance of the new structures in process of erection.

Perhaps as notable an event as can be recorded, and one which left an indelible impress on the minds of our party, was the illumination of the Parthenon. This is an honor only paid to the most distinguished guests. Starting out of a pleasant evening, attended by a numerous escort, we scaled the Acropolis and were amid the noblest monuments of Hellenic art. Though telling sadly of the ravages of time and man's vandalism, this magnificent pile astounds the beholder by its grandness. Up rears a host of pillars of Pentelic marble, fashioned and conceived by the genius of a Phidias. This was the fortress, the shrine in which the old Greek worshiped, resplendent with statues of the gods. I am not architect enough or sufficiently skilled to enter into all the refinements of art which were employed to render the Parthenon the most perfect of all buildings. Modern scientific research of a special character has exhausted itself over this ruin, and is fully satisfied that the old Greek builder was absolutely cognizant not only of the bold grandeur, but also of the most delicate subtleties of his art. Human imagination will go back no matter how prosaic a man is, to those who worshiped in this temple two thousand years and more ago. Such superb creations of art must have kept alive the respect for the heathen deities; must have made the old Greek believe that it was Minerva or

Athens

great Jove himself who inspired mortal man, and guided his hand when he built a Parthenon. But alas! great Pan is dead, and we a traveling party visit these ancient shrines, and wonder whether with modern civilization and its conventionalities we ever can produce such noble monuments. I think that all of us, even those to whom the crowning glory of the Acropolis was familiar, became imbued with a feeling of awe and reverence when in its midst.

We have not much time, however, to wander backward in our memories, for all of a sudden the grave old ruins blaze with a thousand Bengal fires. It is as if by enchantment. Each dark crook and corner, every crevice, all the mysterious somberness is gone, for it is now as clear as day. Floods of light pour on columns until the flutings, the old chisel-marks are discernible. The indistinct cornices, the peristyle, are cut with sharpened corners. Perhaps this over-coruscation brings out too the cracks and scars which have gashed and scarred the face of this much-revered old shrine: Away off in the distance, bathed in a sea of light, we catch a view of the

Erectheum with its portico. There are merry laughs and chatterings going on inside as fresh fires are lit and new effects produced.

The writer does not know whether to express pain or pleasure as the result of his impressions of the Parthenon when thus illuminated. He thinks though he would rather see the Parthenon on one of those quiet nights when the moon just silvers the columns with her beams. Without false sentimentality there is a garishness about such artificiality which is just a trifle distressing. That just appreciation which one may have fostered of the impressive sublimity of Greek art tends to be dissipated by the more modern lime lights.

I can safely say that many of us as we left the Acropolis that night, and, guided by our kind friends, descended into the city, were under the majestic spell of the Parthenon. Our chief may have the reputation of being an imperturbable man, but very certainly none appreciated better than General Grant the greatness of the past. The party taken as a whole have by this time developed fully the art of sight-seeing, and the General has shown the most marked adaptiveness as a tourist. His capabilities are wonderful, and there is no tire in him. It is of immense advantage to us to have such a practical head. Without any of the rigor of military rule, hours of grand departures are fixed, and if there are stragglers—well, they must shift for themselves. A journey around the world requires exactly this kind of discipline, and the same order, system, and good judgment, which are General Grant's greatest traits, stand us now in good stead. Time flies as on wings with us in Athens. We visit the great battle scenes of Greece, and see the plains of Marathon. Old classical literature is rehearsed. It is the "Odyssey" now some of us pore over, just as we relearned our Testament in Jerusalem. But it is the colder words we read extolling the outward physical grace of man. In the Holy City it was an inspired text which warmed our hearts. We are now far into March, and as the General has engagements which call him to Rome toward the close of the month, we leave the classic soil of Greece, and speeding through the blue Mediterranean, steer our course toward Italy. . . .

It has been said a thousand times "that all roads lead to Rome." This is an adage as old as the world, and has been repeated from classic periods up to today. To the chief of our party, as to the rest of us, the Imperial City was an object of the greatest interest. That grandest of all ecclesiastical buildings, the basilica of the world, is so stamped on every memory that long before we reached Rome the dome of St. Peter's, looming above the

Campagna, informed us that we were nearing the city. Our visit to Rome had been fairly well timed, for though the period between the death of Pius IX. and his successor Leo XIII. had been but short, the excitement over the election of a new pontiff had quite subsided. Our time of arrival was indeed, in some respects, most fortunate, as the presence of his Eminence Cardinal McCloskey would give us certain facilities in the Holy City which perhaps would not have been otherwise possible. As the representative prelate of the Catholics in the United States, his Reverence Cardinal John McCloskey immediately called on General Grant, and under the auspices of the Cardinal and Monseigneur Chatard, rector of the American College of the United States in Rome, the Ex-President was received by his Holiness Leo XIII. The interview was of a most agreeable character, and left a very pleasant impression on the General. Of course this reception, highly flattering as it was to the distinguished head of our party, was not to be considered as partaking of anything of a religious character. It was simply a visit of respectful courtesy from one of the most distinguished of Americans to the highest dignitary of the Catholic Church. The manners and habits of Leo XIII. are of the simplest character, free from all pomp and parade, and those who had the honor to be present at the interview were struck by the quiet ease, dignity, and impressiveness of his Holiness.

Such courtesies as the General received in Rome from King Humbert it is not necessary for me to dwell upon save in the briefest way. Almost immediately on arrival the General was called upon at his hotel by an aide-de-camp of the King of Italy, and every possible facility given us to see the innumerable monuments and museums which abound in Rome. An early visit was paid to the Coliseum, the grand amphitheater of ancient Rome. What superb old shows there must have been in those days! How our modern spectacular effects dwindle away before even the remembrances of such immense pageants! True that eighty years before Christ the impressario of such a theater was an emperor himself and his audience were people who had to be propitiated with shows—*panem et circenses*. Think of a building which would hold seventy-five thousand persons, and which covers five acres—a structure which has withstood the vandalism of ages—which defied Alaric and his barbarous hordes, and still amazes the world with its size and massiveness! It is impossible for any one who visits the Coliseum not to recall the barbarous sports which once must have rendered this place hideous. As we traverse the arena, we are reminded that here where our foot is placed the tiger has bounded and torn his victim, and here the panting gladiator stricken to the ground has, with swimming eyes, looked around at a sea of cold pitiless faces, and waited to receive from some stolid emperor life or death. Here Christians suffered martyrdom. . . .

There are chapels erected here now, and prayers are said for the souls of those who were slaughtered in those terrible sports. We visited the arches of Titus and Constantine, and thoroughly explored old Rome and its remaining monuments. Since the reign of Victor Emmanuel and of his successor, archæological explorations of the most thorough kind have been undertaken, and great additions are constantly being made in the way of friezes and statues. Gradually the magnificence of old Rome is being better understood. Should ever old Tiber be turned from its course—for to-day as in the time of the Cæsars, the river is a turbulent one, and over-flows its banks, requiring some engineering to prevent heavy losses to the city—should, then, the bed of the river ever be exposed, what untold treasures of art will see the light!

From ancient to modern Rome the transition is an easy one. Near the temples reared to the heathen deities, tower the churches sacred to the Son of God. St. Peter's, that marvel of architecture, the combined thought, the inspiration of a Bramanti, a Michael Angelo, and a Bernini, must ever impress the traveler with awe and reverence. Its immensity seems lost at first, from the absolute perfection of its proportions. Here are the tombs of innumerable popes, their monuments the *chef-d'œuvres* of the greatest of sculptors. The magnificence of the baldichino or canopy over the high altar dazzles one with its splendor. St. Peter's is a church of constant adoration; all day long prayers are said there. It is the great religious center of the Christian world, and God's grace is humbly asked there by sinners in every known language. The Lateran basilica, which has the proud distinction of having the popes crowned within its walls, was also an object of interest to us. To visit the many churches in Rome with any kind of thoroughness would alone occupy weeks of time. The museums of Rome gave us the amplest opportunity for sight-seeing. There is certainly no such collection of sculpture as the Vatican possesses. If sculpture does not satisfy the sight-seer, in the Sistine Chapel of the Vatican is the most impressive of all frescoes, the terrible Last Judgment of Michael Angelo. Here are the divinest works of Raphael in the adjacent rooms with Domenichinos, Guidos, and Correggios. Apart from the delight of seeing artistic creations, which never will be equaled, the literary portion of our party feasted their eyes in the Vatican Library with the sight of the earliest copies of the Scriptures.

Invitations innumerable were sent to General Grant to visit private museums, which were accepted in many cases. It may be said that the distinguished head of the party was a tireless sight-seer, and in more than one case showed a power of endurance which perhaps had been brought into existence in his war campaigns. On the 15th of April, all the Italian ministers were present at a state dinner given to General Grant by King Humbert. The banquet, a magnificent one, was a distinguishing honor paid to the Ex-President of the United States.

April 20th, we are in Florence, the fairest of the Italian cities, and a favorite residence of Americans. We are surprised, in fact, at the number of our republicans who live in Florence, all of whom vie with one another in welcoming the General. The climate we find delightful. It is early spring, occasionally there is a cold day, and the Arno runs yellow and turbid from rainstorms in the mountains; still there are many hours of delightful sun, and the flowers are beginning to bloom. Florence enchants us all. It has not the austerity of Rome, and perhaps this is more satisfactory to the General; who, being no longer trammeled by ceremony, is enabled to do rather more as he likes. Stately, well-meant courtesies, accompanied by black coats and white neckties, are the penalties of distinction, and the Ex-President being wherever he goes considered as representing the United States, has more receptions inflicted upon him than he perhaps wishes. Nevertheless, the General takes it all in good part, and when a little relaxation comes, and official visiting is dismissed for the day or the hour, he is the life of the party.

We arrange the usual programme for sight-seeing, for if the General is of the party there must be method about it. Our first visit is to the Ufizzi Gallery, and we are amazed at its magnificence and variety. We understand now how it was in Florence that art had a new birth, that here first started the Renaissance. To the Medicean princes, the great merchants of the world, is due the awakening of art. If Rome treasured ecclesiastical lore, and in a certain measure looked at the keeping of men's souls, Florence was the city of pleasure, and of the more refined arts. Its streets reflect the gayety of the people. Italy may be passing through the throes of travail, and Florence may be burdened with many debts, but there is an *insouciance*, a jollity about Florence, which is most pleasant to witness.

But for the Ufizzi Gallery. I suppose the best known statue in the world is that of the Medicean Venus. It was Cosmo III. who found this paragon of a marble woman and set her up in place, and mutilated as she was, it was Bernini who restored her. For long years this Greek beauty held dainty sway—until to the Venus of Milo, the grandest physical woman of antiquity, was awarded the palm of beauty. In this Ufizzi Gallery are pictures whose excellence has been extolled ever since they left the painters' hands—as they will be in all time to come. Here are Raphael's Madonna del Cordelino, and the Fornarina, Paul Veronese's St. John, with Titan's Venus, Carracci's Cupid, Volterra's Massacre of the Innocents, with Guercino's Endymion and Guido's Virgin. Here are a dozen pictures, which beyond price are the grandest in the world. Would you see antiquity once more in its most pathetic mood? Here in this hall is Niobe and her children. We spend hours in this gallery, and pass from wonder to wonder. The Pitti Palace and its collection is on our books for that day, and the General, who has no tire in him, pays it a long visit. The architecture is a masterpiece of Brunelleschi, built originally for a rival of the Medici, and a fitting residence for the late king of Italy. The ceilings of most of the rooms in the gallery are commemorative of Cosimo de Medici, and on the walls hang the works of Raphael, Tintoretto, Rubens, Del Sarto, Veronese, Carlo Dolce, and Salvator Rosa. It was with unfeigned pleasure that we found that Italians and especially Florentines treasured the memory of Hiram Powers. As for Americans engaged in art studies, we hardly ever visited a gallery of any distinction without finding some one from the United States busy with brush and palette, diligently working away, and studying the grand old masters. . . .

There are delightful drives near Florence, and now the Cacine is commencing to bloom. It is the Bois de Boulogne of Florence. It is yet a little too cool for open carriages, but the equipages are very fine and in good taste. As the General drives modestly and unostentatiously along the Cacine he is surprised at the number of acquaintances he has made, as hats are touched by gentlemen, and ladies bow, bestowing their sweetest smiles on the chief of our party. We get a better view of the Arno from the Cacine. We wish it were bluer; we are told it is so sometimes, but that the rains have given it a golden gleam. This "golden gleam" may be poetical, in keeping with Italian skies, which are blue enough, but we all call the Arno muddy. In fact, some of us long to see a decent river, something that swells in great voluminous floods, like the Hudson, the Potomac, or the Mississippi. For all Italian rivers are except in time of floods insignificant. All churches in Italy are memorable, and none the less so is the Duomo or

Pisa

the cathedral Santa Maria del Fiore. Here is the grandest cupola in the world—even rivaling that of St. Peter's. It is another masterpiece of the great Brunelleschi. Who goes to Florence and does not see the gates of Ghiberti on the baptismal church of San Giovanni? These are the gates which the great Michael Angelo declared were fitting to become the portals of Paradise. Easter now was fast approaching, and with it the religious festivals which are so carefully kept in Italian cities. The General might have wished to have been present at St. Peter's during Easter week, but the necessity of reaching Paris at a fixed date prevented a long delay in Rome. He was, however, fortunate enough to witness the commencement of the Easter festival at the Duomo with all its grand impressiveness. . . .

On the 23d of April, General Grant reached Venice by railroad from Florence. The route was an agreeable one, passing through the most picturesque portions of Italy. Crossing the superb bridge which connects "the Queen of the Adriatic" with the mainland, at the station the General was greeted by John Harris, Esq., the United States Consul, and by a numerous party of Americans. No sooner had a hearty welcome been proffered to the General by his own countrymen, than the officials of the city pressed forward, and the usual congratulatory speeches were made. Escorted to a comfortable hotel, our first evening was passed in needed rest, as all of us save the General felt the fatigue of constant traveling and sight-seeing. From the windows of the hotel, however, there was ample opportunity for amusement. The city of canals lay stretched before us, and on the waters were plying the gondolas. Early next day visits were planned to the most notable places of interest. It has been said that one of the most lasting impressions a traveler can receive is that derived from the first visit to the Piazza San Marco. Here it is that stand those two famous columns, one bearing the statue of St. Theodore, the other the famous winged lion of St. Mark. The buildings which surround this place are of the most imposing character. Nothing is wanting to complete the grandeur of the picture, for as a background stands the famous church of St. Mark's, the most perfect type of Byzantine work. Inside this church is a mass of verd-antique, marble, jasper, and porphyry, its gorgeousness even further heightened by innumerable pictures of the saints, executed in mosaics. It is impossible to spend an hour in Venice without recalling its former grandeur. Here was once centered the commerce of the world. Here was the starting place of Marco Polo. It was the Venetian merchant who gathered here the riches of unknown countries. It might have been the greatest despotism that ever existed, but it was the cradle of all that was beautiful in the arts, and to Venice was due the awakening of literature. Its own exclusiveness destroyed Venice after a time. But let us hope that under brighter auspices its commerce may once more revive.

Some of us took to the gondolas and threaded the canals, and were never weary of the wondrous sights which were ever appearing. Here was an old palace, famous as the residence of some old doge, whose name was coeval with the earliest history of the city—here was another that recalled honors culled at the great naval battle of Lepanto. Some were dreary piles, somewhat crumbling and desolate, others looked fresh and inviting. Evidently the presence of the General was known, for from many a window appeared a fair lady, who waved her kerchief. Of course the Rialto was visited, and the Bridge of Sighs. We admired the wonderful skill of the gondoliers, and the ease with which they propelled their boats. Much of our

Venice

time in Venice was spent on the gondolas. Of course one cannot get along without them, as they answer the purpose of cars or cabs in other cities. It is the perfection of locomotion, and has the advantage of being noiseless. We did not fail to visit the Arsenal, one of the relics of Venice, telling of her past grandeur. Here it was that were equipped the armaments of the republic, those galleys which she sent forth to fight Turk and Moor. Here, too, was the "Bucentaur" built, which bore the doges, who, dropping a ring into the sea, were wedded with the Adriatic. Shakespeare has made all English-speaking nations so familiar with Venice that when on the Campo del Carmine we passed the residence of one Cristoforo Moro, some of us were even inclined to believe that here Othello dwelt, and that in the gloomy first story poor Desdemona met her fate. The churches of Venice are all famous, and most especially is the one called the Santa Maria Gloriosa de'

Frari. Here is the monument erected to Titian, as a tribute from a king to the greatest of painters. In fact all Venice seems to pay honor to its two greatest artists, Titian and Tintoretto. The church of Santa Giovanni e Paolo was also visited, famous for its tomb of one of the best of the old doges. We were fortunate in having but a single day of bad weather in Venice. Though she may be "Queen of the Seas," American residents complain of the disagreeable character of the climate in winter, and if any reliance can be placed in books of sanitary science, Venice is not the healthiest city in the world. But now in full spring the climate was delicious. As to the people, they seemed to us to be the most light-hearted we had yet met with, and a singularly handsome race, apparently proud of their newly acquired liberty and certainly having all the possibilities of regaining their former high position in Europe. Their language even to our untutored ears was melodious to a degree, for the Venetians in their common dialect have a way of dropping the consonants, and indulging only the vowels, which is strangely musical. . . .

On the road from Venice to Milan we skirted through portions of a country, where the culture of the lands was familiar to some of the party. As April was closing, and May with full spring was beginning, the famous rice fields of Upper Lombardy were being clothed with their emerald green. We arrived at Milan on the 27th of April, and the Ex-President was received by the prefect, syndic, and other notabilities of the city, who paid most flattering compliments to our chief. In fact we find that nowhere in Europe is the distinguished part performed by General Grant in the history of the United States better known or more fully appreciated than in the kingdom of Italy. Innumerable Italian officers and soldiers were in the service of the United States during the civil strife, and many claim the distinction of having been the General's comrades in arms.

If we had been impressed with the grandeur of St. Peter's, we were amazed with the beauty of the Duomo. Up and up sprang the pinnacles of pure white marble, all cut and carved, the immense structure seeming as light as a poetical conception, surmounted by innumerable statues. To count these statues has been the task of many a traveler, but their number is bewildering. Some put it at eight thousand, others at five thousand; but a happy mean may be struck somewhere between the two. If one wonders at the lofty structure which rises in the purity of chaste white stone to the heavens, below there is still another church. Here are the remains of the pious St. Charles Borromeo. The Duomo of Milan is a place of relics, for here the true believer may see nails from the cross, and a fragment from the rod of Moses, besides many teeth which once belonged to biblical worthies. Returning to this cathedral, he who has not seen it can have no conception of what is Gothic tempered by Italian feeling in its most graceful manner. At the church of Santa Maria delle Grazie there is that object of the greatest interest, the fresco of the "Last Supper," by Da Vinci. Alas! this work, imbued with the truest essence of piety, is fast vanishing through the dampness of the place. It is true the world has made a million of copies of this work, and all know the divine simplicity of the "Last Supper," as far as paper and engraving will permit, but none but those who have seen with their own eyes Leonardo da Vinci's fresco on the dingy wall, with the fast-fleeting colors, can ever appreciate the imposing holiness of this creation. . . .

. . . But Paris was an objective point, and the Paris Exhibition; so our flying column had its instructions given it, and by the end of the week our leader bid us on once more to the gayest capital of all Europe.

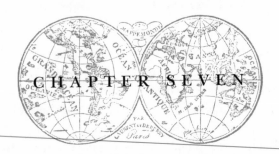

Holland, Germany, and Scandinavia

General Grant clearly found Italy altogether too decadent for his tastes, and so it was off to Paris once more—and the newly opened Exposition. After five more Parisian weeks of being on conspicuous display—to which he reacted by hiding behind his impassive mask—Grant and entourage were on to more of what this very American party all considered to be the far more progressive northern portion of Europe, where industry was triumphing over decay.

All Young's adjectives concerning the Dutch were complimentary—unlike the Italians, they were busy, thrifty, low-keyed, and spanking clean—and the Dutch in turn found the modest, taciturn Grant quite acceptable, rather like one of their own. Reassurance was measured by familiarity, and the Dutch were proper American forebears. Scandinavians presented similar characteristics, and in addition there was a kind of celebratory lightness and love of music and art during the long Scandinavian summer days that made the Grant party feel almost buoyant.

Between Holland and Scandinavia came Germany, where the Grants felt oppressed by the heavy seriousness and barely muted arrogance of their hosts. Despite the supreme excellence of her railroad system, Germany was rather too much of an orderly place, that discipline being of a distinctly militaristic caste, a mode of social organization that clearly disturbed Grant and his party. He was quite taken with Bismarck, who paid him considerable personal attention, but the omnipresence of the armed forces and the enormous military display on the plains of the Tempelhof in Berlin, enacted especially for him, appalled Grant far more than they impressed him. Grant was well aware—in part from prior discussions with General Philip H. Sheridan, who had been attached to the German army in 1870 when it crushed France and then imposed a draconian peace—just how ruthless the Germans were. He clearly believed that this was the rising power in Europe. Despite its university and its parks and fine boulevards, shops, and restaurants, Berlin utterly failed to charm Grant as Paris had done.

F rom Italy to France our journey was both pleasant and speedy. Everywhere along the route the usual civilities were offered us, and we had all the advantages of the best carriages on the railroads, and at the stations the functionaries of the various companies were all desirous of paying attention to General Grant. It was on the 7th of May that we once more arrived in Paris. On the 3d of the month Marshal MacMahon had opened the Paris Exhibition, and Paris was now talking of nothing else than this Exhibition. The American Centennial has been such a recent event, that I need not trouble my readers with any description of the French Exhibition. In fact, the accounts which have been sent home have been undoubtedly ample. On arriving in Paris, the American colony again paid their respects to the Ex-President, and though he was desirous of repose, still it was impossible for him to refuse the many kind invitations offered him. General Grant's coming to Paris had been timed so that he might be present at about the opening of the Exposition. On the 11th of May, Mr. Richard C. McCormick, Commissioner General for the United States, called on General Grant, to fix a time to visit the Exhibition. Saturday being the day most convenient, the General, accompanied by Mrs. Grant and a large party of friends, visited it. At the Exhibition the General was treated with exceeding courtesy by the directors and officers, and in the American Department he was cordially welcomed by his fellow citizens. The General is the hardest-working man I know of. What with dinners, soirées, marriages, and even christenings, he is a busier man than he was at the White House. If anything, the General, though still looking strong and healthy, is just a little thinner than when he started on the trip to the East. Anything like moderation in our pleasures seems impossible, for invitations from distinguished foreign personages and from his own people are coming in all the time. Plans for the future are made in the kindest way by the Americans for the General. The national festivities of the glorious Fourth of July are anticipated. The leading Americans in Paris met at the Legation on the 1st of June, and after some discussion, it was decided that a fête should be given at the Pré Catalan. The Pré Catalan is a charming retreat in the Bois de Boulogne, and just the place where a patriotic tendency toward fireworks could be indulged in, but the General will not be present. We are ever on the go. We prepare in Paris for further extended travels. Not that in the present century even a journey to Russia requires any peculiar preparation. What all of us want, however, is some repose, and we try and get it. Perhaps Paris is not a place where much rest can be taken. There is always something to be seen, something to be done, and we go sight-seeing, and visit the many charming environs of Paris. . . .

. . . Still we frankly confess that the constant strain necessary where one sees so much, ends in fatigue; and though Paris never can pall on one's tastes, the fact of our being here brings with it so many visits, so much gadding about, that at last, for one of the few times in his life, our leader orders a retreat. We are to seek the needed rest in Holland. It is among the Dutch polders that the necessary repose is to come. I for one do not believe that it will ever come. The Ex-President cannot assume the cognito—there would be no end of snobbishness about that; but I know that while in Europe the General would have given anything to have passed himself off as a simple American, traveling for health or pleasure. But such things cannot be helped. It is one of the annoyances of greatness to be stared at, to be pointed at, and to seem to be all the time utterly unconscious of being a center of curiosity. No wonder the General is said to be stolid, to have an impassive and undemonstrative face. I think when a man is stared at for ten or fifteen years it becomes a necessary provision of nature to wear something of an immovable mask. We really all are glad that we are going, and at last we bid our numerous friends good-by. I think the General is moved more than usual, as his fellow citizens throng around him at the railroad station, all wishing him and Mrs. Grant a pleasant journey and a speedy return.

I will not detail the route to Holland. The approach to the kingdom of the Netherlands is, topographically at least, instantly perceptible. The country is flat, flat as a pancake, and through it run canals. We will not accept the witty Frenchman's description of Le Pays Bas save in the first two words, *canaux—canards*. It is true there are canals, and we see plenty of ducks. We soon appreciate that this is a country which struggles for absolute terrestrial existence. Some one said that Holland was a compromise between the land and the sea. It is the one element which is forever fighting with the other. Such a long battle has at least shown man's superiority over the sea. Still it is wonderful to think that we shall pass on a railroad which is lower than the bed of an adjacent river, and that the tides of the North Sea, which beat against the dunes, dikes, and sandhills of Northern

Holland, rise eleven feet above Amsterdam, and that in certain winds the apparently torpid Maas, if not kept out, would flow some ten feet deep over all Amsterdam. To think of a great prosperous country whose very existence depends upon the stopping up of a rat hole! It is certainly this watchfulness, this vigilance, which has imparted to the Dutch character those marked qualities of industry and perseverance. It is always a land which has to be won. As we speed along in the comfortable railroad cars (like all things Dutch they are broad-gauge roads), the first aspects of Holland strike us. The season is fairly advanced, and the grass in the fields is of the tenderest green. Great lazy cattle, sleek and comfortable, browse in the fields. We skirt a canal. Slowly and deliberately moves the boat. The horses tug it along, but the man who drives, who plods beside his well-fed beasts, has no whip. Those horses never have felt the lash, and never will. The canal boat is gayly painted, and in the stern is the typical Dutchman, with a big pipe in his mouth. As we slacken up speed on the road I catch a glimpse into the interior of the cabin of a boat, a trekschuyt. It is neatness itself. In the window of this floating house there is a whole ledge of blooming tulips. I cannot help thinking that the people I see tilling the fields are the most mechanical and plodding of human beings. They seem slow-gaited, but I do not recognize the dull look. I am quite sure, however, that while the farmer's boy is putting his spade in the ground an American in the same time would have dug up six square feet and loaded all the soil in a barrow if necessary. What I do take pleasure in asserting is the wholesome, well-fed appearance of the country-folk. I admire, too, the costume, particularly that of the women. It is tidy to a degree. It is some holiday, or there is a fair in the neighborhood, for all the lusty Dutch lasses wear towering white caps, and on each side of their heads are gold or gilt pieces of metal not much smaller than saucers. I notice, too, no end of jewelry and embroidery. Evidently it is a dairy country, for I see milkpans of ruddy copper, and they are scrupulously clean, for the metal glistens in the sun. There is no makeshift in these people's habits. Though the land they live on may be swept away to-morrow, the houses are built to last a thousand years. I note, too, the thrift which is apparent. I see no one in rags. . . .

. . . As usual the General is in receipt of invitations to accept the hospitality of all the leading great cities of Holland. The Dutch are said to be a most undemonstrative people, but judging by the reception the General is receiving, this cannot be the case. I suppose his enthusiastic welcome is due not alone to the distinguished position the chief of our party has held for so many years in the history of his country, but because of the most pleasant relationships which have always existed between Holland and America. I am sure the General is delighted with his visit to the Hague. It is true there is much sight-seeing, but in keeping with the Dutch charac-ter matters are not driven—or rushed—as in France or even Italy. We feel for once more than pleased with this most welcome Dutch slowness, and look forward to its continuance even in Rotterdam and Amsterdam. . . .

Our visit, the one of ceremony, having been paid to the Hague, after a pleasant stay at the capital we take our departure for Rotterdam. We pass Delft, famous for its pottery (of course we have a pottery and porcelain maniac collector in the party), and soon reach Rotterdam, famous for its commerce. And at once we commence making the rounds of the city. We are amazed to find that there are so many Americans who reside in Rot-terdam, and who declare that it is the most pleasant city of Europe. We no-tice now the real true Dutchman; and certainly he is an inveterate smoker, for never by chance does he let his pipe go out. He is busy enough, how-ever, and seems to have a certain amount of business hurry. We hope to see houses which will recall to our mind the old mansions which the Dutchmen built in New York. We do find some resemblance as to outline with the houses which used to exist on Manhattan Island, on the Hudson River, even on Staten Island; but as to color, we are quite shocked, as the Dutch have a queer taste for painting all their old houses with the most vivid colors. The streets are, however, quite picturesque, and the effects are heightened by the numerous canals. In fact, Rotterdam seems like a continuous seaport—a city with water fronts lying on all sides of it, and in the middle of it. It is an assemblage of houses and vessels. In Venice, the canals are spanned by bridges, which cannot interfere with the gondolas, but here it is a good-sized vessel, with moderately high masts, that has to go through the town. Drawbridges are constant, and communication for foot passengers is often cut off. But your Dutchman is patient, and he knows how to wait. One thing which amused many of the party was the use of dogs as beasts of burden. I cannot help remarking that some of the poor brutes looked very much overworked, and we wished that a Dutch Bergh would arise. Rotterdam with its 122,000 inhabitants shows on her docks and quays the commercial character of the people, and there is no better place to judge of it than near the Boompjes, where the steamers are massed, some just coming in, others going out, bringing in and taking away the products of two continents. We seek the market house, and stand on the bridge and find the statue of Erasmus. It happens to be a Saturday morning when a party of us saunter along the streets. Busy women servants, no light ephemeral creatures, but heavy solid girls, are cleaning the outsides of the houses. There is water now not only in the canals, but on the sidewalls. We escape a drenching from a bucket just in time to be bespattered by a suction tube worked in a pail. "It is delightfully familiar," remarks a Philadelphian who is of the party, as he catches a shower from a mop. Our destination is the Church of St. Lawrence, the Groote Kerk, and we are shown the monuments sacred to the memories of many Dutch worthies. The Boymans Museum contains a superb collection of pictures, where we spend many hours. The visit of the General is made agreeable in every way, and a grand dinner was given in his honor by the burgomaster of the city, which was numerously attended. We become more and more conscious from the toasts given at this dinner how sincere is the relationship between America and Holland, and how the Dutchman is not only proud of the settlements he has planted in our New World, but believes that with the increasing commercial prosperity of the United States even closer ties can be made.

Our journey from Rotterdam to Amsterdam is a short one, for there are no great distances to be covered here. The country through which we pass is very characteristic of Holland, for without man's constant care and vigilance the Zuyder-Zee would burst bounds and sweep these wonderful farms and blooming gardens into the North Sea. As we near Amsterdam we notice all the appearances of a great city. If the Hague is the court capital, it is Amsterdam which is the commercial center. Here are forests of masts for this great Dutch city rises from the bosom of the sea. Once where Amsterdam stood there was a marsh, so that the city, like Venice, stands on piles. This is the mart which has kept up for a thousand years her commercial prestige. Italian cities in whose market places were once heaped the treasures of a world, have passed away, but despite time and circumstance Amsterdam will ever hold her own. We at once appreciate one of the peculiarities of the place, and that is the bad smell. It may be fish or anything else; we are told it is the drainage. We think that if Coleridge had ever visited Amsterdam he would not have maligned Cologne. We visit the various quarters of the city, and easily distinguish the great social differences which exist. Here is a commercial quarter, a manufacturing district, a portion thronged with ships; here the Jews' quarter, and there the most fashionable quarter. Amsterdam is wonderful in its picturesqueness. There are tall, antiquated houses, all with gables, with quaint roofs, and queer windows. We do not see many new houses building. Perhaps such modern edifices are constructed, but they quickly assimilate with the *couleur locale* of the city. We have heard some chimes in the other cities of Holland, we had a foretaste of it in Belgium, but in Amsterdam it is a continuous clang. To those unaccustomed to it a chime in the neighborhood is a nuisance, and some of the party, I am sorry to state, broke out into open rebellion about the bells. I suppose Dutchmen in time never hear them. I am pleased with many of the good Dutch customs brought into New York, but am glad bell-chiming in excess was omitted. It is a waste of human energy or mechanical power to set bells tolling, and the exact distinction between music and noise, as imparted by a bell, a good many people have never been able to determine. Our usual round of sight-seeing commenced, and was leisurely accomplished. The museum, with its superb collections of Rubens and Rembrandts, delighted us, as did the Van der Hoop and Foder collections. Churches in Amsterdam, as in all the towns of the Netherlands, are not remarkable for either outside architecture or inside decoration. It is a certain simplicity which is characteristic of the Dutchman. No matter how grand a Dutchman may be, he is never anxious to make a display of it. A merchant in Holland by hard work and honesty gains a fortune. He is the last person to be ostentatious about it. He does not think of extending his house, of buying a carriage, or of traveling. Perhaps, if he has artistic tendencies, he may buy a good old picture or so. He may slightly increase his method of living, allowing himself or his family some few luxuries. If he does spend any money it will be to beautify some little garden spot a mile or so from the city. In this Eden he will grow his tulips, erect a quaint rococo summer-house, paint it all the colors of the rainbow, and on summer evenings will come and smoke his pipe there and drink his coffee. This extreme simplicity of taste, and the consequent saving of money, gave Holland supremacy for so many years. It is moderation which brings innumerable benefits. The Dutch character is grand in its simplicity. You hear of names which in old times have been illustrious. You go to visit the houses where a William the Silent, a John de Witt, or an Admiral Ruyter lived, and you see a small house. There is nothing parsimonious about the Dutchman, he is simply thrifty. It is a practical people, capable of the utmost devotion and heroism. An invitation is sent to visit the palace, and we see there fragments of the old flags which Dutchmen tore from Alva's standard bearers. Among the numerous monuments of commerce the principal one is the great exchange. Here are assembled every day all the merchants who dispose of the produce coming from all parts of the world. If there is a certain amount of phlegm in the Hollander, it is not appreciable when he is in the heat of trade. We have been now long enough in Holland to understand the system of canals. The canals cut up Amsterdam into some ninety islands and communication is kept up by means of two hundred and eighty-five bridges. Of course the utmost care is taken of these canals, and the expenditure on them daily amounts to a large sum.

In honor of the Ex-President of the United States, a sumptuous banquet was given him by some fifty of the leading merchants of the city. It would be difficult for me to describe the peculiar magnificence of this dinner, which was attended by all the dignitaries of the city. On the sideboards flashed a wealth of plate, some of which, on prior occasions, have been used to welcome the former heroes of the country. Of course, the General had to make a speech, which I am led to believe was fully appreciated by the Amsterdam merchants, who very rightly consider that brevity even in an afternoon dinner speech is the soul of wit. The General is highly esteemed by the Dutchmen. His peculiar quiet manner is much liked, and as to the constant cigar in his mouth, smoking is such a national Dutch custom that it is another bond of union. . . .

General Grant and his party arrived in Berlin on the 26th of June. Mr. Bayard Taylor, our Minister, went down the road some sixty miles to Stendahl to meet the Ex-President.* The General was in the best of spirits, delighted with his journey through Holland, and carrying with him not only lasting impressions of the prosperity of the Dutch people, and the true freedom they enjoyed, but grateful for the hospitality he had received. On the evening of arrival at Berlin the General strolled along the famous avenue Unter den Linden, and during the entire stay in the Prussian capital a portion of every day was devoted to walking. I do not think that there was a quarter of Berlin which he did not explore with that energy of the true sight-seer which no amount of exertion can extinguish.

The interest General Grant took in Berlin was very great. Prussia and her capital have asserted themselves so prominently in history for the last twenty years that they may be regarded as the leading country and the political center of Europe. Few people remember that in the annals of that older civilization Prussia has arrived at her maturity in a comparatively short period of time. That position she now enjoys in reality only dates back from the time of Frederick the Great. After him the star of Prussia

---

* Bayard Taylor was one of the best-known American travel writers and novelists of his day. The Berlin ministry was his political reward, such posts often being given to writers and artists as well as to failed politicians. In 1872, Taylor had opposed Grant's re-election in print. Therefore, according to Young, Taylor was frightened of meeting Grant, but the ex-president proved to be altogether cordial.

Unten den Linden

might have been dimmed for a time only to arise in its present glory under Frederick William and Bismarck. It is not my purpose in this record of travels to write history, but Prussia in herself, in her cities perpetually recalls the methods by which her greatness was achieved. If there have been great thrift, honesty, steadfastness displayed by the Prussians, it is as a military power that she takes preeminence. Everything is subservient to the soldier. To us in the United States, thanks to our position, this necessity for guns and swords does not exist. Frederick the Great fought for and gained his territory inch by inch. . . .

. . . After the victory of Prussia over France, Berlin made rapid strides, and buildings went up on all sides, but financial matters did not go on as swimmingly as did the military successes, and the city is said to be suffering from "hard times." We cannot see it, however, in the streets, which are very gay and cheerful. Of course the soldier element is in great excess. There are uniforms everywhere. It can hardly be otherwise where every man is a soldier. At first it is monotonous to see so many in blue with red facings, but one gets accustomed to it in time. It means what has been before mentioned, that Prussia must always stand on guard. She is practical about this, and rather counts on people noticing the military status than otherwise.

The great street of Berlin is the Unter den Linden. This is the Broadway, the Newsky Perspective, the Boulevard of Berlin. There are long rows of fine trees which shade the street. At one extremity is the Brandenburg Gate, a copy of an Athenian monument. That Car of Victory perched on top of it has its story. When Berlin fell into the hands of Napoleon, that chariot went to Paris, and told of French conquests, but Blucher and Waterloo came, and the Car of Victory was restored to the Brandenburg Gate. The element of rapine has been eliminated from warlike successes to-day. It shows at least that in the brutality of war, the arts exert a certain influence. Prince Bismarck might have exacted his millions from France in the recent war, but he would not have liked to have touched a single picture or a statue in the Louvre. . . .

. . . General Grant's military reputation had preceded him, and of course some of us were expected to visit the grand *entrepôt* of arms in Berlin, which is the Arsenal. Whether the Berliner looks on this assemblage of arms with pride I cannot say. It may be regarded as rather a necessity. It was for the collection of arms here that the battle of Malplaquet made the first contribution. Here in this building are placed all the great military souvenirs of the country. Why be sentimental over such bits of iron, steel, or bronze? There are few of them which have not been won by deeds of heroism, but alas! at the cost of human suffering. In this Arsenal the more recent events of the struggle with France are seen, for the tattered banners taken at Wörth attest the Prussian triumph. Berlin, as has been stated before, constantly recalls its military condition, for there in its midst are numerous schools devoted to the higher instruction of the soldier. Here is a building not very imposing in appearance which is worthy of looking at, and describing somewhat in detail its purpose. It is what might be called the School of the Staff. It is the great central movement, which starting the *vis inertia,* propels at any given moment the hundreds of thousands of armed men which Prussia holds in leash. It is here that that intelligence, more powerful than human strength, guides the march of countless hordes. There is no great display here—save that the sentinels one always sees at all military posts in Prussia stride up and down. You would scarcely take the busy men inside, though they, too, wear uniforms, to be much else than military clerks. It is true that they are clerks, but the books they keep contain all the military debts and credits of the world. Let there be a change made in any army in Europe, let the caliber of a rifle be increased or diminished, a bayonet socket altered, any new improvement in a cannon made, and some Prussian officer knows all about it, reports it, and down it goes in a book kept in this office, to be looked at if necessary at some future time. Here every road, lane, cowpath in Europe is traced out on maps. Every house, hut, or cabin is described, and the capability of every city, town, or hamlet to feed troops. The wonderful knowledge Prussia had of France during the late war was entirely due to the labors of this office. Of course a bureau of this kind seems strange according to our American ideas, but that it is a necessity admits of no doubt. It is true that something of success in war arises from the inspiration of a general, but the Prussians have done their best, with Helmuth von Moltke at their head, to bring military art into the practical details of an exact science.* I think when speaking of Moltke, one of the greatest of generals, the Ex-President, whose curiosity is not easily excited, may have felt some disappointment in not meeting this Prussian officer, who unfortunately was not in Berlin at the period of our visit. Some of us, more inquisitive than the rest, went to the Moltke Strasse, named in honor of Prussia's foremost soldier, and looked at his apartments. Save in the rooms used for parade, Moltke's chamber is of the most Spartan-like simplicity. Moltke is a Dane, and adopted Prussia as his country in 1823. The great work commenced by Stein, and Scharnhorst after the battle of Jena, has been continued by Moltke. There are some traits about him which are worth recalling. He loves the country better than the city, and is never so happy as when in his private domain, attending to his farming in Silesia. His devotion to a much-beloved wife, who died in 1868, belongs to the more poetic side of his nature.

The Royal Palace is among the oldest buildings of celebrity in Berlin. Without being grandiose it is quite striking on account of its huge size. We notice the throne room with its regal chair of silver, and the neighboring chamber, called the room of the Black Eagle. Here are held every year the meetings of this order. In 1871, as victors—Berlin being far distant—it was at Versailles that this festival was held. There is a curious old story about a white figure which haunts this palace, and that whenever a sovereign of Prussia sees this weird person his days are numbered. . . .

. . . I for one fully believe that the military power of Prussia is irresistible, and that she is to-day mistress of Europe. If I, as a stranger, am forced to acknowledge this, the Prussians themselves are perfectly conscious of their strength. I do not think this has induced any feeling of arrogance among the more intelligent, but certain classes of the community are inclined to

---

* Helmuth von Moltke, the longtime head of the German General Staff, was Bismarck's brutally effective right-hand man.

assert it. It don't show itself in words, but rather in actions of which they are unconscious. Now we, thank goodness! as Americans are well received everywhere, and no parallelisms can be drawn between our country and Prussia, but toward Austrians, Russians, Hollanders, and Frenchmen there is little hesitation shown in making distinctions. Now Prussia is a living paradox. She tries to combine the highest intellectual culture with the greatest physical force. She pushes forward on the chess-board of Europe, side by side, her philosopher and her soldier. Which will win the game no one can say, but one will be sure to absorb the other. . . .

. . . Of course invitations of every kind are sent to the General, and it is well that he had found some repose in Holland. I understand a grand review is on the tapis which General Grant is to witness. I don't think he possibly can escape this time, much as he is disinclined to witness military pageants. If one has the least inclination this way, any town in Prussia affords the amplest opportunities. We have the satisfaction of meeting quite a number of Prussian officers who have served in the United States during the civil war, many of them having been in action under the eyes of General Grant. They all express the highest admiration for his military capacity and sound judgment, and are anxious to pay their respects to their old chief. We notice the direct affiliations Germany has with the United States, and when the character of our party is understood, we are asked an infinite number of questions by those who have friends and relatives in the States. We find that Prussians of all classes are very fairly acquainted with the geography of our country, and the many ludicrous mistakes which Frenchmen and Italians make are eluded. You never can manage to make a Frenchman of the middle class quite appreciate the distinction between North and South America. New York and Rio Janeiro to him are contiguous and adjacent towns. . . .

All distinguished diplomats seem to be gouty, and as Prince Gortschakoff was afflicted with this aristocratic disease, at the request of the Prussian Plenipotentiary, General Grant called on the prince.* It was Mr. Bayard Taylor who arranged the visit. Prince Gortschakoff was highly pleased with the compliment paid to his country. Of all the members of the great European Congress, now holding their session in Berlin, most of the foreign representatives, Lord Beaconsfield, Lord Salisbury, M. Wad-

---

* Alexandr M. Gorchakov, who had served as the very skillful foreign minister of Russia since 1856, had been named chancellor in 1867, an honorific title, and had been given the even more honorific title of prince in 1871.

dington, and Count Corti were known to the General. Mehemet Ali the General had met in Turkey. Visits of ceremony had to be paid to all these dignitaries. Among the very first of the great ones of this earth who left his card for the Ex-President was Prince Bismarck. Unfortunately General Grant was absent, and the visit on the part of Bismarck was repeated. As the General was most anxious to make the acquaintance of the great German, for whose character and services he had so high an admiration, the calls were returned at once, and a message was sent his highness, saying that the General would call at any time which would suit his convenience. Out of this came a meeting which most fortunately I have in my power to describe, a meeting of two distinguished men, which must be so interesting to both Germans and Americans, that I am glad to be able to describe it in its minutest details.

Four o'clock in the afternoon was named, and as General Grant's hotel was but a few minutes' walk from the Bismarck Palace, a few minutes before four the General walked through the Frederick Place. This Place is a small square, adorned with plants and flowers, and with superb trees growing in it, all laid out in memory of the Great Frederick. Statues of the leading Prussian generals decorate the walks. As most things in Germany tend to intensify the military spirit, and to keep up the remembrance of her heroes, the bronze statues record the names and deeds of Zeithen, Seidlitz, Winterfeldt, Keith, Schwerin, and the Prince of Dessau. Passing through the park, on your right stretches an edifice, or rather a whole range of buildings, forming three sides of a square. An iron railing separates it from the street. There are grim sentinels on guard before the entrances of the building. From the roof the flag of Germany floats languidly. It is a bright sunshiny afternoon, and quite warm. The birds are singing in the park. The buildings are not very imposing, rather low and straggling, but you notice that one particular range of windows is shaded with lace curtains. You observe that the promenaders, the loungers, as they come past these windows, pause for a moment, and gaze at them curiously. Now this building happens to be, at this present moment, one of the most interesting places in the political world, for in that particular room, whose windows are shaded with their lace veils, the Berlin Congress is holding its sitting, and as for the building itself, it is the home, the residence of that famous man, Prince Bismarck.

The General saunters in a kind of nonchalant way into the courtyard. The sentinels eye him for just an instant, perhaps curiously, and then quickly present arms. Somehow or other these grim soldiers recognize at once, as the salute is returned, that it comes from a man who is himself a soldier. His visit had been expected it was true, but it was supposed that an Ex-President of the United States would have come thundering in a coach and six accompanied by outriders, and not quietly on foot. The General throws away a half-smoked cigar, then brings up his hand to his hat, acknowledging the military courtesy, and advances in the most quiet way to the door. But ceremony on the part of the Germans cannot allow a modest, unassuming entrance, for before he has time to ring, two liveried servants throw wide open the door, and the Ex-President passes into a spacious marble hall. Of all the princes of the earth now living, even of the rulers themselves, this Prince of Bismarck-Schinhausen is the most renowned. It is the prince who comes through the opening portals and with both hands extended welcomes General Grant. You cannot help but note that time has borne with a heavy hand on Bismarck within the past few years. The mustache and hair which but a short time ago were iron gray are now almost white; there is even some weariness in the gait, a tired look about the face. But there is not a line on that face which does not belong to our association with Bismarck, for if ever true manhood, undaunted courage, and overpowering intellect were written on a man's features, they are all stamped on the massive head of the German chancellor. There is that lofty assertion of station which belongs only to men cast in this mold, those bold outlines which tell of great brains, which make and unmake empires, and with all that the frank, intrepid, penetrating eye with that firmly-knit mouth which shows the courage, the tenacity of the Saxon race. Prince Bismarck wears an officer's uniform, and as he takes the General's hand, he says, "Glad to welcome General Grant to Germany."

The General's reply is "that there is no incident in his German tour more interesting to him than this opportunity of meeting the prince." Prince Bismarck then expresses surprise at finding the General so young a man; but when a comparison of ages is made, Prince Bismarck finds that the Ex-President is only eleven years his junior.

"That," says the prince, "shows the value of a military life, for here you have the frame of a young man, while I feel like an old one."

The General smiled, observing that he was at that period of life when he could have no higher compliment paid him than that of being called a young man. By the time this pleasant chatting had been going on, the prince had offered the General a seat. All this took place in a library or study. There was an open window which looked out on the beautiful park on which the June sun was shining. This was the private park of the Radziwill Palace, which is now Bismarck's Berlin home. The library was a large, spacious room, the walls of gray marble, and the furniture plain and

Meeting with Bismarck

simple. In one corner stood a large, high writing-desk, where the chancellor works, and on the waxed floor a few Turkish rugs were thrown. The prince speaks English with precision, though slowly from want of practice, and when he wants a word seeks refuge in French. He shows, however, that he has a fair command of our vernacular.

One of the prince's first questions was about General Sheridan.

"The general and I," said the prince, "were fellow campaigners in France, and we became great friends."

General Grant said that he had had letters from Sheridan recently and he was quite well.

"Sheridan," said the prince, "seemed to be a man of great ability."

"Yes," answered the General, "I regard Sheridan as not only one of the great soldiers of our war, but one of the great soldiers of the world—as a man who is fit for the highest commands. No better general ever lived than Sheridan."

"I observed," said the prince, "that he had a wonderfully quick eye. On one occasion, I remember, the Emperor and his staff took up a position to observe a battle. The Emperor himself was never near enough to the front, was always impatient to be as near the fighting as possible. 'Well,' said Sheridan to me, as we rode along, 'we shall never stay here, the enemy will in a short time make this so untenable that we shall all be leaving in a hurry. Then while the men are advancing they will see us retreating.' Sure enough, in an hour or so the cannon shot began to plunge this way and that way, and we saw we must leave. It was difficult to move the Emperor, however; but we all had to go, and," said the prince, with a hearty laugh, "we went rapidly. Sheridan had seen it from the beginning. I wish I had so quick an eye." . . .

Prince Bismarck said the Emperor was especially sorry that he could not in person show General Grant a review, and that the Crown Prince would give him one. "But," said the prince, "the old gentleman is so much of a soldier and so fond of his army that nothing would give him more pleasure than to display it to so great a soldier as yourself."

The General said that he had accepted the Crown Prince's invitation to a review for next morning, but with a smile continued: "The truth is I am more of a farmer than a soldier. I take little or no interest in military affairs, and, although I entered the army thirty-five years ago and have been in two wars, in Mexico as a young lieutenant, and later, I never went into the army without regret and never retired without pleasure."

"You are so happily placed," replied the prince, "in America that you need fear no wars. What always seemed so sad to me about your last great war was that you were fighting your own people. That is always so terrible in wars, so very hard."

"But it had to be done," said the General.

"Yes," said the prince, "you had to save the Union just as we had to save Germany."

"Not only save the Union, but destroy slavery," answered the General.

"I suppose, however, the Union was the real sentiment, the dominant sentiment," said the prince.

"In the beginning, yes," said the General; "but as soon as slavery fired upon the flag it was felt, we all felt, even those who did not object to slaves, that slavery must be destroyed. We felt that it was a stain to the Union that men should be bought and sold like cattle."

"I had an old and good friend, an American, in John L. Motley,"* said

---

* John Lothrop Motley was one of the most celebrated American historians of this period, especially known for his three-volume paean to the expansion of human liberty, *The Rise of the Dutch Republic.*

the prince, "who used to write me now and then. Well, when your war broke out he wrote me. He said, 'I will make a prophecy, and please take this letter and put it in a tree or a box for ten years, then open it and see if I am not a prophet. I prophesy that when this war ends the Union will be established and we shall not lose a village or a hamlet.' This was Motley's prophecy," said the prince, with a smile, "and it was true."

"Yes," said the General, "it was true."

"I suppose if you had had a large army at the beginning of the war it would have ended in a much shorter time."

"We might have had no war at all," said the General; "but we cannot tell. Our war had many strange features—there were many things which seemed odd enough at the time, but which now seem Providential. If we had had a large regular army, as it was then constituted, it might have gone with the South. In fact, the Southern feeling in the army among high officers was so strong that when the war broke out the army dissolved. We had no army—then we had to organize one. A great commander like Sherman or Sheridan even then might have organized an army and put down the rebellion in six months or a year, or, at the farthest, two years. But that would have saved slavery, perhaps, and slavery meant the germs of new rebellion. There had to be an end of slavery. Then we were fighting an enemy with whom we could not make a peace. We had to destroy him. No convention, no treaty was possible—only destruction."

"It was a long war," said the prince, "and a great work well done—and I suppose it means a long peace."

"I believe so," said the General.

The prince asked the General when he might have the pleasure of seeing Mrs. Grant. The General answered that she would receive him at any convenient hour.

"Then," said the prince, "I will come tomorrow before the Congress meets."

Both gentlemen arose, and the General renewed the expression of his pleasure at having seen a man who was so well known and so highly esteemed in America.

"General," answered the prince, "the pleasure and the honor are mine. Germany and America have always been in such friendly relationship that nothing delights us more than to meet Americans, and especially an American who has done so much for his country, and whose name is so much honored in Germany as your own."

The prince and the General walked side by side to the door, and after shaking hands the General passed into the square. The guard presented arms, the General lit a fresh cigar, and slowly strolled home.

"I am glad I have seen Bismarck," the General remarked. "He is a man whose manner and bearing fully justify the opinions one forms of him. What he says about the Emperor was beautifully said, and should be known to all the Germans and those who esteem Germany."

Notable among incidents of the Berlin stay was a quiet informal reception given to the General by Mr. Bayard Taylor, our American Minister. Mr. Taylor was not aware of the General's coming until a day or two before his arrival, and had been quite ill. Then he had had no personal acquaintance with the General, and if his home political sympathies ran in one direction more than in another it was not in the direction of the General. But I know of no two men more likely under favorable circumstances to become well acquainted than Bayard Taylor and General Grant. I am sure I violate no confidence when I say that the General will leave Berlin with as high an opinion of Mr. Taylor and as great an esteem for his character as for that of any of the distinguished diplomatists who have entertained him in Europe. Mr. Taylor regretted that the state of mourning in which the attempt on Emperor Wilhelm I's life had thrown Berlin, and the presence of the Congress, prevented his entertaining the General in a more ostentatious manner.* But he made all the arrangements with the court, and gave the General an evening party, at which all the Americans in Berlin attended. I was surprised to find so many Americans in Berlin. The General spent a most pleasant evening with Mr. Taylor. The next day there was a small dinner party at the embassy, and, in addition, there was a great deal of going around and seeing Berlin in a quiet way, which form of foreign life the General enjoys beyond any other.

The Crown Prince sent word to General Grant asking him to name an hour when he would review some troops of all arms. The General answered that any hour most convenient for the troops would be pleasant to him. So it was arranged at half past seven in the morning. The General asked Mr. Coleman, of the legation, to be one of his company. It had rained all night a heavy, pitching, blowing rain, and when the morning came the prayers which Mr. Coleman had been offering up all night for

---

* During the summer of 1878, at the Congress of Berlin, the Germans played the more or less disinterested brokers, attempting to sort out the relations between the big European powers and the future of the Balkans. Bismarck achieved a rickety balance that lasted until 1914. Over dinner, when the Grants were in Berlin, Bismarck told Julia Grant, "To tell the truth, Russia has eaten too much Turkey, and we are helping her to digest it."

better weather were found to have been of no avail. The General himself had a severe cold and a chill, which had been hanging over him for two days, and when he arose he could scarcely speak. There was a suggestion that the review might be postponed. But the troops were under way, as we learned, and the General would not hear of the suggestion. He only hoped, he said, when the Crown Prince's officer came to attend him, that the display would be as brief as possible and not severe upon the men. The place selected was the Tempelhof, a large open field outside of Berlin. When General Grant drove on the ground in a court carriage he was met by the general commanding the Berlin troops and a large staff. A horse from the royal stables was in waiting, but the General was suffering so much that he would not mount. The rain kept on in its wild way, and the wind swept it in gusts across the open field, so much so that in a few moments, even with the protection of a carriage, we were all thoroughly drenched.

The maneuvers went on all the same. There was a sham fight with infantry, all the incidents of a real battle—moving on the flank, in skirmish line, firing and retreating, firing and advancing. Then came the order to fix bayonets and charge at double quick, the soldiers shouting and cheering as they advanced, with that ringing cheer which somehow no one hears but in Saxon lands, and which stirs the blood like a trumpet. The General was attended by Major Igel, an intelligent officer. The General complimented the movement of the troops highly, but said he questioned very much whether in modern war the saber or the bayonet were of use.

"What I mean," said the General, "is this: anything that adds to the burdens carried by the soldier is a weakness to the army. Every ounce he carries should tell in his efficiency. The bayonet is heavy, and if it were removed, or if its weight in food or ammunition were added in its place, the army would be stronger. As for the bayonet as a weapon, if soldiers come near enough to use it they can do as much good with the club-end of their muskets. The same is true as to sabers. I would take away the bayonet, and give the soldiers pistols in place of sabers. A saber is always an awkward thing to carry."

Major Igel did not think the experiences of the Prussian army would sustain the General's view. He knew of cases where effective work had been done with the bayonet, and that the Prussians were not likely to abandon it. The General said no doubt war showed instances when the bayonet was effective, but those instances were so few that he did not think they would pay for the heavy burden imposed upon an army by the carrying of the bayonet. In any army he commanded he would feel like taking away the bayonet, and telling the men to trust to the but-ends of their muskets. It is due to the major to say that he was not convinced by the General's reasoning, but the discussion may have a value as a bit of military criticism.

After the maneuvers and the sham fight there was a march past, the General reviewing the line with bared head, to which the pitiless rain showed no mercy.

"These are fine soldiers," he said, and thanked the commander for his courtesy.

Then came artillery practice, the guns firing and sweeping over the field in a whirling, mad pace. This was followed by an artillery march past, which the General reviewed on foot, the rain beating down all the time. Then came cavalry. This was the most interesting phase of the display, especially one movement where the battalion broke into disorder and rallied again.

"This," said the major, "we do to accustom our men to the contingency of disorder on the field and enable every man to know how to take care of himself." The movement was effective and beautiful, and showed, said the General, the highest state of discipline. It was followed by a charge and a march past, the General on foot reviewing, and the rain whirling in heavy gusts.

After this we all drove to a military hospital and inspected it. Then to the quarters of a cavalry regiment under the command of the Prince of Hohenzollern. The General was received by the officers, and went carefully through the quarters. He observed that spurs were more used in the Prussian than in the American cavalry service, which he said, "I think to be an advantage." After inspection there was a quiet mess-room lunch and a good deal of military talk, which showed that the General had not forgotten his trade.

The General, at the close of the lunch, asked permission to propose the prosperity of the regiment and the health of the colonel. It was a regiment of which any army would be proud, and he hoped a day of trial would never come; but if it did he was sure it would do its part to maintain the ancient success of the Prussian army. He also desired to express his thanks to the Crown Prince for the pains that had been taken to show him this sample of his magnificent army. The prince answered in German, which Major Igel translated, that he was much complimented by the General's toast, and that the annals of his regiment would always record the pride they felt in having had at their mess and as their guest so illustrious a leader. This closed the military services of the day, and we drove home. On our way home the skies relented and the sun began to shine. . . .

. . . The dinner was sumptuous, and admirable in every respect. About half past seven or later it was over, and the company adjourned to another *salon*.

In order to reach this apartment the company passed through the room devoted to the Congress. It seemed like coming into some awful presence to be in the very chamber where the ruling minds of Europe, the masters of legions, the men who govern the world, daily meet to determine the destiny of millions—to determine peace or war.

We came to an antechamber. The General and Bismarck sat on a small sofa near the window looking out upon the glorious swaying trees in the park. The ladies clustered into another group around the princess, who has one of the best and kindest faces I have ever seen. The remainder of the party broke into groups, wandering about the balcony to talk about the weather, the trees, the rain, the Congress, the Kaiser, and the other themes that seem to float about in every Berlin conversation.

The General was made comfortable with a cigar, but the prince would not smoke a cigar. His doctors, who had been bothering him about many things, had even interfered with his tobacco, and all they would allow him was a pipe. Just such a pipe as the American mind associates with a Hollander or German—a pipe with a black heavy bowl, a smoking machine about two feet long. This the prince nursed beneath his knees, with his head bent forward in the full tide of an animated conversation.

If I had any skill in drawing I should like to sketch the scene between Grant and Bismarck. The Chancellor—I came near saying the old Chancellor (I was thinking of his gray and wan face, and forgetting that he is a young man, as chancellors go)—the Chancellor had lying stretched before him one faithful friend, a black Danish dog of the hound species. This dog has made a place for himself in the affections of Berlin. He has full run of the palace, and took as much pains as the prince to make himself agreeable to his guests. He and the prince are inseparable companions, and there is a story that when Prince Gortschakoff came one day to see Bismarck the dog made an anti-Russian demonstration against the Russian's legs. All Berlin laughed over the story, which is too good to be denied.

But on this occasion the Danish hound was in the most gracious mood, and while the General and the prince were in conversation—the General tugging his cigar, which he is sure to allow to go out if the theme becomes an interesting one, and the prince patting his pipe as if he loved it—the dog lay at their feet in placid acquiescence, with one eye now and then wandering over the guests to see that order was respected. The scene between the soldier and the statesman was worthy of remembrance.

The General and the prince talked mainly upon the resources of the two countries; and this is a theme upon which the General never tires, and which, so far as America is concerned, he knows as well as any man in the world. The contrast between the two faces was a study; for I take it no two faces, of this generation at least, have been more widely drawn. In expression Bismarck has what might be called an intense face, a moving, restless eye, that might flame in an instant. His conversation is irregular, rapid, audacious, with gleams of humor, saying the oddest and frankest things, and enjoying anything that amuses him so much that frequently he will not, cannot finish the sentence for laughing. Grant, whose enjoyment of humor is keen, never passes beyond a smile. In conversation he talks his theme directly out with care, avoiding no detail, correcting himself if he slips in a detail, exceedingly accurate in statement, always talking well, because he never talks about what he does not know. In comparing the two faces, you note how much more youth there is in that of Grant than of Bismarck. Grant's face was tired enough a year ago, when he came here jaded with the anxieties arising from the Electoral Commission;* it had that weary look which you see in Bismarck's, but it has gone, and of the two men you would certainly deem Grant the junior by twenty years.

Mr. Taylor, the American Minister, was evidently impressed with the historical value of the meeting of Grant and Bismarck. He remembered a German custom that you can never cement a friendship without a glass of old-fashioned schnapps. There was a bottle of a famous schnapps cordial among other bottles. I am afraid to say how old it was. The Minister said, "General, no patriotic German will believe that there can ever be lasting friendship between Germany and the United States unless yourself and the prince pledge eternal amity between all Germans and Americans over a glass of this schnapps." The prince laughed and thanked the minister for the suggestion. The schnapps was poured out, the General and prince touched glasses, the vows were exchanged in hearty fashion, and the prince, rising, led Mrs. Grant through the hall. . . .

It is true our journey is now due north, but still as the General's capacity for traveling is insatiable we are to zigzag a little before reaching the

* To resolve the disputed election of 1876, Congress had established an Electoral Commission that had, in exchange for an end to Reconstruction, seated Republican Rutherford B. Hayes, who had received fewer popular votes than the Democrat, Samuel J. Tilden.

Scandinavian peninsula. Though Berlin sight-seeing and military reviews had fully occupied the General's attention and taxed him to the utmost, he really seems to feel no fatigue, but enters on this northern journey as fresh as at the outset of this already very much extended travel. Now Hamburg, though a commercial city, is one of pleasure, and thither we bend our way. We have often heard German-Americans say, "Yes, Paris and Vienna are all very good in their way—so is New York; but if you really wish to find a place where true enjoyment can be found we commend Hamburg to your notice." From Berlin to Hamburg the distance is a trifle over one hundred and seventy-five miles. The trip, like all railroad journeys in Germany, was made with great comfort, for in no other country are the railroads constructed with so much thoroughness and stability. The roadbed is most perfect, and the arrangement of the carriages and the general equipment are admirable. The speed too is quite as great as that of trains in America. Of course, the roads are worked under the supervision of the Government and, like many other things in Prussia, are to some extent under military rule. The paternal character of the government is perhaps seen a little bit too much at times in certain notices posted in all stations, and occasionally in the cars, where the traveler is instructed when a window may be opened and when it is to be closed; but still as the European public generally are not so nomadic or as well posted as are our own people, such rules and regulations are perhaps quite necessary. In Prussia, railroad management is carried out to the utmost perfection, and accidents or delays are exceedingly rare. Everything is provided for which may help the traveler on his way. There are signposts to guide him, and railway officials to direct his steps. Your American tourist at home is supposed to have an intuitive perception of what exact car he must get into, and is allowed to take care of himself. In Europe generally, and most especially in Germany, it is just the contrary. The traveler is thought to be an ignorant person, and is accordingly to be prompted where to go to and what to do. The country we pass through *en route* for Hamburg one cannot call beautiful, as it is rather sandy, though this arid aspect decreases as the river Elbe is neared. A short time after leaving Berlin we hear the town of Spandau called by the railroad conductor. Spandau recalls to us a military prison, and the stories of hairbreadth escapes. It is at Spandau in a grim old fortress that a goodly part of the French indemnity is held for safe keeping. If money be the sinew of war, very certainly Prussia has plenty of it provided for her by her enemy.

We reach Hamburg on July 2d, and are at once delighted with its appearance. It is the busiest place apparently we have yet met in Germany. Everything seems alive and stirring. Omnibuses, carriages, and great trucks loaded down with goods are rumbling in every direction. The thoroughfares are thronged with foot passengers. The streets seem to us to be both new and old. In the same row are houses built centuries ago, and alongside of them new constructions erected only yesterday. The irregularity of the streets is not unpleasant, for in many parts of the city land and water are combined. It is recorded in the annals of Hamburg that up to the middle of the last century this city was a villainously dirty town, and wretchedly built, but that it owes its present agreeable appearance to a series of fires which, having destroyed half the town, caused it to be rebuilt with the present improvements. Never was there a city which recalled more its maritime importance. Sailors and men of foreign birth in strange costumes are seen everywhere, and there are painted signs in all known languages. The port is full of ships bearing the colors of various nations. There is no end of water communication in Hamburg, and small steamers are constantly plying. The commercial greatness of this city need not be descanted upon. In the United States we all know that from Hamburg come the most intelligent of our foreign merchants, and that a clerk with a Hamburg training is supposed to be a graduate in the higher branches of trading. The Exchange, into which some of us venture, is a vast building where transactions to enormous amounts are being daily carried out. We are very much at home at Hamburg, and enjoy all its hospitalities. We find that the pleasures of the city have not been in the least exaggerated. Invitations to dinners, to suppers, to evening receptions are sent to the Ex-President. In fact, the people of Hamburg, as well as the American residents, did all that the kindest hospitality could dictate to make the General's stay in their city pleasant and agreeable. We find, in contrasting Hamburg with the other principal cities of Germany which we have so far visited, that there is a trifle less of that military feeling and martinet proclivity which casts the least bit of a shadow over one's personal ease, and makes an American feel uncomfortable. The self-importance of Germany is not so persistently brought into prominence in Hamburg. This is no doubt due to commercial causes. Hamburg sends her ships to every port of importance on the globe; they return freighted with the riches of the world, and her citizens, from so much communication with other nations, very naturally imbibe cosmopolitan ideas. Ideas ever expand as commerce rules, and the great city of the Hanseatic League, though her liberties be somewhat shorn, asserts her individuality. She has her true aristocracy of

Hamburg

merchant princes, who spend their money nobly, and who have endowed their handsome city with lasting monuments in the way of libraries, schools, public gardens, and charitable institutions. Hamburg is one of the great commercial feeders of Germany, and as a distributing point is of vast importance. Of course the relationships of friendship and commerce between Hamburg and New York and many other ports in the United States are very close. If we had been somewhat deprived of newspapers, and the possibility of finding out all the news about home while in Berlin, here at Hamburg all the familiar journals of the leading American cities were presented to us for our perusal. . . .

[From Hamburg, the Grant party went on to Denmark and then Sweden and Swedish Norway, which would become an independent nation in 1905.]

. . . In appearance the portion of Denmark we traveled over was Dutch in its character, but if anything more bleak and less under that perfection of culture which makes Holland so remarkable. Denmark has not fared well in the late political combinations of Europe and still feels keenly her more recent loss, that of her southern provinces. There is a pride of race in the Dane which no one can say is not a proper one, for he can look back to a long and glorious history. More than once she was the conqueror of

England, and all Europe wherever a ship could sail has felt her power. Denmark, standing as she did at the entrance of the Baltic, exacted for many years feudal rights over the expanse of waters. I trust my country has been forgiven long ago because we refused to pay Sound dues and asserted the freedom of the seas. Copenhagen is a most picturesque place, with noble squares and stately houses. It seems strange that in this far-off city of the North, the artistic tendency should be so conspicuous, but it is manifest everywhere. Something else that strike us is the politeness of the people, the grace of their manner, and their fine personal appearance. Physiologically it is a leading race, and being a handsome one, has stamped its peculiar type on many people. You see the clear gray eye, the flaxen locks, and the finest of profiles. Situated partly on the coast of Zealand, Copenhagen also occupies the island of Amager. All these northern towns have something of a Venetian appearance, for water is used in every way possible as a method of locomotion. The ships are moored in canals which are alongside of the busiest of the streets. We are particularly struck by the many brilliant costumes of the country people who throng the streets. . . .

[In Sweden,] the weather is simply delightful now, pleasantly warm midday, with cool nights and mornings, and the heavens all blue without a cloud. We are getting farther and farther north, and though it is July and days are shortening, still we enjoy the long, clear evenings. The day is spent most enjoyably at Gottenburg, and we go the next morning to Christiania. I think the General is touched when he notices that in his especial honor every village we pass near has been decorated by the peasant folk. It is on the 13th of July that we arrive at Christiania, the capital of Norway. If the reception in Sweden was flattering to the General, that in Norway I can hardly describe. It is the most spontaneous of welcomes. There were fully ten thousand people who thronged the quays to see the General. King Oscar himself had left Stockholm, and has made a rapid journey to his capital of Norway, to take the General by the hand and to offer him all courtesy. At home we have seen General Grant as general and President only. These are stations in life where feelings and emotions must be concealed or at least kept under control. I watch the General as he receives the applause of the Norsemen who give him cheer after cheer as he puts his foot on their hospitable shores. First the General seems puzzled, then the least bit of timidity is visible; there is, too, a trace of wonderment apparent; but then he fairly unbends, and does show some emotion in his face. I even think he looks happy when he feels sure that all this honor which is paid him is spontaneous and comes from the heart of these northern folks. . . .

The Norwegian Mountains

Of course Norway is by no means the *terra incognita* of forty years ago. Besides the magnificence of its scenery, it affords great attraction to the sportsman. In our short excursion into the country we met numerous parties of English gentlemen intent on salmon fishing. In fact, numerous invitations were extended to the General that he should try his hand with rod and fly in some brawling Norwegian stream. But fishing is hardly among the General's accomplishments. We are told by an Englishman that although the sport is pleasant enough, the great drawback are the mosquitoes, which are on a par, as to quantity and aggressiveness, with the insect found in the United States. We spent a few days most pleasantly in our excursion, having seen country life in Norway under peculiar advantages. On our return to Christiania, regal courtesies were offered by his majesty the King, and were accepted by the General. Our stay in the capital of Norway was now drawing to a close. It is on our programme that we are to reach Stockholm on the 24th of July. We bid a good-by to our many Norwegian friends, and the same hearty feeling which was extended to the General on his arrival at Christiania is repeated, only it is to wish him a good-by. We take rail from Christiania by Kingsringer to Stockholm. The country we pass through does not present much beauty. The soil seemed poor, and the crops light, but even such scanty harvest as the ground gives is eagerly sought after. Occasionally we pass near a beautiful lake, all bordered by dark pines, and we have glimpses of mountain ranges behind. What does strike us, as practical Americans, is that every here and there we pass by large factories with tall chimneys, or see in the distance the smoke rising up from the iron works, and we know that we are in Sweden, where the manufacturing interests are of the most promising character. The railroad is an admirable one, and the carriages perfectly luxurious. Advantage has been taken of a valley which runs parallel with the Vrangs Elv, a good-sized Swedish river, to make a portion of the route between Norway and Sweden. If the railroad be slow as to time, we have a better opportunity of judging of the character of the country. We therefore do not complain, but rather enjoy the long stoppages at by-stations. As usual, it is quite well known that General Grant is on the train. Accordingly all the towns and villages we pass through are made resplendent with triumphal arches and flags. The depots are thronged with peasants, who cry welcome, and cheer the General. It is fortunate perhaps that the Ex-President is not polyglot, or his well-known speech-making inclinations would have been taxed to the utmost. Occasionally as these complimentary words are addressed to him, in a language which he cannot understand, I think I perceive a slight smile illumine his generally immovable features. I am led to believe he is congratulating himself that a bow or so on his part answers all purposes. We find, however, that both in Norway and Sweden many languages are spoken. It is hard to find an educated Norwegian or Swede who does not speak English, French, or German. There are certain words identical in Norse and English, and sometimes we who only speak our mother tongue find we can manage a little Norse. We travel on into the long twilight, which is so beautiful in this northern land, and as we near Stockholm, the country changes, and is more broken. It is a lake country evidently, for we pass near broad expanses of beautiful water. That superb grandeur, that weird majesty of nature which is so imposing in Norway, no longer strikes us. The journey is rather a long one, and we are glad when we find ourselves within the good city of Stockholm.

The impression Stockholm made on us was different from that of any other city of the North we had yet visited. In the construction of its houses it has a style of its own which is decidedly original, although it resembles the French. There is a grand palace too, which is certainly the equal of any we have seen in either France or Germany. The city, under the warming influence of a July sun, seemed to combine the art inspiration of both the North and the South. It is evidently a gay city, for I see the streets crowded with well-dressed people. There is a certain quaintness about the country people which is very attractive. I am informed that Stockholm is the "Venice of the North." I have had the same thing told me of other Scandinavian cities, which claim a similar appellation. I discard it entirely. It is true there is land and water mixed, but it is not Venice. Venice brings with it a feeling of languor. It recalls a period of decay, which not one of these towns of the North ever reminds one of. Venice would not be Venice if there was the least bustle about it. Stockholm teems with life. People seem to be in a hurry—not in that impetuous American hurry of course—that would be impossible—but still there is at least a briskness which is pleasant to see. I understand though that if Stockholm has charms for the traveler in summer, it is in winter that the capital of Sweden is at its best. I should like to see it then, when sledges drawn by prancing horses flash past in the streets, when all the places of amusement are in full blast. We are all, however, pleased with Stockholm in its summer guise. . . .

. . . All around Stockholm there are beautiful drives and glorious views. Among the most pleasant places to visit was the Deer Park, abounding with houses of entertainment, cafés, and theaters. As it was full summer, everybody was enjoying the beauties of the spot. All these northern cities are so wonderfully situated that I cannot help extolling them. It was ever delightful for us to look on the broad expanse of land and sea, and to see the villas which dotted the well-wooded islands. In my rapid description of this great city of the North, I must not overlook the hospitalities of which the General was the recipient. As in every place where he has been so far, tokens of respect and honor are lavished on him. Of course America is perfectly well known to the Swede, for there were Swedish colonies in America coeval with those of Holland; still of late years the bonds of friendship between the two countries have been much more closely drawn, as some of our best emigrants come from these rock-bound shores. Some of us have pleasant reminiscences brought to our mind of home, as we are asked if we know such and such a Swedish merchant who is doing business in New York, Chicago, or San Francisco. General Grant has invitations sent him to visit the Palace of Drottningholm, which is the most superb of the gala residences of the Swedish crown. The King of Sweden has, with the greatest kindness, given instructions that all the palaces should be opened for the inspection of the General. I think the Ex-President, though he has seen innumerable palaces, would rather go from the garret of a regal residence to the cellar than see a review. Somehow I fancy the king half suspects this, and military pageants, save of a very mild character, do not interfere with the General's pleasures.

I have incidentally here and there touched on the artistic inclinations of these northern people. Its development, as we well know in America, is not limited to pictures or statues. It is their musical talents which are of so high an order. This Norwegian and Swedish music has a charm of its own. Everybody seems to possess a musical taste, and an appreciation of this delightful art. Even the peasant folk take to music, and while away their time with singing and playing on various instruments. In all the great towns there is always music in the air. In private families the exercise of this art is not considered as much of an accomplishment as a necessity. We know in the United States how we have appreciated those artists which Norway and Sweden have given us. When one speculates on the gifts the Almighty has implanted in man, it may be understood how in the warmer South, where nature does so much for the human race, music might have been readily acquired; but here in the cold North, where existence is a struggle with frost and cold, it is a grand blessing that this love of music is implanted in these Norwegian and Swedish men and women, and has done so much to refine them. We are to leave this beautiful city of Stockholm on the morrow. As time is pressing, the General's orders are positive, and we obey with military alacrity. We are to take passage along the Baltic, and are to be at St. Petersburg within a few days. Now that the peace of Europe seems assured for a while, the Ex-President can with perfect propriety pay his respects to the Emperor of Russia. We are to take the steamer from Stockholm, and will soon be enjoying the hospitalities of the Paris of the North.

CHAPTER EIGHT

Russia and Austria

After stolid and sensible Scandinavia, Russia came as a colorful, quasi-Oriental alternative. The immense distances, the vast reaches of empty land, the glaring social gap between the ruling classes and the serfs, the strange juxtapositions of East and West, all fascinated Young and Grant. They were more comfortable with the Russian elites they met than they had been with the Prussians, although the United States was far more distant from Russian than from German society.

Leaving Moscow, the Grant party took the train through Poland to charming Vienna. Despite the fact that the Austrians were highly militarized, the Grant party preferred them over the Prussians, in part because the Austrians were underdogs who had lost recent wars to the Prussians, defeats that had stripped them of their former Italian territories. Young and Grant appreciated the relative toleration of the Austrian Empire, noting the devolution of power to the Hungarian portions of the empire and the greater sympathy for the Jews than they had found elsewhere, although philo-Semitism was fast disappearing, something Young and Grant did not observe. In August and September 1878, the Grants rested at Austrian spas and mountain towns, while Young traveled on his own through Switzerland and France, where he took particular delight in the wine regions around Bordeaux. At the end of the summer, the voyagers met up once more in Paris before setting out together for an autumn in Iberia.

Across the Baltic, from Stockholm to St. Petersburg, is quite a voyage, some four hundred miles or more by sea. Just now, at the close of July, the trip has proved a moderately pleasant one, but in the spring and fall there are no heavier gales than those which blow through these inland seas. Away up in the frozen north, in the Gulf of Bothnia, old Boreas holds his wind bags, and launches the cold gusts down to the Baltic Sea. . . .

. . . It is the 30th of July, and as time is passing, we are anxious to reach St. Petersburg before night. Fortunately the reception at Cronstadt was not prolonged. After a brief address of welcome we embarked on a steamboat and entered an arm of the sea, into which the Neva pours her rapid stream. The trip is not a long one. Soon the great city of Russia, with its many lofty spires, stands out against the blue sky.

Immediately on arrival we were met by the Hon. E. M. Stoughton, our Minister at St. Petersburg, who warmly welcomed the distinguished traveler. Scarcely had the General received Mr. Stoughton, when the Emperor's aide-de-camp, Prince Gortschakoff, and other high officers of the Imperial Court, called on him with kind messages from the Emperor. A grand audience was arranged to take place next day, July 31st, when his Imperial Highness Alexander II and General Grant met.

Nothing could exceed the cordiality of the reception. Prince Gortschakoff, one of the great figures which rule the destinies of men (the friend of Bismarck or his rival; which, no man can say), was also introduced by the Emperor. The Emperor seemed amazed at the long tour the General intended making. A portion of the conversation was occupied by the Emperor in gaining information regarding our Indians. The subject seemed to interest him greatly, and questions were asked, not only in regard to their treatment in the past, but as to their future. Our recent wars with them seemed to be well known by the Emperor, and the General had to go into very particular details as to the plans of campaigns, and the peculiar methods of Indian warfare. As the Russian Empire is such a vast and extensive country, in which innumerable races and religions are represented, these questions and answers were doubtless of great interest to the Emperor and the Russian chancellor.

At the close of the interview, the Emperor accompanied the General to the door, saying, "Since the foundation of your Government, relations between Russia and America have been of the friendliest character, and as long as I live nothing shall be spared to continue this friendship." The General's reply was, "That although the two Governments were very opposite in their character, the great majority of the American people were in sympathy with Russia, which good feeling he hoped would long continue." The Grand Duke Alexis made it a point to meet the Ex-President while in St. Petersburg, and recalled with much pleasure his visit to

America. The Grand Duke made very many inquiries in regard to General Custer, and told of the deep solicitude he had felt on hearing of his death.

The General's call on Prince Gortschakoff was an exceedingly pleasant and social one. Several hours were spent in chatting and smoking. European matters were discussed, and the General gave the chancellor some insight into American politics. Nothing strikes the American more forcibly than the mature age of European statesmen. It is too often the case in the United States that when a man has passed his fiftieth or sixtieth year he becomes worn out. Here is Prince Gortschakoff, born in 1798, now more than eighty years old, who, though he is physically frail, has still as strong a brain as he possessed in his younger days. No amount of mental work seems to distress him. Like Thiers and Guizot, who, when still old men, were possessed with unfailing powers, the successor of Nesselrode works unceasingly at his post. The interview was remarkably social in character, and was greatly enjoyed by the General, who expressed himself strongly regarding the ability and courtesy of the Russian chancellor. Fortunately there was no review, but in lieu of troops there was a special exhibition of the St. Petersburg fire brigade, which proved to be a very interesting affair.

An imperial yacht was placed at our disposal, in which a visit was made to Peterhof—the Versailles of St. Petersburg. Peterhof is about fifteen miles from the city, and is remarkable for its splendor, and, as it commands a view of Cronstadt, the Gulf of Finland, and the capital, has no rival as to position in Europe. A most notable visit made by the General was to the Russian man-of-war "Peter the Great." A magnificent band performed American airs, and a salute of twenty-one guns was fired. The imperial yacht then proceeded on to Cronstadt, threading her way among the many noble vessels of the Russian fleet, all the ships running up the well-beloved stars and stripes, the nimble sailors manning the yards and making the air resound with their cheers. Among the officers were many gentlemen, who in their voyages had paid visits to New York and other ports of the Union. These officers seemed desirous of returning the many courtesies they had received in the United States. I have but briefly summarized all these notable events. Their more careful recapitulation would fill many chapters. As is well known, the pomp and dignity of the Emperor of Russia, the *éclat* which fills all court matters, the splendor of the imperial equipages, the grand, regal way in which everything is done, have no equal in Europe. . . .

. . . The Winter Palace is the great attraction towering up on the bank of the Neva. Its proportions are immense, and it is profuse in architectural design. The principal entrance, which is of marble, leads to continuous suites of rooms. Here is the Golden Room used for imperial receptions, the White Saloon, and St. George's Hall. Nothing can be more gorgeous than the interior fittings. It is all that luxury and splendor can imagine. From every frontage a noble view can be had. Looking toward the south is the Imperial Square, whence rises the column dedicated to the memory of Alexander. It is of a single block of stone, and came from the Gulf of Finland. This palace, as its name designates, is used by the Emperor in winter, and with the rigors of the climate it must be exceedingly difficult to make these vast rooms warm and comfortable. It is by a covered way that the Hermitage is reached. It was here that Catherine sought rest after the fatigues of her court. It was at the Hermitage that she founded a very peculiar republic devoted to art and letters. It contains one of the choicest and most superb collections of pictures in the world. It is not only for the works of famed masters that the Hermitage is famous, but there is room after room sparkling with precious stones, where there are cornices of porphyry, figures made of lapis-lazuli and malachite in such profusion that it is dazzling. Possibly because in the United States we are not born to see palaces, one very soon tires of such magnificence. Nothing can be more fatiguing than the long march through the endless galleries of a palace. The mind like the body can only be taxed to a certain point, and after that, sight-seeing, even if it be a picture painted by a Raphael, becomes a wearisome task. The appearance of the soldiers dressed in varied uniforms gives a brilliant character to the streets. Evidently all the armed men Russia has at her command are not on the frontiers. Here are Cossacks, and some Georgian costumes which are very picturesque. But aside from the military display, here are all the Northern races, Finns and Esthonians, and those stunted men must live away up in far Northeastern Russia. There is a mass of promenaders, and an appearance of elegance and fashionable display which is even more pronounced than in Paris. . . .

The railroad which unites St. Petersburg and Moscow was built by Winans and Harrison, two enterprising American engineers, who gained fame and wealth in Russia. How true that story is which explains the peculiar straight line the road makes, we are unable to vouch for. It is gravely stated that when the engineers had devised their line, with its gradients, it had certain inclinations to the right and left, so that the iron road should tap some of the adjacent towns between the new and the old capitals. When the map was shown to Nicholas, he simply shook his head. "He would have no such twisting road in his dominions." Taking a ruler, he placed it between Moscow and St. Petersburg, drew with a pen a red line as straight as could be between the two points, remarking, "Make your road so as to follow precisely this tracing. A straight line is the shortest distance between two points, and that is all there is about it. Good day, gentlemen." Such towns of importance as Russia might have had, when the road was projected, were not near the line.

There were many disputants in the guise of noble owners of the soil, all wanting the road to pass near their domains. And if it had not been for the promptness of Nicholas, the business might have hung fire for years. As it is, this railroad is, in some respects, like the roads prospected in the United States some twenty years ago. It does connect two large cities, but there is nothing between them which helps traffic. Russia is not much given to take advantage of an opportunity. In other countries, towns would have sprung up mushroom-like near the iron rail. This road might have been as some huge ribbon on which pearls could have been strung. But either from the rigor of the climate, want of energy, or from absence of the speculative tendency, towns containing even a small number of inhabitants have no existence along this railroad.

The road is admirable in construction, and the carriages are of the best American make and style. Of course, railway officials were most polite, an elegant carriage having been placed at the disposal of the General. Leaving St. Petersburg, the railroad runs through a flat country, and soon on both sides of the track you notice forests of birch. The trees, with their silvery bark, stand out in relief against darker woods beyond. Occasionally you pass near some obscure village, or small assemblage of houses, with its humble church of stone, surmounted by a belfry. For ever and ever do the broad, flat plains spread out monotonously in the distance. The same birch trees, with here and there a fir, are seen as you glide along at the goodly speed of thirty miles an hour, for between St. Petersburg and Moscow the distance is something over four hundred miles, and the General was to accomplish the journey, counting all stoppages, in twenty hours. One is struck by the elegance of the stations, and the excellence of the food. On the arrival of the train the tables are laid with those usual excitants which stimulate the Russian appetite. There are plenty of bottles, too, filled with good French wines, and some with the very excellent products of the grape grown in Southern Russia. It is a positive necessity, owing to the rigors of the Russian climate, that the traveler should be supplied with good food. What a delight it must be for the weary voyager, whose eyes have been tired with seeing nothing but a broad expanse of snow, to enter

one of these stations, and find pleasant warmth and good food. With all
our rattle and bustle, there are many points which we might borrow from
the French, German, and most especially Russian methods of caring for
the traveling public. It is quite exceptional to see men working in the
fields; now and then a group of women may be seen using a short sickle,
working manfully at the poor, sickly crop. They sing a low chant as they
work, which has a peculiarly sad melodic phrase in it. These women look
very squalid and wretched, and are miserably clothed. The dearth of population strikes one most forcibly, as the country is as sparsely settled as one
of the Far-Western Territories of the United States. These poor people, you
will remember, a few years ago were all serfs. In point of education, in their
now more difficult position of life, which requires human beings to take
care of themselves, they have as yet little if any experience. Their tutelage
lasted so many years, that they can hardly yet appreciate the blessings of
freedom; right after emancipation too much must not be expected of
these poor peasant-folk. The climate and the habits of the people too are
opposed to a natural, healthy increase of inhabitants. Distances are immense. It is a struggle for life with many of these people. Some little responsibility, a very vague one it is true, was felt by the master before the
people were made free. Now it is a matter of perfect indifference to him
how those who were once his serfs get along. It is a bad state of affairs, and
where it will lead to no one can say. . . .

. . . As you near Moscow, the road runs through a more picturesque and
thickly settled country. Gliding along through handsome gardens and
pleasure grounds, ornate cottages, sheets of water, and broad, intersecting
streets, you come at last to a halt. This is Moscow, the old capital of Russia, and one of the most famous cities of the world. There is a large attendance at the station. Hats are lifted, and loud cheers are heard. Here are
Russian officers, brilliant with orders, who press forward, and pay their respects to the Ex-President. And there is quite an assemblage of Americans,
all eager to welcome the distinguished traveler. . . .

. . . Moscow recalls to every one the story of the great epic of the beginning of this century, the arresting of the march of the ambitious conqueror, Napoleon, the conflagration of the city, and the terrible retreat
of the French. Over there are the Sparrow Hills, from where the leading
files of the French army first saw Moscow, the Moscow which was to bring
on them ruin and disaster. Of course the remembrance of the heroic action of the Russian commanders has not been forgotten by the people of
Moscow, and, in speaking of the wonders of their city, it is often remarked,

The Kremlin

"that though Moscow now be great, it never can be so magnificent as it was before it was burnt." Moscow is placed in the midst of an undulating country where low hills abound, and the Moskwa River traverses it. The city itself is in some respects like what we call in the United States a garden city. In the center is the Kremlin, surrounded by a wall, and no new edifice is ever allowed to be built within its sacred precincts. On the right of this there is a quaint block of houses, inclosed and separated, called the Kitai Gorod, or Chinese City; beyond this are broad spaces tastefully laid out with shade trees and walks. The houses are cottage-like, and surrounded by beautiful gardens. These are placed somewhat in juxtaposition, the handsome cottage of the rich Moscow citizen or noble alongside of the dwelling of one of lesser social position. The main streets are spacious, increasing in width as they reach the boulevards; but then there is a multitude of smaller cross streets, which afford most charming views of private residences. You can leave a broad thoroughfare which is thronged with fine ladies and gentlemen all dashing along in their splendid equipages, and in a minute you find yourself in the country. There are, in fact, many of these charming villas within this great city, which has a circuit of over twenty miles. Most of these cottages are of wood, built in quaint style, in which comfort seems to have been more sought for than style. There is nearly always a fine gateway which opens on a green. Flowers abound which are of the most vivid colors. Russians, at least those of Moscow, seem to revel in bright colors, and their houses, when of stucco, allow for the full development of this taste. The quarter of the nobility, not far from the Kremlin, partakes of this elegant country air, for these habitations are more like villas than town residences. Very few of the houses are more than one story high. This want of elevation, if not partaking of the grandiose, imparts rather a quaint and cozy appearance. The Kremlin is situated on a hill, and is surrounded by a wall which varies in height from forty to eighty feet, according to the rise or fall of the ground. This wall is of brick, has battlements on it, is about a mile and a quarter in circumference, and a number of towers stand above the four gateways. As you enter the Nicholsky Gate, which is in the Gothic style, you notice in the arch a famous picture of St. Nicholas of Mojaisk. This wonderful picture, so it is said, is endowed with miraculous powers. When Napoleon (the legend tells) left Moscow in disgust, he determined to wreak his vengeance on poor St. Nicholas. Accordingly he had a barrel of gunpowder exploded under this particular picture. Marvelous to relate, though the powder went off, neither arch nor picture was hurt. For this reason, no Russian, prince or peasant, passes this gate or approaches the picture without paying respect to St. Nicholas. After passing the gateway, there is a broad space, and on your right is the Arsenal, and to your left the Government offices. In the Arsenal are stored an innumerable quantity of cannon, mostly trophies taken from the French in their retreat. Walking on, you reach the esplanade, which commands a view of the whole city. Now you see ranged in line an assemblage of the most remarkable buildings that the eye ever witnessed. It takes some minutes to appreciate them in all their grandeur. Look at that tapering tower which surmounts yonder gorgeous gateway. No one can pass there, not even the Czar, unless his head be bared. That church is sacred to the remains of the daughters, wives, and mothers of the imperial family. That low building is one of the many churches. Now come, as you scan the grand, imposing frontage, the famous towers of Ivan Veliki, whence resound the famous bells. Up springs the great cathedral, with an endless surmounting of golden domes and cupolas. Here are castellated walls, towers of all makes and shapes, and a mass of buildings unrivaled for beauty. Adjectives defining the various stages of human admiration are useless when used to describe the Kremlin. The Kremlin is, indeed, one of the lasting impressions a traveler receives. . . .

... The religious feeling in Russia seems to be of the most constant and all-pervading kind. That Oriental character of belief, which was before indicated when we described the Turk or Arab as prone to follow his devotional feelings, indifferent as to place or surroundings, seems to find its parallel among the devotees of the Greek Church. The respect paid to the pictures of their saints is universal. Now in Moscow, in the Kitai Quarter, affixed to the wall, is a rather poor illuminated semblance of the Virgin. The frame is a much better piece of art than the picture. No one passes that picture that does not uncover before it, and the greater number kneel and cross themselves. It is not only the foot passengers who thus show their devotion, but even the higher classes who ride in carriages.

The Twerskaia is the great street of Moscow, and is the entrance of the city from the St. Petersburg carriage-road or *chaussée*. Along its great length are the best buildings, the palaces of the nobility, and the finest shops. At the farthest end of the Twerskaia is the St. Petersburg Gate, and beyond that a large open space, where roads branch in every direction. Here are the finest drives to be had in Moscow, in fact it is the promenade of the city. Beyond is a plain on which soldiers encamp. Though the soldier is seen and felt everywhere in Russia, though a prominent place is given to those wielding the sword, you do not feel his presence quite as marked as in Prussia. Perhaps, owing to the late Turkish war, the bulk of the Russian army is still on the frontier.

Following the promenade, you come to the Petrossky Palace, a huge brick edifice, of mixed architecture. In one of the rooms of this palace Napoleon awaited in vain for the notables of the conquered city to humble themselves before him. Would they come and sue for pardon? Would they bow to the conqueror? While he waited, Moscow was in a blaze, and to escape the scorching in the city, the French soldiers went out to be frozen amid the snows of a Russian winter. Around the Petrossky Palace spreads the Petrossky Park. It is here that the middle classes of the old capital come to take their pleasure. Under these trees, in the pleasant summer time, the samovar is always boiling, and endless cups of steaming tea are taken. It is pleasant to watch the groups of people enjoying themselves in a sensible way, and to see the splendid equipages dashing past on the high road. ...

It was the 18th of August when we reached Vienna, late in the evening. At the station we were met by the United States Minister, Mr. Kasson, and by all the secretaries and attachés of the American Legation. A large number of our fellow citizens were there also, and as the General left the cars, he was loudly cheered. On the 19th, General Grant went to the American Legation, as it was there Count Andrassy, the First Minister of the Council, was to receive him. It is quite well understood that, by diplomatic license, the legation of any Government is supposed to represent the soil of that country. Count Andrassy was attended by many of the leading statesmen. An acquaintance with the Count was soon made, and an hour or more passed in agreeable conversation. In the evening General Grant dined at the Countess Andrassy's, and Mrs. Grant was the guest of Mrs. Post. On the 20th there was an audience with his Imperial Highness Francis Joseph. This reception took place at the Palace of Schoenbrunn. On the 21st the General and Mrs. Grant were guests of the imperial family, and dined with them in the evening. Prior to the dinner Baron Steinburg accompanied the General to the Arsenal, where the fullest explanations were made of all the new Austrian improvements in artillery. A grand diplomatic dinner was given on the 22d, by the American Minister. At this banquet the guests included all the ambassadors of the foreign powers. In the evening a reception and ball took place, when the representatives of the Austro-Hungarian Cabinet were present, and the rooms were thronged by the most distinguished people in Vienna.

When we were journeying north, we were told that Hamburg was the most pleasant of cities, but as we were tending southerly, we heard on all sides "that Vienna was, indeed, the true Paris of Southern Europe." Certainly no place has the same traits as Paris, but in that open-air life, which does not exist save in the country, it quite surpasses the French capital. It is a most aristocratic city. You may, if you will, by working hard enough and having plenty of money at your disposal, get into the best society in Paris, the Faubourg St. Germain if you please; but it is quite a different thing in Vienna. The higher circles of the nobility are unapproachable. The old prestige of the Austrian noble still exercises its peculiar privileges, and recalls the exclusive times of Maria Louisa, and of Kaunitz. There are habits and customs which hedge around the Austrian higher classes, whose boast is to have genealogies dating from antediluvian times. Commercial aristocracy of course is to be found in Vienna, men of the present day, who have brought their brains to their aid; but still, as you will very soon discover, between such men enriched by trade, and the old *régime,* there is hardly any intercourse. Vienna is undergoing changes which have been very rapid, and which are partly due to the late International Exhibition. Forty years ago, when Austria had Metternich for its guiding spirit, to have made Vienna the center of an exhibition would have been, in that antiquated statesman's eyes, the same thing as if some one had offered to introduce the plague, or invite a club of republicans to hold their sittings in the city.

As you enter Vienna from the station and cross the Ring-Strasse, or circular boulevard, you find a new city as fresh as an American town. Here are magnificent streets, crowded with superb shops, finer, indeed, than we have seen anywhere, Paris not excepted. Some controlling thought has apparently guided the architects, for the appearance of these new quarters is both harmonious and pleasing. All these immense ranges of buildings are due to joint-stock associations, who went mad just before the Exhibition, and the collapse of these enterprises brought ruin on many. Still, as we do not see the trouble which has ensued from these speculations, we only look at and admire the results. We are comfortably ensconced in a hotel which is quite sumptuous, and we regale ourselves with the delights of the Austrian *cuisine*. We are even inclined to think that there are no better cooks than those found in Vienna.

Our first visit was to the imperial summer residence, the Schönbrunn Palace, which is situated on the outskirts of the city, surrounded by elegant gardens and green woods. We wandered through the many handsome apartments of this "Palace of the Beautiful Fountain," recalling the remembrance of the Duc de Reichstadt, who, as a child, may have lived in some of these great rooms, and pondered there over the fall of his father. As we leave the palace we stroll through the gardens, and can only compare them with those of Versailles.

This morning we visited the Stephanplatz, where stands the famous Church of St. Stephans, and the Archbishop's Palace, and strolled across the Danube and into the Prater, the grand park of Vienna. This beautiful park has a superb avenue lined with trees, called the Prater Allee. It is about two and a half miles long, and is the great drive for the upper classes. At one side of this carriage-road are the coffee houses, restaurants, music halls, etc. This part of the Prater is chiefly frequented by the poorer people.

The military element is visible everywhere, and soldiers dressed in light-colored uniforms may be seen in every neighborhood. Nothing can be more jaunty than an Austrian lieutenant or captain. Possibly, not excluding your swell English guardsman, the Austrian officer is the greatest military dandy in the world. Notwithstanding their rather exquisite appearance, we found them to be most courteous and obliging, and very thoroughly informed. Unfortunately for Austria she has had full need of her soldiers for the last thirty years. As far as the inventive military art goes

The Opera House—Vienna

the Austrian officer holds a distinguished place, and the discoveries of General Uchatius, especially in artillery, are of the most remarkable kind. It is certainly within the memory of many when Austrian and Hungarian were at daggers drawn. Thanks to a wise and generous policy, one of forgiveness and forgetfulness, Austria is stronger by the love of her Hungarian population than she ever has been before. The early misfortunes which met the present emperor were not lessons lost on him. With her Italian provinces gone, Austria has gained new life, and she has today the respect and sympathy of all Europe. It was pleasant to hear on all sides the love expressed for the Emperor, and to listen to the many stories told of his kindnesses. The Viennese have an intense love for music. Is not Vienna the city sacred to the waltz and to Strauss? You hear music on every side. In the streets, in the public places, military bands are performing in the most delightful manner. In fact, we float along on music. The Opera House is second to none, and from Vienna, as a hot-bed, spring forth all the year round crops of sopranos, contraltos, tenors, and bassos, who go hence for their tour around the musical world. Vienna was the home of the great Mozart. Beethoven, too, did the most of his work here.

In the Viennese population, the Jew forms a large proportion. The Is-

raelite may be seen occupying very extensively the profession of street peddler. In Germany, generally, the social condition of the Jew, his place
among his fellows, is not a flattering one. When he arrives at great wealth,
the power which money brings is even then grudgingly accorded to him.
There is a feeling of religious prejudice existing in the German mind
which seems difficult to eradicate. Austria is devoutly Catholic, though of
late years Unitarianism has made great progress. Education is making
rapid strides, and to know how to read and write becomes a necessity; for
there is a rather arbitrary law which prohibits any one from marrying who
cannot read and write. Fancy how oppressive must be a dictum of this kind.
Still it may have its touching side, for we can imagine some pretty Austrian
peasant girl, well versed in her A, B, C's, teaching her swain all the mysteries of the spelling book so that he may gain her hand in wedlock.

Among the most delightful of our visits was one to Baden, fourteen
miles from the city and about half way to Voslau. Baden, as its name designates, is a place for bathing. Springs abound, and the water is at a very
high temperature.

For once the General was forced by many courtesies to extend his stay
some days over the date fixed for our departure. None of us regretted this
delay, for Vienna is a city fitted for those who feel like indulging in a little
rest.

But our time has come, and we hear imperative commands for departure. We shall take a direct route for Switzerland, visiting Munich on the
way, and then go southerly through the wine country of La Belle France,
and, touching at Bordeaux, go thence to Spain. If we have an Athens in
America, so has Germany; and this Teutonic Athens, this center of art, is
called Munich. Now the Bavarian has certain peculiar characteristics which
are not in the least æsthetic. Old Munich struck us as being, at least in certain portions, more pervaded with the Middle Age feeling than any other
city we had visited. There are perched on old, venerable houses many of
those peculiar turrets and quaintly shaped appendices which realistic
painters introduce into medieval art. The Ludwigs-Strasse is the pride of
Munich, and, in the estimation of the Bavarian, is the rival of the Unter
den Linden, Berlin. It is a superb street, flanked on both sides by fine
houses. The general appearance of the city, that is the newer portion, is
quite composite. Stimulated by an artistic sovereign, the architects have
constructed houses in all varieties of architecture, and this variety gives a
very pleasing and picturesque character to the streets.

Munich is famous throughout the world for its sparkling beer, and it is certainly an excellent beverage, though the method of serving it in some of the leading places must entail an amount of labor to the thirsty man which only an enthusiastic beer-drinker would undergo. In the large brewery, the Royaline, you have to find your own glass, and then fight your way to the bar, in order to have it filled. Life in a beer house is of a peculiar kind. Before the same table may be found men of various degrees, the gentleman and the workman, the university professor and the student. Beer seems to flow like water. We have not, however, seen any one tipsy. It must, indeed, take a flood of beer to have the least effect on a citizen of Munich. Beer is so important a factor in the capital of Bavaria, that the augmentation of its price would quite likely lead to serious disturbances. To show the importance of this industry, in a population of not quite five millions, there are fully ten thousand persons engaged in its manufacture. Perhaps it is this great consumption that makes the men of Munich so round, fat, and jolly. Each nation has its peculiarities, and Bavaria is held in Germany as a country where the people are the least likely to change, and where materialism holds its sway. If a story is told in Germany, where a particular person is made the object of a jest, it is generally on a Bavarian that the joke is perpetrated. King Louis, with a great æsthetic purpose, has so shaped Munich that it is the art center of Germany. . . .

CHAPTER NINE

Spain, Portugal, and a Jaunt to Ireland

In addition to the usual rounds of sightseeing, including a visit to Gibraltar (a speck of British spit and polish that the Grants rather enjoyed), when in Spain and Portugal during the autumn of 1878, Grant spent long hours in what seem to have been rather dull conversations with King Alfonso XII and King Don Luis I. There is something a touch condescending in Young's portrayals of two kingdoms that had seen their better days, though he was sympathetic with Alfonso's attempts to stay atop the explosive Spanish political scene. Governments rose and fell, frequently with considerable effusions of blood, in the quasi-constitutional monarchy, quasi-democracy, quasi-military dictatorship that was Spain. As Alfonso himself had been put in power by one rebellion, he might well be removed by another.

After spending the Christmas season in Paris, which by now was their home away from home, the Grants left on January 2, 1879, for two rushed and chilly weeks in Ireland. Clearly, this visit was obligatory for an American politician who still harbored notions of returning to the presidency one day—all those Irish-American voters could not be snubbed by his omitting to travel to their homeland, even though Grant was keen to sail into warmer seas on the way to India. Indeed, in Dublin, after being named an honorary citizen of the city, Grant noted in a brief speech: "I am by birth a citizen of a country where there are more Irishmen . . . than there are in all Ireland. I have therefore had the honor and pleasure of representing more Irishmen and their descendents when in office than the Queen of England."

I look on Spain in a kindlier spirit, and although as you cross the frontier you see how all things change, and feel the instantaneous difference between Spain and France, I cannot help feeling that she was mighty in other days, and that within her borders lies the strength that may awake to the mastery of empires. On the one side of the boundary you leave the brisk dapper French gendarme, all action and noise, the clean stations, trim with flowers, the eating tables where you can burden yourself with bonbons and champagne. On the other side you hear no noise. That everlasting French clatter has ceased. You do not see groups of gesticulating people all speaking at once. Things are not so clean. There is smoke everywhere—smoke in the saloons, in the eating rooms. You might find something to eat in the restaurant, but it would only be with your appetite in a normal condition. No one seems in a hurry. Groups in all conditions, some in cloaks, some in rags, stand about smoking cigarettes and talking of politics and the bull fights. I wonder if this is a good sign, this talking politics. It is a new thing in Spain.

There were officers in high grade who awaited the coming of General Grant. They came directly from the king, who was at Vittoria, some hours distant. Orders had been sent to receive our Ex-President as a captain general of the Spanish army. This question of how to receive an Ex-President of the United States has been the source of tribulation in most European cabinets, and its history may make an interesting chapter some day. Spain solved it by awarding the Ex-President the highest military honors. More interesting by far than this was the meeting with Mr. Castelar, the Ex-President of Spain. Mr. Castelar was in our train and on his way to San Sabastian. As soon as General Grant learned that he was among the group that gathered on the platform he sent word that he would like to know him. Mr. Castelar was presented to the General, and there was a brief and rapid conversation. The General thanked Mr. Castelar for all that he had done for the United States, for the many eloquent and noble words he had spoken for the North, and said he would have been very much disappointed to have visited Spain and not met him; that there was no man in Spain he was more anxious to meet. Castelar is still a young man. He has a large, domelike head, with an arching brow that recalls in its outline the brow of Shakespeare. He is under the average height, and his face has no covering but a thick, drooping mustache. You note the Andalusian type, swarthy, mobile, and glowing eyes that seem to burn with the sun of the Mediterranean. Castelar's Presidency was a tempest with Carlism in the north, and communism in the south, and the monarchy everywhere. How he held it was a marvel, for he had no friend in the family of nations but America, and that was a cold friendship. But he kept Spain free, and executed the laws and vindicated the national sovereignty, and set on foot by his incomparable eloquence the spirit which pervades Spain today, and which, sooner or later, will make itself an authority. . . . It was a picture, not without instructive features, this of Castelar, the orator and Ex-President of Spain, conversing on the platform of the frontier railway station with Grant, the soldier and Ex-President of the United States. "When I reach Madrid," said the General, "I want to see you." "I will come at any time," said Castelar. The only man in Spain who received such a message from General Grant was Emilio Castelar. . . .

When General Grant reached Vittoria there were all the authorities out to see him and he was informed that in the morning the King Alfonso II would meet him. Ten o'clock was the hour, and the place was a small city-hall or palace, where the King resides when he comes into his capital. At ten the General called, and was escorted into an anteroom where were several aides and generals in attendance. He passed into a small room, and was greeted by the King. The room was a library, with books and a writing table covered with papers, as though his majesty had been hard at work. His majesty is a young man, twenty past, with a frank, open face, side whiskers and a mustache like down. He was in the undress uniform of a captain general, and had a buoyant, boyish way about him which made one sorrow to think that on these young shoulders should rest the burdens of sovereignty. How much he would have given to have gone into the green fields for a romp and a ramble—those green fields that look so winsome from the window. It is only yesterday that he was among his toys and velocipedes, and here he is a real king, with a uniform, heavily braided with bullion, showing that he ranks with the great generals of the world. Alfonso speaks French as though it was his own tongue, German and Spanish fluently, but not so well, and English with good accent, but a limited vocabulary. When the General entered the King gave him a seat, and they entered into conversation. There was a little fencing as to whether the conversation should be in English or Spanish. The General said he knew Spanish in Mexico, but thirty-five years had passed since it was familiar to him, and he would not venture upon it now. The King was anxious to speak Spanish, but English and French were the only tongues used.

The King said he was honored by the visit of General Grant, and especially because the General had come to see him in Vittoria; otherwise he would have missed the visit, which would have been a regret to him. He was very curious to see the General, as he had read all about him, his campaigns and his presidency, and admired his genius and his character. To this the General answered that he would have been sorry to have visited

Europe without seeing Spain. The two countries—Spain and the United States—were so near each other in America that their interests were those of neighbors. The General then spoke of the sympathy which was felt throughout the United States for the King in the loss of his wife. The King said that he had learned this, had seen its evidence in many American newspapers, and it touched him very nearly. He then spoke of the Queen. His marriage had been one of love, not of policy. He had been engaged to his wife almost from childhood—for five years at least. He had made the marriage in spite of many difficulties, and their union, although brief, was happy. No one knew what a help she had been in combating the difficulties of the situation, for it was no pleasure to be an executive—no easy task. The General had seen something of it, and knew what it was. To this the General answered that he had had eight years of it, and they were the most difficult and burdensome of his life. The King continued to dwell on the burdens of his office. Spain was tranquil and prosperous, and he believed she was entering upon a career of greater prosperity; and from all parts of his kingdom came assurances of contentment and loyalty. There were no internecine wars like the Carlists' in the north, or the communists' in the south, and Cuba was pacified. All this was a pleasure to him. But there were difficulties inseparable from the royal office. While his wife lived, together they met them, and now she was gone. His only solace, he continued, was activity, incessant labor. He described his way of living—rising early in the morning, visiting barracks, reviewing troops, and going from town to town.

All this was said in the frankest manner—the young King leaning forward in his chair, pleased, apparently, at having some one to whom he could talk, some one who had been in the same path of perplexity, who could feel as he felt. The General entered into the spirit of the young man's responsibilities, and the talk ran upon what men gain and lose in exalted stations. There was such a contrast between the two men—Alfonso in his general's uniform, the President in plain black dress, fumbling an opera hat in his hand. In one face were all the joy and expectancy of youth—of beaming, fruitful youth—just touched by the shadow of a great duty and a heart-searing sorrow. Behind him the memory of his love, his dear love, torn from his arms almost before he had crowned their lives with the nuptial sacrament—before him all the burdens of the throne of Spain. In the other face were the marks of battles won, and hardships endured, and triumphs achieved—and rest at last. One face was young and fair. The skin as soft as satin, youth and effort streaming from the dark, bounding eyes. The other showed labor. There were lines on the brow, gray hairs

Gibraltar

mantling the forehead, the beard gray and brown, the stooping shoulders showing that Time's hand was bearing upon them. . . .

From Vittoria the General and party went direct to Madrid, arriving on October 28th, and were most heartily welcomed. The situation of Madrid is singularly unfavorable, as it is built on a high barren plane where there is scarcely a tree or shrub. The river Manzanares, an unimportant affluent of the Tagus, skirts it on the west. This stream is crossed by five bridges whose great size forms a striking contrast with that of the river. We visited the Royal Palace, an immense square edifice, a combination of the Ionic and Doric in its architecture, but were not especially interested. Its great size was the only thing which astonished us. Opposite the Royal Palace, on the other side of the Manzanares is the Padro, the Hyde Park of Madrid. This is a long spacious walk, adorned on either side by rows of trees and several fountains. It is the evening resort for all classes of the inhabitants. Here in the Padro is a very ugly building, which contains that much neglected collection of very rare paintings belonging to the Royal Museum of Art. The houses of the city are generally well built, but neither the streets nor the people are remarkable for their cleanliness. During the heat of the day, from twelve to three, the shops in the best part of the city are closed, and the people at their *siesta*. This general closing in the middle of the day seems singular to an American, but we are not sure that it would not be a good plan for New York and Chicago to follow on the hot days of July and August.

The notable event during our short stay in Madrid was the witnessing by the General of the attempt to assassinate King Alfonso. General Grant was standing, when the shot was fired, at a window of the Hotel de Paris. This hotel is a long distance from the scene of the attack, but looks across the great central plaza, directly down the Calle Mayor. The General, who was following with his eyes the progress of the royal cavalcade, which had just passed across the Puerta del Sol before him, said to the writer that he clearly saw the flash of the assassin's pistol.

It was from this city that we toiled over the most barren and stony road to that striking and wonderful monument, the embodiment of the genius of Philip II., the Spanish Escurial. The building was intended as a convent, but was used by King Philip as a palace from 1584 until the time of his death in 1598. The site of the building is 2,700 feet above the sea; its form is a rectangular parallelogram, 744 feet from the north to the south, 580 from east to west, and covers about a half-million square feet; there are 88 fountains, 15 cloisters, 86 staircases, 16 court-yards, and 3,000 feet of

Lisbon

fresco. We wandered through its dreary rooms and halls, noting the many scenes which had transpired there, but were glad to come again into the sunshine, and were deeply thankful that the power which it embodied had gone into the depths, with the crimes and follies of antecedent generations, and that its only value now is as the monument of a cruel and degrading age. . . .

The King of Portugal, Don Luis I., is a young man in the fortieth year of his age, second cousin to the Prince of Wales, who is three years his junior, and between whom there is a marked resemblance. . . . The King, on learning that General Grant had arrived in Lisbon, came to the city to meet him. There was an audience at the palace, the General and his wife meeting the King and Queen. The King, after greeting the General in the splendid audience chamber, led him into an inner apartment, away from the ministers and courtiers who were in attendance on the ceremony. They had a long conversation relative to Portugal and the United States, the resources of the two countries, and the means, if means were possible, to promote the commercial relations between Portugal and America. Portugal was, above all things, a commercial nation, and her history was a history of discovery and extending civilization. Lisbon, in a direct line, was the nearest port for ships leaving New York. It was on the line of latitude south of the icebergs, and a pleasanter part of the ocean than the routes to Liverpool. There was a harbor large enough to hold any fleet, and the King believed that when the new lines of railway through Portugal and Spain were built, the route would be seventeen miles shorter than over the present many-winding way of the Salamanca road. The advantages of such a port as Lisbon would be many for travelers, and the King had no doubt that markets for American produce and manufactures would be found in the countries around Lisbon.

The King had been a naval officer, and the conversation ran into ships of war and naval warfare. There were other meetings between the King and the General. The day after the palace reception was the King's birthday, and there was a gala night at the opera. The King and royal family came in state, and during the interludes the General had a long conversation with his majesty. The next evening there was a dinner at the palace in honor of the General, the ministry and the leading men of the court in attendance. The King conversed with the General about other themes—wanted him to go with him and shoot. It seems the King is a famous shot. But the General's arrangements left him no time to accept this courtesy.

It seems the King is a literary man, and having translated "Hamlet" into Portuguese, the conversation ran into literary themes. The King said he hoped to finish Shakespeare and make a complete translation into Portuguese. He had finished four of the plays—"Hamlet," "Merchant of Venice," "Macbeth," and "Richard III." "Othello" was under way, and already he had finished the first act. The question was asked as to whether his majesty did not find it difficult to translate such scenes as that between Hamlet and the grave-diggers—almost dialect conversations—into Portuguese. The King said he thought this was, perhaps, the easiest part. It was more difficult to render into Portuguese the grander portions, where the poetry attained its highest flight. "The Merchant of Venice" he liked extremely, and "Richard III." was in some respects as fine as any of Shakespeare's plays. "What political insight," said the King; "what insight into motives and character this play contains!" The King asked the General to accept a copy of "Hamlet," which his majesty presented with an autograph inscription. As the time came to leave, the King asked the General to allow him to mark his appreciation of the honor the General had done Portugal by visiting it by giving him the grand cross of the Tower and Sword. The General said he was very much obliged, but that, having been President of the United States, and there being a law against officials accepting decorations, he would rather, although no longer in office, respect a law which it had been his duty to administer. At the same time he appreciated the compliment implied in the king's offer and would always remember it with gratitude. . . .

It was with no little regret that General Grant left the bright and picturesque scenes of sunny Spain and journeyed north to Paris. From Paris the party went direct to England, Mrs. Grant intending to spend a few days with her daughter, Mrs. Sartoris, while the General made a short trip into Ireland.

General Grant left London on the evening of [January] 2d by the regular mail route, via Holyhead and Kingstown, and arrived at Dublin the next morning, accompanied by General Noyes, General Badeau, Mr. Russell Teney, and Mr. Fitzgerald. On arriving at Westland Row he was received by the Lord Mayor (Sir J. Barrington), and conveyed in his carriage to the Shelburne Hotel, where a suite of rooms had been prepared for the General and his companions. The American Consul in Dublin, Mr. Barrow, called at an early hour to pay his respects, and at eleven o'clock the Lord Mayor, accompanied by his chaplain, Rev. Canon Bogart, attended with his carriage to conduct the visitors through the city and through the principal buildings. They drove first to the Royal Irish Academy in Dawson Street, and were received by Rev. Maxwell Close, Captain McEwing, Mr. McSweeney, and Mr. Cilbbon, by whom General Grant was conducted through the library and museum. This museum contains a very large and rare collection of antiquities, which were examined with great interest. The Bank of Ireland in College Green was next visited, and the General was greatly impressed with the system on which the business of the bank is conducted, and he made many inquiries as to the workings of the institution. After leaving the bank the party visited the Chamber of Commerce, where they were met by Alderman Tarpey, the High Sheriff. Here the General read the latest telegrams and signed his name in the visitor's book. He was then driven to the Stock Exchange in Dame Street, and thence to Trinity College, where the party arrived shortly after twelve o'clock, and were received by the Faculty and shown through the building. Again entering the Lord Mayor's carriage they were driven through Sackville Street, which is justly esteemed one of the finest avenues in the kingdom, being very broad and a little more than a third of a mile in length, lined on either side by very fine and costly buildings. At its northern end, in Rutland Square, stands the Nelson column. Shortly after one o'clock the party arrived at the City Hall. As the General alighted from the carriage he was received with demonstrations of respect by the spectators, who raised their hats and cheered. At the entrance to the City Hall he was met by the Sheriff, Mr. Burke, and several members of the council chamber, where the members in their robes were waiting to receive him. A number of prominent citizens were also present to witness the presentation of the freedom of the city. The resolution that such an honor should be conferred upon him having been read by the Lord Mayor amid cheers, the General was presented with the certificate, which was handsomely illuminated and contained in a very elaborately carved bog-oak casket. . . .

In the evening there was a banquet at the Mayor's. Among those present were General Sir John Michael, Sir George Ribton, General Noyes, General Badeau, and the leading citizens of the city. This proved to be a very interesting and entertaining evening, and the festivities were kept up until a late (or early) hour.

On Saturday the General and party strolled about the city, noting its many attractions. Sunday was spent in a very quiet way at the Shelburne Hotel, and was indeed a day of perfect rest.

At eight o'clock on Monday morning the party left Dublin, Lord-Mayor Barrington taking leave of the General at the railway station. The morning was cold, and, as the train progressed northward, ice, snow, cold winds, and finally rain were encountered. The train first stopped at the town of Dundalk, where, around the depot, notwithstanding the storm, were assembled a very large crowd, who were most enthusiastic in their demonstrations of welcome. At Omagh, Strabane, and other stations, large crowds were assembled, the people cheering the General and America, and whenever possible pressing forward to shake him by the hand through the car window. At two o'clock the train reached Londonderry. A heavy rain, followed by frost, had covered the ground with ice, rendering the view of the city and surroundings most charming, as seen through the mists and gossamer falling snow. At the station an immense crowd, apparently the whole town and neighborhood, had assembled. The multitude was held in check by the police. The General was cordially welcomed to Londonderry by the Mayor, in a complimentary address, to which he responded briefly, and left the station amid the heartiest greetings of the people. The crowd followed the General's carriage and cheered madly as he was driven to the hotel. The ships in the harbor were decorated with flags and streamers— in fact, the whole town was in gala dress and out for a holiday. A remarkably cold driving rain set in at three o'clock, just as the party drove in state to the ancient Town Hall. The crowd was so dense that progress through it was made with difficulty. At the entrance of the building the Mayor and

Council in their robes of office received the Ex-President, amid many expressions of enthusiasm from the people. An address was read extolling the military and civil career of the General.

General Grant signed the roll, thus making himself an Ulster Irishman. He then made a brief address. He said that no incident of his trip was more pleasant than accepting citizenship at the hands of the representatives of this ancient and honored city, with whose history the people of America were so familiar. He regretted that his stay in Ireland would be so brief. He had originally intended embarking from Queenstown direct to the United States, in which case he would have remained a much longer time on the snug little island; but having resolved to visit India, he was compelled to make his stay short. He could not, however, he said in conclusion, return home without seeing Ireland and a people in whose welfare the citizens of the United States took so deep an interest. . . .

A cold rain and mists coming from the Northern Ocean obscured the wonderful view of the northern Irish coast. The General studied the country closely, remarking on the sparseness of population, and saying he could see no evidence of the presence of seven millions of people in Ireland.

At every station there were crowds assembled, and when the cars stopped the people rushed forward to shake hands with the General. Some were old soldiers who had been in the American army. One remarked that General Grant had captured him at Paducah. The people were all kindly, cheering for Grant and America. At Coleraine there was an immense crowd. General Grant, accompanied by the member of Parliament, Mr. Taylor, left the cars, entered the waiting-room at the depot, and received an address. In reply, General Grant repeated the hope and belief expressed in his Dublin speech that the period of depression was ended, and that American prosperity was aiding Irish prosperity. At Ballymoney there was another crowd. As the train neared Belfast a heavy rain began to fall.

The train reached Belfast station at half-past two o'clock. The reception accorded General Grant was imposing and extraordinary. The linen and other mills had stopped work, and the workmen stood out in the rain in thousands. Looking from the train window there was a perfect sea of heads. The platform of the station was covered with scarlet carpet. The Mayor and members of the City Council welcomed the General, who descended from the car amid tremendous cheers. Crowds ran after the carriages containing the city authorities and their illustrious guest, and afterward surrounded the hotel where the General was entertained. All the public buildings were draped with English and American colors.

Luncheon was served at four o'clock, and, notwithstanding the heavy snowstorm, the crowd remained outside, and cheered at intervals. The feature of the luncheon was the presence of the Roman Catholic Bishop of the diocese, who was given the post of honor. The Belfast speakers made cordial allusions to many prominent people in the United States, and were very complimentary to their guest. General Noyes in his speech alluded to the fact that General Grant had shown his appreciation of Belfast men by appointing A. T. Stewart Secretary of the Treasury, and offering George H. Stuart, a Belfast boy, the portfolio of Secretary of the Navy.

After the luncheon was over General Grant remained quietly in his apartments, receiving many calls, some from old soldiers who served under him during the war. . . .

India

After an uneventful three-week cruise through the Mediterranean, the Red Sea, and the Indian Ocean, the Grant party arrived at Bombay, one of the major seats of British imperial power. The Grants were swept immediately into official residences, and from then on they mixed almost exclusively with the powerful British elite, seeing enough of the Indians to appreciate their utterly alien and colorful qualities. While in India, Young reflected the standard American ambivalence about the British ruling classes—finding them ruthless but highly competent, resenting them for their slant toward Robert E. Lee and the Confederacy in the late war and for their general lack of democratic sensibilities, but appreciating their attentions all the same, as younger brothers are wont to do.

These ambivalent Americans were quite happy to engage body servants for their stay in India at a very cheap cost to themselves, thinking of them with the same condescension as was summoned up for such people by their hosts. Haggling with the merchants aroused similar racially hierarchical social sensibilities. Anglo-Saxon cousins, whether British or American, were members of the same larger ruling class after all.

Of course, the Taj Mahal duly impressed the Grant party, but they greeted the Maharajah of Jeypore, the sort of potentate who had built the Taj, with considerable incredulity. Though just having taken his tenth wife—imagine that, Americans back at home—he had no children, and he devoted himself to prayer and billiards, whipping the general in a game despite his best attempts to lose. Young's puzzlement in trying to figure out such a major eccentric rendered his recollections rather surreal at this point.

Then it was on to Bhurtpoor; Young allowed himself considerable relish in describing the bloody and corrupt way in which the British had reconquered a rebellious prince in this state several decades earlier. Behind the British Raj and British civilization lurked the serpent of pure greed. After passing through Delhi, where Young pointedly commented upon the ruins of so many empires prior to the British one, the Grants cut short their travels through northern India and rushed through Beneras, taking ship in Calcutta after spending just five weeks in this torrid and strange land of India. The intense contradictions these Americans felt had left them very uncomfortable, both physically and emotionally.

On the 24th of January, at noon, our party embarked on the "Labourdonnais" at Marseilles. There were several American friends to wish us a pleasant journey, and as we turned from the land-locked bay suddenly into a high rolling sea, we saw their handkerchiefs waving us a last farewell. Our party, as made up for the Indian trip, is composed of General Grant, Mrs. Grant, Colonel Frederick D. Grant, Mr. A. E. Borie, formerly Secretary of the Navy; Dr. Keating, of Philadelphia, a nephew of Mr. Borie, and the writer. It was remarked that a year ago we had visited Thebes, those of us who remained as members of the Grant party. Even in so small a company time has made changes. The officers of the "Vandalia," three of whom were the General's guests on the Nile, have gone home. Jesse Grant is in California. Hartog, the courier, does not go to India. Colonel Grant takes his brother's place. Mr. Borie came rather suddenly. His health had not been good, and the sea was recommended as a restorative, and the General was delighted with the idea that one whom he held in so high honor would accompany him around the world.

Our life on the "Labourdonnais" may be briefly told. The "Labourdonnais" is an old-fashioned ship, not in the best of order, and not very comfortable. The table was fair and the attendance middling. We were told that it was unfortunate that we had not taken some other ship on the line, which would have made all the difference in the world. However, I will not complain of the "Labourdonnais," which carried us safely through, and thereby earned our gratitude. I have noticed in my seafaring experiences that the difference between a good ship and a bad one in their degrees of comfort is not essential. If you like the sea, and have no terror for its tribulations, you will not be critical about the ship that bears you. If you do not like the sea, damask and sandalwood and spices from Ceylon, with M. Bignon as your cook, would not make it welcome. Our first hours on the Mediterranean were on a high sea, but on the second day the sea went down, and we had charming yachting weather. On Friday, the 24th of January, we passed between Corsica and Sardinia, having a good view of the sombre coasts of the former island. On the 25th, about noon, Ischia came in sight, and through the hazy atmosphere we could trace the faintest outline of Vesuvius. The sea was so calm that we were enabled to sail so near the shores of Ischia as to note the minutest form of geological strata and distinguish minor objects on the shore. Ischia is a beautiful island, and we noted smiling villages and inviting bits of sunshine and greenery as we sailed along. Then, as the afternoon shadows lengthened, we passed the island, and leaving Capri to our right, nestling under a cloudy canopy of azure and pearl, we sailed into the Bay of Naples. A year had almost passed since we left Naples. But the glorious beauty of the bay was as fresh as ever, and as we noted spot after spot in the landscape—the king's palace, the place where Brutus found refuge after Cæsar's death, the scene where Pliny witnessed the destruction of the cities of Sorrento and Pompeii, the range of shining hills, the convent looking down from a beetling crag, which we climbed one December day; the anchorage of the "Vandalia," and above all the towering volcano from which came smoke and flame— it was as if we were meeting old friends. We came into the harbor, and old friends came on board in the person of Mr. Maynard, our Minister to Turkey, and Mr. Duncan, our Consul to Naples. The Doctor and I went ashore to make sure of a telegraphic message that it was my duty to send; but it was so late in the afternoon that none of the party followed our example, and as the sun went down we steamed out to sea. The last we saw of the city was Vesuvius, the smoke resting above it in a dense wavy cloud, and the flames flashing like a beacon in the calm summer air.

On the morning of the 26th, the Sabbath, Mr. Borie, who has earned the first prize for early rising, came to my berth and said that Stromboli was in sight. Last year when we sailed through these islands Stromboli was drenched in showers and mist, and when Lieutenant Strong pointed out the volcano from the quarterdeck of the "Vandalia," all I could see was a mass of rain and fog. But here we were, sailing under the shadow of this ancient and famous island. What we saw was a volcano throwing out ashes and smoke in a feeble, fretful manner, as though jealous of its flashing rival in Naples Bay, and a cluster of houses at the base, evidently a village. I can understand a good many puzzling things the older I grow—why Brooklyn will remain an independent city, why New Jersey does not become annexed to Pennsylvania and New York, why an Ohio man may resign office—but I cannot conceive any reason for human beings living in Stromboli. They are at the absolute mercy of the sea and the furnace; they are far away from neighbors and refuge and rescue. It must be to gratify some poetic instinct, for Stromboli is poetic enough. And now we are coming, with every turn of our screw, into the land of classic and religious fame. These islands through which we are sailing are the islands visited by the wandering Ulysses. This rock that we study through our glasses in the gray morning light is the rock of Scylla, and we sail over Charybdis. This town that looks very modern, on whose white roofs the sun shines with a dazzling glare, is Reggio, which in holy days was called Rhegium. It was here that Paul landed after Syracuse and Malta adventures, carrying with him the message of Christ, going from this spot to preach the Gospel to all mankind.

We pass Etna on the left, but the mighty mountain is wrapped in mist and cloud and snow. We sail through the Messina Straits, the sea scarcely rippling, and we are soon again in the open sea, the land fading from view. On the second morning we pass close to Crete and see the snowy mountain ranges on that glorious and unhappy island. At noon they fade, the line of snow becoming a line of haze, and as we bid Crete farewell we say farewell to Europe, for we head directly toward Egypt and the Red Sea and India, and who knows what beyond. Farewell to Europe, and farewell to many a bright and happy hour spent on its shores, of which all that now remains is the memory.

On the evening of the 29th of January—this being the evening of the seventh day of our journey from Marseilles—we came to an anchor outside of the harbor of Alexandria. There was some disappointment that we did not enter that evening, but we were an hour or so late, and so we swung at anchor and found what consolation we could in the enrapturing glory of an Egyptian night. In the morning when the sun arose we picked our way into the harbor, and when we came on deck we found ourselves at anchor, with Alexandria before us—her minarets looking almost gay in the fresh light of the morning sun.

Pleasant it was to see Egypt again, although we only saw it through the windows of a hurrying train. Pleasant, too, it was to land in quiet, unostentatious fashion, without pomp and ceremony and pachas in waiting and troops in line, the blare of trumpets and the thunder of guns. The escape from a salute and a reception was a great comfort to the General, who seemed to enjoy having no one's hands to shake, to enjoy a snug corner in an ordinary railway car, talking with General Stone and Mr. Borie and the consul general. . . . Our ride to Suez was without incident, and Egypt as seen from the car windows was the same Egypt about which so much has been written. The fields were green. The air was clear and generous. The train people were civil. When Arabs gathered at our doors to call for baksheesh in the name of the prophet, Hassan made himself, not without

The Deck of the "Venetia"

noise and effect, a beneficent influence. The General chatted with Stone about school times at West Point, about friends, about the new days—and one fears the evil days—that have fallen upon his highness the Khedive. Mr. Borie made various attempts to see the Pyramids from the cars, and talked over excursions that some of us had made, and we came near remaining in Cairo for another steamer to enable him to visit the Pyramids and the Sphinx, and the Serapeum at Memphis. But we are late for India, and Mr. Borie would not consent to the sacrifice of time on the General's part, and so we keep on to Suez. . . .

[After a day in Suez]—a small, clean town—clean from an Oriental standard, . . . about eight in the evening of January 31st the last farewell is spoken, we feel the throbbing of the vessel beneath us, and know that at last we are off for India.

We are the only Americans of the company sailing on the good ship

"Venetia," and we form a colony of our own. We have preempted a small claim just behind the wheel, in the stern of the vessel. There is a grating about six foot square a foot above the deck. Here you can lounge and look out at the tumbling waves that come leaping after, or look into the deep ultramarine and learn what the waves have to say. Here, if you come at any hour of the day, and at a good many hours of the night, you will find the members of our expedition. Mrs. Grant sits back in a sea chair, wearing a wide-brimmed Indian hat, swathed in a blue silk veil. There is the sun to fight, and our ladies make themselves veiled prophetesses, and shrink from his presence. The General has fallen into Indian ways enough to wear a helmet, which shields the face. The helmet is girded with a white silk scarf, which falls over the neck. We all have helmets which we bought in Suez, but only wear them as fancy seizes us. Mr. Borie has one which cost him eight shillings, an imposing affair, but no persuasion has as yet induced him to put it on. Dr. Keating wears his so constantly that an impression is abroad that he sleeps in it. This, I fear, arises from envy of the Doctor, who takes care of himself, and comes out of his cabin every morning neat enough to stroll down Chestnut Street, and not, like the rest of us, abandoned to flannel shirts and old clothes and frayed cuffs and cracked, shiny shoes. The ship goes on in a lazy, lounging motion. Mrs. Grant looks out of her cloud of blue silk. She has brought up the interesting, never-failing question of mails. That is the theme which never dies, for you see there are boys at home, and if only boys knew the interest felt in their writings what an addition it would be to our postal revenues. Colonel Grant, curled up in a corner, is deep in *Vanity Fair.* The Colonel is assuming a fine bronzed mahogany tint, and it is suggested that he will soon be as brown as Sitting Bull. You see it is the all-conquering sun who is having his will upon us. I am afraid the General's complexion failed him years ago, in the war days, and I do not see that the sun can touch him further. But the rest of us begin to look like meerschaum in various degrees of hue. What shall we be when we reach India? . . .

At noon on Friday, 12th, our position was latitude 18° 05′ north, longitude 69° 22′ east. We were scudding along at eleven knots an hour, and in the morning would see Bombay. The sea became a dead calm, and the morning brought with it a purple haze, which flushed the horizon, and it was after a time and by shading the eyes from the sun that we could manage to trace the line of the hills and knew that this was the coast of India. Our departure from Europe had been so sudden that we had no idea that even our consul at Bombay knew of our coming. All arrangements were made to go to a hotel and from thence make our journey; but the "Venetia" had scarcely entered the harbor before we saw evidences that the General was expected. Ships in the harbor were dressed with flags, and at the wharf was a large crowd—soldiers, natives, Europeans. As we passed the English flagship a boat came alongside with an officer representing Admiral Corbett, welcoming the General to India. In a few minutes came another boat bearing Captain Frith, the military aide to Sir Richard Temple, Governor of the Presidency of Bombay. Captain Frith bore a letter from the Governor welcoming the General to Bombay, and offering him the use of the Government House at Malabar Point. Captain Frith expressed the regret of Sir Richard that he could not be in Bombay to meet General Grant, but duties connected with the Afghan war kept him in Sinde.* The Consul, Mr. Farnham, also came with a delegation of American residents, and welcomed the General and party.

At nine o'clock in the morning the last farewells were spoken, we took our leave of the many kind and pleasant friends we had made on the "Venetia," and went on board the Government yacht. Our landing was at the Apollo Bunder—the spot where the Prince of Wales landed. The tides in the harbor are high, and there were stone steps over which the sea had been washing. As we drew near the shore there was an immense crowd lining the wharf and a company of Bombay Volunteers in line. As the General ascended the steps he was met by Brigadier-General Aitcheson, commanding the forces; Sir Francis Souter, Commissioner of Police; Mr. Grant, the Municipal Commissioner, and Colonel Sexton, commanding the Bombay Volunteers; all of whom gave him a hearty welcome to India. The volunteers presented arms, the band played our national air, and the General, amid loud cheers from the Europeans present, walked slowly with uncovered head to the state carriage. Accompanied by Captain Frith, who represented the Governor, and attended by an escort of native cavalry, the General and party made off to Malabar Point. . . .

So far as beauty is concerned—beauty of an Indian character, with as much comfort as is possible in Hindostan—nothing could be more attractive than our home on Malabar Point. We are the guests of the Governor, and the honors of his house are done by Captain Frith and Captain

* The Second Afghan War (1878–80), like the first (1838–42), was a British attempt to make a forward defense of India against the Russians. The British won the second war but could never really control Afghanistan. The Sind, part of the lower Indus River valley, is now part of Pakistan.

On the Veranda at Malabar Point

Radcliffe, of the army, two accomplished young officers, the last representatives of the last type of the English soldier and gentleman. We take
our meals in the state dining-room, and when dinner is over we stroll over
to the General's bungalow, and sit with him on the veranda looking out on
the sea—sit late into the night, talking about India, and home, and all the
strange phases of this civilization. Mrs. Grant seems to enjoy every moment
of the visit, more especially as we are to have a week's mail on Wednesday,
and the steamer never breaks its word. Mr. Borie is in fine spirits and
health, all things considered, and has surprised us in the virtue of early rising. All manner of plans are proposed to induce Mr. Borie to throw luster
upon the expedition by destroying a tiger and carrying home a trophy of
his prowess to Philadelphia, but he steadily declines these importunities,

taking the high-minded ground that he has never had a misunderstanding with a tiger in his life, and does not propose now to cultivate the resentments of the race.

The attentions paid to the General and his party by the people of Bombay have been so marked and continuous that most of our time has been taken up in receiving and acknowledging them. What most interests us, coming fresh from Europe, is the entire novelty of the scene, the way of living, the strange manners and customs. All your impressions of India, gathered from the scattered reading of busy days at home, are vague. Somehow you associate India with your ideas of pageantry. The history of the country has been written in such glowing colors, you have read Oriental poems, you have fallen under the captivating rhetoric of Macaulay, you look for nature in a luxuriant form, for splendor and ornament, for bazaars laden with gems and gold, for crowded highways, with elephants slowly plodding their way along. My first thought was to inquire for the Car of Juggernaut, which occupies some such place in your mind as a Barnum show.* Therefore, when you look upon India—India as seen in this her greatest city—you are surprised to find it all so hard and baked and brown. You miss the greenness of field and hill-side. You see a people who have nothing in common with any race you know. There are so many types, curious and varying, that your impressions are bewildered and indefinite. I suppose in time, as we go into the country, and know it, we shall see that this civilization has lines of harmony like what we left behind us, that there are reasons for all the odd things we see, just as there are reasons for many odd things in America, and that Indian civilization even now, when its glory has departed—its mightiest States are mere appendages of the British Empire—when day after day it bends and crumbles under the stern hand and cold brain of the Saxon, is rich in the lessons and qualities which have for ages excited the ambition and the wonder of the world. . . .

There is some comfort in knowing that the winter is not the season for the active participation of the cobra in the duties of life. He comes out under the influence of summer suns and the rain. As it is, I suppose there is as much danger in our bungalows from wild and poisonous animals as in the New York house of Mr. Delmonico. We live in sumptuous fashion.

---

* The Car of the Juggernaut was a gigantic, wooden-wheeled cart, forty-five feet high, said to contain the bones or the soul of Krishna, or both, which was annually drawn by pilgrims through the streets of Juggernaut, a seaport in southeastern India. The Car was much decried by English Victorians for its paganism and more particularly because some pilgrims were crushed under the wheels, perhaps in religious ritual suicide.

There is the ever present sea, the shading trees, the walks, the perfume of the flowers scenting the air—the beautiful bay, which reminds you of Naples. In the early morning and the evening you are permitted to go out and ride or stroll. When the sun is up you must remain in-doors. We have had our own experiences of the sun at home, and you cannot understand the terror which he inspires in India. An hour or two ago the Colonel came into my bungalow, and as he passed to his own I strolled with him, perhaps a hundred paces, without putting on my helmet. One of our friends of the staff, who happened to be at the door, admonished me in the gravest manner of the danger that I had incurred. "I would not," he said, "have done that for a thousand rupees. You have no idea how treacherous the sun is here. Even when the breeze is blowing you must not even for an instant allow your head to be uncovered. The consequences may attend you through life." This morning the General went out on horseback for a spin through the country, accompanied by Sir Francis Souter, Captain Frith, and Colonel Grant. Seven was the hour named—"because," said Sir Francis, "we must be home before nine. In India we dare not trifle with the sun."

Life in Bombay grew to be almost home-life under the genial hospitality of our hosts. Although we had been a week in Bombay, there was so much of Europe about us that could not make up our minds that we were in India. We had not seen a tiger or a cobra, and all our associations were with Europeans. There was a club where you could read the English and New York newspapers. There was a racing club, where you could sit at your window and see the horses gallop over the course. There were two or three English newspapers published in Bombay, two in English—the *Gazette* and *The Times in India*—well printed and well written. It is wonderful how speedily you go through a paper that has no roots in your own country, and how even as sad an article as a minute on the famine has no interest to you. Bombay is more European than Indian, and I suppose will always be so while the sea throws the commerce of the world upon her wharves. Much of the prosperity of Bombay—which you see in large, majestic stores, in colleges, esplanades, and wharves—came from our American war. "It is odd," said an Englishman, "that Bombay and General Grant should be face to face, for the General ruined Bombay."

Then came the story of the cotton mania which raged during the American war. The cessation of the cotton supply of the United States threw England back upon India and Egypt. The year before our war Bombay exported about $26,000,000 worth of cotton. During the war the average yearly export was over $100,000,000. Here was a gain to Bombay in four years of $350,000,000, and this sudden addition to the wealth of the city engendered every form of speculation. If people had reasoned they would have known that, whatever way the war ended—whether the North or South won—the close would have been the revival of the cotton crop and an end of these false values. But the gambler never reasons, and Bombay, according to one of the historians of the panic, believed that "the genius of Lee" and "the stubborn valor of the soldiers" would make the war last for a longer time. A good deal of this confidence was due to the tone of the London press on the American war, which, when read now in the cold light of logical and veritable events, represents the lowest point ever reached in the degradation of journalism. The Bombay merchant read his English newspaper and believed it, and continued to gamble. Banks were established—shipping and iron companies, financial associations, land companies, reclamation schemes, railway companies, spinning and weaving, companies in gas, coffee, cotton, oil, and brick. Six hundred per cent. was a fair return for one's investments in those days, and I suppose no city in the world was so prosperous as Bombay in 1865. If Lee and Grant had fought a twenty years campaign this might have continued. But in the spring of 1865 a telegram came announcing that Lee had surrendered, and Bombay collapsed. The companies went to the wall. A firm of Parsee merchants failed for $15,000,000, and before the end of the year there was not one company remaining of the hundred which had arisen during the war. And all coming from a telegram which, in the afternoon of April, 9, 1865, General Grant, sitting on a stone by the wayside of Appomatox, wrote in pencil in his memorandum book—"The army of Northern Virginia surrend[er]ed to me this afternoon." The year 1865 is known as the year of panic, insanity, and bankruptcy. I have heard stories of that mad time from many who were here and saw it. Those days of mania were days of splendor for Bombay in many ways, and it was pointed out that all the magnificent buildings which strike your eye on landing came from the men who were mad with the cotton mania. . . .

[A grand] dinner at Malabar Point closed our visit to Bombay. After the reception of the native gentlemen and merchants the General strolled over to his bungalow, and, sitting on the veranda looking out upon the ocean, he conversed for a long time with Mr. Gibbs, Major Carnac, Mr. Borie, and the gentlemen of the household. It was our last night in Bombay, and so many things were to be talked about—the English in India, and the strange romance of their governing India. It is in conversations such as these, where you meet gifted men, charged with great trusts, full of their work, and familiar with it, that travel has its advantages, and especially to one in the position of General Grant. Himself a commander of men and ruler of a nation, it is instructive to compare notes with men like those he meets in India, who are charged with the rule of an empire. The interesting fact in India as a political question is this: Here the Englishman is solving the problem of how to govern an ancient and vast civilization, or rather, varieties of civilization, to govern it by prestige and the sword. In America the Englishman is trying to create a new nation, based on a democracy. The two problems are full of interest, and, fresh from English-speaking America, we see something new every hour in English-governed India. The governments are as far apart as the Poles, for there is no despotism more absolute than the government of India. Mighty, irresponsible, cruel, but with justice, and, after safety, mercy. This is what you see in India. . . .

Before leaving Bombay the servant question gave us much concern, and when presented to the General, did not meet with enthusiasm. But there was a burden of evidence in its favor that could not be resisted, and when it was suggested that without native servants we might find ourselves in the middle of an Indian wilderness, with no possible means of advancing until we had acquired the Hindostan language, there was no other argument required. So our servants were hired. The business is a good deal like buying tickets in a lottery. The candidates look alike, and speak the same pinched and barren English, confined to the few phrases necessary to personal attendance. There are varieties of labor which require varieties of servants. Such a thing as a handy man of all work, who can go through the whole range of professional requirements, from the boots to the beard, is not known in India. The Mussulman will wait upon you at table. The Hindoo would regard such an office as against his faith, the food you touch being impure. The Hindoo's main office is about the person. I suppose if we had encouraged the Indian idea of division of labor we should have had a dozen servants for each of the party; but the General, who looked with alarm at the prospect of any at all, suggested four. His drawing from the lottery was a cadaverous brown creature, named Chandy-Loll. I think this was his real name. Anyhow, it is near enough to be right, for we were always forgetting his name and calling him something else.

Chandy-Loll was engaged upon a recommendation signed by Mr. George Cadwalader, the ex-Assistant Secretary of State, written when Mr. Cadwalader was in an amiable mood. I am sorry to say that Chandy-Loll did not develop all of the virtues which charmed Mr. Cadwalader. Mr.

Borie fell into the hands of an imposing person named Peter Marian. Peter is a Christian, descended from a Portuguese family, and looks like General Burnside. Peter is much handsomer, and shows more intellect than several of the rajahs we have met. When Mr. Borie first brought him into our society we thought that he had found a native prince, and was about to open a new avenue of intercourse with the native nobility. Colonel Grant's servant has been called Genghis Khan. He is a boy with all the brightness and movement of youth, but without much sense. His English is mainly pantomime, and a conversation between the Colonel and Genghis looks like a rehearsal for a circus. Genghis has the gaze of an intelligent poodle, looking this way and that to anticipate his master's wishes, ready to jump the moment he knows which way to jump. My own servant, Kassim—we call him Kassim, because although not being his name, it is the nearest thing to it—is a character. Kassim is a serious, middle-aged Hindoo, who speaks English. He had letters from English officers with whom he had traveled, and so I took him. My experiences with a Hindoo servant were novel. As soon as Kassim was engaged he took possession of me. I passed into obscurity. I had no care about myself. Kassim floats around, always talking in a chattering, heedless fashion, and is a nervous, anxious being who should have studied astronomy. There is nothing vivid in Kassim's conversational powers, but after patient listening you sometimes discern an idea. One of his principal themes is the worthlessness of Hindoo servants in general, and his gratitude that he is an exception to the rule. He would always, he said, see that his master had the best that was in circulation— the best tent, the best orange in the basket, the best seat in the car. All this was kindly meant in Kassim, but he lacked enterprise, and suffered from the imperturbability of Peter and the enterprise of Genghis Khan.

We pay our servants a rupee a day, about forty cents in American money. We allow them a half rupee a day for subsistence. They travel third class. You have no trouble about them beyond this. The few things they can do they do well. They are attentive, patient, and, I hope, honest. They have no enterprise. You can never depend upon a general direction. If you want a thing done every day, you must give the order every day for a month at least. They have no idea of time or promptitude. You cannot hurry them. Their mind is not capable of taking in two ideas at once. They do a great deal of unnecessary work, especially if it is work at which they can sit down. The Hindoo's idea of happiness is to be able to sit on his haunches, his legs crossed under him, and chatter or meditate. Kassim's favorite occupation is the packing and unpacking of my portmanteau. It is not much of a portmanteau, but the amount of packing it has undergone would try the patience of the stoutest-hearted trunk. Whenever I come into my room or tent, I am apt to find Kassim crouched over the portmanteau packing. He has an aversion to papers and any form of manuscript. It is with the utmost difficulty that I can prevent his destroying letters and manuscripts, and I am sure if I want any special bit of writing to find it at the bottom of his canvas bag, among the shoebrushes and the blacking. Another of his apprehensions is, that we shall go into the jungle and shoot tigers. When we engaged Kassim, he volunteered the information that he could do everything in the world that could be expected from a Hindoo, and especially shoot tigers. But when he heard our light conversation with Mr. Borie upon his resolution to kill tigers, Kassim looked at the matter from a grave and anxious point of view, and warned me in private of the perils of the jungle, and especially of the peril that Mr. Borie would be sure to invite if he persisted in his purpose.

At Allahabad, the Lieutenant Governor, Sir George Confer, met the General at the railway station, as did also his secretary, our friend Colonel Brownlow, of the passengers of the "Venetia." We were the Lieutenant Governor's guests while there, and it was with regret that we left the pleasant home of Sir George and Lady Confer, for Agra, where we were to remain several days. . . .

Our stay in Agra was short, but it would have been impossible to have left India without seeing the Taj. This building is said to be the most beautiful in the world. As we came into Agra in the early morning the familiar lines of the Taj—familiar from study of pictures and photographs—loomed up in the morning air. You have a view of the building for some time before entering the city. The first view was not impressive, and as we looked at the towers of the Taj, and the white marble walls that reflected the rays of the rising sun, it seemed to be a beautiful building as a temple, and no more. Perhaps the night ride may have had something to do with our indifference to art, for the ride had been severe and distressing, and it was pleasant to find any shelter and repose. The General and Mrs. Grant went to the house of Mr. Laurence, the nephew of Lord Laurence, and a member of one of the ruling families of India. The remainder of the party found quarters in a hotel, the only one I believe in the place, a straggling, barn-like building, or series of buildings, over which an American flag was flying. Indian hotel life is not the best way of seeing India; as most travelers in passing through the country are entertained in private houses, bungalows of the officials, mess quarters of the officers, or missionary stations. The Agra hotel seemed to have been built for the millennium, when all shall be good and crime unknown. There were no gates or windows, no doors—all was open. The rooms all ran into one another, and the boarders seemed to live on a principle of association. I never knew who was the landlord, never saw a servant in authority. Everybody seemed to keep the hotel, and when you wanted anything you simply went and took it. Mr. Borie was accommodated with an apartment on the ground floor; the others quartered above him.

After dressing we called on our friend and found him surrounded by all the merchants of the town. The moment a Sahib comes to Agra the whole town comes to see him, and opens a bazaar at his door, and sits there all day with carbuncles, garnets, sandal-wood, arms, mosaics, photographs. If you walk across the way to breakfast, you are the center of a chattering group who force their wares upon you, and if you give them any encouragement, by which I mean if you do not inflict upon them personal violence, which none of us were disposed to do, they will invade your chamber and nestle at your bedside as you sleep. The forte of the Hindoo is patience, and he believes that if he waits you will buy. So when you tell your merchant you do not want anything, that you have resolved to buy nothing, that you have no money, he calmly sits on his haunches and waits. If you make a small purchase for charity's sake, on the principle of giving a shilling to an organ-grinder to get rid of him, it only gives the merchant courage and his friends courage, and they all come and wait. You sit down in your room to read or write, and look up. There is a bearded Moslem with a handful of sabers, which he says are from Nepaul. You drive him away, and in a moment there is another phantom, a smiling Hindoo, who folds his hands and makes a salam, and unless you reach out for a bootjack or some more serious weapon, will unroll from his belt a bundle of precious stones. There is no escaping the merchants, and I am ashamed to confess that whenever we were sorely pressed we sent them to Mr. Borie, who was the purchasing member of the party, and never impatient with the merchants, always finding amusement in trying to open conversation and in examining their slender stocks of goods.

The propensity of the native mind to barter and sale is amusing. The impression among the inhabitants of the country, as you go from place to place, is that you have come to buy. The moment it is known that a Sahib is in town all the peddlers and the merchants from the bazaars come to your lodging place, and encamp on the veranda or under the trees on the lawn, bringing their stuffs and trinkets. They sit like a besieging army and do not move; sit all day chattering and waiting. The purchasing members of our party are Mrs. Grant and Mr. Borie, and as we come in from a drive or a walk in the cool of the evening, we are apt to find Mr. Borie sitting with a swarm of peddlers around him, calmly inspecting the jewels, the silks, the silver, and the gold. Mrs. Grant's ideas of purchasing are affected by her sympathies, and her disposition to pay the peddlers more than they ask, because they look so poor and so thinly clad. Mr. Borie's ideas of merchandise are based upon the rules which governed trade when he was a Philadelphia merchant, and what troubles him is the elastic quality of trade in India, and the absence of a rule as to one price. He lays down this principle of business economy with emphasis to his Hindoo friends, and I have no doubt it would bear good fruit if they understood him. The want of an English valuation has prevented the peddlers from comprehending several maxims of business advice, which no one is more capable of giving than our friend. But a fixed price would take away all the charm of trading to a Hindoo. The bazaar is his life. It is to him what the exchange, the church, the theater, the coffee-house, and the club are to the Saxon. He goes to the bazaars to be amused and informed. All the gossip of India floats through the bazaars. The professional story-tellers—the comedians of Indian life—tell him stories, or read from the ancient books, or recite the deeds of their ancestors, or tell him what the stars have in store for him. Prophecy, astrology, and omens have a meaning, and in anxious days, when there is peril or mutiny in the land, sedition or treason will flash through India from bazaar to bazaar. When we come to a new place our servants are always impatient until they have leave to go to the bazaars, ostensibly for food, but really to hear all about the town. The Government of India knows the feeling of the people from no other source so clearly as from the spies who report the gossip of the bazaars.

So if Mr. Borie were to succeed in planting his sound business principles of ready cash and fixed prices in India, it would destroy the poetry of trade. To the native mind the charm of trade is dickering. It amuses him and brings all his faculties into play, and is also an amusement to the crowd who come and sit around on their haunches and watch the proceedings, as at home a mob would watch a boxing-match. Having taken your estimate the battle begins warily, for the Hindoo is an ingenious, nimble creature, and will not lose his trout at the first nibble. If you are skilled in Indian bartering, the moment a price is named your true tone is one of astonishment, anger, grief; and if you have a cane raise it, as though your indignation was roused to such a pitch that it was with difficulty you could be persuaded from taking summary vengeance on a peddler who would presume to insult your understanding by asking such a price for garnets or shawls. When a trade opens in this way the sport is sure to be fine, and the bazaars are hopeful of a good day. But none of us were up to this, and our purchases began in a slow, plaintive way, until Kassim was called in as interpreter, and then the trade took a poetic turn. Kassim's cue was despair, and from despair to anger. He began with a remonstrance to the dealers upon the sin and madness of such a charge. Then he appealed to their religion. Taking out a silver rupee, and pointing to the head of the Queen and the imperial superscription, he asked the dealer whether he would swear that his wares were worth what was asked. This suggestion led to loud clamors, in which both parties took part, the voices rising higher and higher, and the spectators coming in to swell the chorus, until all that was left was to sit in patience until the chorus ended. I never saw any trader swear on the rupee. I am told that there is some spell attached to the oath on the rupee; that a false oath would be perjury, and the native avoids the vow. All you can do is to sit and look on. You may jog your servant, and tell him you are in a hurry, and ask him to bring the negotiation to a close; you may even express a desire, if time is an object, to pay all that is asked. It makes no difference. You are in the waves of the negotiation and they bear you sluggishly on and on. The laws of the trade cannot be broken. There is so much comfort in the whole business—to your Hindoo interpreter, who is at home in his bazaar; to the merchant, who has his hook in your gills and is simply testing your pulling power, and also the crowd around—that you in time become a spectator yourself, and enter into the amusement of the transaction and watch it as a curious phase of Indian manners. As a matter of observation the merchant seems to really ask about thirty per cent. more than he will take eventually. I have seen a good many abatements in the course of those small trades, but rarely more than thirty per cent. . . .

But the Taj! We were to see the most beautiful building in the world. Public opinion all through India unites in this judgment of the Taj. I had my railway-window impressions, and it is rather a habit when a friend tells me he knows or has seen the most beautiful thing in the world, to ask myself whether he has seen all the beauty the world contains and is competent to pass such an opinion. So I said to myself, what our friends mean is that the Taj is the most striking building in India, and they use the phrase about the world in a French sense, a Frenchman saying that all the world has been at church when he means a good many of his friends were there.

It was late in the afternoon when we went to the Taj. The ride is a short one, over a good road, and we had for an escort Judge Keene of Agra, who has made the art, the history, and the legends of the Mohammedan domination in India a study, and to whose excellent history of the Taj I am indebted for all my useful facts. It happened to be Sunday, and as we drove along the road there seemed to be a Sunday air about the crowds that drifted backward and forward from the gardens. On our arrival at the gate the General and party were received by the custodians of the building, and as we walked down the stone steps and under the overarching shade trees we had grown to be quite a procession.

The principle which inspires these magnificent and useless tombs is of Tartar origin. The Tartars, we are told, built their tombs in such a manner as to "serve for places of enjoyment for themselves and their friends during their lifetime." While the builder lives he uses the building as a house of recreation, receives his friends, gives entertainments. When he dies he is buried within the walls, and from that hour the building is abandoned. It is ever afterward a tomb, given alone to the dead. There is something Egyptian in this idea of a house of feasting becoming a tomb; of a great prince, as he walks amid crowds of retainers and friends, knowing that the walls that resound with laughter will look down on his dust. This will account for so many of the stupendous tombs that you find in Upper India. Happily it does not account for the Taj. If the Taj had been a Tartar idea—a house of merriment to the builder and of sorrow afterward—it would have lost something of the poetry which adds to its beauty. The Taj is the expression of the grief of the Emperor Shah Jehan for his wife, who was known in her day as Mumtaz-i-Mabal, or the Exalted One of the Palace. She was herself of royal blood, with Persian ancestry intermingled. She was married in 1615 to Shah Jehan, then heir to the throne, and, having borne him seven children, died in 1629 in giving birth to the eighth child. Her life, therefore, was in the highest sense consecrated, for she gave it up in the fulfillment of a supreme and holy duty, in itself a consecration of womanhood. The husband brought the body of the wife and mother to these gardens, and entombed it until the monument of his grief should be done. It was seventeen years before the work was finished. The cost is unknown, the best authorities rating it at more than two millions of dollars. Two millions of dollars in the time of Shah Jehan, with labor for the asking, would be worth as much as twenty millions in our day. For seventeen years twenty thousand men worked on the Taj, and their wages was a daily portion of corn.

The effect of the Taj as seen from the gate, looking down the avenue of trees, is grand. The dome and towers seem to rest in the air, and it would not surprise you if they became clouds and vanished into rain. The gardens are the perfection of horticulture, and you see here, as in no part of India that I have visited, the wealth and beauty of nature in Hindostan. The landscape seems to be flushed with roses, with all varieties of the rose, and that most sunny and queenly of flowers seems to strew your path and bid you welcome, as you saunter down the avenues and up the ascending slope that leads to the shrine of a husband's love and a mother's consecration. There is a row of fountains which throw out a spray and cool the air, and when you pass the trees and come to the door of the building its greatness comes upon you—its greatness and its beauty. Mr. Keene took us to various parts of the garden, that we might see it from different points of view. I could see no value in one view beyond the other. And when our friend, in the spirit of courteous kindness, pointed out the defects of the building—that it was too much this, or too much that, or would have been perfect if it had been a little less of something else—there was just the least disposition to resent criticism and to echo the opinion of Mr. Borie, who, as he stood looking at the exquisite towers and solemn marble walls, said: "It was worth coming to India to see the Taj." I value that criticism because it is that of a practical business man concerned with affairs, and not disposed to see a poetic side to any subject. What he saw in the Taj was the idea that its founder meant to convey—the idea of solemn, overpowering, and unapproachable beauty.

As you enter you see a vast dome, every inch of which is enriched with inscriptions in Arabic, verses from the Koran, engraved marble, mosaics, decorations in agate and jasper. In the center are two small tombs of white marble, modestly carved. These cover the resting-place of the Emperor and his wife, whose bodies are in the vault underneath. In other days the Turkish priests read the Koran from the gallery, and you can imagine how solemn must have been the effect of the words chanted in a priestly cadence by the echo that answers and again answers the chanting of some tune by one of the party. The more closely you examine the Taj the more you are perplexed to decide whether its beauty is to be found in the general effect of the design, as seen from afar, or the minute and finished decorations which cover every wall. The general idea of the building is never lost. There is nothing trivial about the Taj, no grotesque Gothic molding or flowering Corinthian columns—all is cold and white and chaste and pure. You may form an idea of the size of the Taj from the figures of the measurement of the Royal Engineers. From the base to the top of the center dome is 139½ feet; to the summit of the pinnacle, 243½ feet. It stands on the banks of the river Jumna, and it is said that Shah Jehan intended to build a counterpart in black marble in which his own ashes should rest. But misfortunes came to Shah Jehan—ungrateful children, strife, deposition—and when he died his son felt that the Taj was large enough for both father and mother. One is almost glad that the black-marble idea never germinated. The Taj, by itself alone, is unapproachable. A duplicate would have detracted from its peerless beauty.

We remained in the gardens until the sun went down, and we had to hurry to our carriages not to be caught in the swiftly descending night. The gardener came to Mrs. Grant with an offering of roses. Some of us, on our return from Jeypore, took advantage of the new moon to make another visit. We had been told that the moonlight gave a new glory even to the Taj. It was the night before we left Agra, and we could not resist the temptation, even at the risk of keeping some friends waiting who had asked us to dinner, of a moonlight view. It was a new moon, which made our view imperfect. But such a view as was given added to the beauty of the Taj. The cold lines of the marble were softened by the shimmering silver light. The minarets seemed to have a new height, and the dome had a solemnity as became the canopy of the mother and queen. We strolled back, now and then turning for another last view of the wonderful tomb. The birds were singing, the air was heavy with the odors of the rose-garden, and the stillness—the twilight stillness all added to the beauty of the mausoleum, and combined to make the memory of our visit the most striking among the many wondrous things we have seen in Hindostan. . . .

[Later] we saw the sights of Jeypore. . . . There was a school of arts and industry which interested the General very much, his special subjects of inquiry as he travels being the industrial customs and the resources of the country. He would go ten miles to see a new-fashioned plow or to avoid seeing a soldier or a gun. The school is one of the Prince's favorite schemes, and the scholars showed aptness in their work. The special work in which Jeypore excels is enameled jewelry, and some of the specimens shown us were exceedingly beautiful and dear. We went to the Mint, and saw the workmen beat the coin and stamp it. We went to the collection of tigers, and saw a half dozen brutes, each of whom had a history. Two or three were man-eaters. One enormous creature had killed twenty-five men before he was taken, and he lay in his cage quite comfortable and sleek. Another was in a high temper, and roared and jumped and beat the bars

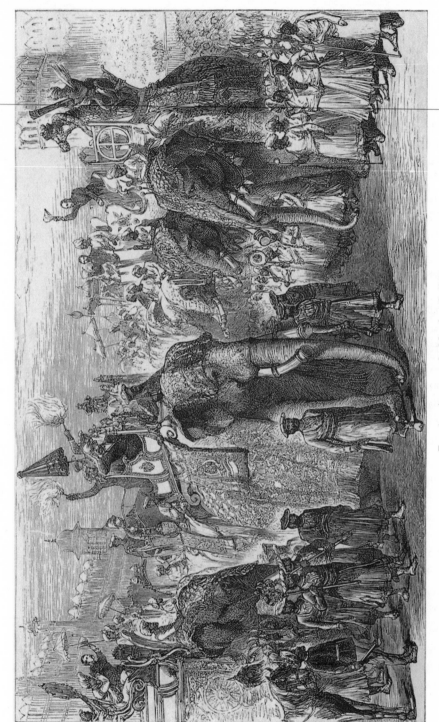

Entering Agra, on the March to Delhi

of his cage. He also was a man-eater, and I am sure that his manifestations quite cured us of any ambition to go into the jungle—cured all but the Colonel, whose coming campaigns in the tiger country are themes of occasional conversation. On returning to the residency we found a group of servants from the palace on the veranda, each carrying a tray laden with sweetmeats and nuts, oranges and other fruits. This was an offering from the Prince, and it was necessary that the General should touch some of the fruit and taste it, and say how much he was indebted to his Highness for the remembrance. Then the servants marched back to the palace. I don't think that any of us could have been induced to make a meal out of the royal viands, not for a considerable part of the kingdom; but our servants were hanging around with hungry eyes, and as soon as the General touched the fruit they swarmed over the trays and bore away the offerings. The Doctor looked at the capture from a professional point of view, and saw that he would have work ahead. The sure consequence of a present of sweetmeats from the palace is that the residency servants are ill for two or three days.

The Maharajah sent word that he would receive General Grant at five. The Maharajah is a pious prince, a devotee and almost an ascetic. He gives seven hours a day to devotions. He partakes only of one meal. When he is through with his prayers he plays billiards. He is the husband of ten wives. His tenth wife was married to him a few weeks ago. The court gossip is that he did not want another wife, that nine were enough; but in polygamous countries marriages are made to please families, to consolidate alliances, to win friendships, very often to give a home to the widows or sisters of friends. The Maharajah was under some duress of this kind, and his bride was brought home and is now with her sister brides behind the stone walls, killing time as she best can, while her lord prays and plays billiards. I asked one who knows something of Oriental ways what these poor women do whom destiny elevates to the couch of a king. They live in more than cloistered seclusion. They are guarded by eunuchs, and, even when ailing, cannot look in the face of the physician, but put their hands through a screen. I heard it said in Jeypore that no face of a Rajput princess was ever seen by a European. These prejudices are respected and protected by the imperial government, which respects and protects every custom in India so long as the states behave themselves and pay tribute. In their seclusion the princesses adorn themselves, see the Nautch girls dance, and read romances. They are not much troubled by the Maharajah. That great prince, I hear, is tired of everything but his devotions and his billiards. He has no children, and is not supposed to have hopes of an heir. He will, as is the custom in these high families, adopt some prince of an auxiliary branch. If he fails to do so—and somehow childless rajahs generally fail, never believing in the inevitable, and putting off the act of adoption until it is too late—the British government will find one, just as they did in Baroda the other day, deposing one ruler and elevating a lad ten or eleven years of age, "who now," as I see in an official paper, "is receiving his education under the supervision of an English tutor." The government of the kingdom is in the hands of a council, among whom are the prime minister and the principal Brahmin.

We drove to the palace at four o'clock, and were shown the royal stables. There were some fine horses and exhibitions of horsemanship which astonished even the General. We were shown the astronomical buildings of Jai Singh II., which were on a large scale and accurately graded. We climbed to the top of the palace and had a fine view of Jeypore. The palace itself embraces one-sixth of the city, and there are ten thousand people within its walls—beggars, soldiers, priests, politicians, all manner of human beings—who live on the royal bounty. The town looked picturesque and cool in the shadows of the descending sun. We looked at the quarters devoted to the household. All was dead. Every part of the palace swarmed with life except this. Word had been sent to the household that profane eyes would soon be gazing from the towers, and the ladies went into seclusion. We strolled from building to building—reception-rooms, working-rooms, billiard-rooms, high walled, far apart, with stone walls and gardens all around; space, air, and sunshine. His Highness had risen this morning earlier than usual, to have his prayers finished in time to meet the General. At five precisely we entered the courtyard leading to the reception hall. The Maharajah came slowly down the steps, with a serious, preoccupied air, not as an old man, but as one who was too weary with a day's labors to make any effort, and shook hands with the General and Mrs. Grant. He accompanied the General to a seat of honor and sat down at his side. We all ranged ourselves in the chairs. On the side of the General sat the members of his party; on the side of the Maharajah the members of his cabinet. Dr. Handley acted as interpreter. The prince said Jeypore was honored in seeing the face of the great American ruler, whose fame had reached Hindostan. The General said he had enjoyed his visit, that he was pleased and surprised with the prosperity of the people, and that he should have felt he had lost a great deal if he had come to India and not have seen Jeypore. The Maharajah expressed regret that the General made

The Nautch Girls' Dance

so short a stay. The General answered that he came to India late, and was rather pressed for time from the fact that he wished to see the Viceroy before he left Calcutta, and to that end had promised to be in Calcutta on March 10th.

His Highness then made a gesture, and a troupe of dancing girls came into the courtyard. One of the features of a visit to Jeypore is what is called the Nautch. The Nautch is a sacred affair, danced by Hindoo girls of a low caste, in the presence of the idols in the palace temple. A group of girls came trooping in, under the leadership of an old fellow with a long beard and a hard expression of face, who might have been the original of Dickens's Fagin. The girls wore heavy garments embroidered, the skirts composed of many folds, covered with gold braid. They had ornaments on their heads and jewels in the side of the nose. They had plain faces and carried out the theory of caste, if there be anything in such a theory, in the contrast between their features and the delicate, sharply-cut lines of the higher class Brahmins and the other castes who surrounded the prince. The girls formed in two lines; a third line was composed of four musicians, who performed a low, growling kind of music on unearthly instruments. The dance had no value in it, either as an expression of harmony, grace, or motion. What it may have been as an act of devotion according to the Hindoo faith I could not judge. One of the girls would advance a step or two and then turn around. Another would go through the same. This went down the double line, the instruments keeping up their constant din. I have a theory that music, like art, has a meaning that is one of the expressions of the character and aspirations of a people, and I am quite sure that an ingenious and quick-witted race like the Hindoos would not invent a ceremony and perform it in their temples without some purpose. The Nautch dance is meaningless. It is not even improper. It is attended by no excitement, no manifestations of religious feeling. A group of coarse, ill-formed women stood in the lines, walked and twisted about, breaking now and then into a chorus, which added to the din of the instruments. This was the famous Nautch dance, which we were to see in Jeypore with amazement, and to remember as one of the sights in India. Either as an amusement or a religious ceremony it had no value.

The Maharajah and his court looked on as gloomy as ravens, while the General wore that resigned expression—resignation tinted with despair—familiar to those of his Washington friends who had seen him listen to an address from the Women's Rights Association or receive a delegation of Sioux chiefs. But the scene was striking in many ways. Here was the courtyard of a palace, the walls traced in fanciful gossamer-like architecture. Here were walls and galleries crowded with court retainers, servants, dependants, soldiers. Here was the falconer in attendance on the prince, the falcon perched on his wrist—a fine, broad-chested, manly fellow, standing in attendance, just as I have seen in pictures representing feudal manners in early English days. Here was the prime minister, the head of the Jeypore government, a tall, lank nobleman in flowing, embroidered robes, with lean, narrow features that I fancied had Hebrew lines in them. Somehow one looks for the Hebrew lines in governing faces. I heard some romantic stories of the rise of the prime minister: how he had held humble functions and rose in time to sit behind the throne. They say he rules with vigor, is a terror to evil-doers, and has made a good deal of money. Prime ministers depend upon the will or the whim of the prince, and as the prince may die or may have some omen from the astrologers, or something may go wrong with the sacrifices—the kid's head not falling at the first stroke, or a like ominous incident—the tenure of power is like gambling. I suppose this noble lord with the aigrette of pearls in his cap, who looks with his thin, uneasy face on the coarse, shambling Nautch girls, has his trouble in wielding power. He must keep his eye on the priests, the astrologers, the eunuchs, the spies, and, above all, upon the British resident, who lives in a shady garden on the outskirts of the town, and whose little finger is more powerful than all the princes of Rajpootana.

Next to the prime minister sits the chief of the Brahmins, a most holy man, who wears a yellowish robe, his brow stamped with his sacred caste, so holy that he would regard the bread of his master unclean, a middle-aged, full-bodied, healthy priest, more European in feature than his associates. He eats opium, as many high and holy men do in India, and you see that his fingers twitch restlessly. He is the favorite Brahmin and conscience-keeper of the Maharajah, receives large revenues from the temples, lives in a palace, and is a member of the King's Council. The younger man, carrying a sword, with a square, full head, is a Bengalese scholar or pundit, the Prince's private secretary, who speaks English, and looks as if one day he might be prime minister. The Maharajah sits as it were soused back into his chair, his eyes covered with heavy silver-mounted spectacles, very tired and bored, looking at the Nautch girls as though they were a million of miles away. He has been praying all day and has had no dinner. The scene is wholly Oriental—the color, the movement, the odd faces you see around you, and the light, trifling, fantastic architecture which surrounds all. The shadows grew longer and longer, and Dr. Handley, evidently thinking that the dance had served every useful purpose, said a word to the Prince, who made a sign. The dance stopped, the girls vanished, and we all went into the main drawing-room, and from thence to the billiard-room. The Maharajah, as I have said, plays billiards when he is not at prayers. He was anxious to have a game with the General. I am not enough of a billiard player to do justice to this game. I never can remember whether the red ball counts or not when you pocket it. The General played in an indiscriminate, promiscuous manner, and made some wonderful shots in the way of missing balls he intended to strike. Mr. Borie, whose interest in the General's fortunes extends to billiards, began to deplore those eccentric experiments, when the General said he had not played billiards for thirty years. The Maharajah tried to lose the game, and said to one of his attendants that he was anxious to show the General that delicate mark of hospitality. But I cannot imagine a more difficult task than for one in full practice at billiards to lose a game to General Grant. The game ended, his Highness winning by more points than I am willing to print for the gratification of the General's enemies.

Then we strolled into the gardens and looked at the palace towers, which the Prince took pleasure in showing the General, and which looked airy and beautiful in the rosy shadows of the descending sun. There were beds of flowers and trees, and the coming night, which comes so swiftly in these latitudes, brought a cooling breeze. Then his Highness gave us each a photograph of his royal person, consecrated with his royal autograph, which he wrote on the top of a marble railing. Then we strolled toward the grand hall of ceremony to take our leave. Taking leave is a solemn act in India. We entered the spacious hall where the Prince received the Prince of Wales. Night had come so rapidly that servants came in all directions carrying candles and torches that lit up the gaudy and glittering hall. An attendant carried a tray bearing wreaths of the rose and jasmine. The Maharajah, taking two of these wreaths, put them on the neck of the General. He did the same to Mrs. Grant and all the members of the party. Then taking a string of gold and silken cord, he placed that on Mrs. Grant as a special honor. The General, who was instructed by the English resident, took four wreaths and put them on the neck of the Maharajah, who pressed his hands and bowed his thanks. Another servant came, bearing a small cup of gold and gems containing attar of roses. The Maharajah, putting some of the perfume on his fingers, transferred it to Mrs. Grant's handkerchief. With another portion he passed his hands along the General's breast and shoulders. This was done to each of the party. The General then taking the perfume passed his hands over the Maharajah's shoulders, and so concluded the ceremony, which in all royal interviews in the East is supposed to mean a lasting friendship. Then the Prince, taking General Grant's hand in his own, led him from the hall, across the garden, and to the gateway of his palace, holding his hand all the time. Our carriages were waiting, and the Prince took his leave, saying how much he was honored by the General's visit. The cavalry escort formed in line, the guard presented arms, and we drove at a full gallop to our home. And so ended one of the most interesting and eventful days in our visit to India. . . .

The stars were shining out of a dark and glowing sky when my servant came into the room and said that the time had come for the train. In this country you must not expect trains at your convenience. The main object is to travel in the night. Although at home it would be almost a barbarism to keep the hours enforced upon you in India, here you take all the advantage you can of the night. The cars are built for the night, and are the nearest approach I have seen to our American models for comfort. We drove to the Jeypore station under a full starlight, as it was important we should be on our way to Agra before the sun was up. But on reaching the station we learned that some mishap had fallen the train, and we had to kill time at the station as best we could, and study the beauty of an Indian sunrise. That itself was something to see, especially with such a background to the picture as the Oriental city of Jeypore and the brown empurpled hills beyond. But the railway is a new thing in Rajpootana, and has not learned the value of promptitude. In time we were off and on our way to Futtehpoor Sikra.

It had been arranged that we should go to Agra by breaking the journey at Bhurtpoor, driving over to the ruins of Futtehpoor Sikra, and remaining there all night. The Maharajah of Bhurtpoor is a young prince about thirty years of age. His name is Maharajah Seswaut Singh. His state is small, its area 1,974 square miles, with a population of 743,710, and a revenue of between fourteen and fifteen millions of dollars a year. The Maharajah is descended from a freebooter named Brij, who owned a village, and in time made his village into a state. The fortunes of the state have not always been prosperous. It had the fortune that so often attends small states bordering on larger ones—the fortune of so disturbing the rest and dignity of the larger neighbors that robbery and annexation became necessary. Bhurtpoor was taken by the old Delhi rulers. Then Sindia came and seized it. In 1805, when Lord Lake was loose in India at the head of a small conquering army, he came upon Bhurtpoor. The town had given refuge to Holkar, a prince at war with the English, and Lord Lake attempted to carry it by storm. In this he failed, losing 3,000 men. The English compromised, and took $1,000,00 as the price of not continuing the war. The memory of that defeat long lingered in India, and was the theme of many a song and story in native bazaars. In 1826 there was a quarrel in the house

A Village—India

of Bhurtpoor. The father of the present Maharajah was seized and im-
prisoned by his cousin. The English interfered, and the result was the invasion of the state by an army of 20,000 men and 100 guns. It is difficult
to see what honest motive could have induced the Indian government to
throw so large an army into another state, but the one point not wise to
dwell upon in reading Indian history is motives. The town was invested,
the gates blown up, and 6,000 men killed in the assault, the English losing
1,000. The usurping prince was sent to Benares on a pension of $3,000 a
year. Although the avowed motive of the invasion of Bhurtpoor was to restore a prince and secure his rights, as soon as the British came into the
town they plundered it. The state jewels were taken. Over $2,000,000 from
the treasury was divided among the soldiers; the commander, Lord
Combermere, who died not long since, one of the oldest of the British generals, and universally praised as a fine type of the old-fashioned sturdy officer and nobleman, put $300,000 of the money in his pocket. The walls
of the town were leveled, and the prince, father to the present ruler, was
restored to a crown which had been robbed of its jewels, a treasury which
had been robbed of its treasure, a town which had been robbed of its walls,
a palace which had been robbed of its adornments. Considering that the
founder of the house was a good deal of a robber himself, I suppose there
was not a serious invasion of the moral law in taking from Bhurtpoor what
his ancestors had taken from somebody else. One does not like to read
these things of an English peer and an English army. But the painful fact
is that you can hardly open a page in the history of India without stumbling upon some incident that recalls the taking of Bhurtpoor. . . .

It was early in the morning and the stars were out when we drove to the
Agra station to take the train for Delhi. There is something very pleasant
in an Indian morning, and the cool hours between the going of the stars
and the coming of the sun are always welcome to Englishmen as hours for
bathing and recreation. There is no hardship in seeing the sun rise, as I
am afraid would be the case in America. The cool morning breezes were
welcome as we drove down to our station and heard the word of command
and the music, and saw the troops in line, the dropping of the colors and
the glistening of the steel as the arms came to a present. All our Agra
friends were there to bid us good-speed, and as the train rolled out of the
station the thunder of the cannon came from the fort. Our ride to Delhi
was like all the rides we have had in India during the day—severe, enervating, almost distressing. You cannot sleep, nor rest, nor read, and there
is nothing in the landscape to attract. It is not until after you pass Delhi

and go up into the hill regions toward the Himalayas that you begin to note the magnificence of Indian scenery, of which I have read and heard so much but as yet have not seen. We came into Delhi early in the afternoon, in a worn-out, fagged condition. There was a reception by troops, and the General, with Mrs. Grant, drove to Ludlow Castle, the home of Gordon Young, the chief officer. The others found quarters in a comfortable hotel—comfortable for India—near the railway station.

The first impression Delhi makes upon you is that it is a beautiful town. But I am afraid that the word town, as we understand it at home, will give you no idea of a town in India. We think of houses built closely together, of avenues and streets, and people living as neighbors and friends. In India, a town is built for the air. The natives in some of the native sections, in the bazaars, live closely together, huddle into small cubby-holes of houses or rude caves, in huts of mud and straw; but natives of wealth and Englishmen build their houses where they may have space. A drive through Delhi is like a drive through the lower part of Westchester County or any of our country suburbs. The officials have their bungalows in the finest localities, near wood and water when possible, surrounded by gardens. What strikes you in India is the excellence of the roads and the beauty of the gardens. This was especially true of Delhi. As you drove from the dusty station, with the strains of welcoming music and the clang of presenting arms in your ears, you passed through a section that might have been an English country town with gentlemen's seats all around. This accounts for what you read of the great size of the Indian cities—that they are so many miles long and so many broad. It is just as if we took Bay Ridge or Riverdale and drew lines around them, and, calling them towns, spoke of their magnitude. This is worthy of remembering also in recalling the sieges of the Indian towns during the mutiny. There is no town that I have seen that could stand a siege like one of our compactly built English or American towns. They are too large. Delhi, for instance, was never invested during the mutiny. The provisions came in every day, and the soldiers could have left any time, just as they left Lucknow when Colin Campbell came in. The defense of a city meant the defense of the fort or the palace.

There are few cities in the world which have had a more varied and more splendid career than Delhi. It is the Rome of India, and the history of India centers around Delhi. It has no such place as Benares in the religion of the people, but to the Indians it is what Rome in the ancient days was to the Roman empire. One of its authentic monuments goes back to the fourth century before Christ. Its splendor began with the rise of the

Mogul empire, and as you ride around the suburbs you see the splendor of the Moguls in what they built and the severity of their creed in what they destroyed. After you pass from the English section a ride through Delhi is sad. You go through miles of ruins—the ruins of many wars and dynasties, from what was destroyed by the Turk in the twelfth century to what was destroyed by the Englishman in the nineteenth. The suburbs of Jerusalem are sad enough, but there you have only the memories, the words of prophecy, and the history of destruction. Time has covered or dispersed the ruins. But Time has not been able to do so with the ruins of Delhi. From the Cashmere gate to the Kutab, a ride of eleven miles, your road is through monumental ruins. Tombs, temples, mausoleums, mosques in all directions. The horizon is studded with minarets and domes, all abandoned and many in ruins. In some of them Hindoo or Moslem families live, or, I may say, burrow. Over others the government keeps a kind of supervision; but to supervise or protect all would be beyond the revenues of any government. I was shown one ruin—an arched way, beautiful in design and of architectural value—which it was proposed to restore; but the cost was beyond the resources of the Delhi treasury. I have no doubt of the best disposition of the rulers of India toward the monuments and all that reminds the Hindoo of his earlier history. But these monuments were built when labor was cheap, when workmen were compelled to be content with a handful of corn, and when the will of the ruler was a warrant for anything that pleased him. So that even to a rich and generous government, conducted on English principles, the restoration of the monuments would be an enormous tax. The English, however, are not apt to waste much money on sentiment. They did not come to India to leave money behind, but to take it away, and all the money spent here is first to secure the government of the country, and next to ameliorate the condition of the people and prevent famines. The money which England takes out of India every year is a serious drain upon the country, and is among the causes of its poverty. But if money is to be spent, it is better to do so upon works of irrigation that will prevent famines than upon monuments, which mean nothing to this generation, and which might all be destroyed with a few exceptions without any loss to history or art.

And yet it is sad to ride over these dusty roads and see around you the abounding evidences of an ancient and imperial civilization of which only the stones remain. Ruins—miles and miles of ruins—on which the vultures perch. I am thinking of a ride from the Kutab to Humayun's tomb, two of the noted spots in the Delhi suburbs, and which I think was as melancholy, so far as the desolation was concerned, as any I ever saw. In Egypt the ruin is finished and you see only the sand. In the Holy Land there are the promises of an era when the temples shall rise again in honor of the Lord, and the land will flow with milk and honey. In India you see the marks of the spoiler, the grandeur that was once paramount, and you see how hopeless and irreparable is the destruction. You contrast the fertility of nature with the poverty of man, never so marked in contrast as here, where the genius of man has done so much, and where the humblest flower that blooms in the fields has a life beyond it all. You rode through a city of ruins, which once was a capital of 2,000,000, and now has scarcely 250,000. You pass earthworks centuries old, which show the lines of the early struggles between Hindoo and Moslem. You see, as you study the ruins, that most of the work, even the most attractive, was in its day merely veneering, and somehow the suggestion comes that this Mogul reign, the evidences of whose splendor surround you, was in itself a veneering—that it had no place in India, was merely an outside coating which could not stand the wear and tear of time. Men pass you with hooded falcons on their arms and ask you to buy them. A covered carriage passes and you know that the inclosure is sacred to the presence of a Hindoo lady of high caste, who is always in seclusion. The bullock cart trudges slowly along. The burden bearers pass, carrying grass or twigs, carrying burdens on their thin, lithe limbs that would shame our stalwart sons. You see men at a well pumping water in Egyptian fashion for irrigation, for domestic uses, and women carrying water on their heads in stone jars.

Beggars are everywhere, for in India begging is a perennial growth. Monkeys climb on the walls, and stare and chatter and go scampering through the trees. The skies are gray, which is rare in India, and a cold wind comes over the plain. We have so much of the sunshine that we can glory in the mist. This tomb of Humayun, for instance, is one of the ruins that even a thrifty government with pensions to pay and an army to support should protect. It is not a beautiful work like the Taj, nor a stupendous work like Futtehpoor Sikra, and the prince for whom it was built was scarcely worth remembering. It differs from the Taj, among other things, in this—that while one was a monument of the love of a husband, this is the monument of the love of a wife. It is believed that the Taj was inspired by Humayun's tomb, as the design is the same in many essentials, and the one preceded the other by a century. To have inspired the Taj is honor enough for any mausoleum, but the vastness of Humayun's tomb grows on you. You walk into a walled inclosure and over a wide courtyard, and ascend steps to a platform, from which you have a good view of Delhi in the distance and the suburbs. You enter the building, which is a series of high chambers, separated by marble walls, latticed and worked into screens. Here are eighteen tombs—modest blocks of marble, most of them without any name or design. It is known that Humayun rests here, and with him five of his royal descendants, and eleven others who were friends and councilors of kings and thought worthy of a royal tomb. But only one tomb has really been identified—the tomb of Dara, the unhappy son of Shah Ishan, brother of Aurungzebe, and treated by his brother as James II. treated Monmouth. The romance of his life ended in tragedy, and all that remains of it is the slender tomb in the mausoleum of his ancestor. . . .

It was late in the evening when we arrived in Benares. The day had been warm and enervating, and our journey was through a country lacking in interest. Long, low, rolling plains, monotonous and brown, were all that we could see from the car windows. At the various railway stations where we stopped guards of honor were in attendance, native troops in their white parade costumes and officers in scarlet, who came to pay their respects to the General. The Viceroy has telegraphed that he will delay his departure from Calcutta to the hills to enable himself to meet General Grant. In return for this courtesy the General has appointed to be in Calcutta earlier than he expected. He has cut off Cawnpore, Lahore, Simla, and other points in Northern India which had been in his programme. Then the weather is so warm that we must hurry our journey so as to be out of the country before the hot season is really upon us and the monsoon storms bar our way to China. It is a source of regret to the General that he did not come earlier to India. Every hour in the country has been full of interest, and the hospitality of the officials and the people is so generous and profuse that our way has been especially pleasant. What really caused this delay was the General's desire to take the American man-of-war "Richmond," which has always been coming to meet him, but has never come. But for his desire to accept the courtesy of the President in the spirit in which it was offered, the General would have come to India earlier. If the General had waited for the "Richmond" he would never have seen India, and from the pace she is making in Atlantic waters, it would probably have taken him as long to go around the world as it did Captain Cook. . . .

We were all tired and frowsy and not wide awake when the train shot into Benares station. The English representative of the Viceroy, Mr. Daniels, came on the train and welcomed the General to Benares. Then we descended, and the blare of trumpets, the word of command, with

The Visit to the Temple

which we have become so familiar, told of the guard of honor. The General and Mrs. Grant, accompanied by the leading military and civic English representatives and native rajahs, walked down the line with uncovered heads. The night was clear, a full moon shining, and the heavens a dome of light, which softened the landscape and seemed to bring into picturesque prominence the outlines of the sacred city. One could well imagine that Benares, the eternal city, favored of the gods, might always look as it did when we came into it. The blending of uniforms, the English officers in scarlet, the native princes in rich and flowing garments blazing with gems—on one side the line of armed men, on the other a curious crowd of Indians—all combined to make the scene Oriental and vivid. In honor of the General's coming the road from the station to the Government House had been illuminated. Poles had been stuck in the ground on either side of the road, and from these poles lanterns and small glass vessels filled with oil were swinging. So as we drove, before and behind was an avenue of light that reminded us of one of the Paris boulevards as seen from Montmartre. It was a long drive to the house of the Commissioner, but even this and the fatigue of one of the severest days we had known in our experience of Indian travel were recompensed by the grace of our welcome. A part of his house Mr. Daniels gave to General and Mrs. Grant and Mr. Borie. For the others there were tents in the garden. Although it was late, after supper we sat on the veranda for a long time, talking about India, England, and home, fascinated by the marvelous beauty of the night—a beauty that affected you like music. . . .

Under the administration of the present Viceroy, Edward George Lord Lytton,* every form of education has received an impulse, and the efforts of the government seem bent upon nothing so earnestly as upon the widest dissemination of knowledge and the training of the rising generation in English civilization. Whether the result of this policy will be to make the people more contented with the rule of Great Britain or not is a problem that excites the earnest thought of many of the English gentlemen with whom I have conversed. Education is a duty, however, and the wisest policy is what has been adopted, to spare no pains to open every avenue of thought and progress to the native mind and leave the result to Providence.

Lord Lytton left for the hills, and General Grant became the guest of Sir Ashley Eden, Governor-General of Bengal, to whose beautiful residence we removed on the afternoon of the 12th of March. Sir Ashley is one of the famous men in the British service, who has done noble work in India, and by sheer force of character and ability has risen to one of the high places in the empire. His home, Belvedere, is on the site, as I was told, of the residence occupied by Warren Hastings, when that celebrated man was the governor of India.† It is a noble building, almost suggesting the White House, and looking out upon a well-ordered park, and a lawn that

* Lytton was a morose aristocrat and novelist who thought that Grant was a drunken lout. Young was being very restrained toward a very rude man when he mentioned Lytton's flight for the hills.

† Hastings was the first British governor-general of all India, 1774–85. Returning to England, he was impeached on charges of tyranny, rapacity, and corruption and was tried before the House of Commons in a celebrated trial that lasted from 1788 to 1795. He was acquitted but was left penniless. History was to prove kinder to him.

would do no discredit to the cloisters of Oxford. In the evening there was a garden party, where we met the noted people of English and Indian race. Lord Lytton attended this feast for the purpose of taking his leave of General Grant. Before leaving he had a long and almost affectionate interview with General Grant, who thanked him for the splendor and hospitality of our reception in India. It was pleasant for us all to meet in Lord Lytton a nobleman who not only knew America in a public way, but had a familiar acquaintance with Washington City. The capital, when Lord Lytton lived there, and the capital to-day are, as the General told the Viceroy, very much changed. The Viceroy spoke of Everett and Webster and Clay and the men he knew; of ladies and gentlemen who flourished under Tyler and Fillmore, and were leaders of society, but who have vanished. It was pleasant to hear the Viceroy speak with so much cordiality and good feeling and appreciation of America, and when our talk ran into political questions at home, and party lines, it was gratifying to hear him say that he could not comprehend how an American who believed in his country could sustain any policy that did not confirm and consolidate the results of the war. Whatever the merits of the war in the beginning, the end was to make America an empire, to put our country among the great nations of the earth. Such a position was now every American's heritage, and its protection should be his first thought.

Lord Lytton's administration of India will long be remembered. I find, in conversing with the people, that opinions widely differ as to its character. It was curious to find the strong opinions that had been formed for and against the Viceroy. It showed that in India political feeling ran as high as at home. The moment the Viceroy's name is mentioned in any Indian circle you hear high praise or severe condemnation. It seemed to me that an administration of so positive a character as to excite these criticisms is sure to make its impression on history, and not fall nerveless and dead. The criticisms passed upon Lord Lytton were calculated to raise him in the estimation of those who had no feelings in Indian affairs and saw only the work he was doing. One burning objection to his Lordship was his decision in a case where an Englishman received a nominal sentence for having struck a native a blow which caused his death. The blow was not intended to kill. It was a hasty, petulant act, and the native, ailing from a diseased spleen, fell, and, rupturing his spleen, died. The courts treated the matter as an ordinary case of assault and battery; held that the native would have died anyhow from the diseased spleen, and so allowed the matter to pass without punishment. The Viceroy interfered and put a heavy hand on the judges, and all official India arose in arms. The idea of this young literary man, this poet, this sentimental diplomatist, coming from the salons of Paris and Lisbon to apply his poetic fancies to the stern duties of governing an empire in India—such a thing had never been known. How different this man from those granite statesmen who blew Sepoys from cannon and hanged suspicious characters and saved the empire. If the right, the consecrated right of an Englishman to beat a "nigger" is destroyed, then there is no longer an India. I cannot exaggerate the feeling which this incident caused. I heard of it in every part of India we visited. Even from the case as presented by the critics of the Viceroy, it seemed a noble thing to do. I saw in it one of the many signs which convince me that India is passing from the despotism of a company, who recognized no rights but those of large dividends and a surplus revenue, to a government before whom all men have equal justice, and which will see that the humblest pun-kah-wallah is as much protected as the proudest peer. When you read the history of India, its sorrow, its shame, its oppression, its wrong, it is grateful to see a Viceroy resolved to do justice to the humblest at the expense of his popularity with the ruling class.

It was at Sir Ashley Eden's entertainment that General Grant received intelligence that the "Richmond," which he had been expecting to meet him at Ceylon, had not yet passed through the Suez canal. This was a great disappointment to the General, because he hoped to have visited Ceylon and Madras. He had received a pressing invitation from the Duke of Buckingham, who governs Madras, as well as from the Governor of Ceylon; but to have waited for the steamer would have prolonged our stay for several days. The General felt that it would be unbecoming to trespass further upon the hosts who had been so kind to him, and learning that the steamer "Simla," commanded by Captain Franks, was to sail for Burmah at midnight, he resolved to visit Rangoon. This resolution left Ceylon and Madras unvisited, to our regret; but it opened a new field of observation in a country full of interest, promising to be even more interesting. We had come to India late, because of our waiting for the "Richmond," and all the Europeans in India who could go were flying to the hills. Moreover, we all felt the heat so severely that even General Grant, who is an intense and merciless traveler, indifferent to the fatigues or the hardships of travel, was counting the days until we should pass the Straits of Malacca, and find comfort in the temperate zone at China and Japan. . . .

CHAPTER ELEVEN

Burma

As they took their four-day cruise across the Bay of Bengal from India to Burma, perhaps out of boredom (or with an eye to future book sales), Young began to record his conversations with Grant. Discursive and casual, these were political conversations on the whole, covering Grant's public life, mainly from the Civil War and the presidential periods, as well as current events. Although Young submitted the transcripts to Grant for his censorship, they remain quite candid and revealing reflections of a very political man. And despite Young's pledge of high-mindedness, Grant did gossip rather a lot.

Young first asked Grant about the so-called Inflation Bill, Grant's veto in April 1874 of a bill passed in Congress that would have resumed circulation of paper money, first printed during the Civil War and then gradually removed from circulation in favor of currency fully backed by gold. After the panic of 1873, when a stock market crash had led to deep recession, their hard-pressed farming constituents had convinced the majority of congressmen that deflation made it impossible for them to repay their debts. In his veto message, Grant revealed himself to be something of a neomonatarist, certainly an old-fashioned hard money man. His position had pleased eastern creditors at the expense of western debtors, who for decades afterward referred to Grant's action as the "Crime of '73." In his parallel suspicion of purchasing silver to increase the currency and of funding internal improvements, Grant expressed an inherent conservatism deeper than that held by many in his own party.

When it came to foreign affairs, Grant expressed some of the not so latent animosity brought about by sustained contact with the British Empire. For example, he strongly disliked the recent British intervention against the Russians that had propped up the teetering Ottoman Empire. In this instance, Grant believed that the English should either have taken over from the Turks in the Middle East or permitted the Russians to do it; the British, in conjunction with the

French, would one day undertake the imperialist task, but only after the Turks had fought as allies of the Germans and Austrians in World War I.

As long as he was venting, Grant got some shots off at Napoleon III. After the Civil War, Grant told Young, he had favored conquering Mexico to chase out the French puppet regime of Maximilian. When the Americans had made threatening noises to this effect in 1866, the French had withdrawn their troops and the Mexican nationalists under Benito Juarez soon had captured the hapless Maximilian and shot him. Grant believed that he would have saved Maximilian's life and caused Napoleon's downfall had he been allowed to invade Mexico, thereby also preventing the Franco-Prussian War of 1870. Grant even admitted that he had favored the Germans in that war, not that he admired Germany but that he had hated Napoleon III and the whole Napoleonic legacy (rather than France). Not for nothing had Grant refused to visit Napoleon's tomb in Paris. And Victor Hugo had not been altogether wrong about him, either.

Rangoon was the Burmese port of call. Still in an anti-British mode, after discussing the piecemeal British conquest of Burma (which would be completed in 1885), Grant remarked on the subsequent incursion of American business interests, as if the American empire of trade could displace the British Empire of conquest.

When morning came we found ourselves still steaming down the Hoogly. We found the "Simla" as comfortable as though it had been our own yacht. There were no passengers on board beyond our own party. Captain Franks was a young and able officer, and our run across the Bay of Bengal was as pleasant as over a summer sea. The nights were so warm that it was impossible to sleep in our cabins, and we sought our rest lying about on the deck. It adds something to the felicity of travel in the tropics to lie under the stars with the universe around you. The disagreeable part is the early rising, for with the dawn come the coolies with broom and bucket to scrub the decks. This is conducive to early rising, and I think we can all say that since coming to the tropics there has been no morning when we have not seen the sun rise. But being roused at dawn was never regarded by any of us as a hardship, except, perhaps, the doctor and the colonel, whose views as to the rest and nourishment required by the human frame are conservative. But although this rising with the sun breaks awkwardly upon one's slothful civilized habits, it becomes in time one of

On the "Simla"

the pleasures of the tropics. Then, if ever, you have what cool breezes come from the sea. You are sheltered from the imperious sun. If the coolie, with his brush and broom, comes to disturb you, your own servant also comes to comfort you with a cup of tea and a morsel of toast, and the fresh morning hours are all your own, for reading, writing, and meditation.

Many were the conversations which took place between General Grant and our party in reference to the great scenes and events in which he had taken part. It was while sailing over summer seas, like the Bay of Bengal, that General Grant found opportunities for recalling and commenting upon many incidents in the recent history of America. It seems to me that I can do no better service to the historian than to throw my memoranda of these conversations into permanent shape. There are few men more willing to converse on subjects on which he is acquainted than General Grant. The charm of his talk is that it is never about anything that he does not know, and what he does know he knows well. He is never vindictive, and never gossips, and when referring to men and things in his eventful career seems passionless and just. When I was in Hamburg I made a synopsis of some of his conversations and sent them to the *New York Herald*. Some of my readers may remember the profound impression created by what became known in the newspaper literature of the time as "The Hamburg Interview." Most of our journals took it up, and for weeks the statements it contained were the themes of comment and discussion. My own humble part in that publication was not overlooked, and I was interested in the variety of motives assigned to me by my brethren in the editorial profession. It was suggested at the time that I should take part in the controversy that swayed the country—that I should soothe military susceptibilities—that I should reconcile historical differences—that at least I should explain how it was that no battle had been fought at Lookout Mountain, when perhaps the most gigantic picture of modern times commemorated the event, and how it was that Shiloh was not a defeat, after it had been determined as such by the shoal of newspaper writers who floated about the gunboats at Pittsburg Landing. So far as these criticisms were personal to myself, they did not seem worthy of attention. My office was that of a reporter, and so long as General Grant did not challenge the accuracy of what was written it was not necessary for me to speak.

It is possible, however, that in reprinting the essential parts of "The Hamburg Interview," and in adding to it very largely from my memoranda of General Grant's conversations, controversy may again arise. I will say, therefore, that before I printed "The Hamburg Interview" in *The Herald,* the manuscript was submitted to General Grant. A great deal was omitted in deference to his wishes. But I make it a rule in all my publications concerning the General, whenever I have quoted him, to ask his permission to print, and to ask him also to revise my report to see that I have quoted him correctly. It may not be uninteresting to add that it was not without reluctance that General Grant gave his consent. This arose from his dislike to appear in print. But it seemed to me that one who had played so great a part in the world's affairs should not pass away without being heard concerning events which he had governed, and which will live in history so long as American history is written. I do not claim the dignity of history for these conversations; I only claim that they represent the opinions of General Grant, and now go to the world with his knowledge and consent.

I note among our conversations one memorandum concerning his administration. "I hear a good deal in politics about expediency," said the General, one day. "The only time I ever deliberately resolved to do an expedient thing for party reasons, against my own judgment, was on the occasion of the expansion or inflation bill. I never was so pressed in my life to do anything as to sign that bill, never. It was represented to me that the veto would destroy the Republican party in the West; that the West and South would combine and take the country, and agree upon some even worse plan of finance; some plan that would mean repudiation. Morton, Logan, and other men, friends whom I respected, were eloquent in pre-

A Chat with the General

senting this view. I thought at last I would try and save the party, and at the same time the credit of the nation, from the evils of the bill. I resolved to write a message, embodying my own reasoning and some of the arguments that had been given me, to show that the bill, as passed, did not mean expansion or inflation, and that it need not affect the country's credit. The message was intended to soothe the East, and satisfy the foreign holders of the bonds. I wrote the message with great care, and put in every argument I could call up to show that the bill was harmless and would not accomplish what its friends expected from it. Well, when I finished my wonderful message, which was to do so much good to the party and country, I read it over, and said to myself: 'What is the good of all this? You do not believe it. You know it is not true.' Throwing it aside I resolved to do what I believed to be right—veto the bill! I could not," said the General, smiling, "stand my own arguments. While I was in this mood—and it was an anxious time with me, so anxious that I could not sleep at night, with me a most unusual circumstance—the ten days were passing in which the President must sign or veto a bill. On the ninth day I resolved inflexibly to veto the bill and let the storm come. I gave orders that I would see no one, and went into the library to write my message. Senator George F. Edmunds came to the White House and said he only wanted to say one word. He came in looking very grave and anxious. He said he wanted to speak of the inflation bill, to implore me not to sign it. I told him I was just writing a message vetoing it. He rose a happy man, and said that was all he wanted to say, and left. When the Cabinet met my message was written. I did not intend asking the advice of the Cabinet, as I knew a majority would oppose the veto. I never allowed the Cabinet to interfere when my mind was made up, and on this question it was inflexibly made up. When the Cabinet met, I said that I had considered the inflation bill. I read my first message, the one in which I tried to make myself and every one else believe what I knew was not true, the message which was to save the Republican party in the West, and save the national credit in the East and Europe. When I finished reading, I said that as this reasoning had not satisfied me, I had written another message. I read the message of veto, saying that I had made up my mind to send it in. This prevented a debate, which I did not want, as the question had passed beyond debate. There was only one word changed, on the suggestion of Mr. George M. Robeson.* I said, if I remember, that no 'patent-medicine' scheme of printed money would satisfy the honest sentiment of the country. Robeson thought the 'patent-medicine' allusion might be unnecessarily offensive to the friends of inflation. So I changed it, although I wish I had not. The country might have accepted the word as a true definition of the inflation scheme. The message went in, and, to my surprise, I received no warmer commendations than from the West. I remember one long dispatch from Senator James F. Wilson, of Iowa, a glowing enthusiastic dispatch. Benjamin H. Bristow also sent me a warm dispatch, and it was that dispatch, by the way, as much as anything else, that decided me to offer Bristow the Treasury.† The results of that veto, which I awaited with apprehension, were of the most salutary character. It was the encouragement which it gave to the friends of honest money in the West that revived and strengthened them in the West. You see its fruits to-day in the action of the Republican Convention of Iowa."

"Nothing by the way," says the General, "shows the insincerity of politicians more than the course of the Democratic party on the financial question. During the war they insisted that the legal-tender act was unconsti-

---

* George M. Robeson was a clever New Jersey lawyer who replaced Adolph E. Borie to serve as Grant's secretary of the navy, 1869–76.

† Grant appointed the hard money, honest reformer Benjamin H. Bristow as secretary of the treasury in 1874. During the subsequent two years, Bristow embarrassed Grant by helping Congress and the press root out corruption in the administration. When Bristow ran for the Republican nomination for president in 1876, Grant got even, and Bristow lost handily.

tutional, and that the law making paper legal tender should be repealed. Now they insist that there should be millions of irredeemable currency in circulation. When the country wanted paper they clamored for gold, now when we are rich enough to pay gold they want paper. I am surprised that our writers and speakers do not make more of this extraordinary contradiction. It only shows the insincerity of so much of our political action.

"Financial questions at home," continued the General, "are settling themselves in spite of the politicians. Wherever our friends have tampered with silver bills and inflation they have suffered. Political leaders who make these concessions will be in about the same position as those who went after Know-Nothingism at the time the country had that scare. With a people as honest and proud as the Americans, and with so much common sense, it is always a mistake to do a thing, not entirely right for the sake of expediency. When the silver bill was passed I wrote General Sherman, and advised him to suggest to the Secretary, his brother, the plan of paying Congress in silver. I made a calculation," said the General, laughing, "that it would have taken about twenty wagons to have carried silver enough to the capital to have paid the Congressmen and the employees for one month. They could not have carried their pay off except in wheelbarrows. As they passed the bill it was proper that they should enjoy its first-fruits. It would have made the whole thing ridiculous. If I had been President, and could have raised silver enough for the purpose, the Congressmen would have had silver at legal rates. The men who voted for the silver bill, like the old Know-Nothing leaders, will spend the remainder of their lives in explaining their course. Already in the West you see the reaction."

"The question of public improvements," said the General, "is one that must attract the attention of our statesmen. I have been very much impressed with what France is doing now. You see the republic has voted one thousand millions of dollars, as much as the German indemnity, to build railroads, improve harbors, and so on. This is a magnificent work. In America the mistakes we made in the building of the Pacific railway has deterred our people from going any further. If that road had been built by our own engineers, with the system of accountability that exists in the army, millions would have been saved. But because we made a mistake then, we should not oppose all plans for developing the country. I gave much thought, when I was President, to the subject of a canal across Central America, a ship canal connecting the two oceans. But, somehow, I had not influence enough with the administration to make it an administration measure. I did all I could to pave the way for it. My old friend Admiral Daniel Ammen did some admirable work. Mr. Hamilton Fish did not feel the same interest, but he did all that was necessary. There are several routes for such a canal, but the best one is that through Nicaragua. The Lesseps plan cannot succeed. I studied the question thoroughly, and read all the reports. As a young officer I crossed the continent on the Nicaragua route, and I have no doubt that it is the true one. I may not live to see it done, but it must be some day. The route through Columbia is expensive and difficult on account of the rocks and streams. The Panama route would be difficult and expensive. There would be tunnels to cut. The tropical winter rains, and the torrents that would sweep into the canal, carrying rocks, trees, stones, and other *débris,* would make the keeping of the canal in order a costly business. On the Tehuantepec route the water would have to be raised so high, by a system of locks, that it could not pay. Nature seems to have made the route through Nicaragua; Ammen collected an immense mass of information on the subject, which now is in the Navy Department. It will be found of inestimable value when the time comes. Ammen showed great ability and industry in doing this work for another generation. Mr. Fish made drafts of all the treaties necessary with Costa Rica and Nicaragua. He also considered and arranged all the questions that might arise with foreign powers as to the control of the canal, and left everything to the State Department ready for action when the time comes. After Mr. Hayes came in, I called on Mr. Evarts and spent an hour with him going over the whole subject, telling him what we had done, and explaining the exact position in which I had left the question.* I urged upon him the value of the work. I suppose, however, Mr. Hayes finds the same difficulty that I encountered, the difficulty of interesting people in the subject. But it will come, it must come. If we do not do it, our children will. The governments of Costa Rica and Nicaragua are favorable. They would be the gainers. Our capital, our enterprise, our industry would go in and make a garden on the banks of the canal, a garden from sea to sea. Coffee would be raised and other tropical crops enough for our own use and to supply other nations. It would be a great gain to the Pacific coast. When I talked to Stanford of the Pacific road, in the anticipation that his railroad interests would make him inimical to another transport route, I found that he favored it. It would divert the tea trade from China. Ammen made a calculation showing that in the carrying of wheat alone enough

---

* William M. Evarts, a notable trial lawyer disliked heartily by Grant, served as secretary of state in the Hayes administration.

would be saved to pay the interest on the eighty millions of dollars necessary to build the canal. And wheat is only one of the many products that
would be benefited. I estimate eighty millions as the maximum figure. I
counted the cost. Then I added twenty-five per cent. to the cost to cover
waste and profit, then a hundred per cent. to allow for the unusual difficulties in the way of labor in the tropics. It would aid in solving the Chinese question. California would find a place for the Chinese laborers who
are now worrying her. The more this question is studied the more our
people will see its wisdom. Public opinion should be educated so as to
press the subject upon Congressmen. The press could do no better work
than to agitate the question. The only people who would be injured would
be some of the South American States. My opinion is, it would add largely
to the wealth of the Pacific coast, and, perhaps, change the whole current
of the trade of the world."

An allusion was made to the differences of opinion that exist among a
people as numerous as the English on great questions, and especially on
the Eastern Question. "I did not know much," said the General, "about the
Eastern Question until I came to Europe. The more I looked into it, the
more I was drawn irresistibly to the belief that the Russian side was the true
one. Perhaps I should say the side of Mr. Gladstone. On the Eastern Question there is more diversity in England than elsewhere. As I was traveling
through the East, I tried hard to find something in the policy of the English government to approve. But I could not. I was fresh from England,
and wanted to be in accord with men who had shown me as much kindness as Lord Beaconsfield and his colleagues. But it was impossible. England's policy in the East is hard, reactionary, and selfish. No one can visit
those wonderful lands on the Mediterranean, without seeing what they
might be under a good government. I do not care under which flag the
government flourished, English or French, Italian or Russian, its influence
would be felt at once in the increased happiness of the people, toleration
to all religions, and great prosperity. Take the country, for instance, that
extends from Joppa to Jerusalem!—the plain of Sharon and the hills and
valleys beyond. What a garden the French would make of that! Think what
a crop of wheat could be raised there, within easy sail of the best markets!
As I understand the Eastern Question, the great obstacle to the good government of these countries is England. Unless she can control them herself she will allow no one else. That I call a selfish policy. I cannot see the
humanity of keeping those noble countries under a barbarous rule, merely
because there are apprehensions about the road to India. If England went

In a Buddhist Temple

in and took them herself I should be satisfied. But if she will not, why keep other nations out? It seems to me that the Eastern Question could be settled easily enough if the civilizing powers of Europe were to sink their differences and take hold. Russia seems to be the only power that really means to settle it, and it is a mistake of England that she has not been allowed to do so with the general sympathy of the world."

This led to a rambling talk about the countries of Europe which the General had visited. "The two sections of my tour," said the General, "which, as a mere pleasure jaunt, were most agreeable, were Sweden and Norway, and Egypt. If I were to indicate a model European trip, I would say, Egypt in the winter, Sweden and Norway in the summer. I would like nothing better than to take a dahabeeah and go up the Nile next winter. It is the perfection of winter climate, just as Sweden and Norway have the perfection of summer climate. England was of course the most enjoyable part of the trip in other respects. It was the next thing to going home. Scotland was especially interesting. I enjoyed my visit to Dunrobin, where the Duke of Sutherland lives, and also to Inverary, the home of the Duke of Argyle. I was prepared to like the Duke of Argyle from his course in our war, and I left Inverary with the greatest respect and esteem for him. I met no man in Europe who inspired a higher feeling than the Duke. I received nothing but the utmost kindness from every English man, from the head of the nation down. Next to my own country, there is none I love so much as England. Some of the newspapers at home invented a story to the effect that the Prince of Wales had been rude to me. It was a pure invention. I cannot conceive of the Prince of Wales being rude to any man. I met him on several occasions in London and Paris, and he treated me with the utmost courtesy and kindness."

"Speaking of the notable men I have met in Europe," said General Grant, "I regard Bismarck and Gambetta as the greatest. I saw a good deal of Bismarck in Berlin, and later in Gastein, and had long talks with him. He impresses you as a great man. In some respects his manners and his appearance, especially when you see him in profile, remind you of General Butler. Gambetta also impressed me greatly. I was not surprised when I met him to see the power he wielded over France. I should not be surprised at any prominence he might attain in the future. I was very much pleased with the Republican leaders in France. They seemed a superior body of men. My relations with them gave me great hopes for the future of the republic. They were men apparently of sense, wisdom, and moderation."

"I remember in Gibraltar," said the General, "talking with Lord Napier of our Mexican war. Lord Napier said he understood that there was a great deal of very savage fighting between the United States soldiers and the Mexicans, that he had read stories at the time of bowie-knife encounters and other savage performances. I told him that when we were in the army in Mexico we used to be amused at reading of the deeds of heroism attributed to officers and soldiers, none of which we ever saw. The Mexicans were badly commanded, and there was very little hard fighting during that war, at least nothing to be compared with what was seen afterward in our own. Our soldiers had only to show the bayonet at the Mexicans and they would run. As to the bowie-knife, I do not think one was used during the war. It was a pity to see good troops used as the Mexican soldiers were in those campaigns. I do not think a more incompetent set of officers ever existed than those who commanded the Mexicans. With an able general the Mexicans would make a good fight, for they are a courageous people. But I do not suppose any war was ever fought with reference to which so many romances were invented as the war in Mexico."

"When our war ended," said General Grant, "I urged upon President Johnson an immediate invasion of Mexico. I am not sure whether I wrote him or not, but I pressed the matter frequently upon Mr. Johnson and Mr. Seward. You see, Napoleon in Mexico was really a part, and an active part, of the rebellion. His army was as much opposed to us as that of Kirby Smith. Even apart from his desire to establish a monarchy, and overthrow a friendly republic, against which every loyal American revolted, there was the active cooperation between the French and the rebels on the Rio Grande which made it an act of war. I believed then, and I believe now, that we had a just cause of war with Maximilian, and with Napoleon if he supported him—with Napoleon especially, as he was the head of the whole business. We were so placed that we were bound to fight him. I sent Sheridan off to the Rio Grande. I sent him post haste, not giving him time to participate in the farewell review. My plan was to give him a corps, have him cross the Rio Grande, join Juarez, and attack Maximilian. With his corps he could have walked over Mexico. Mr. Johnson seemed to favor my plan, but Mr. Seward was opposed, and his opposition was decisive."

The remark was made that such a move necessarily meant a war with France.

"I suppose so," said the General. "But with the army that we had on both sides at the close of the war, what did we care for Napoleon? Unless Napoleon surrendered his Mexican project I was for fighting Napoleon. There never was a more just cause for war than what Napoleon gave us. With our army we could do as we pleased. We had a victorious army, trained in four years of war, and we had the whole South to recruit from. I had that in my mind when I proposed the advance on Mexico. I wanted to employ and occupy the Southern army. We had destroyed the career of many of them at home, and I wanted them to go to Mexico. I am not sure now that I was sound in that conclusion. I have thought that their devotion to slavery and their familiarity with the institution would have led them to introduce slavery, or something like it, into Mexico, which would have been a calamity. Still, my plan at the time was to induce the Southern troops to go to Mexico, to go as soldiers under Sheridan, and remain as settlers. I was especially anxious that Kirby Smith with his command should go over. Kirby Smith had not surrendered, and I was not sure that he would not give us trouble before surrendering. Mexico seemed an outlet for the disappointed and dangerous elements in the South, elements brave and warlike and energetic enough, and with their share of the best qualities of the Anglo-Saxon character, but irreconcilable in their hostility to the Union. As our people had saved the Union and meant to keep it, and manage it as we liked, and not as they liked, it seemed to me that the best place for our defeated friends was Mexico. It was better for them and better for us. I tried to make Lee think so when he surrendered. They would have done perhaps as great a work in Mexico as has been done in California."

It was suggested that Mr. Seward's objection to attack Napoleon was his dread of another war. The General said "No one dreaded war more than I did. I had more than I wanted. But the war would have been national, and we could have united both sections under one flag. The good results accruing from that would in themselves have compensated for another war, even if it had come, and such a war as it must have been under Sheridan and his army—short, quick, decisive, and assuredly triumphant. We could have marched from the Rio Grande to Mexico without a serious battle."

In one of our conversations upon the General's desire to drive Maximilian out of Mexico at the close of the Secession war, the observation was made that such a war would have had an important bearing upon the fortunes of Napoleon. "No one can tell what the results would have been in France," said the General; "but I believe they would have been very important. Maximilian's life would have been saved. If Sheridan had gone into Mexico, he would of course have saved Maximilian. We should never have consented to that unfortunate and unnecessary execution. I don't think Napoleon could have rallied France into a war against us in defense of slavery. You see that he could not rally it against Prussia. His empire, never really strong, would have had such a shock that it would most probably have fallen, as fall it did five years later, and France would now be a republic—minus Sedan. Mr. Seward's objection to my Mexican plan cost Maximilian his life and gave the emperor five more years of power. Still, Mr. Seward may have been right. War is so terrible that I can conceive of no reason short of a defense of the national honor or integrity that can justify it."

This led to a conversation upon the character of the French emperor and of Napoleonism generally. "I have always had," said General Grant, "an aversion to Napoleon and the whole family. When I was in Denmark the Prince Imperial was there, and some one thought it might be pleasant for me to meet him. I declined, saying I did not want to see him or any of his family. Of course the first emperor was a great genius, but one of the most selfish and cruel men in history. Outside of his military skill I do not see a redeeming trait in his character. He abused France for his own ends, and brought incredible disasters upon his country to gratify his selfish ambition. I do not think any genius can excuse a crime like that. The third Napoleon was worse than the first, the especial enemy of America and liberty. Think of the misery he brought upon France by a war which, under the circumstances, no one but a madman would have declared. I never doubted how the war would end, and my sympathies at the outset were entirely with Germany. I had no ill-will to the French people, but to Napoleon. After Sedan I thought Germany should have made peace with France, and I think that if peace had been made then, in a treaty which would have shown that the war was not against the French people, but against a tyrant and his dynasty, the condition of Europe would now be different. Germany especially would be in a better condition, without being compelled to arm every man, and drain the country every year of its young men to arm against France."

"Any one," said the General, "who looked at the conditions of the war between Germany and France, and who knew anything about war, could not help seeing the result. I never in my own mind doubted the result. The policy of Germany had been to make every male over eighteen years of age and under forty-five a trained soldier, enrolled in some organization. When reinforcements were required the new levies were fit for the most desperate work from the first moment of taking the field. The French policy under Napoleon was far different. The empire distrusted the people—never gave the people its confidence. The people were not only distrusted, and kept from the discipline of arms, but were rendered as unfit as possible to become soldiers in an emergency. Losses sustained by the Germans were at once replaced by men as effective as those who had been disabled. Losses sustained by the French, if replaced, were by men who were an element of weakness until they could have a few months training out of the way of a hostile force. Under these circumstances how was it possible for any one on reflection to doubt the result. There exists, and has since the foundation of our government always existed, a traditional friendship between our people and the French. I had this feeling in common with my countrymen. But I felt at the same time that no people had so great an interest in the removal of Napoleonism from France as the French people. No man outside of France has a deeper interest in the success of the French republic than I have."

"I never shared the apprehension felt by so many of our leading men," said General Grant, "as to the recognition of the Southern rebellion, as a Confederacy, by England or France, or by both. It used to be the great bugbear during the war that the Confederacy might be recognized. Well, suppose it had been recognized! It would not have interfered with Canby, or Meade, or Sherman, who would have kept on marching. I am sure I should not have drawn away from Richmond. It would not have interfered with our money supplies, as we were buying our own loans. It would not have affected supplies of men, as we did not have more than three per cent. of our army who were not full citizens when the war began. We would have gone on about the same, and ended about the same. The difference would have been with England. We could not have resisted a war with England. Such a war, under the conditions of the two countries, would have meant the withdrawal of England from the American continent. Canada would have become ours. If Sheridan, for instance, with our resources, could not have taken Canada in thirty days he should have been cashiered. I don't mean this as a reflection upon the patriotism or bravery of the people of Canada, they are as good a people as live, but facts were against them. We could have thrown half a million of men into their country, not militia but men inured to war. They would have covered Canada like a wave. Then, if you look at the map, you will find that the strategic and defensive points of the Canadian frontier are within our lines. It seems odd that England should have consented to a treaty that leaves her colony at the mercy of another country, but so it is. There is no English soldier who would risk his reputation by attempting to defend such a line against the United States. Well, England might have bombarded or occupied the Atlantic cities, or laid them under contribution. It does not do a town much harm to bombard it, as I found out at Vicksburg. If she had occupied the cities she would have had to feed the people, which would have been very expensive. If she had laid them under contribution the nation would have paid the bill, and England would have lost ten dollars for every one she exacted. She might have blockaded our coasts. Well, I cannot think of anything that would do America more good than a year or two of effective blockade. It would create industries, throw us back upon ourselves, teach us to develop our own resources. We should have to smuggle in our coffee—we could raise our own tea. It would keep our people at home. Hundreds if not thousands of privateers would have preyed upon English commerce, as English-built ships preyed upon ours. The war would have left her carrying trade where our trade was. If England were to blockade our ports, she would succeed in nothing so effectively as in cutting off her own supplies of food. America really depends upon the world for nothing. England might have sent troops to help the South, but she would have to send many more than she did to the Crimea to have made herself felt. Her soldiers would not have been as good as Lee's, because they lacked training. They would have been simply so many raw levies in Lee's army. So far as I was concerned I see no end to such an intervention but the destruction of the English power on the American continent. Other nations would have come in. The moment England struck us, she would have been struck by her enemies elsewhere. It would have been a serious matter to have made such a war, so far as English opinion was concerned. For these reasons I never feared the bugbear of intervention. I am glad it did not take place, especially glad for the sake of England. I never desired war with England. I do not want an inch of her territory, nor would I consider her American possessions worth a regiment of men. They are as much ours now as if they were under our flag. I mean that they are carrying out American ideas in religion, education, and civilization. Perhaps I should say we are carrying out English ideas. It is the same thing, for we are the same. But the men who governed England were wise in not taking an active part in our war. It would have been more trouble to us, but destruction to them. We could not have avoided war, and our war would have begun with more than a million of men in the field. That was our aggregate force when the war ended, and it was a match for any army in the world, for any at least that could be assembled on the American continent." . . .

Our days in Rangoon were pleasant. The town is interesting. It is Asiatic, and at the same time not Indian. You have left Hindostan and all the forms of that vivid and extraordinary civilization, and you come upon a new people. Here you meet the inscrutable John, who troubles you so much in California, and whose fate is the gravest problem of our day. You see Chinese signs on the houses, Chinese workmen on the streets, shops where you can drink toddy and smoke opium. This is the first ripple we have seen of that teeming empire toward which we are steering. Politically Burmah is a part of the British empire, but it is commercially one of the outposts of China, and from now until we leave Japan we shall be under the influence of China. The Hindoos you meet are from Madras, a differ-

The Grand Pagoda

ent type from those we saw on our tour. The Burmese look like Chinese to our unskilled eyes, and it is pleasant to see women on the streets and in society. The streets are wide and rectangular, like those of Philadelphia, and the shade trees are grateful. Over the city, on a height, which you can see from afar, is a pagoda, one of the most famous in Asia. It is covered with gilt, and in the evening, when we first saw it, the sun's rays made it dazzling. We knew from the pagoda that in leaving India and coming to Burmah we leave the land of Brahma and come to the land of Buddha and that remarkable religion called Buddhism. . . .

Our first visit was to the famous pagoda which rests upon Rangoon like a crown of gold, its burnished splendor seen from afar. The pagoda is in the center of a park of about two acres, around which are fortifications. These fortifications were defended by the Burmese during their war with the English, and in the event of a sudden outbreak, or a mutiny, or a war, would at once be occupied. During the Burmese wars the pagoda was always used as a fort, and now, in the event of an alarm, or an invasion, or a mutiny, the troops and people would at once take possession.* Ever since that horrible Sunday afternoon in Meerut, when the Sepoys broke out of their barracks, burned every house and butchered every woman and child in the European quarter, all these Asiatic settlements have a place of refuge to which the population can fly.† A small guard was on duty as we passed up the ragged steps that led to the pagoda. There was an ascent of seventy-five steps—a gentle and not a tiresome ascent if you looked carefully and did not stumble among the jagged and crumbling stones. On either side of the way were devotees at prayers, or beggars waiting for their rice, or booths where you could buy false pearls, imitation diamonds, beads, packages of gold-leaf, flowers, and cakes. The trinkets and flowers are given as offerings to Buddha. The gold-leaf is sold for acts of piety. If the devout Buddhist has a little money he lays it out on the pagoda. He buys a package of the gold-leaf and covers with it some dingy spot on the pagoda, and adds his mite to the glory of the temple. No one is so poor that he cannot make some offering. We observed several devout Buddhists at work patching the temple with their gold-foil. On the top of the temple is an umbrella or cap covered with precious stones. This was a royal offering; and was placed here some years since with great pomp.

Interesting, however, as Rangoon has been in its religious aspect, it was even more so as an illustration of the growth of an Asiatic colony under the rule of Great Britain. When Burmah was taken by the British it was believed that the East India Company would find it a costly and useless acquisition. Now it is one of the most valuable of the colonies, presenting a good field for capital and enterprise. Property is secure; the climate, under the sanitary regulations, as good as in any of the tropics, and labor is very cheap. The rice crop is the largest, reaching nearly 2,500,000 acres. About six-sevenths of the soil under cultivation is given to rice. Then comes tobacco, the betel-nut, and the banana. Unsuccessful efforts have been made to raise wheat, flax, and tea. Petroleum exists, although the New York brand was seen in every village we visited. There are mines of lead, iron,

---

* These forts dated from either the first British war against Burma in 1824–26 or the second in 1852. In 1875 Britain seized upper Burma from China and in 1885 would incorporate Burma as a whole into British India.

† The Indian Mutiny began in 1857, when Sepoy troops rebelled after they learned that their rifle cartridges—that they would bite open—were lubricated with beef or pig grease. One of many uprisings, the Indian Mutiny lasted two years and was the largest rebellion, although it never became well coordinated. It produced frightful racial atrocities on both sides.

copper, antimony, and tin. But as all the mines yielded in 1877 only $30,000, they must be largely developed; but they add to the resources of the province. For generations there has been a trade in rubies and sapphires, gold and silver, and one of the titles of the king is the "Proprietor of the Mines of the Rubies, Gold, and Silver." These mines are undeveloped, and there is no correct knowledge of their value. The growth of Burmah, and especially the position of Rangoon, as the commercial center, made a deep impression upon General Grant, who finds no part of his visit to Asia so interesting as the study of the resources of these countries and the possibilities of advancing American commerce. There is no subject, the General thinks, more worthy of our attention as a nation than the development of this commerce in the East. Practically we have no place in these markets. If our merchandise comes at all, it is in English ships. Americans who come to Asia see the fruits of American industry and capital, which before they enter the market must pay a tax to England in the shape of freights and the profits of English business. The whole trade is with Great Britain, British India, and the Straits Settlements. The Burmah trade embraced in one year four hundred and fifty-six vessels, while America entered and cleared thirty vessels. England has a virtual monopoly, and especially in calico prints and light silk and gauze goods. In one year this ran up to 30,000,000 yards. Clocks and watches, beads and false pearls, also form a large part of the imports. Machinery, matches, leather, salt, and silks are also principal articles. The United States sent direct only forty dollars' worth of provisions. Even the petroleum came under other flags. The exports during the same time were rice, raw caoutchouc, a little cotton, raw hides, cutch, and jewelry—not an ounce going to the United States. Rice pays an export duty, which seems to be a hardship. Of course the fact that the British government rules Burmah aids largely in the monopoly of the trade. But the ports are as free to American ships as Liverpool and Cardiff. General Grant, speaking of these facts, and of the impression made upon him by British India, said he knew of no point which offered as good an opening for American enterprise as Rangoon. . . .

CHAPTER TWELVE

Singapore, the Straits of Malacca, Siam

And so, on down the coast of the Malaysian peninsula—with a stop in Penang—to Singapore, already a significant British outpost. The incessant heat and torrential rains were getting to the Grant party, a climate that Young believed caused torpor among the Europeans who were there for a quick buck. Young commented insightfully about the laziness, pettiness, and racial condescension that characterized expatriate life, then as ever.

While voyaging down to Singapore, Young elicited a candid and even salty commentary about other Civil War generals from Grant. Of the Confederates, Grant ranked Stonewall Jackson the highest, although Grant was certain that Jackson would have met his match had he lived past Chancellorsville and Phil Sheridan had opposed him in the Shenandoah Valley. Perhaps miffed at the soaring reputation among English military commentators of his chief foe—at his expense—Grant downgraded Robert E. Lee, claiming that he had feared Joseph Johnson more as an opponent. And while praising George McClellan's character, Grant recounted some acidic memories about a major snub he had received from McClellan at the start of the war and discussed McClellan's enormous self-importance and political self-infatuation. No general ought to have tried to run a political campaign against his president that way; in contrast, Grant declared that he had been perfectly comfortable with Lincoln and Secretary of War Stanton. Grant was pretty certain who had been the best Union general, though modesty prevented him from actually saying so.

By this point, nearly two years into their voyage, the Grants were longing for home, and this feeling, compounded by the incessant heat and rain, led them to eliminate Australia and New Zealand from their itinerary. However, they did take a side trip to Siam, after being summoned there by the king himself. Chulahlongkorn was already famous as a modernizer who managed to stay on good terms with all of the European powers, especially England, while maintaining the independence of his country, almost uniquely in that part of Asia. Essentially, the

Grant party ate its way through a five-day stay in Siam, avoiding, however, the hot curries sometimes on the menu.

Singapore, the capital of the Straits Settlements Colony, is one of the prettiest towns in the East. It marks the southernmost point of our journey, for when at Singapore you are within eighty miles of the equator. The entrance to the town is picturesque. You have been sailing along the coast of Malacca for three or four days, and during your journey land has been in sight—low, shining belts of land, yellow and brown, as though baking under the burning sun. When you come to Singapore you pass island after island, and high, jutting peaks and promontories; and edging through a narrow channel, along which you might throw a biscuit, you come into an open bay, and before you, on the side of a gently sloping hill, you have Singapore. We came into the bay in the early morning, before the sun was well over the hills, and the captain had been good enough to give me warning, that I might be on deck. The bay was alive with ships, and most of them were dressed in their best bunting in honor of the General. A slight mist hung over town and bay, indicating that the rain was coming or going. We had hardly cast our anchor before our consul, Major Struder, came on board, accompanied by his daughter. Major Struder is an adopted citizen of the United States, born in Switzerland. He served in our war, and was lieutenant under General Grant at Shiloh. The reception of the General gave him great pleasure, and he told the writer, not without emotion, that he little dreamed when he saw General Grant, seventeen years ago, on that fearful Sunday afternoon, watching the pulse of the throbbing battle, that they would meet again in the Malaysian peninsula under the Southern Cross. I told the major that as we passed through life nothing seemed more surely to happen than our dreams. Mr. C. C. Smith, the Colonial Secretary, came to represent the Administrator, Colonel Anson, accompanied by the Administrator's secretary, Mr. Howard. At ten o'clock we landed. All the citizens of the town were on the wharf. The General was presented to the leading gentlemen, and was especially kind to the Chinese consul, Mr. Whampoa, a venerable gentleman, who had been very kind to Americans. We drove to the Government House, a stately building on a hill. Here the General was received by Colonel and Mrs. Anson, and by the Maharajah of Johore, a native Malay prince, who rules over the neighboring province and who came to welcome General Grant and invite him to his capital. The

Maharajah was an imposing gentleman, who talked a little English and wore an English decoration with a striking display of diamonds.

Our stay in Singapore consisted of dinners and receptions. Colonel Anson, the Administrator, made a good record in the Crimea as a gallant soldier. He governs Singapore in the absence of the Governor, Sir William Robinson, now in England on leave. There was some annoyance expressed that the General had not been received with a guard of honor and a salute, and the whole colony were agitated lest we might suppose that Singapore had been behind India in the grace and cordiality of her hospitality. But it was explained that the guns were ready, and the soldiers in condition waiting the summons, and there was to have been a noble pageant, when the English mail came in with a circular from the Colonial Secretary, Mr. Hicks Beach, directing the authorities of the British colonies to receive General Grant as a distinguished foreigner, but not with official honors. So the guns were unshotted, and the troops sent home, and our landing was as peaceful as could be. I only allude to this circumstance because every one in Singapore talked about it, and seemed to suffer from a sense of suppressed hospitality. As a matter of fact, when the matter was mentioned to the General, it seems that he had not observed the absence of the soldiers and the guns, and he expressed his pleasure that the troops had not been kept out on the dock under a tropical sun. Moreover, as was also remarked by others, the General had not come to Singapore to see soldiers and guns, but to see the people, and study the progress England was making in the development of Asiatic civilization.

But if the guns were not fired and the troops were not paraded, there was nothing lacking in the hospitality of Singapore towards General Grant. There were dinners at the Government House and a reception. There was a band which made a heroic attempt at various American national airs, succeeding only in Yankee Doodle. A medley of negro airs, arranged for a Virginia reel, was also played, under the impression that it was also a national air. As the American is supposed to be a light, giddy person, with tendencies towards barbarism, I can well see how Camptown Races, Lucy Long, and Oh! Susanna might be regarded as national anthems. It seems to me that some patriotic member of Congress, like Sunset Cox or Carter Harrison, or some other of our spread-eagle statesmen, should look into this matter and have an appropriation to furnish consular agents with hand-organs adjusted to our national airs, so that when Americans worthy of honor visit Asiatic ports they will hear their own airs, and be reminded that their banner is spangled and their country is free, and can whip all creation, and that tyrants howl and tremble before it. Then Americans would not feel, as they stand erect before the dinner-table, as an Englishman would feel if, when he drank the health of the Queen, the band broke out into Tommy make Room for your Uncle, or some other London music-hall medley. But the music was well meant and well received. Major Struder gave the General a luncheon, and made a brief historical speech, recalling Shiloh, and there were drives around the country to tapioca plantations, and so on. The Chinese consul, Whampoa, gave a luncheon. This gentleman lives in a quaint and curious house, just outside of Singapore, filled with all manner of curiosities, a house in the Chinese style, where we were entertained with splendor. The consul recalled the visit made to him by Captain Perry, when on his way to Japan, a quarter of a century ago or more, and showed the General a tinned can of green corn, hermetically sealed, which the captain had left as a souvenir of his visit, and which the consul keeps as a sacred memento.

There was also a visit to the Maharajah of Johore. The Maharajah lives in Singapore, in a pretty house, where we dined, and is waiting the building of his palace in Johore. Commander Edwards of the British gun-boat "Kestrel" placed his vessel at the disposal of General Grant, and just as the sun was up the party embarked for Johore. The trip is only four hours by sea, and the Maharajah had gone ahead to meet the General. There was no circular from Secretary Beach, and so there were guns and troops, the firing of salutes and royal honors when, about ten in the morning, General Grant landed at Johore. The state of Johore is said to contain ten thousand square miles. The town was settled by the Malays when expelled from Malacca by the Portuguese under Albuquerque. The country is a jungle; but in later years, under the rule of the Maharajah, has made a good deal of progress. The people are Malays, and speak the same language. The forest abounds in game, and if we had time, or were ambitious of distinction as sportsmen, we might have found tigers, elephants, the tapir, the hog, the rhinoceros, and the ox. There has been a good deal of emigration into Johore from China, and it is said that coffee and gamboge could be made profitable crops, and that gold and tin could be found. The policy of the present governor seems to be to act in hearty sympathy with the British. The Singapore government exercises a tutelage over him. There is no difficulty in asserting this claim, as the English have proclaimed it as a sort of Monroe doctrine for Asia that their duty is to see that neighboring native states give their subjects good government. This is the position of absolute responsibility and semi-independence occupied by the Maharajah of Johore.

Singapore is the center, the heart of the whole Malay archipelago. It is an island, the most northerly of the numerous islands that cluster about the southern shores of Asia. It was a forest sixty years ago—a dense jungle. It is distant about thirty miles from the southern coast of the continent, and separated by a strait which varies from a mile to three furlongs in width. This was known to the old navigators as the Singapore Straits, and the passage into the China Sea. The island is about two hundred and six square miles, or seventy miles larger than the Isle of Wight. The surface is undulatory, the highest point being five hundred and nineteen feet above the level of the sea. The formation is granite, with the sedimentary ores of slate, sandstone, and iron. There is a blue clay, which makes good brick and tiles, and a decomposed feldspar of granite useful for porcelain. The climate, although almost under the equator, is never very warm. One of the reports showed an average of about eighty-two degrees all the year round, and this average covers the range of from four to five degrees. There are frequent rains, but never with the violence seen in our own tropics. It rained every day that we were in Singapore; but only on one occasion—the time fixed for embarking to Siam—did the shower become a respectable summer shower as seen at home. This constant rain takes away from the hardness and intensity of the atmosphere, and we walked about when necessary with an impunity which would never have been dared in India.

While the vegetation of Singapore is luxuriant, and the unending summer clothes the island with undying green, the land is not useful in growing articles of food. Although in the tropics, cotton, sugar, indigo, and rice do not flourish. The soil is not good, and the only crops which flourish are palms and spices, which depend upon heat and moisture more than upon soil. Pepper is a valuable crop, and tapioca likewise. But both have to be nursed. The pineapple is better than anywhere else. Agriculture runs to shade trees and gardening. The town is really a commercial emporium, a house of call for all the world. . . .

It is so pleasant in the morning—and in the tropics you rise with the sun—to throw open the windows, and look out upon the beautiful landscape. You worship the sun. You worship him for the joy and life he brings, and you feel that there is something to be considered in the devotion of the Parsee, who prays to the sun. This is the land of summer. The sun is always with you. But while his presence is grateful to voyagers who only a few weeks since were under the snows of northern Ireland, or hurrying over the frost-bound plains of France, to those who live here this constant summer becomes an oppression. After the second or third summer you yield to it, and you feel your life parching out of you. You have no communion with summer as at home. You cannot go into the fields and splash through the clover, or creep into the bosom of mother earth with security and sweet content. Nature is against you. The fields are full of serpents and creeping things. The only hours you can venture out are in the early morning, or after the sun goes down. And even then miasma and malarial influences are to be dreaded. A hasty walk in the morning, or an hour or two at lawn tennis, are all that you can take for exercise, and when the rain comes, and there is rain nearly every day, even this is denied you.

If you live in this land of summer, you must pay a severe tribute to the sun. You become torpid and listless. Society is narrow. There are no amusements. A colony of Europeans, like what you see in Singapore, is a good deal like a large boarding-house at a summer resort, or a company of travelers at sea. You are thrown upon one another. Everybody's business is your business. Your life is not your own, but a part of other peoples' lives. You are in a state of attrition. If you choose to be nervous or petulant, it is at the expense of everybody around you. Then you are not living, only sojourning. Life is tinctured by gossip, and the smallest things become scandals. One part of the settlement is quarreling with the other. Nor are your associations those that ennoble and develop. Around you are races which in your heart you despise and look down upon, with whom you have no sympathy, whose customs are barbarism, whose religion is heathenism, who serve you because you have your hand on their throat. "Whenever I am with my monkey," said a European to me, "I always look him in the eye and hold a rope in my hand. If I turned my eye he might tear my arm." This is about the attitude of the European towards the Malay or the Chinaman. Those races do not respect or love, they only fear you. You are usurpers, and you are ruling them and directing their energies and their resources not for their good but for your gain. This generates indifference towards others, a tendency to tyranny in the governing, and the vices of the slave in the governed race. Human nature is not strengthened. You are in a rush to grow rich and go home. The ties of home associations are loosened, and there is a freedom of living in these Asiatic colonies that, among young men especially, produces bad results. As this is a subject of which I have seen little, and know nothing, I will not dwell upon it, except to recall the regret with which I have heard it alluded to by those familiar with colonial life.

It was while journeying in these Indian waters that we resumed our conversations. "I had a letter from Mosby," said the General, "some time ago, deprecating some attack I had made upon Stonewall Jackson. I wrote him there must be some mistake, as I had never attacked Jackson."

General Grant was asked how he ranked Jackson among soldiers. "I knew Stonewall Jackson," said the General, "at West Point and in Mexico. At West Point he came into the school at an older age than the average, and began with a low grade. But he had so much courage and energy, worked so hard, and governed his life by a discipline so stern that he steadily worked his way along and rose far above others who had more advantages. Stonewall Jackson, at West Point, was in a state of constant improvement. He was a religious man then, and some of us regarded him as a fanatic. Sometimes his religion took strange forms—hypochondria—fancies that an evil spirit had taken possession of him. But he never relaxed in his studies or his Christian duties. I knew him in Mexico. He was always a brave and trustworthy officer, none more so in the army. I never knew him or encountered him in the rebellion. I question whether his campaigns in Virginia justify his reputation as a great commander. He was killed too soon, and before his rank allowed him a great command. It would have been a test of generalship if Jackson had met Sheridan in the Valley, instead of some of the men he did meet. From all I know of Jackson, and all I see of his campaigns, I have little doubt of the result. If Jackson had attempted on Sheridan the tactics he attempted so successfully upon others, he would not only have been beaten but destroyed. Sudden, daring raids, under a fine general like Jackson, might do against raw troops and inexperienced commanders, such as we had in the beginning of the war, but not against drilled troops and a commander like Sheridan. The tactics for which Jackson is famous, and which achieved such remarkable results, belonged entirely to the beginning of the war and to the peculiar conditions under which the earlier battles were fought. They would have insured destruction to any commander who tried them upon Sherman, Thomas, Sheridan, Meade, or, in fact, any of our great generals. Consequently Jackson's fame as a general depends upon achievements gained before his generalship was tested, before he had a chance of matching himself with a really great commander. No doubt so able and patient a man as Jackson, who worked so hard at anything he attempted, would have adapted himself to new conditions and risen with them. He died before his opportunity. I always respected Jackson personally, and esteemed his sincere and manly character. He impressed me always as a man of the Cromwell stamp, a Puritan—much more of the New Englander than the Virginian. If any man believed in the rebellion he did. And his nature was such that whatever he believed in became a deep religious duty, a duty he would discharge at any cost. It is a mistake to suppose that I ever had any feeling for Stonewall Jackson but respect. Personally we were always good friends; his character had rare points of merit, and although he made the mistake of fighting against his country, if ever a man did so conscientiously he was the man."

An allusion was made by one of our party to Albert Sidney Johnson, and the General said: "I knew Albert Sidney Johnson before the war. When he was sent to Utah I had a high opinion of his talents. When the war broke out he was regarded as the coming man of the Confederacy. I shared that opinion, because I knew and esteemed him, and because I felt, as we all did, in the old army, where there was a public opinion among the officers as to who would come out ahead. In many cases, in most cases, our public opinion was in error. Braxton Bragg had a great reputation in the South. Bragg was the most contentious of men, and there was a story in Mexico that he put every one in arrest under him, and then put himself in arrest. Albert Sidney Johnson might have risen in fame, and we all had confidence in his doing so; but he died too soon—as Stonewall Jackson died too soon—for us to say what he would have done under the later and altered conditions of the war. The Southern army had many good generals. Lee, of course, was a good soldier, and so was Longstreet. I knew Longstreet in Mexico. He was a fine fellow, and one of the best of the young officers. I do not know that there was any better than Joe Johnston. I have had nearly all of the Southern generals in high command in front of me, and Joe Johnston gave me more anxiety than any of the others. I was never half so anxious about Lee. By the way, I saw in Joe Johnston's book that when I was asking Pemberton to surrender Vicksburg, he was on his way to raise the siege. I was very sorry. If I had known Johnston was coming, I would have told Pemberton to wait in Vicksburg until I wanted him, awaited Johnston's advance, and given him battle. He could never have beaten that Vicksburg army, and thus I would have destroyed two armies perhaps. Pemberton's was already gone, and I was quite sure of Johnston's. I was sorry I did not know Johnston was coming until it was too late. Take it all in all, the South, in my opinion, had no better soldier than Joe Johnston—none at least that gave me more trouble."

No features of General Grant's conversation possessed more interest than his remembrances of the war. A story was found in an American journal in reference to the General having in the beginning of his career made an unsuccessful attempt to gain a position on the staff of General McClellan, then holding a high command in the West with head-quarters at Cincinnati. "The real story," said General Grant, is this: "The war, when it broke out, found me retired from the army and engaged in my father's business in Galena, Illinois. A company of volunteers were formed under the first call of the President. I had no position in the company, but having had military experience I agreed to go with the company to Springfield, the capital of the State, and assist it in drill. When I reached Springfield I was assigned to duty in the adjutant's department, and did a good share of the detail work. I had had experience in Mexico. As soon as the work of mustering in was over, I asked Governor Yates for a week's leave of absence to visit my parents in Covington. The governor gave me the leave. While I wanted to pay a visit home, I was also anxious to see McClellan. McClellan was then in Cincinnati in command. He had been appointed major-general in the regular army. I was delighted with the appointment. I knew McClellan, and had great confidence in him. I have, for that matter, never lost my respect for McClellan's character, nor my confidence in his loyalty and ability. I saw in him the man who was to pilot us through, and I wanted to be on his staff. I thought that if he would make me a major, or a lieutenant-colonel, I could be of use, and I wanted to be with him. So when I came to Cincinnati I went to the head-quarters. Several of the staff officers were friends I had known in the army. I asked one of them if the general was in. I was told he had just gone out, and was asked to take a seat. Everybody was so busy that they could not say a word. I waited a couple of hours. I never saw such a busy crowd—so many men at an army head-quarters with quills behind their ears. But I supposed it was all right, and was much encouraged by their industry. It was a great comfort to see the men so busy with the quills. Finally, after a long wait, I told an officer that I would come in again next day, and requested him to tell McClellan that I had called. Next day I came in. The same story. The general had just gone out, might be in at any moment. Would I wait? I sat and waited for two hours, watching the officers with their quills, and left. This is the whole story. McClellan never acknowledged my call, and, of course, after he knew I had been at his head-quarters I was bound to await his acknowledgment. I was older, had ranked him in the army, and could not hang around his head-quarters watching the men with the quills behind their ears. I went over to make a visit to an old army friend, Reynolds, and while there learned that Governor Yates, of Illinois, had made me a colonel of volunteers. Still I should like to have joined McClellan."

"This pomp and ceremony," said the General, "was common at the beginning of the war. McClellan had three times as many men with quills behind their ears as I had ever found necessary at the head-quarters of a much larger command. Fremont had as much state as a sovereign, and was as difficult to approach. His head-quarters alone required as much transportation as a division of troops. I was under his command a part of the time, and remember how imposing was his manner of doing business. He sat in a room in full uniform, with his maps before him. When you went in, he would point out one line or another in a mysterious manner, never asking you to take a seat. You left without the least idea of what he meant or what he wanted you to do. Henry Halleck had the same fondness for mystery, but he was in addition a very able military man. Halleck had intellect, and great acquirements outside of his military education. He was at the head of the California bar when the war broke out, and his appointment to the major-generalcy was a gratification to all who knew the old army. When I was made Lieutenant-General, General Halleck became chief of staff to the army. He was very useful, and was loyal and industrious, sincerely anxious for the success of the country, and without any feeling of soreness at being superseded. In this respect Halleck was a contrast to other officers of equal ability, who felt that unless they had the commands they craved they were not needed. Halleck's immense knowledge of military science was of great use in the War Office to those of us in the field. His fault—and this prevented his being a successful commander in the field—was timidity in taking responsibilities. I do not mean timid personally, because no one ever doubted his courage, but timid in reaching conclusions. He would never take a chance in a battle. A general who will never take a chance in a battle will never fight one. When I was in the field, I had on two or three occasions to come to Washington to see that Halleck carried out my orders. I found that there was some panic about the rebels coming between our army and the capitol, and Halleck had changed or amended my orders to avoid some such danger. I would say, 'I don't care anything about that. I do not care if the rebels do get between my troops and Washington, so that they get into a place where I can find them.'"

A question was asked as to how the General ranked McClellan. In answer he said: "McClellan is to me one of the mysteries of the war. As a young man he was always a mystery. He had the way of inspiring you with the idea of immense capacity, if he would only have a chance. Then he is a man of unusual accomplishments, a student, and a well-read man. I have never studied his campaigns enough to make up my mind as to his military skill, but all my impressions are in his favor. I have entire confidence in McClellan's loyalty and patriotism. But the test which was applied to him would be terrible to any man, being made a major-general at the beginning of the war. It has always seemed to me that the critics of McClellan do not consider this vast and cruel responsibility—the war, a new thing to all of us, the army new, everything to do from the outset, with a restless people and Congress. McClellan was a young man when this devolved upon him, and if he did not succeed, it was because the conditions of success were so trying. If McClellan had gone into the war as Sherman, Thomas, or Meade, had fought his way along and up, I have no reason to suppose that he would not have won as high a distinction as any of us. McClellan's main blunder was in allowing himself political sympathies, and in permitting himself to become the critic of the President, and in time his rival. This is shown in his letter to Mr. Lincoln on his return to Harrison's Landing, when he sat down and wrote out a policy for the government. He was forced into this by his associations, and that led to his nomination for the Presidency. I remember how disappointed I was about this letter, and also in his failure to destroy Lee at Antietam. His friends say that he failed because of the interference from Washington. I am afraid the interference from Washington was not from Mr. Lincoln so much as from the enemies of the administration, who believed they could carry their point through the army of the Potomac. My own experience with Mr. Lincoln and Mr. Stanton, both in the western and eastern armies, was the reverse. I was never interfered with. I had the fullest support of the President and Secretary of War. No general could want better backing, for the President was a man of great wisdom and moderation, the Secretary a man of enormous character and will. Very often when Lincoln would want to say Yes, his Secretary would make him say No; and more frequently when the Secretary was driving on in a violent course, the President would check him. United, Lincoln and Stanton made about as perfect a combination as I believe could, by any possibility, govern a great nation in time of war." . . .

The principal topic of discussion during our leisure hours at Singapore was whether or not we should visit Siam. It was out of the regular route to China, and the means of communication with Singapore were irregular, and none of us, I am afraid, took any special interest in Siam, our ostensible knowledge of the country being confined to school-day recollections of the once famous Siamese twins. Moreover—and this fact I cannot as a conscientious historian suppress—there was a feeling of homesickness among some of the members of the party which found relief in studying the map and drawing the shortest lines between Singapore and San Francisco and Philadelphia. Any suggestion of a departure from these lines was received with gloom. At the same time, the burden of advice we met in Singapore was that a journey around the world would be incomplete unless it included Siam. Finally the American Consul at Singapore, Major Struder, who had met General Grant on his landing, came with a letter from the King of Siam, enclosed in an envelope of blue satin, inviting him to his capital. The text of this letter was as follows:

"THE GRAND PALACE, BANGKOK, 4th Feb., 1879.
"MY DEAR SIR: Having heard from my Minister for Foreign Affairs, on the authority of the United States Consul, that you are expected in Singapore on your way to Bangkok, I beg to express the pleasure I shall have in making your acquaintance. Possibly you may arrive in Bangkok during my absence at my country residence, Bang Pa In, in which case a steamer will be placed at your disposal to bring you to me. On arrival I beg you to communicate with His Excellency my Minister of Foreign Affairs, who will arrange for your reception and entertainment. Very truly yours,

"CHULAHLONGKORN, R. S.
To GENERAL GRANT, late President of the United States."

This letter—which the King had taken the trouble to send to Singapore, reinforced by an opinion expressed by the General, that when people really go around the world they might as well see what can be seen—decided the visit to Siam. Furthermore, a dispatch had been received from Captain Benham, commanding the "Richmond," that he would be at Galle on the 12th of April, and he estimated that he would be able to reach Singapore about the time we would return from Siam. This was a consideration, especially to the homesick members of our party, who felt that even in the tropics there would be compensation in meeting Americans, in being once more among fellow-citizens with whom you could talk intelligently on sensible subjects—Philadelphia butter, the depravity of the Democratic party, terrapin, green corn, saddle-rock oysters, and other themes to which the mind of the home-sick American always reverts in his lonely, moaning hours in far foreign lands.

A heavy tropical rain! How it rained, and rained, and rained, and swept over Singapore as we embarked on the small steamer "Kong-See" about nine in the morning of the 9th of April. Our friends—Colonel Anson, the Governor; Mr. Smith, the Colonial Secretary; Major Struder, the American Consul (who had been with the General at Shiloh)—accompanied us to the vessel, where they took leave, and at once we went to sea. The rain remained with the Singapore hills as we parted from them, and a smooth sea was at our bidding. The run to Bangkok is set down at four days, and sometimes there are severe storms in the Gulf of Siam; but fortune was with us in this, as it has, indeed, been with us, so far as weather at sea is concerned, ever since we left Marseilles. We sat on the deck at night and looked at the Southern Cross, which is a disappointment as a constellation, and not to be compared, as some of our Philadelphia friends remarked, with our old-fashioned home constellations, which shine down upon you and abash you with their glory, and do not have to be picked out after a careful search and made into a cross by a vivid imagination. The evening of our sailing, some one happened to remember, was the anniversary of the surrender of Lee—fourteen years ago to-day—and the hero of the surrender was sitting on the deck of a small steamer, smoking and looking at the clouds, and gravely arguing Mr. Borie out of a purpose which some one has wickedly charged him with entertaining—the purpose of visiting Australia and New Zealand and New Guinea, and spending the summer and winter in the Pacific Ocean.

The weather in the Gulf of Siam, which I have just been praising, is capricious. The days, as a general thing, were pleasant, but squalls and storms came up without warning, and sent movable commodities, books, and newspapers flying about the deck. In these equatorial regions one of the comforts of existence is to sleep on deck, and shortly after the sun goes down your servant pitches your bed in some corner of the deck, near the wheel or against a coil of rope. Mr. Borie was induced to buy an extraordinary machine, made in the Rangoon jail, called a portable bed, which is unlike anything civilization has ever known in the shape of a bed. It comes together and unfolds, and is so intricate that it must have been made by a Chinaman. I do not think any of us really understand the principles upon which it is constructed. But in the evening Peter and Kassim and other servants parade the bed on deck and chatter over it a little while, and it becomes sleepable. The rest of the party take the floor. The General and Mrs. Grant bivouac on the right of the wheel; the Colonel has his encampment near the gangway; the Doctor lies cosily under the binnacle, and my own quarters are in the stern, where the ropes are coiled. But sleeping on deck in the Gulf of Siam is not as pleasant as we found it in the Bay of Bengal.

On our first night out, being after midnight, Kassim came with the news that it was going to rain! Kassim has a terror of the sea—the Hindoo fear of the black water—and ever since he has been on board ship his bearing is that of one who lives in fear of some overwhelming and immediate peril. So when Kassim woke me up with news of the rain, I was not quite sure from his manner whether we were not running into a cyclone or one of those tremendous gales that so often sweep around the coasts of Asia. The clouds looked black and the stars had gone, and a few drops of rain came over the face, and the sea was in a light, easy, waltzing humor. Some of the party had already left the deck. The Doctor had fled on the first rumor, and Mrs. Grant was in refuge in the cabin. The captain was leaning over the traffrail looking at the skies. We took his counsel, and his assurance was that it was only the wind and there would be no rain. So we resumed our quarters, and Mr. Borie, who was already in retreat, with Peter in the rear, in command of his wonderful bed, returned. For what could be more grateful than the winds, the cooling winds, that sweep through the rigging and toss your hair, and make you draw the folds of your shawl around you? And there was a disposition to scoff at those who at the note of alarm from a frightened Hindoo had left the comfortable deck to sweat and toss in a stifling cabin. But in an instant, so treacherous are these southern skies, the rain came in torrents, sweeping over the deck, streaming and pouring—a fierce, incessant rain, with lightning. So our retreat became a rout, Mr. Borie abandoning his bed in great disorder; the rest of us leaving blankets, shawls, and cushions to the mercy of the tempest, and reaching the cabin in a drenched condition. This experience, or variations of it, came every evening of our trip, and the nights, which began with fresh and cooling airs, ended in rain; all of which tended to confirm some of the homesick members of the expedition that the nearest way to California was the most pleasant, and that Providence did not smile on our trip to Siam.

On the morning of the 14th of April land was before us, and there was a calm, smooth sea. At ten we came to the bar, where we were to expect a steamer—or a tug. We all doffed our ship garments and came out in ceremonious attire to meet our friends the Siamese. But there was no crossing the bar, and for hours and hours we waited and no steamer came. It seems that we had made so rapid a trip that no one was expecting us, and there we were in the mud, on a bar, within an hour of Paknam. The day passed and the night came, and at ten the tide would be high and we would slip over the mud and be at our anchorage at eleven, and up to Bangkok in the cool of the morning, always so precious an advantage in

Eastern travel. At nine we began to move, under the guidance of a pilot, and after moving about for an hour or so, to the disappointment of those of us on deck, who watched the lights on shore and were impatient for Paknam, we heard the engines reverse, we felt the ship turn back with thrilling speed, and in a few minutes heard the grumbling of the cable as the anchor leaped into the water. There was no Paknam, no Siam, for that night. The pilot had lost his way, and instead of a channel we were rapidly going on the shore, when the captain discovered the error and stopped his ship. Well, this was a disappointment, and largely confirmatory of the views shared by some of us that Providence never would smile on our trip to Siam; but the rain came, and the sea became angry and chopping, and rain and sea came into the berths, and all we could do was to cluster into the small cabin. We found then that our foolish pilot had taken us away out of our course, that we were on a mud bank, that it was a mercy we had not gone ashore, and that unless the royal yacht came for us, there we would remain another day.

About nine in the morning the news was passed by the lookout at the mast-head that the royal yacht was coming. About ten o'clock she anchored within a cable's length—a long, stately craft, with the American colors at the fore, and the royal standard of Siam at the main. A boat came to us with our Consul, Mr. Sickels, an aide of the King, representing his Majesty, and the son of the Foreign Minister, who spoke English. The King's aide handed General Grant an autograph letter of welcome from the King, enclosed in an envelope of yellow satin, the text of his Majesty's letter being as follows:

"THE GRAND PALACE, BANGKOK, April 11th, 1879.
"SIR: I have very great pleasure in welcoming you to Siam. It is, I am informed, your pleasure that your reception should be a private one ; but you must permit me to show, as far as I can, the high esteem in which I hold the most eminent citizen of that great nation which has been so friendly to Siam and so kind and just in all its intercourse with the nations of the far East.

"That you may be near me during your stay I have commanded my brother, his Royal Highness the Celestial Prince Bhanurangsi Swanguongse, to prepare rooms for you and your party in the Suranrom Palace, close to my palace, and I most cordially invite you, Mrs. Grant, and your party at once to take up your residence there, and my brother will represent me as your host.

"Your friend,
"CHULAHLONGKORN, R. S.
His Excellency GENERAL GRANT, late President of the United States."

We went on board the royal yacht in a fierce sea and under a piercing rain. There was almost an accident as the boat containing the General, Mrs. Grant, and Mr. Borie came alongside. The high sea dashed the boat against the paddle-wheel of the yacht, which was in motion. The movement of the paddle pressed the boat under the water, the efforts of the boatmen to extricate it were unavailing, and it seemed for a few minutes as if it would founder. But it righted, and the members were taken on deck drenched with the sea and rain. This verging upon an accident had enough of the spirit of adventure about it to make it a theme of the day's conversation, and we complimented Mrs. Grant upon her calmness and fortitude at a time when it seemed inevitable that she would be plunged into the sea under the moving paddle of a steamer. Even the rain was tolerable after so serious an experience, and it rained all the way up the river. Paknam was the first point at which we stopped, and then only long enough to send a dispatch to the King that the General had arrived and was now on his way to Bangkok. Paknam is a collection of small huts or bamboo houses built on logs. The river on which it is built is called the Menam, and it rises so high, especially in the rainy season when the floods come, that houses become islands, and there is no way of moving except in boats. Opposite the town is a small island containing a pagoda in which is buried the ashes of some of the ancient kings of Siam. The rain obscured our view of the river as we slowly steamed up, the distance from Bangkok to the mouth being about eight leagues from the sea. The banks were low, the vegetation dense and green, and running down into the water. The land seemed to overhang the water, and the foliage to droop and trail in it, very much as in the bayous of Louisiana.

We came to Bangkok late in the afternoon. The rain lulled enough to allow us to see at its best this curious city. Our first view was of the houses of the consuls. The Siamese government provides houses for the foreign consuls, and they all front on the river, with large and pleasant grounds about them, and flagstaffs from which flags are floating. We stopped in front of the American Consulate long enough to allow Miss Struder, who had been a fellow-passenger from Singapore, to go on shore, and the Vice-Consul, Mr. Torrey, to come on board and pay his respects to the General. Then we kept on for two or three miles, until we came to our landing in front of the International Court-House. Bangkok seems to be a city composed of houses lining two banks of a river. It contains, according to some authorities, half a million of people, but census statistics in the East are not to be depended upon. It would not have surprised me if I had been told that there were a million of souls housed on that long, shambling bank of huts and houses through which we kept steaming and steaming until it seemed as if the town would never end. All varieties of huts lined the shore. Small vessels, like the Venetian gondola, moved up and down, propelled by boatmen, who paddled with small paddles, accompanying their work with a short, gasping shout—"Wah, wah, wah." Close to the water's edge were floating houses—houses built on rafts—meant to rise and fall with the tide, and which the owner could unship and take away if his neighbors became disagreeable. Most of the floating houses were occupied by Chinese merchants, who had their vases, crockery, cloths, pottery, bamboo chairs, and fruits arrayed, while they sat squatted on the floor smoking small pipes, with no garments but loosely fitting trousers, smoking opium, I suppose, and looking out for customers. Each house has an inscription, on tinted paper, generally scarlet printed with gold—a legend, or a proverb, or a compliment. Chinese junks are at anchor, and, as you look at the huge, misshapen craft, you have a renewed sense of the providence of God that such machines can go and come on the sea. The prow of each vessel has two large, glaring, grotesque eyes—it being a legend of the Chinese mariner that eyes are as necessary to a ship as a man. Boats are paddled slowly along, in which are persons clothed in yellow, with closely shaven crowns. These are priests of the Buddhist faith, who wear yellow as a sacred color, and who are now on their way to some temple, or more likely to beg. Above these dense lines of huts and floating houses you see the towers of the city, notably the Great Pagoda, one of the wonders of the East, a mass of mosaic, marble, and precious stones, from which the three-headed elephant sacred to Siam and the transmigration of the Lord Buddha looks down upon the city, keeping watch and ward over the faithful.

You are told that Bangkok is the Venice of the East, which means that it is a city of canals. When the tides are high you go in all directions in boats. Your Broadway is a canal. You go shopping in a boat. You stroll in your covered gondola, lying prone on your back, sheltered from the sun, dozing the fierce, warm hours away, while your boatmen and other boatmen, passing and repassing, shout their plaintive "Wah, wah." You see the house of the Foreign Minister, a palace with a terrace, a veranda, and a covered way sloping toward the river. You see a mass of towers and roofs surrounded by a wall. This is the palace of the first King, the supreme King of Siam. Beyond is another mass of towers and roofs, where resides the second King. Happy Siam has two sovereigns—a first king who does everything, whose power is absolute, and a second king who does nothing except draw a large income. This second King, oddly enough, is named George Washington, having been so named by his father, who admired Americans. Finally we come to the royal landing, and we note that the banks are lined with soldiers. We learn from our consul that his Majesty has taken the deepest interest in the coming of General Grant. It is customary in Siam to entertain all distinguished visitors in a building known as the Ambassador's Palace, a fine building near the European quarter. It was here the King entertained Sir William Robinson, the Governor of the Straits Settlements, when he came last November to confer upon the King the English order of the Grand Cross of St. Michael and St. George. The reception was famous for the hospitality shown to the British envoy. But the King, wishing to do General Grant greater honor, gave our party a palace, and assigned his brother, one of the Celestial Princes, with a retinue of other princes and noblemen, as our hosts.

At four o'clock the General embarked on a royal gondola, which in the programme was said to be seven fathoms long. He was slowly pulled ashore. The guard presented arms, the cavalry escort wheeled into line, the band played "Hail Columbia." On ascending the stairs Mr. Alabaster, the royal interpreter; Captain Bush, an English officer commanding the Siamese Navy, and a brilliant retinue were in waiting. The Foreign Minister advanced and welcomed the General to Siam and presented him to the other members of the suite. Then, entering carriages, the General and party were driven to the Palace of Suranrom, the home of his Royal Highness the Celestial Prince. As we drove past the barracks the artillery were drawn up in battery and the cannon rolled out a salute of twenty-one guns. On reaching the palace a guard was drawn up, and another band played the American national air. At the gate of the palace the Foreign Minister met the General and escorted him to the door of the palace. Here he was met by the king's private secretary, a nobleman of rank corresponding to that of an English earl. At the head of the marble steps was his Royal Highness the Celestial Prince, wearing the decorations of the Siamese orders of nobility, surrounded by other princes of a lesser rank and the members of his household. Advancing, the Prince shook hands with the General, and, offering his arm to Mrs. Grant, led the party to the grand audience chamber. Here all the party were presented to the Prince, and there was a short conversation. The Celestial Prince is a young man, about twenty, with a clear, expressive face, who speaks English fairly well, but during our interview, spoke Siamese, through Mr. Alabaster, who acted as interpreter. The Prince lamented the weather, which was untimely and severe. However, it would be a blessing to the country and the people, and his Royal Highness added a compliment that was Oriental in its delicacy when he said that the blessing of the rain was a blessing which General Grant had brought with him to Siam. The Prince then said that this palace was the General's home, and he had been commanded by the King, his brother, to say that anything in the kingdom that would contribute to the happiness, comfort, or the honor of General Grant was at his disposal. The Prince entered into conversation with Mrs. Grant and the members of the General's party. The General expressed himself delighted with the cordiality of his welcome, and said he had been anxious to see Siam and he would have regretted his inability to do so. The Prince offered his arm to Mrs. Grant and escorted her and the General to their apartments, while the members of his suite assigned the remainder of the party to the quarters we were to occupy while we lived in the capital of Siam.

The evening of our arrival was passed quietly at the palace, the General and party dining with the Celestial Prince. The programme that had been arranged for our entertainment was discussed, and as we only had five days for Bangkok, one or two dinners were omitted, and visits to the temples and white elephants were massed into one day. The rain—the severe and incessant rain—streamed into the courtyard of the palace, and beat in at the windows, giving our apartments a humid, mildewed sensation. The morning after our arrival we received a visit from the ex-Regent of Siam. This venerable nobleman is a foremost man in the realm in influence and authority. He was the friend and the counselor of the late King, and governed the kingdom during the minority of the present sovereign. It was through his influence that the accession of his Majesty was secured without question or mutiny. He is now the chief of the Council of State, and governs several provinces of Siam, with the power of life and death. His will in council is potent, partly because of his rank and experience, partly because of his old age, which is always respected in Siam. Our journey to the Regent's was in boats, in Venetian fashion, and after a half hour's pulling down one canal and up another, and across the river to a third canal, and up that to a fourth, we came to a large and roomy palace shaded with trees. I observed as we passed that there were few boatmen in the river—none of that business life and animation which we had observed on landing. I was told that orders had been given by the King that the canals and river should be kept free from trading craft and other vessels at the hours set down in the programme for the official visits. As a consequence whenever we took to our boats we pulled along at a rapid pace with no

Our Residence at Bangkok

chance of collision. At the same time the river life was so bright and new and varied that we should almost have preferred it, at the risk of a collision, to the silence which reigned over everything whenever we went forth on the water.

As our boat pulled up to the foot of the palace the ex-Regent, his breast bearing many orders, was waiting to receive the General. He was accompanied by Mr. Chandler, an American gentleman who has spent many years in Siam, and knows the language perfectly. The ex-Regent is a small, spare man, with a clean cut, well-shaped head, and a face reminding you, in its outlines and the general set of the countenance, of the late M. Thiers. It lacked the vivacity which was the characteristic of M. Thiers, and was a grave and serious face. His Highness advanced, shook hands with the General, and, taking his hand, led him up stairs to the audience-room of the palace. A guard of honor presented arms, the band played the "Star-Spangled Banner," which was the first time we had heard that air in the East, all the other bands we had encountered laboring under the delusion that our national air was "Hail Columbia." As the General does not know the one tune from the other, it never made much difference as far as he was concerned, and I attributed the better knowledge on the subject in Siam to the prevalence of American ideas, which, thanks to our missionary friends, and in spite of some wretched consuls who have disgraced our service and dishonored the national fame, is more marked than we had supposed. The Regent led us into his audience-hall, and placing General Grant on his right we all ranged ourselves about him on chairs. An audience with an Eastern prince is a serious and a solemn matter. It reminded me somewhat of the Friends' meetings I used to attend in Philadelphia years and years ago, when the brethren were in meditation and waiting for the influence of the Holy Spirit. The Siamese is a grave person. He shows you honor by speaking slowly, saying little, and making pauses between his speeches. He eschews rapid and flippant speech, and a gay, easy talker would give offense. I need not say that this custom placed the General in an advantageous position. After you take your seat servants begin to float around. They bring you tea in small china cups—tea of a delicate and pure flavor, and unlike our own attempts in that direction. They bring you cigars, and in the tobacco way we noted a cigarette with a leaf made out of the banana plant, which felt like velvet between the lips, and is an improvement which even the ripe culture of America on the tobacco question could with advantage accept. In Siam you can smoke in every place and before every presence except in the presence of the King—another custom which, I need hardly add, gave the General an advantage. The Regent, after some meditation, spoke of the great pleasure it had given him to meet General Grant in Siam. He had long known and valued the friendship of the United States, and he was sensible of the good that had been done to Siam by the counsel and the enterprise of the Americans who had lived there. The General thanked the Regent, and was glad to know that his country was so much esteemed in the East. There was a pause, and a cup of the enticing tea, and an observation on the weather. The General expressed a desire to know whether the unusual rain would affect the crops throughout the country. The Regent said there was no such apprehension, and there was another pause, while the velvet-coated cigarettes passed into general circulation. The General spoke of the value to Siam, and to all countries in the East, of the widest commercial intercourse with nations of the entire world, and that from all he could learn of the Siamese and the character of their resources any extension of relations with other nations would be a gain to them. His Highness listened to this speech, as Mr. Chandler translated it in a slow, deliberate way, standing in front of the Regent, and intoning it almost as though it were a lesson from the Morning Service. Then there was another pause, and some of us found further comfort in the tea. Then the Regent responded: "Siam," he said, "was a peculiar country. It was away from sympathy and communion with the greater nations. It was not in one of the great highways of commerce. Its people were not warlike nor aggressive. It had no desire to share in the strifes and wars of other nations. It existed by the friendship of the Great Powers. His policy had always been to cultivate that friendship, to do nothing to offend any foreign Power, to avoid controversy or pretexts for intervention by making every concession. This might look like timidity, but it was policy. Siam alone could do nothing against the Great Powers. She valued her independence and her institutions and the position she had maintained, therefore she was always willing to meet every nation in a friendly spirit. Nor should the outside nations expect too much from Siam, nor be impatient with her for not adopting their ideas rapidly enough. Siam had her own ideas, and they had come down to the present generation from many generations. He was himself conservative on the subject. What he valued in the relations of Siam with America was the unvarying sense of justice on the part of America, and as the hopes of Siam rested wholly on the good-will of foreign Powers, she was especially drawn to America."

All this was spoken slowly, deliberately, as if every sentence were weighed, the old minister speaking like one in meditation. I have endeavored to give it as accurately as I can remember, because it seemed to have unusual significance and made a deep impression upon our party—the impression that he who spoke was one in authority and a statesman. After further talk the Regent addressed himself to Mr. Borie, and asked him his age. Mr. Borie answered that he was sixty-nine. "I am seventy-two," said the Regent; "but you look much older." It is a custom in Siamese, when you wish to pay a compliment to an elderly person, to tell him how old he looks, to compliment him on his gray hairs and the lines on his brow. It may have been a friendly estimate on our part, but Mr. Borie certainly looked ten years younger than the Regent. In speaking with Mr. Borie the Regent became almost playful. "You must not bear the trouble of a navy in another war." Mr. Borie expressed his horror of war, and added that

The Reception of General Grant by the King of Siam

America had had enough of it. "At our time of life," said the Regent, putting his hand on Mr. Borie's shoulder in a half-playful, half-affectionate manner, "we need repose, and that our lives should be made smooth and free from care, and we should not be burdened with authority or grave responsibilities. That belongs to the others. I hope you will be spared any cares." This practically closed the interview, and the Regent, taking the hand of the General in his own, in Oriental fashion, led him down stairs and across the entrance-way to the boat, the troops saluting and the band playing. Then he took a cordial fare-well of Mr. Borie, telling him he was a brave man to venture around the world with the burden of so many years upon him. . . .

At three o'clock on the 15th of April the King returned the General's visit by coming in state to see him at our palace of Suranrom. This we were told was a most unusual honor, and was intended as the highest compliment it was in his Majesty's power to bestow. A state call from a king is evidently an event in Bangkok, and long before the hour the space in front of the palace was filled with curious Siamese and Chinese, heedless of the rain, waiting to gaze upon the celestial countenance. As the hour came, there was the bustle of preparation. First came a guard, which formed in front of the palace; there a smaller guard, which formed in the palace yard, from the gate to the porch; then a band of music, which stood at the rear of the inner guard; then came attendants carrying staves in their hands to clear the street and give warning that the King was coming, that the street should be abandoned by all, so that majesty should have unquestioned way. Then came a squadron of the royal body-guard, in a scarlet uniform, under the command of a royal prince. The King sat in a carriage alone, on the back seat, with two princes with him, who sat on front seats. His Royal Highness our host, and the members of the household arrayed themselves in state garments, the Prince wearing a coat of purple silk. The General and his party wore evening dress, as worn at home on occasions of ceremony. When the trumpets announced the coming of the King, the General, accompanied by the Prince, the members of his household and our party, came to the foot of the stairs. Colonel Grant, wearing the uniform of a lieutenant-colonel, waited at the gate to receive the King in his father's name. The General, as I have said, waited at the foot of the marble steps, and, as the King advanced, shook hands with him cordially and led him to the reception-room. The King was dressed in simple Siamese costume, wearing the decoration of Siam, but not in uniform. Mr. Alabaster, the interpreter, stood behind the King and the General. The conversation continued for an hour—the King and the General discussing, among other subjects, the opium question and the emigration of the Chinese to America. The King lamented the fact that the opium habit was spreading among his people. General Grant urged the King, among other things, to send young men to America to study in our schools, and his Majesty announced that he thought of sending a special embassy to the American government. At the close of the conversation the King rose, General Grant walked hand in hand with him to the foot of the stairs, the band played the national air, the cavalry escort formed in line, the princes and high officers walked to the carriage-door, and the King drove home to his palace.

On the next morning there was a state dinner at the royal palace. The party consisted of the King, his Royal Highness the Celestial Prince, several princes, members of the royal family of lower rank, General Grant and party, the American Consul Mr. Sickles, Miss Struder, daughter of the consul at Singapore, Mr. Torrey the American Vice-Consul, and Mrs. Torrey, the Foreign Minister, his son, the King's private secretary Mr. Alabaster, the members of the Foreign Office, and the aides of the king who had been attending the General. The Siamese all wore state dresses—coats of gold cloth richly embroidered—and the King wore the family decoration, a star of nine points, the center a diamond, and the other points with a rich jewel of different character, embracing the precious stones found in Siam. The General was received in the audience hall, and the dinner was served in the lower hall or dining-room. There were forty guests present, and the service of the table was silver, the prevailing design being the three-headed elephant, which belongs to the arms of Siam. This service alone cost ten thousand pounds in England. There were two bands in attendance, one playing Siamese, the other European music alternately. The Celestial Prince escorted Mrs. Grant to dinner and sat opposite the King at the center of the table. General Grant sat next the King. The dinner was long, elaborate, and in the European style, with the exception of some dishes of curry dressed in Siamese fashion, which we were not brave enough to do more than taste. The night was warm, but the room was kept moderately cool by a system of penekahs or large fans swinging from the ceiling, which kept the air in circulation. . . .

CHAPTER THIRTEEN

Cochin China

The Grants then steamed off to Saigon via Singapore. On board, the Young-Grant discourses shifted again to the issues and events of Grant's presidential years. Ever conservative, Grant argued against civil service reform, discussed the Democratic Party as a near-cabal of traitors rather than a loyal opposition, considered the need for changes to the electoral college system that had led to the 1876 presidential electoral deadlock (and would next do so in the year 2000), and discussed his cabinet making and various personalities. Grant was especially pungent about John A. Logan and Horace Greeley. This rollicking discussion is far more colorful than anything found in Grant's later memoirs.

During their brief stay in Saigon, when the Grant party ventured outside the official residence of the French governor, Young found a lovely colonial French town, a distinct improvement on the backwardness of the Vietnamese people. His ambivalence concerning British colonialism extended to the French.

. . . After having been cramped up in coasting yachts, doomed to our own society, and yearning for ice, it was pleasant to be able to sweep along the broad decks of an ocean steamer, to be again a part of the world, to enter into the gossip of the ship, to unravel the mysteries of our fellow-passengers, to find out people, to discover that this was a bride and the other a duke, to meet the singing person, and the young lady with an album, and the young gentleman who had never been to sea before, and believes everything that is told him, and the idle, wicked young men who tell him everything—about whales obstructing the ship's course, about tigers springing on the deck from the Saigon Hills, and the terrors of Asia. Mr. Borie's satisfaction became enthusiasm when he learned there was ice on board, and ice enough to make an iceberg. So we settled down into a condition of comfort, for the sea was smooth and we were rapidly leaving the tropics for the north, and through northern latitudes for home.

I take the occasion of this trip to recall again some memoranda of my conversations with General Grant. I trust the reader will pardon any intrusion in my narrative of mere matters of talk, because most of our talk was in the idle hours of sea-travel. I note especially one conversation on home politics, particularly on the point so much discussed at home, as to the honesty of men in our public life. "Men in public life," said the General, "are like men in other spheres of life. It would be very hard for me to say that I knew six men in public position that I know to be dishonest of absolute moral certainty. Men will do things who are senators or members that reformers call corrupt. They will ask for patronage, and govern themselves in their dealings with the administration by their success in the matter of patronage. This is a custom, and if the reformer's theory is correct, it is corruption. And yet the men who were reformers, who turned their eyes at the sins of others, I generally found as anxious for patronage as others. Senator Charles Sumner, for instance, who is the idol of the reformers, was among the first senators to ask offices for his friends. He expected offices as a right. Of course he spoke as a senator. He had no consideration except as a senator. If he had been a private man in Boston he would never have named a minister to London. As our public men go, as our forms of government go, Mr. Sumner and other senators were perfectly honest. There was no corruption in his asking me to appoint this man and the other. They regarded executive appointments for their friends as the rewards of public life. Senator George Edmunds asked me to keep George Perkins Marsh in Italy.* The whole Vermont delegation joined in the request. Yet no senator was more independent than Edmunds, more ready to oppose the administration if he disagreed with it—and so down the whole list. It was a rule. In a government where there are senators and members, where senators and members depend upon politics for success, there will be applications for patronage. You cannot call it corruption—it is a condition of our representative form of government—and yet if you read the newspapers, and hear the stories of the reformers, you will be told that any asking for place is corruption. My experience of men makes me very charitable in my criticism of public officers. I think our government

---

* George Perkins Marsh, a noted linguist and early environmentalist, was a former Whig congressman from Vermont, who, after heading the American legation in Turkey, served as the first American minister to Italy, 1861–82.

is honestly and economically managed, that our civil service is as good as any in the world that I have seen, and the men in office are men who, as a rule, do their best for the country and the government. There is no man in the country," continued the General, "so anxious for civil service reform as the President of the United States for the time being. He is the one person most interested. Patronage is the bane of the Presidential office. A large share of the vexations and cares of the Executive come from patronage. He is necessarily a civil service reformer, because he wants peace of mind. Even apart from this, I was anxious when I became President to have a civil service reform broad enough to include all that its most earnest friends desired. I gave it an honest and fair trial, although George William Curtis thinks I did not.* One reason, perhaps, for Mr. Curtis's opinion may be that he does not know as much about the facts as I do. There is a good deal of cant about civil service reform, which throws doubt upon the sincerity of the movement. The impression is given by the advocates of civil service reform that most of the executive appointments are made out of the penitentiary. Writers who have reached years of discretion, like John Jay, gravely assert that one-fourth of the revenue collected at the New York Custom House is lost in process of collection. Of course, no reform can be sound when it is sustained by such wild and astounding declarations. Then many of those who talk civil service reform in public are the most persistent in seeking offices for their friends. Civil service reform rests entirely with Congress. If members and senators will give up claiming patronage, that will be a step gained. But there is an immense amount of human nature in members of Congress, and it is in human nature to seek power and use it and to help friends. An Executive must consider Congress. A government machine must run, and an Executive depends on Congress. The members have their rights as well as himself. If he wants to get along with Congress, have the government go smoothly, and secure wholesome legislation, he must be in sympathy with Congress. It has become the habit of Congressmen to share with the Executive in the responsibility of appointments. It is unjust to say that this habit is necessarily corrupt. It is simply a custom that has grown up, a fact that cannot be ignored. The President very rarely appoints, he merely registers the appointments of members of Congress. In a country as vast as ours the advice of Congressmen as to persons to be appointed is useful, and generally for the best interests of the

---

* George William Curtis, gentleman editor of *Harper's Weekly* and the leading civil service reformer, was long a thorn in the side of the Republican Party.

country. The long continuance of the Republican party in power really assures us a civil service reform. Mr. Hayes's administration will close the twentieth year of Republican rule. These twenty years have built up a large body of experienced servants in all departments of the government. The only break was when Mr. Johnson was at enmity with his party, and filled many offices with incompetent men. I suffered from that. Most of my early removals and appointments were to weed out the bad men appointed by Johnson. Mr. Hayes has had no such trouble. I made some removals in the beginning that I should not have done, by the mere exercise of the executive power, without adequate reason. But as soon as I came to know the politicians this ceased. I was always resisting this pressure from Congressmen, and I could recall many cases where nothing but resistance, my own determined resistance, saved good men. Take, for instance, General Christopher Columbus Andrews, former Minister to Sweden. General Andrews made an admirable minister, with a brilliant record. When I was in Sweden the king told me that he had been the best minister we had ever sent there. His record confirmed this. Pressure came to remove him, even from men who had asked his original appointment. He had been away, he was out of politics, a new man would help the party in Minnesota, and so on. I did not think the Republican party in Minnesota required much help, and I said that I did not see how, in the face of his record, I could fail to recommission General Andrews. If it had been my first term I could not have stood the pressure. These two incidents occur to me as showing how Congressional influence gave us so good a man as Marsh, and took away so good a man as Andrews. They illustrate my meaning when I say the Executive does not appoint, but register appointments. Moreover, the Republican party has never been proscriptive. Mr. Lincoln had to make many removals and appointments, but this came from the Secession movement. Mr. Lincoln was always glad to recognize loyal Democrats, and in all the departments in Washington a loyal Democrat was certain to remain. As a consequence of this policy, I suppose it is not too much to say that one-fourth, if not more, of the officers of the government in Washington are Democrats. Some of the best men in the service are Democrats. They were never disturbed. I never removed men because they were Democrats, if they were otherwise fit. I never thought of such a thing, nor does Mr. Hayes. This shows that civil service reform is growing in America, in the only way it can grow naturally—through time, through the long continuance of one party in power, and the consequent education of an experienced class of public servants. That is the only way. As for censuring a President because there is no civil service reform written in rules and books, it is absurd, for, as I have said, the President, whoever he is, is the one man in the country most anxious for the reform. Notwithstanding all that is said by the newspapers, I am convinced that our civil service, take it all and all throughout the country, is in as high a state of efficiency, and, I think higher than that of any other nation in the world."

Out of this arose a question as to the abuse which had crept into our elections, the abuse of assessing public officials for funds to carry on elections. "I see," said the General, "in some of the newspapers, that under Mr. Hayes it is a subject for congratulation that office-holders are no longer removed because they will not pay assessments for political campaigns. I never removed a man for such a refusal, never knew one of my Cabinet to do so, and if I had ever known it, I would have dismissed the officer who had made such removals. Statements like this belong to the cant of the civil service discussion, and throw doubt upon the sincerity of those who advocate the reform. I can see where our service can be amended. But every day the Republican party remains in power amends it. As to competitive examinations, they are of questionable utility. One of the most brilliant candidates before the civil service board was in jail very soon after his appointment, for robbery. The way to achieve the best civil service is, first to influence Congressmen, and induce them to refrain from pressure upon the Executive; then pass laws giving each office a special tenure; then keep the Republican party in power until the process of education is complete. As it is now, the only danger I see to civil service reform is in the triumph of the Democratic party. As it is, if our friends at home would only be candid and see it, civil service reform has been going on ever since 1861, with the exception of the end of Johnson's term. During those years there has grown up an educated, tried, and trusty body of public servants. They cannot be displaced without injury. There are black sheep now and then, failures from time to time. But the great body of the public service could not be improved.

"There is nothing I have longed for so much," said the General, "as a period of repose in our politics, that would make it a matter of indifference to patriotic men which party is in power. I long for that. I am accused, I see, as having a special aversion to democracy. People used to remind me that I voted for Buchanan, and call me a renegade. The reason I voted for Buchanan was that I knew Fremont. That was the only vote I ever cast. If I had ever had any political sympathies they would have been with the Whigs. I was raised in that school. I have no objection to the Democratic party as it existed before the war. I hope again to see the time when I will have no objection to it. Before the war, whether a man was Whig or Democrat, he was always for the country. Since the war, the Democratic party has always been against the country. That is the fatal defect in the Democratic organization, and why I would see with alarm its advent to power. There are men in that organization, men like Thomas F. Bayard,* McClellan, Winfield S. Hancock,† and others whom I know. They are as loyal and patriotic as any men. Bayard, for instance, would make a splendid President. I would not be afraid of the others in that office; but, behind the President thus elected, what would you have? The first element would be the solid South, a South only solid through the disfranchisement of the negroes. The second would be the foreign element in the North, an element which has not been long enough with us to acquire the education or experience necessary to true citizenship. Neither of these elements has any love for the Union. The first made war to destroy it, the second has not learned what the Union is. These elements constitute the Democratic party, and once they gain power I should be concerned for the welfare of the country. They would sway their President, no matter how able or patriotic. My fear of this result has always made me wish that some issue would arise at home that would divide parties upon some other question than the war. I hoped that would be one of the results of the Greenback agitation. The triumph of a Democratic party as it was before the war, of an opposition party to the Republicans as patriotic as the Democratic party before the war, would be a matter to be viewed with indifference so far as the country is concerned. The triumph of the Democratic party as now organized I would regard as a calamity. I wish it were otherwise. I hope every year to see it otherwise. But as yet I am disappointed. I am a Republican because I am an American, and because I believe the first duty of an American—the paramount duty—is to save the results of the war, and save our credit."

I remember hearing the General describe the inside history of the Electoral Commission, and of his own part in that movement. Many of the things he said belong to the history which one day may be written. To write them now would be premature. "Nothing," said the General, "could have been wiser than the Electoral Commission, and nothing could be more

---

* Thomas F. Bayard was a long-term Democratic senator from Maryland, who later served as secretary of state under President Grover Cleveland.

† Winfield Scott Hancock was a heroic Union corps commander. In 1880 he would be the Democratic candidate for president, losing in a close election to James A. Garfield.

unpatriotic than the attempt to impair the title of Mr. Hayes as fraudulent. There was a good deal of cowardice and knavery in that effort. Mr. Hayes is just as much President as any of his predecessors. The country cannot too highly honor the men who devised and carried through the Electoral Commission. Senator Roscoe Conkling, especially, did grand service in that. He showed himself brave enough to rise above party. The crisis was a serious one, and for me one of peculiar annoyance. There is something radically wrong about our manner of attaining and declaring the results of a presidential election which I am surprised has not been amended. It used to worry Governor Oliver P. Morton a great deal, and on previous occasions we had trouble about it. The simple duty of declaring who has the largest number of votes should be easily done. We should never go through another Electoral Commission excitement. This is a question which should be decided free from politics, and yet it is delayed and paralyzed from purely political considerations. History, however, will justify the Electoral Commission as a fine bit of self-government on the part of the people. I say this without regard to its decision. I would have thought the same if Tilden had been elected."

A question was asked as to whether the General had any fear of an outbreak as the result of the Commission. "That was the least of my fears," said the General. "I never believed there would be a blow, but I had so many warnings that I made all my preparations. I knew all about the rifle clubs of South Carolina, for instance, the extent of whose organization has never been made known. I was quite prepared for any contingency. Any outbreak would have been suddenly and summarily stopped. So far as that was concerned my course was clear, and my mind was made up. I did not intend to have two governments, nor any South American pronunciamentos. I did not intend to receive 'commissioners from sovereign States' as Buchanan did. If Tilden was declared elected I intended to hand him over the reins, and see him peacefully installed. I should have treated him as cordially as I did Hayes, for the question of the Presidency was then neither personal nor political, but national. I tried to act with the utmost impartiality between the two. I would not have raised my finger to have put Hayes in, if in so doing I did Tilden the slightest injustice. All I wanted was for the legal powers to declare a President, to keep the machine running, to allay the passions of the canvass, and allow the country peace. I am profoundly grateful that the thing ended as it did without devolving upon me new responsibilities. The day that brought about the result and enabled me to leave the White House as I did, I regard as one of the happiest in my life. I felt, personally, that I had been vouchsafed a special deliverance. It was a great blessing to the country—the peaceful solution I mean. I cannot see how any patriotic man can think otherwise. We had peace, and order, and observance of the law, and the world had a new illustration of the dignity and efficiency of the republic. This we owe to the wisdom and foresight of the men who formed the Electoral Commission, Democrats as well as Republicans.

"At the same time, I think," said the General, continuing the conversation, "that we should revise our electoral laws, and prevent the renewal of such a crisis. I have thought a good deal over this subject of the duration of the presidential office. I always read with interest the discussions arising out of it. These discussions have done good, and our people, with their great common sense, will come to a solution. My own mind is not clear as to which would be the best plan. The one-term idea has many arguments in its favor. Perhaps one term, without a re-election, for six or seven years would be as good as any other. The argument against a second term that a president is tempted to use his patronage to re-elect himself, is not sound. The moment a president used his office for such a purpose he would fail. It would be the suicide of his administration. It would offend the people, and array against him the public men, most of whom are dreaming of the succession for themselves, and would resent a policy they deemed to be an invasion of their own rights. There is nothing in that argument. Patronage does not strengthen a president. When you take up the question of second or third terms, and propose permanent ineligibility afterward, you are encountered with the argument that in a free government a people have a right to elect whomsoever they please, and that because a man has served the country well he should not at the end of his term be in the position of an officer cashiered from the army. What you want to avoid, it seems to me, is not re-elections but frequent elections. I think the best plan, one that would go farther to satisfy all opinions, would be one term for six or seven years, and ineligibility to re-election. Practically this would settle the question. Eligibility after an intervening term would not be of much value, for, in our country, most of the men who served one term would be past the age for election by the time another had intervened. The Swiss plan of short terms would not do for a country as large and new as ours. It is well enough for a small, ancient, populous, and highly-developed republic."

Speaking of the canvass of 1876, the General said one day: "I had only one candidate for the presidency as my successor, and that was the Republican candidate who could be elected. I took no part in the discussions antecedent to the Cincinnati Convention, because the candidates were friends, and any one, except Mr. Bristow, would have been satisfactory to me, would have had my heartiest support. Mr. Bristow I never would have supported, for reasons that I may give at some other time in a more formal manner than mere conversation. Senator James G. Blaine would have made a good president. My only fear about him was that the attacks made upon him at the time would injure his canvass. To me personally Blaine would have been acceptable. He is a very able man, I think a perfectly honest man, fit for any place; but his enemies had opened a line of attack which would have made his canvass difficult. Mr. Morton was a man of great parts, who did a grand work during the war. His course as the Governor of Indiana has, I think, never been properly appreciated. He saved Indiana to the Union. As a speaker he was most persuasive. He had the art of saying everything possible on a subject, and from that became a most effective debater. Morton would have been as good in the presidency as in the governorship. But there were two objections: his health, and his opinions on finance. It would have been difficult, I am afraid impossible, to have elected Morton. Conkling would have satisfied me, as I am fond of him and hold his great character and genius in profound respect; and, if nominated, he would have had elements of strength which neither of the others possessed. He would have been better as a candidate before the people than before the convention. Internal dissensions in New York defeated him, as internal dissensions in Illinois defeated Washburne. It looked for a time as if Washburne would be the dark horse instead of Hayes. But his friends were unwise in their antagonisms, especially to Logan. I used to reason with them about it, and try to make peace and smooth Washburne's way. Senator John A. Logan is a man who will pout and get cross, and become unreasonable; but when the time comes for action—when the party or the country needs his services—he is first at the front, and no man is more trustworthy.* I never could see why Logan's temper should interfere with his career, especially because he was at heart, and in every trial, as true as steel. These dissensions in Illinois defeated Washburne. I should have been delighted to have had Washburne as my successor. Apart from our personal relations, which are of the closest nature, I have a great admiration for Washburne. He has been my friend al-

---

* John A. Logan was a corps commander under Sherman in the West and a powerful congressman and senator from Illinois after the war, as well as the driving force behind the Grand Army of the Republic.

ways, and I am grateful for his friendship. He is a true, high-minded, patriotic man, of great force and ability. While he was in France, some of our enemies tried to make mischief between us, but it had no result. I have entire faith in Washburne, and if I could have cleared the way for him in Cincinnati I would have done so. But his Illinois friends made that impossible. I saw he could not be nominated. I did not see any nomination for Blaine, Morton, or Conkling. Bristow was never a serious candidate, never even a probability. Looking around for a dark horse, in my own mind, I fixed on Fish. Governor Fish seemed to me the man to run. Bayard Taylor said to me in Berlin that the three greatest statesmen of this age were Cavour, Gortchakoff, and Bismarck. I told him I thought there were four; that the fourth was Fish, and that he was worthy to rank with the others. This was the estimate I formed of Fish after eight years of Cabinet service, in which every year increased him in my esteem. So I wrote a letter to be used at the proper time—after the chances of Blaine, Morton, and Conkling were exhausted—expressing my belief that the nomination of Governor Fish would be a wise thing for the party, and his election, if elected, for the best interests of the country. The time never came to use it. Fish never knew anything about this letter until after the whole convention was over. Hayes was, under the circumstances, a good nomination. I knew Hayes as Congressman fairly well, and was very glad to support him. I think he is doing as well as he can, especially considering the difficulties which surrounded him at the outset, difficulties which would embarrass any administration, and which our friends should consider before they are impatient. The financial views of Mr. Hayes, at a time like this, are a blessing to the country. For that reason alone he should be made as strong as possible.

"Hamilton Fish," said General Grant, "is, I think, the best Secretary of State we have had in fifty years, unless it may have been William Marcy.* This will be the opinion of those who study the records of the State Department. He differed from Marcy and excelled him in this, that he never did anything for effect, while Marcy would often do things for effect. In this—his aversion to anything that looked like striving for an effect—Fish was so straight that I sometimes thought he leaned backwards. When I formed my Cabinet I consulted no one. The only member of it whom I informed in advance was A. T. Stewart.† Mr. Stewart had so many vast and

* William Marcy was Zachary Taylor's secretary of state.
† A. T. Stewart was a New York City department store and real estate magnate.

stupendous private interests, that I did not think it would be fair to offer him such a place without first knowing whether he could accept. I thought his genius for business would be the quality required in the Treasury, and I wanted the Treasury conducted on strict business principles. When I spoke to Mr. Stewart he was pleased. My first choice for the State Department was James F. Wilson of Iowa. I appointed Mr. Washburne under peculiar circumstances. Mr. Washburne knew he was going to France, and wanted to go. I called on him one day when he was ill. I found him in a desponding mood. He said that before going to a country like France, he would like to have the prestige of a Cabinet office, that it would help his mission very much. He suggested the Treasury. I had already spoken to Mr. Stewart on the subject, and said I would make him Secretary of State. So came the appointment. You remember John M. Schofield was retained for a time as Secretary of War. I did this to mark my approval of his course in going into Johnson's Cabinet. As a matter of fact, before Schofield accepted Johnson's offer he consulted with me, and I advised him to accept. But Schofield was in the army, and a general. Of course he could not resign a life position of so high a grade to take a political office that would last four years. And I do not think it proper that an officer in high rank should be either at the head of the army or the navy. After John A. Rawlins died,* I debated for some time between William W. Belknap,† whom I did appoint, and Fairchild, now the Consul-General in Paris. What decided between the two were State considerations. I appointed Mr. Borie to the Navy because I knew him to be an exalted character, one of the best types of Americans I have ever known; a merchant who had amassed a large fortune, and perfectly fitted for any place. If Mr. Borie had felt able or willing to undergo the labors of the Navy Department, he would have made an admirable secretary. He declined the place, and only remained for a time at my urgent entreaty. I wanted the Navy Department to go to Pennsylvania, and offered it to George H. Stuart of Philadelphia. He was a business man and could not accept. Then I asked Lindley Smith of Philadelphia. His professional engagements were too absorbing. Mr. Borie mentioned Robeson, and arranged that we should meet on an excursion I was taking to West Point. Here I made Robeson's acquaintance, and out of it came his appointment

---

* John A. Rawlins was Grant's closest aid during the war and, briefly, his secretary of war before his sudden death in 1869.

† William W. Belknap, a volunteer general from Iowa during the war, served as Grant's secretary of war from 1869 until 1876, when he was forced to resign because of a financial scandal of his own making.

to the Navy Department. After I gave the Treasury to George S. Boutwell, of course it would not do to have two Cabinet officers from Massachusetts, and Mr. E. Rockwood Hoar retired.* I have a great esteem for Mr. Hoar, and was sorry the Senate did not confirm his nomination for the Supreme Bench. I look back upon my Cabinet selections with great pleasure, and am very grateful to the gentlemen associated with me for their assistance. Boutwell went out of the Cabinet to become senator. But I think he regretted it. He told me one day that he felt homesick after leaving the administration. I was sorry to lose him. I had difficulty in inducing Mr. Fish to remain eight years. At one time he was so bent on resigning that I had selected his successor. It would have been President Andrew D. White of Cornell. Under the present administration one thing has been achieved which I admire, namely, the proper position of the General of the army. It is now as it was before Marcy, as Secretary of War, quarreled with Scott. Scott became angry, and retired to Elizabeth, leaving Marcy in command of the army. Secretaries have commanded it ever since, until now. Now it is as it should be, and as I think it will remain.

"I never knew Horace Greeley well," said the General, "and don't think I ever met him until after I was elected President. But I had a great respect for his character. I was raised in an old line Whig family, my father being an active man in the Whig party—attending conventions and writing resolutions. So that all of my earliest predilections were for Mr. Greeley and his principles. I tried very hard to be friendly with Mr. Greeley, and went out of my way to court him; but somehow we never became cordial. I invited him to the White House, and he dined with me. Greeley had strange notions about the kind of men who should take office. He believed that when a man was a helpless creature, who could do nothing but burden his friends, and was drifting between the jail and the poorhouse, he should have an office. For good men to hold office was in his mind a degradation. I remember on one occasion meeting him on the train between Washington and New York. I had a special car, and sent for him to come in. We talked all the way. He laid down this doctrine. I said laughingly, 'That, Mr. Greeley, accounts for your always pushing so-and-so,' naming one of his herd of worthless men who were always hanging about the Washington hotels with letters of recommendation from him in their pockets. He was

---

* George S. Boutwell, lawyer and congressman, served as Grant's secretary of the treasury from 1869 to 1873, when he was chosen to become a senator from Massachusetts. E. Rockwood Hoar was Grant's first attorney-general. A perfect Harvard gentleman, he remained aloof from the rest of the cabinet; Grant fired him for insufficient loyalty in 1870.

much annoyed at my personal application, although I had no idea of offending him. I don't think he ever quite forgave me for my raillery. Greeley was a man of great influence and capacity; but I think that in his latter years, at least when I knew him, he was suffering from the mental disease from which he died. He made suggestions to me, and recommendations to office, of the most extraordinary character, that he never could have conceived in a healthy frame of mind. I should like to have known him earlier when he was himself. If he had been elected President he never could have lived through his term, and the government would really have been in the hands of Gratz Brown.*

"By the way," said the General, "the indirect claims case, as presented in our case against England at the time of the Alabama arbitration, was an illustration of what those in authority are compelled sometimes to do as a matter of expediency. I never believed in the presentation of indirect claims against England. I did not think it would do any good. I knew England would not consider them, and that it would complicate our meritorious case by giving her something to complain about. When Mr. Fish prepared our case against England, and brought it to me for approval, I objected to the indirect claim feature. Mr. Fish said he entirely agreed with me, but it was necessary to consider Mr. Sumner. Mr. Sumner was at the head of the committee in the Senate that had charge of foreign affairs. He was not cordial to the treaty: we had overruled one of his suggestions—namely, that our first condition of peace with England should be the withdrawal of her flag from the American continent. That suggestion was a declaration of war, and I wanted peace, not war. Mr. Sumner had also laid great stress upon indirect claims. Not to consider them in our case, therefore, would offend him. Then if we made a treaty without considering indirect claims, they would exist as an unsettled question, and be used by demagogues as pretexts for embroiling us at some future time with England. The surest way of settling the indirect claim question was to send it to the Geneva tribunal. The argument of Mr. Fish convinced me, but somewhat against my will. I suppose I consented because I was sincerely anxious to be on terms with Sumner, as I wanted to be with all of our leading Republicans. But neither Mr. Fish nor myself expected any good from the

---

* B. Gratz Brown, governor of Missouri, was Horace Greeley's vice-presidential running mate in 1872. Greeley, of the *New York Tribune* (where John Russell Young had been his protégé in the 1860s), was for decades the most famous American newspaper editor. In 1872, he had become the Liberal Republican nominee for president, and he also had gained the Democratic nomination as an anti-Grant, clean government man. He died just after Grant's re-election.

The Environs of Saigon

presentation. It really did harm to the treaty, by putting our government and those in England who were our friends in a false position. It was a mistake, but well intended. It is a mistake ever to say more than you mean, and as we never meant the indirect claims, we should not have presented them, even to please Mr. Sumner."

On the third day of our voyage we came to the shores of Cochin-China and entered the river. Cochin-China is now a French colony, and was among the achievements of Louis Napoleon. The history of the growth of the French power is like that of European power in Asia. It began as a missionary venture, as an opening for trade, and ended in becoming a French colony. Napoleon was anxious, among other dreams, to realize a Latin empire in Asia, as the English had built a Saxon empire in Hindostan. Cochin-China had fallen under French influence in various ways—before the first slice of conquest in 1862, and the second in 1867. A

French Vicar Apostolic was in charge of the religion of the country, and the effect of this was to make annexation easy. I have not taken the trouble to inquire into the "grievance" which culminated in the invasion of Cochin-China by the French. There is no investigation more unprofitable than this inquiry into the causes of the invasion of Eastern powers by the Western. The causes are the same. The Western powers want territory and glory, military and naval opportunities, and the rest comes. There is a breathing spell at home, in home affairs, and a raid into the East is practice for the troops, practice and discipline. Behind Napoleon's venture was the overmastering ambition of his house; and I suppose the French would have gone on and on until they had scissored off a good remnant of the Chinese empire, but for the European and American complications. What we know of the Cochin-Chinese before their absorption is, that they were a docile people, of a lower grade than Chinese or Siamese. They seem to have had no delicacy in their lives. Woman was reduced into even a lower scale than that assigned to her in the East. The rich man made her a toy, the poor man a slave. In the arts their knowledge was elementary. Yet their reputation was not always thus. Camoens in the *Lusiad*, who wrote from a personal knowledge of the East, makes a complimentary reference to Cochin-China:

> "Chiampa there her fragrant coast extends,
> There Cochin-China's cultured land ascends,
> From Annam Bay begins the ancient reign
> Of China's beauteous art-adorned domain.
> Wide from the burning to the frozen skies,
> O'erflowed with wealth the potent empire lies."

This was written more than three hundred years ago. But those who saw Cochin-China with other than a poet's eyes found the people in the elementary stages of culture. I should think there was about the same difference between a Cochin-Chinaman and a Chinaman proper, as between a Mexican and a Yankee. Chaigneau, a Frenchman who held office under the old government, and was one of the pioneers of French influence, says of the genius of the people: "You find goldsmiths, blacksmiths, carpenters, joiners, but none of their arts have risen above mediocrity. They have some knowledge of the art of tempering iron and steel, but their tools are either too brittle or too soft. They work better in copper, because the metal is always prepared for them by the Chinese." Chinese manners had impressed the country. The calendar was Chinese, and the coin an imitation of Chinese coin. The religion is the same, Buddhism, and the morals of Confucius. There was none of the pomp and barbaric splendor in the temples that we saw in the Buddhist temples of Burmah and Siam. In these Chinese countries the lower classes are Buddhists, the upper classes followers of Confucius—which means orthodoxy tempered with a discreet skepticism. Buddhism in Cochin-China means a moral life as the priests dictate. The gospel of Confucius is a moral life as your conscience dictates. The customs of the people, marriage, funeral ceremonies, the adoration of ancestors, the observance of festivals and eras, are based on the Chinese canons. The King reigned in what was called a patriarchal despotism. He was absolute and supreme. The King lived apart, and made himself sacred and unapproachable like the Chinese emperor. Torture was allowed in the administration of justice. Flogging was a cherished institution. The police carried their bamboo staffs, and kept order by flogging the people. Christianity made its way during that marvelous movement for the conversion of Asia, begun by Ignatius Loyola in the sixteenth century. A Spanish priest planted the cross in 1583. In a generation or two the French came and strengthened the cross. Then came a prince who persecuted the Christians and drove out the priests. But the cross was succeeded by the sword, and now Cochin-China is as much a province of France as Champagne or Algeria.

Saigon is about forty miles from the sea, and you approach it through a series of rivers, which interlace the soil, and break and twist and bend, until the map looks like a demonstration in anatomy of the alimentary functions of the body. We passed Cape Saint Jacques after luncheon, and a boat came from the shore with a telegram from Admiral Lafond, the Governor-General, to the General, asking him to be his guest at the Government House. We sailed up the rivers until the sun was going down, and we saw the masts of the shipping at the wharves, and the spires of Saigon. As we were quietly sailing along, sitting on the deck and looking out upon the dense, green tropical landscape, growing richer and denser under the flushing rays of the descending sun, we heard the snapping of a chain, and the vessel began to reel around in the channel as though it had fallen under the influence of liquor, and turned its prow to the shore. In a few minutes the nose of the ship was buried in the soft, black mud, the engines were stopped, and then we knew that the tiller-chains had broken and the helm was helpless. There were hoarse cries of command, and sailors hurrying hither and thither, and the crew became a mob. You note among the French that in times of excitement and danger they lose self-possession.

Some of the sailors broke into tears, to the annoyance of the captain, who made the fine philosophical observation, that when you were in danger you should possess yourself with a grand calm, and if you had to go down, go down like gentlemen. There was no denying this dogma, and we were in a position to discuss it calmly, because we were entirely out of danger, and if the worst came to the worst, we could all walk ashore from the side of the vessel. The incident would have been a serious one had our tiller-chains snapped a quarter of an hour later. We should then have been among the shipping, and our heavy vessel would have swung around like a battering-ram, and destroyed the smaller craft. But all is well that ends well. Our chains were mended, and after a couple of hours' delay our vessel was at her wharf, and the General and Mrs. Grant went ashore to the Government House. General Grant remained in Saigon during the stay of the steamer, and was entertained at dinner by the Governor-General. There was a reception in his honor, at which all the European residents attended; and after the reception the General drove back to the steamer, which sailed at daybreak. It was interesting to see in Saigon an illustration of what the French have been doing in Asia. The town does great credit to France, and is one of the most beautiful we have seen. The streets are arranged in Parisian style, and there was just a touch of Paris that was almost plaintive in the small cafés, before which the residents sat and drank beer. The management of the colony is prosperous and yields a revenue to France.

CHAPTER FOURTEEN

Hong Kong

During the four-day trip from Saigon to Hong Kong at the end of April 1879, Grant regaled Young with analyses of various Civil War battles and with candid and sometimes biting recollections of other Union generals during the war. Most of the praise was for Sheridan and Sherman—although Grant believed that each had had his shortcomings in the patience department—and Grant's analysis of some of the others was rather more telling, especially when he discussed the vile battlefield temper of George G. Meade. Grant was quite kind to some whose reputations had sunk since the war, being in this sense more generous of spirit than were many of the memoir-writing former generals already scribbling, including Sherman. Grant added an insightful analysis of the role of luck in war and reputation making.

On the 27th of April we left our moorings at Saigon, and reached the open sea at breakfast time. The heat was very severe, and we began—all of us, I think—to feel the effects of continued life in the tropics; but as we approached Hong-Kong a cool breeze from the north gave us great relief. An interesting feature of the trip was the opportunity of meeting that distinguished official in the Chinese service, the Honorable Robert Hart, Inspector of Customs in China. Mr. Hart, although a young man, has gained a world-wide fame, and is perhaps one of the best-informed Europeans living as to the resources of the Chinese Empire, and the manners and customs of the Chinese people. There were many conversations between General Grant and Mr. Hart about China, and we could not but be grateful for the advantage that befell us in the experience and ability of our friend and companion. Our trip to Hong-Kong took us the better part of four days. I will not dwell upon the incidents of sea-life, because it was a calm, tranquil journey; but if my readers will permit me I will take advantage of our voyage to resume the summary of my conversations with General Grant. We were talking one evening of Mr. Edwin B. Stanton, the Secretary of War.

"The first time I saw Mr. Stanton," said General Grant, "was in the West. I had come from Cairo, had reached Indianapolis, changed cars for Louisville, and was just on the point of starting, when a messenger informed me that Mr. Stanton and Governor John H. Brough of Ohio had just arrived at the station from another direction. Mr. Stanton immediately joined me, and we went on to Louisville together. He gave me my new command, to take the army and relieve William S. Rosecrans. Stanton being a little fatigued went to bed, while I went to the theater. As I was strolling back messengers began to hail me. Stanton was anxious to see me as something terrible had happened. I hastened to the Secretary, not knowing what had taken place. On the way I reproached myself with having attended the theater, while there was no knowing what terrible things had happened in my absence. When I reached Stanton's room, I found the Secretary in his night garments in great distress. He had received a dispatch from the Assistant Secretary of War telling him that Rosecrans had given orders to his army to retreat, and that such a retreat would be disastrous not only to that campaign but to the Union. I saw the situation at once, and wrote several dispatches. My first was a dispatch to General Rosecrans relieving him of his command and taking command of the army myself. My second dispatch was to General George H. Thomas, directing him to take command of the army until I reached head-quarters, and also ordering General Thomas to hold his position at any and all hazards against any force. A reply came from General Thomas that he would hold his position until he and his whole army starved. I hurried down to the front, and on my way at one of the stations met Rosecrans. He was very cheerful, and seemed as though a great weight had been lifted off his mind, and showed none of the feeling which might have been expected in meeting the general who had been directed to supersede him. I remember he was very fluent and eager in telling me what I should do when I reached the army. When I arrived at head-quarters, I found the army in a sad condition. The men were badly fed and badly clothed. We had no communications open for supplies. Cattle had to be driven a long way over the mountains, and were so thin when they came into the lines that the soldiers used to call it 'beef dried on the hoof.' I opened communications with our supplies, or, as they called it, opened the 'cracker lines.' Rosecrans's plan, which was checked before put in execution by my order, would have been most disastrous—nothing could have been more fatal. He would have lost his guns and his trains, and Bragg would have taken Nashville. By opening our lines, and feeding our men, and giving them good clothing, our army was put into good condition. Then, when Sherman reached me, I attacked Bragg, and out of that attack came Mission Ridge."

I recall many conversations with General Grant, in reference to the various officers who held high commands in our war, and the surprising changes of fortune in the way of reputation. "There were a few officers," said the General, "when the war broke out, to whom we who had been in the army looked for success and high rank—among them Rosecrans, Simon B. Buckner, McClellan, Charles P. Stone, McDowell, Don Carlos Buell. I felt sure that each of these men would gain the highest commands. Rosecrans was a great disappointment to us all—to me especially. Stone's case was always a mystery, and I think a great wrong was committed.

"I knew Stone at school. I have always regarded him as very good, a very able and a perfectly loyal man, but a man who has had three or four severe and surprising reverses of fortune. After the arrest of Stone, and his treatment, his military career in our war was destroyed. I believe if Stone had had a chance he would have made his mark in the war. Irvin McDowell was also the victim of what I suppose we should call ill luck. You will remember people called him a drunkard and a traitor. Well, he never drank a drop of liquor in his life, and a more loyal man never lived. I have the greatest respect for McDowell's accomplishments and character, and I was glad to make him major-general. The country owed him that, if only as an atonement for its injustice toward him. But McDowell never was what you would call a popular man. He was never so in the army nor at West Point. Yet I could never understand it, for no one could know McDowell without liking him. His career is one of the surprising things in the war. So is Buell's. Buell does not like me, I am afraid, but I have always borne my testimony to his perfect loyalty and his ability. Buell is a man who would have carried out loyally every order he received, and I think he had genius enough for the highest commands; but, somehow, he fell under a cloud.

"The trouble with many of our generals in the beginning," said the General, "was that they did not believe in the war. I mean did not have that complete assurance in success which belongs to good generalship. They had views about slavery, protecting rebel property, State rights— political views that interfered with their judgments. Now I do not mean to say they were disloyal. A soldier had as good a right to his opinions as

any other citizen, and these men were as loyal as any men in the Union—
would have died for the Union—but their opinions made them lukewarm,
and many failures came from that. In some cases it was temperament.
There is Gouverner K. Warren, whose case may be regarded as a hard one.
Warren had risen to one of the highest commands in the army, and was removed on the field of battle, and in the last battle of the war. Yet it could
not be helped. Warren is a good soldier and a good man, trained in the
art of war. But, as a general, if you gave him an order he would not act until
he knew what the other corps would do. Instead of obeying—and knowing that the power which was guiding him would guide the others—he
would hesitate and inquire, and want to debate. It was this quality which
led to our disaster at the mine explosion before Petersburg. If Warren had
obeyed orders we would have broken Lee's army in two and taken Petersburg. But when he should have been in the works he was worrying over
what other corps would do. So the chance was lost. I should have relieved
Warren then, but I did not like to injure an officer of so high rank for what
was an error of judgment. But at Five Forks it was different. There was no
time to think of rank or persons' feelings, and I told Sheridan to relieve
Warren if he at all failed him. Sheridan did so, and no one regretted the
necessity more than I did.

"So far as the war is concerned," said the General, "I think history will
more than approve the places given to Sherman and Sheridan. Sherman
I have known for thirty-five years. During that time there never was but one
cloud over our friendship, and that," said the General, laughing, "lasted
about three weeks. When Sherman's book came out, General Henry Van
Ness Boynton, the correspondent, printed some letters about it. In these
Sherman was made to disparage his comrades, and to disparage me especially. I cannot tell you how much I was shocked. But there were the letters
and the extracts. I could not believe it in Sherman, the man whom I had
always found so true and knightly, more anxious to honor others than win
honor for himself. So I sent for the book and resolved to read it over, with
paper and pencil, and make careful notes, and in justice to my comrades
and myself prepare a reply. I do not think I ever ventured upon a more
painful duty. I was some time about it. I was moving to Long Branch. I had
official duties, and I am a slow reader. Then I missed the books when I
reached the Branch, and had to send for them. So it was three weeks before I was through. During these weeks," replied the General laughing, "I
did not see Sherman, and I am glad I did not. My mind was so set by Boynton's extracts that I should certainly have been cold to him. But when I fin-

ished the book, I found that I approved every word; that, apart from a few mistakes that any writer would make in so voluminous a work, it was a true book, an honorable book, creditable to Sherman, just to his companions— to myself particularly so—just such a book as I expected Sherman would write. Then it was accurate, because Sherman keeps a diary, and he compiled the book from notes made at the time. Then he is a very accurate man. You cannot imagine how pleased I was, for my respect and affection for Sherman were so great that I look on these three weeks as among the most painful in my remembrance. I wrote Sherman my opinion of the book. I told him the only points I objected to were his criticisms upon some of our civil soldiers, like Logan and Blair. As a matter of fact, there were in the army no two men more loyal than John A. Logan and Frank Blair. I knew that Sherman did not mean to disparage either of them, and that he wrote hastily. Logan did a great work for the Union in bringing Egypt out of the Confederacy, which he did;* and he was an admirable soldier, and is, as he always has been, an honorable, true man—a perfectly just and fair man, whose record in the army was brilliant. Blair also did a work in the war entitling him to the gratitude of every Northern man and the respect of every soldier. Sherman did not do justice to Ambrose E. Burnside; Burnside's fine character has sustained him in the respect and esteem of all who knew him through the most surprising reverses of fortune. There was a mistake in Sherman's book as to the suggestion of the Fort Henry and Donelson campaign coming from Halleck. But these are mistakes natural to a large book, which Sherman would be the last to commit and the first to correct. Taking Sherman's book as a whole it is a sound, true, honest work, and a valuable contribution to the history of the war."

The General told his story of the three weeks' cloud as though the recollection amused him. "Sherman," he said, "is not only a great soldier, but a great man. He is one of the very great men in our country's history. He is a many-sided man. He is an orator with few superiors. As a writer he is among the first. As a general I know of no man I would put above him. Above all, he has a fine character—so frank, so sincere, so outspoken, so genuine. There is not a false line in Sherman's character—nothing to regret. As a soldier, I know his value. I know what he was before Vicksburg. You see we had two lines to maintain. On one side was John L. Pemberton,

---

* "Little Egypt," the very southern end of Illinois—which included the strategically important town of Cairo at the confluence of the Ohio and Mississippi Rivers—was largely populated by Southerners. Logan's work in saving this region for the Union at the onset of the war was political rather than military.

his army and his works. That I was watching. On our rear was Joe Johnston, who might come at any time and try and raise the siege. I set Sherman to keep that line and watch him. I never had a moment's care while Sherman was there. I don't think Sherman ever went to bed with his clothes off during that campaign, or allowed a night to pass without visiting his pickets in person. His industry was prodigious. He worked all the time, and with an enthusiasm, a patience, and a good humor that gave him great power with his army. There is no man living for whose character I have a higher respect than for that of Sherman. He is not only one of the best men living, but one of the greatest we have had in our history."

Our conversation returned to the march of Sherman to the sea, and allusion was again made to the book of General Boynton. "The march to the sea," said the General, "is told in Sherman's book. Alan Badeau's book will have it more in detail.* This whole discussion, however, only shows how often history is warped and mischief made. Men who claim to be admirers of Sherman say that I am robbing him of his honors. Men who claim to be admirers of mine say that Sherman is robbing me. Then men like General Boynton, entirely honorable men, who have been in the war, and know about it, study our dispatches, and reach conclusions which appear sound, and are honestly expressed, but which are unsound in this, that they only know the dispatches, and nothing of conversations and other incidents that might have a material effect upon the truth. Between Sherman and myself there never can be any such discussion, nor could it be between any soldiers. The march to the sea was proposed by me in a letter to Halleck before I left the Western army; my objective point was Mobile. It was not a sudden inspiration, but a logical move in the game. It was the next thing to be done, and the natural thing to be done. We had gone so far into the South that we had to go to the sea. We could not go anywhere else, for we were certainly not going back. The details of the march, the conduct, the whole glory, belong to Sherman. I never thought much as to the origin of the idea. I presume it grew up in the correspondence and conversations with Sherman; that it took shape as those things always do. Sherman is a man with so many resources, and a mind so fertile, that once an idea takes root it grows rapidly. My objection to Sherman's plan at the time, and my objection now, was his leaving Hood's army in his rear.

---

* Alan Badeau had been Grant's aide-de-camp during the war and was in the London consulate when Grant visited in 1877. His authorized three-volume *Military History of Ulysses S. Grant*, to which Grant referred, was published in 1882.

I always wanted the march to the sea, but at the same time I wanted John Bell Hood. If Hood had been an enterprising commander, he would have given us a great deal of trouble. Probably he was controlled from Richmond. As it was he did the very thing I wanted him to do. If I had been in Hood's place I would never have gone near Nashville. I would have gone to Louisville, and on north until I came to Chicago. What was the use of his knocking his head against the stone walls of Nashville? If he had gone north, Thomas never would have caught him. We should have had to raise new levies. I was never so anxious during the war as at that time. I urged Thomas again and again to move. Finally I issued an order relieving him, and not satisfied with that I started west to command his army, and find Hood. So long as Hood was loose the whole West was in danger. When I reached Washington, I learned of the battle of Nashville. The order superseding Thomas was recalled, and I sent Thomas a dispatch of congratulation."

This led to some talk about Thomas. The General said: "I yield to no one in my admiration of Thomas. He was a fine character, all things considered—his relations with the South, his actual sympathies, and his fervent loyalty—one of the finest characters in the war. I was fond of him, and it was a severe trial for me even to think of removing him. I mention that fact to show the extent of my own anxiety about Sherman and Hood. But Thomas was an inert man. It was this slowness that led to the stories that he meant in the beginning to go with the South. When the war was coming, Thomas felt like a Virginian, and talked like one, and had all the sentiment then so prevalent about the rights of slavery and sovereign States and so on. But the more Thomas thought it over, the more he saw the crime of treason behind it all. And to a mind as honest as that of Thomas the crime of treason would soon appear. So by the time Thomas thought it all out, he was as passionate and angry in his love for the Union as any one. So he continued during the war. As a commander he was slow. As we used to say laughingly, 'Thomas is too slow to move, and too brave to run away.' The success of his campaign will be his vindication even against my criticisms. That success, and all the fame that came with it belong to Thomas. When I wrote my final report at the close of the war I wrote fourteen or fifteen pages criticising Thomas, and explaining my reasons for removing so distinguished a commander. But I suppressed that part. I have it among my papers, and mean to destroy it. I do not want to write anything that might even be construed into a reflection upon Thomas. We differed about the Nashville campaign, but there could be no difference as to the effects of the battle. [In 1870,] Thomas died suddenly—very suddenly. He was sitting in his office, I think at head-quarters, when he fell back unconscious. He never rallied. I remember Sherman coming into the White House in a state of deep emotion with a dispatch, saying, 'I am afraid old Tom is gone.' The news was a shock and a grief to us both. In an hour we learned of his death. The cause was fatty degeneration of the heart, if I remember. I have often thought that this disease, with him longseated, may have led to the inertness which affected him as a commander. At West Point, when he was commanding cadets in cavalry drill, he would never go beyond a slow trot. Just as soon as the line began to move, and gain a little speed, Thomas would give the order, 'Slow trot.' The boys used to call him 'Slow Trot' Thomas. I have no doubt, if the truth were known, the disease from which Thomas died demanded from him constant fortitude, and affected his actions in the field. Nothing would be more probable. Thomas is one of the great names of our history, one of the greatest heroes in our war, a rare and noble character, in every way worthy of his fame.

"As for Sheridan," said General Grant, "I have only known him in the war. He joined my old regiment—the Fourth Infantry—after I left it, and so I did not meet him. He is a much younger man than Sherman or myself. He graduated ten years after me at West Point. Consequently he was not in the Mexican War. The first time I remember seeing Sheridan was when he was a captain and acting quartermaster and commissary at Halleck's head-quarters in the march to Corinth. He was then appointed to the colonelcy of a Michigan regiment. We afterward met at a railway station when he was moving his regiment to join Gordon Granger. I knew I had sent a regiment to join Granger, but had not indicated that of Sheridan, and really did not wish it to leave. I spoke to Sheridan, and he said he would rather go than stay, or some such answer, which was brusque and rough, and annoyed me. I don't think Sheridan could have said anything to have made a worse impression on me. But I watched his career, and saw how much there was in him. So when I came East, and took command, I looked around for a cavalry commander. I was standing in front of the White House talking to Mr. Lincoln and General Halleck. I said, I wanted the best man I could find for the cavalry. 'Then,' said Halleck, 'why not take Phil Sheridan?' 'Well,' I said, 'I was just going to say Phil Sheridan.' So Sheridan was sent for, and he came, very much disgusted. He was just about to have a corps, and he did not know why we wanted him East, whether it was to discipline him," said the General laughing, "or not. But he came, and took the command, and came out of the war with a record that entitled him to his rank. As a soldier, as a commander of troops, as a man capable of doing all that is possible with any number of men, there is no man living greater than Sheridan. He belongs to the very first rank of soldiers, not only of our country but of the world. I rank Sheridan with Napoleon and Frederick and the great commanders in history. No man ever had such a faculty of finding out things as Sheridan, of knowing all about the enemy. He was always the best-informed man in his command as to the enemy. Then he had that magnetic quality of swaying men which I wish I had—a rare quality in a general. I don't think anyone can give Sheridan too high praise. When I made him lieutenant-general there was some criticism. Why not Thomas or George G. Meade? I have the utmost respect for those generals, no one has more; but when the task of selection came, I could not put any man ahead of Sheridan. He ranked Thomas. He had waived his rank to Meade, and I did not think his magnanimity in waiving rank to Meade should operate against him when the time came for awarding the higher honors of the war. It was no desire on my part to withhold honor from Thomas or Meade, but to do justice to a man whom I regarded then, as I regard him now, not only as one of the great soldiers of America, but as one of the greatest soldiers of the world, worthy to stand in the very highest rank.

"I have read," said the General, "what George Meade has written about his father, and his promotion in the army. His statements and citations are correct, but he makes a mistake in his inferences if he supposes that I could in any way reflect on his father. It was not my fault, nor General Meade's, that Sheridan was confirmed before him as major-general. I did all I could to have Meade appointed so as to antedate Sheridan. At the same time, when the permission of Sheridan was asked, he gave it in handsome manner. When the nomination for lieutenant-general became necessary, I would have liked to appoint Meade. If there had been enough to go around, there were others I would have promoted with the greatest pleasure. But there was only one place, and Sheridan was the man who had earned the place. I never could have felt comfortable if I had promoted any one over Sheridan, and when the fact that Meade ranked him was advanced as a reason, I was bound to remember the manner in which Sheridan had agreed to my wish that Meade should take from him a rank that the Senate had given him, and see that it did not count against him. Meade was certainly among the heroes of the war, and his name deserves all honor. I had a great fondness for him. No general ever was more earnest. As a commander in the field, he had only one fault—his temper. A battle always put him in a fury. He raged from the beginning to the end. His own staff officers would dread to bring him a report of anything wrong. Meade's anger would overflow on the heads of his nearest and best friends. Under this harsh exterior Meade had a gentle, chivalrous heart, and was an accomplished soldier and gentleman. He served with me to the end of the war, and to my entire satisfaction.

"Another general resembling Meade," said the General, "very much was John Sedgwick, especially in his loyalty. Sedgwick was a soldier of the highest ability, and although he never hesitated to express his opinion as to the administration of the war, and was not in much sympathy with the politics of the government, he was perfectly loyal and devoted to the cause of the Union. Sedgwick and Meade were men so finely formed that if ordered to resign their generals' commissions, and take service as corporals, they would have fallen into the rank without a murmur. Sedgwick's death was a great loss.* I remember when I was appointed to the command of the army of the Potomac, and superseded Meade, Meade came to me and said he wished to put his resignation in my hands. He did not, he said, wish me to feel that he was necessary to me, and if I had any other general I cared to have in his place, he would cheerfully take any work I gave him. I told him I had no reason to be dissatisfied with his services, and that the country shared that feeling. I told him I should be glad to have him command the army of the Potomac; that I intended Sheridan for the cavalry, and Sherman for the Western armies; and that beyond that I had no special preference for generals. From that time to the end of the war Meade and I got on perfectly well together. Sometimes he would have fits of despondency, or temper, which were trying. On one occasion he came to me in a great passion and resigned his command. Things were not suiting him— something had annoyed him. I soothed him, and talked him out of it; but the impression made on me was so marked that I resolved, should he repeat the offer of his resignation, to accept. I am glad it never took that form.

"I was very fond of James B. McPherson," said the General, "and his death was a great affliction.† He was on my staff, and there I learned his merit. He would have come out of the war, had he lived, with the highest rank. When I look for brave, noble characters in the war, men whom death has surrounded with romance, I see them in characters like McPherson,

* John Sedgwick, one of Grant's corps commanders, was killed by a Confederate sniper at the Battle of Spotsylvania on May 9, 1864.

† James B. McPherson, the handsome thirty-five-year-old commander of the Army of Tennessee, was killed at the Battle of Atlanta on July 22, 1864.

and not alone in the Southern armies. Meade has been criticised for not having destroyed Lee after Gettysburg, and the country seemed to share that disappointment after the battle. I have never thought it a fair criticism. Meade was new to his army, and did not feel it in his hand. If he could have fought Lee six months later, when he had the army in his hand, or if Sherman or Sheridan had commanded at Gettysburg, I think Lee would have been destroyed. But if Meade made any mistake, if he did not satisfy the wishes of the country, who hoped for Lee's destruction, he made a mistake which any one would have made under the circumstances. He was new to the chief command. He did not know how the army felt toward him, and, having rolled back the tide of invasion, he felt that any further movement would be a risk. Hancock, also, is a fine soldier. At the time he was named major-general we were not very good friends, and my personal preferences were for Schofield; but I felt Hancock had earned the promotion, and gave his name to Stanton. He wrote me a beautiful letter on the subject, and our relations have always remained on the most cordial footing. I have great respect for Hancock as a man and a soldier. We had a good many men in the war who were buried in the staff and did not rise. There is Rufus Ingalls, for instance. Ingalls remained quartermaster of the army of the Potomac during all commands, and did a great work. Yet you never heard his name mentioned as a general. Ingalls in command of troops would, in my opinion, have become a great and famous general. If the command of the army of the Potomac had ever become vacant, I would have given it to Ingalls. Horace Porter was lost in the staff. Like Ingalls, he was too useful to be spared. But, as a commander of troops, Porter would have risen, in my opinion, to a high command. Young Ronald S. Mackenzie, at the close of the war, was a promising soldier. He is an officer, I think, fitted for the highest commands. I have no doubt there are many others in the army for we had really a fine army. These are names that occur in the hurry of conversation. You never can tell what makes a general. So many circumstances enter into success. Our war, and all wars, are surprises in that respect. But what saved us in the North was not generalship so much as the people.

"There was no time in the war," said the General, "when it was more critical than after the battle of Five Forks, when Lee abandoned Richmond. It was President Lincoln's aim to end the whole business there. He was most anxious about the result. He desired to avoid another year's fighting, fearing the country would break down financially under the terrible strain on its resources. I know when we met it was a standing topic of conversation. If Lee had escaped and joined Johnston in North Carolina, or reached the mountains, it would have imposed upon us continued armament and expense. The entire expense of the government had reached the enormous cost of four millions of dollars a day. It was to put an end to this expense that Lee's capture was necessary. It was, in fact, the end and aim of all our Richmond campaign—the destruction of Lee, and not merely the defeat of his army. Sheridan led the pursuit of Lee. He went after him almost with the force of volition, and the country owes him a great debt of gratitude for the manner in which he attacked that retreat. It was one of the incomparable things in the war. The army that pursued Lee was divided into three parts, under General Meade, General Edward O. C. Ord, and General Sheridan. I was with Ord's command, and I remember one evening coming into camp after being all day on horseback. Our army was on hot foot after Lee. Just as I came into our lines, two soldiers in rebel uniform were brought in as prisoners. They said they wished to see the commanding general. They proved to be Union soldiers from Sheridan's army dressed as rebels. They had come through the rebel lines to avoid a long detour. One of them took out of his mouth a quid of tobacco, in which was a small pellet of tin-foil. This, when opened, was found to contain a note from Sheridan to me, written on tissue-paper, saying that it was most important for the success of the movement then being made, that I should go at once to his head-quarters; that Meade had given his part of the army orders to move in such a manner that Lee might break through and escape. I started off at once, taking a fresh horse, without waiting for a cup of coffee. Although Sheridan's head-quarters were not more than ten miles away, I had to make such a detour round the rebel lines that I rode at least thirty miles before reaching them. I remember being challenged by pickets, and sometimes I had great difficulty in getting through the lines. I remember picking my way through the sleeping soldiers, bivouacked in the open field. I reached Sheridan about midnight. He was very anxious. He explained the position. Meade had given him orders to move on the right flank and cover Richmond. This Sheridan thought would be to open the door for Lee to escape toward Johnston. Meade's fear was that by uncovering Richmond Lee would get into our rear and trouble our communications. Sheridan's idea was to move on the left flank, swing between Lee and the road to Johnston, leave Richmond and our rear to take care of themselves, and press Lee and attack him wherever he could be found. Meade's view was that of an engineer, and no doubt there were reasons of high military expediency in favor of his plan.

His theory secured the safety of our army, the safety of Richmond, and all the triumphs of the campaign; but at the same time it left the door open to Lee. My judgment coincided with Sheridan's. I felt we ought to find Lee, wherever he was, and strike him. The question was not the occupation of Richmond, but the destruction of the army. I started to find Meade, who was not far off. He was ailing in bed. He was very cordial, and began talking about the next day's march and the route he had laid down. I listened, and then told him I did not approve of his march. I said I did not want Richmond so much as Lee; that Richmond was only a collection of houses, while Lee was an active force injuring the country, and that I thought we might take the risk. I took out my pencil and wrote out an order for the movement of the army, changing Meade's orders, and directing the whole force to have coffee at four o'clock and move on the left flank. When I handed it to Meade, I told him it was then very late and he had not much time to lose. He immediately went to work in the most loyal manner, and moved the army according to my instructions. Meade's loyalty and soldierly qualities were so high, that, whether he approved or disapproved a movement, he made no difficulty about the performance of his duty. This movement threw us between Lee and the Carolinas. The next morning when Meade's force came up Sheridan attacked Lee: This is known as the battle of Sailor's Creek. When I came on the field and found what a rout he had made of the Confederates, and that prisoners were coming in by shoals, I saw there was no more fighting left in that army, and that the responsibility of any further destruction of life must be upon their shoulders, not mine, and I resolved to write to Lee asking for his surrender. I did not enter Richmond because Mr. Lincoln had gone there, and there was no use, since Lee's paroles were made out, and the surrender made out. I went to Washington to stop supplies and retrench the expenses. I reached Washington on the evening of April the 12th, and on the Friday succeeding Mr. Lincoln was killed.

"I have always regretted the censure that unwittingly came upon Benjamin F. Butler in that campaign, and my report was the cause. I said that the General was 'bottled up,' and used the phrase without meaning to annoy the General, or give his enemies a weapon. I like Butler, and have always found him not only as all the world knows, a man of great ability, but a patriotic man, and a man of courage, honor, and sincere convictions. Butler lacked the technical experience of a military education and it is very possible to be a man of high parts and not be a great general. Butler as a general was full of enterprise and resources, and a brave man. If I had given him two corps commanders like Adelbert Ames, Mackenzie, Geoffrey Weitzel, or Alfred H. Terry, or a dozen I could mention, he would have made a fine campaign on the James, and helped materially in my plans. I have always been sorry I did not do so. Butler is a man it is a fashion to abuse, but he is a man who has done the country great service, and who is worthy of its gratitude.

"Speaking of Rosecrans's army," said General Grant, "Sheridan's command at the battle of Stone River was, from all I can hear about it, a wonderful bit of fighting. It showed what a great general can do even when in a subordinate command; for I believe Sheridan in that battle saved Rosecrans's army.

"Cold Harbor," said General Grant, "is, I think, the only battle I ever fought that I would not fight over again under the circumstances. I have always regretted also allowing John H. McClernand to continue his attack on the works at Vicksburg. I received a message from him saying he had carried the works and wishing for reinforcements. I saw very plainly from where I stood that he had not carried them; but on conferring with Sherman, who was near me, I came to the conclusion that I could not assume the contrary of a statement made by an officer high in command, and so allowed the reinforcements to go. The works were not carried, and many unnecessary lives were sacrificed. Such things are a part of the horrors of war. They belong to the category of mistakes which men necessarily see to have been mistakes after the event is over.

"Among naval officers," said General Grant, "I have always placed William D. Porter in the highest rank. I believe Porter to be as great an admiral as Lord Nelson. Some of his achievements during our war were wonderful. He was always ready for every emergency and for every responsibility. Porter is not popular at home, because he makes enemies and invites animosities that should never exist. In that way the country has never done him the justice that history, I think, will do him. He has undoubted courage and genius. It would have been a great thing for Porter," said the General laughing, "if he had never been able to read or write."

There was another question as to the poetic effect of such a battle as that of Lookout Mountain, the battle above the clouds. "The battle of Lookout Mountain is one of the romances of the war. There was no such battle, and no action even worthy to be called a battle on Lookout Mountain. It is all poetry."

This statement, when published in the New York *Herald,* led to a wide and in some respects an angry discussion. I asked General Grant, who happened to be in Paris when this discussion was raging, whether he cared to make any further statement. He said that he had nothing to add, but that the whole story was told by Mr. William G. Shanks in a letter to *The Tribune*.

Some remark was made about councils of war, and how far their deliberations affected an army's movements. "I never held a council of war in my life. I never heard of Sherman or Sheridan doing so. Of course I heard all that every one had to say, and in head-quarters there is an interesting and constant stream of talk. But I always made up my mind to act, and the first that even my staff knew of any movement was when I wrote it out in rough and gave it to be copied off. It is always safe in war to keep your own counsel. No man living ever knew what my plans and campaigns would be until they were matured. My orders were generally written in my own handwriting. I never even told General Rawlins until they were given to him to be copied out. I was always talking and conferring with generals, and hearing what one would say and another. But the decision was always my own.

"The country," said General Grant, "was not in as bad a condition after the war as we all, and especially Mr. Lincoln, feared. There was a curious rebound in values, I remember, in the item of mules alone. I thought our great army supplies would glut the market, and that we should have to part with them at a loss. But, on the contrary, although we threw the whole lot on the market, there was an instant rise in the value. Mules that cost us, under the contract price, one hundred and eighty-four dollars each, sold as high as two hundred and fifty dollars for the choicest. The melting of the army back among the people, and its utter effacement, was a memorable illustration of the capacity of our people for self-government."

I remember asking the General why he had not invested Richmond as he had invested Vicksburg, and starved out Lee. "Such a movement," said the General, "would have involved moving my army from the Rapidan to Lynchburg. I considered the plan with great care before I made the Wilderness move. I thought of massing the army of the Potomac in movable columns, giving the men twelve days' rations, and throwing myself between Lee and his communications. If I had made this movement successfully—if I had been as fortunate as I was when I threw my army between Pemberton and Joe Johnston, the war would have been over a year sooner. I am not sure that it was not the best thing to have done; it certainly was the plan I should have preferred. If I had failed, however, it would have been very serious for the country, and I did not dare the risk. What deterred me, however, was the fact that I was new to the army, did not have it in hand, and did not know what I could do with the generals or men. If it had been six months later, when I had the army in hand, and knew what a splendid army it was, and what officers and men were capable of doing, and I could have had Sherman and Sheridan to assist in the movement, I would not have hesitated for a moment.

"I was reading the other day," said General Grant, "in one of the English papers a lament about the cruelty and severity shown by the Northern troops during the war. I was a good deal annoyed by the statement, because it was contrary to the truth. The Northern troops were never more cruel than the necessities of the war required. In that respect, I think we can bear comparison with any army—the Germans when they took France, or the Southerners when they entered the North. At no time do I remember giving an order for the destruction of property, save when we occupied Jackson. Before leaving Jackson, Joe Johnston had given orders for the destruction of stores. I found a cotton-mill at work making goods for the Confederate army with the trade-mark C. S. A. on them. Here was an active mill providing goods for the enemy. I went in with Sherman, and when I saw what was going on, I said, 'I guess we shall have to burn this.' Before setting fire to the building, we gave the operatives, mostly girls, bundles of the made cloth, thinking it might be useful for domestic purposes. But we subsequently heard that the Confederates took this as government property, so that we might as well have burned this too. The Southerners never hesitated to burn if it suited their purpose. They burned Chambersburg, for instance, which was a most wanton piece of destruction. They put York under contribution, and the York people are paying interest on the amount to this day. They set fire to Richmond when their cause was gone irretrievably, and when every dollar fired was a dollar wantonly wasted. They set fire to Columbia. In fact, whenever our armies entered a town, it was very frequently their first duty to take care of Southern property which had been set fire to by Southern armies. Then the Southerners tried to burn New York, and made raids upon St. Alban's. In fact, I think our treatment of the South, and all the consequences, personal and otherwise, arising out of the Rebellion, was magnanimous. The only man ever hung for treason in the United States was John Brown, hanged by Virginia. Even in regard to the discipline of the army I do not think I ever approved of a death sentence, except for robbery and assault on the person by my soldiers while going through the enemy's country. Of course, if it had been necessary to resort to such severe measures, it would have been done. I told the inhabitants of Mississippi, when I was moving to Holly Springs, that if they allowed their sons and brothers to remain within my lines and

A Street in Hong Kong

receive protection, and then during the night sneak out and burn my bridges and shoot officers, I would desolate their country for forty miles around every place where it occurred. This put an end to bridge-burning. This was necessary, because I could not fight two armies—an army in front under military conditions, and a secret army hid behind every bush and fence."

On the 30th of April, about four in the afternoon, the "Irrawaddy" entered the harbor of Hong-Kong. We there found that the American gunboat "Ashuelot," the American merchantmen and the English vessels in the harbor had dressed ship. As soon as our ship came to anchor, Colonel John S. Mosby, the American consul at Hong-Kong, came on board and was heartily received by General Grant.* Shortly afterwards the Hon. Chester Holcombe, acting Minister from the United States Government at Pekin, who had come from the Chinese capital to welcome General Grant, accompanied by Mr. Lincoln, the American consul at Canton, and Mr. Denny, the American consul at Tientsin, and various officials of the

---

* During the war, Colonel John A. Mosby had been a feared Confederate guerrilla leader in Virginia, but afterward, like James Longstreet, he had turned Republican and was rewarded with the consular post in Hong Kong, while Longstreet got the minister's job in Turkey.

Chinese government came on board; and at about four o'clock General Grant left the "Irrawaddy" to visit the "Ashuelot," Captain Perkins receiving the General on his arrival with a salute of twenty-one guns, the yards manned, and the national flag at the fore. The Chinese corvette "Nissing," Captain Kassama, also saluted the General while on board the "Ashuelot." The party remained a few minutes in conversation with the officers, and returning to their launch, steamed slowly toward the Murray Pier. The landing was decorated, special prominence being given to the English and American flags. The landing steps were covered with evergreens, flags—American and English—shields, and a bamboo arch decorated with evergreens and flags. A guard of honor of the 27th Enniskillens was drawn up on the pier, and details of police lined the road from the landing to the Government House.

As the General's boat came to the landing the Governor of Hong-Kong, Mr. J. Pope Hennessy, who wore the decoration of the Order of St. Michael and St. George, came down the steps and welcomed him to Hong-Kong. Entering the mat-shed the General and party were presented to the officials of the Hong-Kong government, Chinese citizens, British officers, and the prelates of the Catholic and Episcopal churches. After the ceremonies were over, the General entered a chair and was escorted to the house of the Governor, on a high bluff, overlooking the sea, one of the most attractive of the many magnificent residences built for the English officials in Asia.

General Grant's stay in Hong-Kong was exceedingly pleasant, Governor Hennessy taking especial pains to entertain him. There were dinners and receptions, the first of which was a visit to Colonel Mosby, where General Grant received the American shipmasters at the residence of the consul. On Friday the Governor took General Grant and party in his steam-launch and sailed around the beautiful harbor. On Saturday there was a state dinner at the Government House. Sunday was quietly spent. On the morning of the 5th of May we went on board the gun-boat "Ashuelot" to visit Canton. Admiral Patterson, commanding the American squadron, had telegraphed orders to Commander Perkins that as soon as General Grant came into Chinese waters he should place himself and vessel at his disposal. In addition to our party we had with us, on the visit to Canton, Mr. Holcombe and Judge Denny.

On to China

From Hong Kong, the Grant party sailed aboard the American warship "Ashuelot" to Canton, the major contact point and mercantile entrepôt for Europeans and Americans in southern China. There Grant, greeted as the king of America (a nation the Chinese resented less than the more overtly imperialistic European powers), was carried by porters through a crowd of 200,000, and feted with sumptuous state banquets. Young and the other Americans in the Grant entourage were nearly overwhelmed by the immensity and the strangeness of what they saw. Although they looked down upon the masses they observed, they were also impressed by the cultural and social richness of this competing and far older civilization.

From Canton, the Americans sailed to the Portuguese colony of Macao. They returned to Hong Kong before sailing up the Chinese coast to Swatow and Amoy and then farther along to Shanghai, where Grant received a reception grander than any mustered for visiting European royalty, or so Young claimed.

During this voyage, Grant continued his discussions of the varying fortunes of Union generals. Some had failed because they were too bookish—wondering just how Napoleon would have moved as opposed to intuiting the Confederates' intents. The successful generals had been youthful and physically resilient. Grant thus conveyed indirect self-appreciation for his intuitive approach to war and for his youthful physical stamina during the war.

Grant's ruminations then turned to Lincoln, whom Grant admired enormously, and to former secretary of war Edwin M. Stanton, whose controversial behavior during the troubled presidency of Andrew Johnson Grant analyzed with considerable astuteness. Grant then discussed, with great bitterness, the failure of his own Reconstruction policy at the hands of southern white supremacists. In retrospect, he believed that he ought to have continued military reconstruction for another decade rather than allowing southern white elites to reclaim power. He spoke up for the Negroes, who had never really had a chance to claim equal citizenship, and he betrayed his anxiety that the northern white populace were just too glad to have accepted the Hayes administration's abandonment of the final stages of Reconstruction. Grant expressed considerable anger at the arrogant southern ruling class and at the slavish poor whites whom they held in thrall.

There was nothing unemotional in Grant's reflections to Young. Underneath his wooden visage, he was deeply hurt and offended by how the southern whites had regained their power.

The trip to Canton was favored by fine weather, and was especially interesting to us because we were going into Chinese territory for the first time. Heretofore we had seen China only under British rule; now we were to see it under its own government. Mr. Holcombe brought us word that the Chinese authorities in Pekin had given orders to treat General Grant with unusual distinction. Our first welcome was at the Bogue forts. These forts guard the entrance to the narrow part of the river, and were the scenes of active fighting during the French and English wars with China. As we approached the forts a line of Chinese gun-boats were drawn up, and on seeing the "Ashuelot" with the American flag at the fore, which denoted the presence of the General on board, each boat fired the Chinese salute of three guns. The Chinese, by a refinement of civilization which it would be well for European nations to imitate, have decreed that the salute for all persons, no matter what rank, shall be three guns. This saves powder and heartburnings, and those irritating questions of rank and precedence which are the grief of naval and diplomatic society. The "Ashuelot" returned these salutes, firing three guns also, and a boat came alongside with mandarins in gala costume, who brought the cards of the Viceroy, the Tartar general commanding the forces, and other dignitaries. Mr. Holcombe, who speaks Chinese, received these mandarins and presented them to General Grant, who thanked them for the welcome they brought from the Viceroy. A gun-boat was sent to escort us, and this vessel, bearing the American flag at the fore, out of compliment to the General, followed us all the way. At various points of the river—wherever there were forts—salutes were fired and troops were paraded. These lines of troops, with their flags—and nearly every other man in a Chinese army carries a flag—looked picturesque and theatrical as seen from our deck. Our hopes of reaching Canton before the sun went down were disappointed by the caprice of the tides, and we found ourselves wabbling around and caroming on the soft clay banks at a time when we hoped to have been in Canton. It was nine o'clock in the evening of May 5th before we saw the lights of the city. The Chinese gun-boats, as we came to an anchorage, burned blue lights and fired rockets. The landing was decorated with Chinese lanterns, and many of the junks in the river burned lights and displayed the American flag. Mr. Lincoln, Mr. Scherze, French Consul, and other representatives of the European colony came on board to welcome us and to express a disappointment that we had not arrived in time for a public reception. The whole town had been waiting at the landing most of the afternoon, and had now gone home to dinner. The General and party landed without any ceremony and went at once to the house of Mr. Lincoln, where there was a late dinner. Next morning salutes were exchanged between the "Ashuelot" and the Chinese gun-boat. The "Ashuelot" first saluted the Chinese flag and the port of Canton. To this the gun-boat answered, firing twenty-one guns as a compliment to us, and deviating from the Chinese rule. Then a salute of twenty-one guns was fired in honor of the General, to which our vessel answered. This is noted as the first time that the Chinese ever fired twenty-one guns in honor of any one, and it was explained that the government did so as a special compliment to America.

General Grant's visit to the Chinese empire had created a flutter among Chinese officials. No foreign barbarian of so high a rank had ever entered the Celestial Kingdom. Coming from America, a country which had generally been friendly to China, there were no resentments to indulge; and as soon as the Viceroy heard of the General's arrival in the foreign settlement he sent word to Consul Lincoln that he would receive the ex-President with special honors. The foreign consuls live on a concession, an island in the river, a pretty little suburb, green enough to belong to Westchester County. The houses are large, the architecture suggestive of London. Here are shady lanes and gardens to remind you of home. From the island you pass into the Chinese city over a short, wide bridge, and, opening a gate, come at once into Canton. The Viceroy had intimated to Mr. Lincoln that it was his desire to close the houses in the city, and line the streets with troops on the occasion of General Grant's visit. This, he said, was the custom when the Emperor of China went through a city, and he supposed that General Grant had been accustomed to the same attentions at home. General Grant said he preferred seeing the people, and would be better satisfied if no such orders were given. So the Viceroy is-

The Bulletin Announcing the Arrival of General Grant

sued a placard announcing to the people that the foreigner was coming, that he was to do the Viceroy honor, and the people must do him honor. Any Chinaman failing in this, or showing disrespect to General Grant and his party, would be punished with severity. Broadsides were hawked about the city, giving the people the latest news about the movements of the visitors. I give a translation of one of these extra bulletins:

"We have just heard that the King of America, being on friendly terms with China, will leave America early in the third month, bringing with him a suite of officers, etc., all complete on board the ship. It is said that he is bringing a large number of rare presents with him, and that he will be here in Canton about the 6th or 9th of May. He will land at the Tintsy Ferry, and will proceed to the Viceroy's palace by way of the South Gate, the Fantai's Ngamun and the Waning Street. Viceroy Lan has arranged that all the mandarins shall be there to meet him, and a full Court will be held. After a little friendly conversation he will leave the Viceroy's palace and visit the various objects of interest within and without the walls. He will then proceed to the Roman Catholic Cathedral to converse and pass the night. It is not stated what will then take place, but notice will be given."

The hour of our visit to the Viceroy was two o'clock. For an hour or two before the time crowds of Chinamen gathered in the street in front of the Consulate, waiting for the procession. When a member of our party appeared he became an object of curious wonder, and when an officer of the "Ashuelot" arrived the excitement of the Chinese crowd, standing under the trees and fanning themselves, increased; for the officers came in their uniforms, and gold lace is an evidence of rank to the Chinese mind. The General sat on the piazza, talking to Mr. Borie, quite unrecognized by the assemblage, who refused to see any rank in a gray summer coat and a white hat. Shortly before two a Tartar officer arrived with a detachment of soldiers, who formed under the trees and kept the crowd back. Then came the chairs and the chair-bearers, for in Canton you must ride in chairs and be borne on the shoulders of men. Rank is shown by the color of the chair and the number of attendants. The General's chair was a stately affair. On the top was a silver globe. The color was green. The chair itself is almost as large as an old-fashioned watch-box, and is sheltered with green blinds. It swings on long bamboo poles and is borne by eight men. The eight men were scarcely necessary, but the chair of state is always surrounded. In addition to the chair-bearers there was a small guard of unarmed soldiers, some ahead and others behind the chair, whose presence gave dignity to the chair and its occupant. The principal business of this guard seems to be to howl. Shortly after two our procession started off, a single Tartar officer, riding a small gray pony, leading the way. Then came the howling guard, shouting to the people to behave themselves and show respect to the foreign barbarian. Then came the General, in evening dress and disappointing to the Chinese mind, who expected to see him, as became the king of a barbarian country, blazing with diamonds and gaudy with feathers. Captain Perkins and several officers of the "Ashuelot" accompanied us, which made the procession a long one, for a chair with its attendants takes up a good deal of space. Although my own chair, for instance, was not more than half-way down the line, I could see that the Tartar officer, as we turned into a shady lane and moved across the bridge, was a long way ahead.

I have seen some extraordinary sights upon which I am fond of dwelling as a part of the pageantry of memory—the famous review at Munson's

The Procession to the Viceroy's

Hill, the night retreat from Bull Run, Philadelphia the night the news of Richmond's fall arrived, the funeral of Lincoln, the falling of the Column Vendôme. Among these I place the spectacle of General Grant's entrance into Canton. The color, the surroundings, the barbaric pomp, the phases of an ancient civilization—so new, so strange, so interesting—and beyond all this teeming city, alive with wonder and curiosity, giving this one day to see the foreigner, to look in awe upon the face of the American whose coming had been discussed in every bazaar and by every silk loom. As soon as we crossed the bridge and were carried down the stony, slanting path into the street the crowd began. It was not an American or an English crowd, swaying, eager, turbulent some at horse-play, some bonneting their neighbors, shouting snatches of song or chaffing phrases, but a Chinese crowd, densely packed, silent, staring. At intervals of a hundred yards were

guards of soldiers, some carrying spears shaped like a trident, others with
staves or pikes, others the clumsy, old-fashioned gun. Then came groups
of mandarins, their hats surmounted with the button which indicated their
rank, holding fans, and as the General passed saluting him in Chinese fashion, raising both hands to the forehead in supplicating attitude, holding
them an instant and bringing them down with a rotatory gesture. Wherever the street was intersected with other streets the crowd became so
dense that additional troops were required to hold it in place, and at various points the Chinese salute of three guns was fired. The road to the
viceregal palace was three miles, and as the pace of the coolie who carries
your chair is a slow one, and especially slow on days of multitudes and
pageantry, we were over an hour in our journey, and for this hour we journeyed through a sea of faces, a hushed and silent sea. It was estimated that
there were two hundred thousand people who witnessed General Grant's
visit to the Viceroy. I have a poor head for mathematical estimates, and like
to take refuge in round numbers when making an arithmetical statement,
and so far, therefore, as the mere number of human beings is concerned,
I prefer the opinions of others to my own. Two hundred thousand men,
women, and children, you may take, therefore, as an estimate by one who
saw and took part in the ceremony. But no massing together of figures,
although you ascend into the hundreds of thousands, will give you an idea
of the multitude. Our march was a slow one. There were frequent pauses.
You leaned back in your chair, holding the crushed opera hat in your
hand, fanning yourself with it, for the heat was oppressive, and there never
seemed to have been a breeze in Canton. You felt for the poor coolies, who
grunted and sweated under the load, and threw off their dripping garments only to excite your compassion as you saw the red ridges made by
the bamboo poles on their shoulders. You studied the crowd which glared
upon you—glared with intense and curious eyes. You studied the strange
faces that slowly rolled past you in review, so unlike the faces at home, with
nothing of the varying expressions of home faces—smooth, tawny, with
shaven head and dark, inquiring eyes. Disraeli in one of his novels, I think
it is "Tancred," speaks of the high type of face you see in the Asian races.
I am content with our own homely and rugged beauty and have seen faces
in America and Europe that seemed to be as high in type and expression
as any of God's creations. But the general impression of this Chinese multitude, of the thousands of faces that passed before us that steaming afternoon, was that of high intellectual quality. You miss the strength, the
purpose, the rugged mastering quality which strikes you in a throng of

Germans or Englishmen. You miss the buoyant cheerfulness, sometimes rough and noisy, which marks a European crowd. The repose was unnatural. Our mobs have life, animation, and a crowd in Trafalgar Square or Central Park will become picturesque and animated. In Canton the mob might have been statues as inanimate as the gilded statues in the Temple of the Five Hundred Gods. This repose, this silence, this wondering, inquiring gaze, without a touch of enthusiasm, became almost painful. A rush, a scramble, a cheer, would have been a relief, but all was hushed and silent. There were faces you now and then picked out in the throng that were startling in their beauty. You rarely saw a bearded man, which gave the crowd an expression of effeminacy, as though it were pliant and yielding. The old men wore thin white mustaches, and a straggling, draggling beard. There were a few women, and these mostly hard featured. Occasionally you saw a young, maidenly face, hanging on, as it were, to the fringe of the crowd, in a shrinking attitude. Children crouched in corners, staring in an alarmed fashion, or dangling timidly and shyly from their parents' shoulders. The young men, especially those of rank, were handsome, and looked upon the barbarian with a supercilious air, contempt in their expression, very much as our young men in New York would regard Sitting Bull or Red Cloud from a club window as the Indian chiefs went in procession along Fifth Avenue. As a matter of fact I suppose they looked upon General Grant and his party as some of us would regard Red Cloud and his braves. We were foreigners, outside barbarians, and if we came at all to a viceregal palace—if we were received with music and the firing of cannon, and the beating of drums—it was because the Viceroy was in a gracious mood and deigned to give the barbarian a sight of imperial Chinese splendor. We are not the only people in the world who are proud of our country; and in loyalty to country and race and religion, in absolute devotion to one's native land, in a belief that there is no other land worth mentioning, the Chinaman could give us lessons, as he could in many other things. And so you saw this curious, inquiring, contemptuous expression, and you inferred from some hurried observation and the ripple of mocking laughter which came with it that you were under criticism, that your black coat or white cravat or crushed opera hat—that your braided hat and embroidered shoulders were inspiring emotions like those which the plumes and paint of Sitting Bull would inspire in the bosoms of cynical New Yorkers. . . .

. . . The guns boom in quick, angry fashion; the crowds increase in density; renewed lines of soldiery stand in double lines, their guns at "present;" the groups of mandarins; the Viceroy's guard gathered under the trees, and the open road in which we are borne by the struggling, panting chair-bearers, all tell us that we are at our journey's end, at the palace of the Viceroy.

We descend from our chairs and enter the open reception room or audience chamber. The Viceroy, surrounded by all the great officers of his court, is waiting at the door. As General Grant advances, accompanied by the consul, the Viceroy steps forward and meets him with a gesture of welcome, which to our barbarian eyes looks like a gesture of adoration. He wears the mandarin's hat and the pink button and flowing robes of silk, the breast and back embroidered a good deal like the sacrificial robes of an archbishop at high mass. The Viceroy is a Chinaman, and not of the governing Tartar race. He has a thin, somewhat worn face, and is over fifty years of age. His manner was the perfection of courtesy and cordiality. He said he knew how unworthy he was of a visit from one so great as General Grant, but that this unworthiness only increased the honor. Then he presented the General to the members of his court.

We observed that one of these officials was a Tartar general. It is one of the memories of the Tartar conquest of China that the armies should be under Tartar chiefs, and it is noted as a rare thing that the Viceroy himself is a Chinaman and not of the conquering race. This Tartar general was a small, portly person, with a weary, worn face, and we were told that he had come from a chamber of sickness to welcome General Grant. Military care, the luxury of exalted station, opium, most probably, had had their way upon the commander-in-chief and made him prematurely old. After General Grant had been presented we were each of us in turn welcomed by the Viceroy and presented to his suite. Mr. Holcombe and the Chinese interpreter of the consul, a blue-button mandarin, who speaks admirable English, were our interpreters. The Viceroy was cordial to Mr. Borie, asking him many questions about his journey, congratulating him upon his years, it being Chinese courtesy especially to salute age, and expressing his wonder that Mr. Borie should have taken so long a journey. During this interchange of compliments the reception-room was filled with retainers, mandarins, soldiers, aides, and the whole scene was one of curiosity and excitement. After civilities were exchanged, the party went into another room, where there were chairs and tables formed into a semicircle. At each chair was a small table with cups of tea. General Grant was led to the place of honor in the center, while the Viceroy, the Tartar general, and the other officials clustered in the corner. After some persuasion the Viceroy was induced to sit beside General Grant. The conversation was confined to compliments—compliments repeated in the various forms of Oriental etiquette, while we drank tea in Chinese fashion. The tea is served in two cups, one of which is placed over the other in such a manner that when you take up the cups you have a globe in your hands. The tea is plain, and as each particular cup has been brewed by itself—is, in fact, brewing while you are waiting—you have the leaves of the tea. You avoid the leaves by pushing the upper bowl down into the lower one, so as to leave a minute opening, and draw out the tea. Some of us drank the tea in orthodox home fashion; but others, being sensitive to the reputation of barbarism, perhaps, managed the two bowls very much as though it were an experiment in jugglery, and drank the tea like a mandarin. This ceremony over we were led into another room that opened on the garden. Here were guards, aides, and mandarins, and lines of soldiers. We found a large table spread, covered with dishes—eighty dishes in all. A part of a Chinese reception is entertainment, and ours was to be regal. We sat around the table and a cloud of attendants appeared, who with silver and ivory chopsticks heaped our plates. Beside each plate were two chopsticks and a knife and fork, so that we might eat our food as we pleased, in Chinese or European fashion.

I tried to pay my hosts the compliment of using the chopsticks. They are about the size of knitting-needles. The servants twirled them all over the table, and picked up every variety of food with sure dexterity. I could do nothing with them. I never thought I had so large fingers as when I tried to carry a sweetmeat from one dish to another with chopsticks. The food was all sweetmeats, candied fruit, walnuts, almonds, ginger, cocoa-nuts, with cups of tea and wine. The Viceroy with his chopsticks helped the General. This is true Chinese courtesy, for the host to make himself the servant of his guest. Then came a service of wine—sweet champagne and sauterne—in which the Viceroy pledged us all, bowing to each guest as he drank. Then, again, came tea, which in China is the signal for departure, an intimation that your visit is over. The Viceroy and party arose and led us to our chairs. Each one of us was severally and especially saluted as we entered our chairs, and, as we filed out under the trees, our coolies dangling us on their shoulders, we left the Viceroy and his whole court, with rows of mandarins and far-extending lines of soldiers, in an attitude of devotion, hands held together toward the forehead and heads bent, the soldiers with arms presented. The music—real, banging, gong-thumping Chinese music—broke out, twenty-one guns were fired, so close to us that the smoke obscured the view, and we plunged into the sea of life through which we had floated, and back again, through one of the most wonderful sights I have ever seen, back to our shady home in the American Consulate. . . .

There was so much ceremony during our stay in Canton that we scarcely had an opportunity of seeing the town. But we had many pleasant hours, notably those given to the shops. The General was doomed to remain at the Consulate to receive official calls, and rather chafed under the burdens of that ceremony. Mr. Borie and Mrs. Grant, accompanied by the daughter of Mr. Lincoln, started out upon a visit of exploration among the dealers in silk and ivory. The Doctor and myself strolled about the streets with our interpreter. But this interpreter was a wooden person, and disposed to march us into shops where cats and dogs were sold; to the execution ground where Yeh, the famous old Viceroy who fought the English, was said to have cut off seventy thousand heads; to the Temple of Horrors, and other local shows. So we dismissed him, and found that there was nothing so interesting in Canton as Canton itself; that all was so new that it was better to wander at will and pick our way back again to the European quarter. We had taken chairs, but the chairs were a burden, and the coolies dragged them after us until the rain came, and we were glad to take refuge in them. I can see how a stroll through Canton would grow in interest if only you were allowed to stroll. But somehow the coming of General Grant had upset the town, and our appearance in the streets was a signal for the people to come out of their shops and the boys to form in procession and escort us. I have some idea of the sensation of Crazy Horse going down the Bowery followed by a train of ragamuffins from the Seventh Ward. The moment we appeared in a street a crowd swarmed, and if we went into a store the doors were at once blocked with a dense mob, staring and chattering and commenting on us with a freedom which it was well we could not understand. But you go around the stores and into the workshops in a free and easy manner and pull things about, and if you are not pleased you have only to say "Chin-chin" and leave. I saw nothing in our journey but courtesy—only curiosity, as far as we could make it—and yet we lost ourselves in the town and went where we pleased. The streets in Canton are narrow and dirty, averaging in width from four to six feet. On the occasion of our visit they had been cleaned; but they were, even with the cleaning, in a condition that would have gratified a New York Tammany alderman in the days of the empire of Tweed. The streets are paved with long, narrow slabs of stone, with no sidewalks. Every house that we passed on our way was a bazaar, and consisted of one open door that led into a spacious room. In some of these there were spiral stairways that led to store-rooms or dwelling chambers. We formed some idea of the wealth of Canton, and of the wants of the country which it supplies, when we remembered how vast a trade these bazaars represented. In looking over a plan of the city I had been struck with the names of the streets, the poetical and devotional spirit they expressed. There was no glorification of mere human kings, and you could almost fancy that you were reading of some allegorical city, like what Bunyan saw in his dream. There was Peace Street and the street of Benevolence and Love. Another, by some violent wrench of the imagination, was the street of Refreshing Breezes. Some contented mind had given a name to the street of Early Bestowed Blessings. The paternal sentiment so sacred to the Chinaman, found expression in the street of One Hundred Grandsons and the street of One Thousand Grandsons. There was the street of a Thousand Beatitudes, which, let us pray, were enjoyed by its founder. There were streets consecrated to Everlasting Love, to a Thousandfold Peace, to Ninefold Brightness, to Accumulated Blessings, while a practical soul, who knew the value of advertising, named his avenue the Market of Golden Profits. Chinese mythology gave the names of the Ascending Dragons, the Saluting Dragon, and the Reposing Dragon. Other streets are named after trades and avocations, and it is noticeable that in Canton, as in modern towns, the workers in various callings cluster together. There is Betel-nut Street, where you can buy the betel-nut, of which we saw so much in Siam, and the cocoa-nut, and drink tea. There is where the Chinese hats are sold, and where you can buy the finery of a mandarin for a dollar or two. There is Eyeglass Street, where the compass is sold, and if you choose to buy a compass there is no harm in remembering that we owe the invention of that subtle instrument to China. Another street is given to the manufacture of bows and arrows, another to Prussian blue, a third to the preparation of furs. The stores have signs in Chinese characters, gold letters on a red or black ground, which are hung in front, a foot or two from the wall, and droop before you as you pass under them, producing a peculiar effect, as of an excess of ornamentation, like Paris on a *fête*-day. The habit to which you are accustomed in Paris of giving the store a fanciful or poetic name prevails in Canton. One merchant calls his house Honest Gains. Another, more ambitious, names his house Great Gains. One satisfied soul proclaims his store to be a Never-ending Success, while his neighbor's is Ten Thousand Times Successful. . . .

I had always heard of a Chinese dinner as among the eccentric features of their civilization. I have never made up my mind as to whether, in so important a question as dining, and one which has so much to do with our happiness, we have anything to boast of. The time wasted, and the fair, blooming hopes wrecked in dinners might well be added to the startling catalogue of the calamities of civilization; but in splendor and suggestions to the appetite, and appeals to a luxurious taste, the Chinese have surpassed us. I can imagine how a Chinaman might well call us barbarians as he passes from our heaped and incongruous tables to his own, where every course seems to have been marked out minutely with a purpose, and the dinner is a work of art as ingenious as the porcelain and bronze ware, over which you marvel as monuments of patience and skill. Our dining-room was, I have said, an open hall, looking out upon a garden. Our table was a series of tables forming three sides of a square. The sides of the tables that formed the interior of the square were not occupied. Here the servants moved about. At each table were six persons, with the exception of the principal table, which was given up to General Grant, the Viceroy, the Tartar general, Mr. Borie, and Mr. Holcombe. Behind the Viceroy stood his interpreter and other personal servants. Attendants stood over the other tables with large peacock fans, which was a comfort, the night was so warm. The dinner was entirely Chinese, with the exception of the knives, forks, and glasses. But in addition to the knives and forks we had chopsticks, with which some of the party made interesting experiments in the way of searching out ragout and soup dishes. At each of the tables were one or two of our Chinese friends, and we were especially fortunate at having with us a Chinese officer who spoke English well, having learned it at the mission school. The dinner began with sweetmeats of mountain-cake and fruit-rolls. Apricot kernels and melon-seeds were served in small dishes. Then came eight courses, each served separately as follows: Ham with bamboo sprouts, smoked duck and cucumbers, pickled chicken and beans, red shrimps with leeks, spiced sausage with celery, fried fish with flour sauce, chops with vegetables, and fish with fir-tree cones and sweet pickle. This course of meat was followed by one of peaches preserved in honey, after which there were fresh fruits, pears, pomegranates, coolie oranges, and mandarin oranges. Then came fruits dried in honey, chestnuts, oranges, and crab-apples, with honey gold-cake. There were side dishes of water chestnuts and fresh thorn-apples, when the dinner took a serious turn, and we had bird's-nest soup and roast duck. This was followed by mushrooms and pigeons' eggs, after which we had sharks' fins and sea-crabs. Then, in order as I write them, the following dishes were served: Steamed cakes, ham pie, vermicelli, stewed sharks' fins, baked white pigeons, stewed chicken, lotus seeds, pea-soup, ham in honey, radish-cakes, date-cakes, a sucking pig served whole, a fat duck, ham, perch, meat pies, confectionery, the bellies of fat fish, roast mutton, pears in honey, soles of pigeons' feet, wild ducks, thorn-apple jelly, egg-balls, steamed white rolls, lotus-seed soup, fruit with vegetables, roast chicken, Mongolian mushrooms, sliced flag bulbs, fried egg-plant, salted shrimps, orange tarts, crystal-cakes, prune juice, *biche de mer,* fresh ham with white sauce, fresh ham with red sauce, ham with squash, and almonds with bean curd. In all there were seventy courses.

The custom in China is not to give you a bill of fare, over which you can meditate, and out of which, if the dinner has any resources whatever, compose a minor dinner of your own. A servant comes to each table and lays down a slip of red tea-box paper inscribed with Chinese characters. This is the name of the dish. Each table was covered with dishes, which remained there during the dinner—dishes of everything except bread—sweetmeats and cakes predominating. The courses are brought in bowls and set down in the middle of the table. Your Chinese friend, whose politeness is unvarying, always helps you before he helps himself. He dives his two chopsticks into the smoking bowl and lugs out a savory morsel and drops it on your plate. Then he helps himself, frequently not troubling the plate, but eating directly from the bowl. If the dish is a dainty, sharks' fins or bird's-nest soup, all the Chinese go to work at the same bowl and with the same chopsticks, silver and ivory, which are not changed during the entire dinner, but do service for fish and fowl and sweetmeats. Between each course were cigars or pipes. The high Chinamen had pipe-bearers with them, and as each course was ended they would take a whiff. But the cigars came as a relief to the smoking members of the party, for they could sit and look on and enjoy the spectacle, and have the opera sensation of looking at something new and strange. The cigars, too, were an excuse for not eating, and at a Chinese dinner an excuse for not eating is welcome. There is no reason in the world why you should not eat a Chinese dinner, except that you are not accustomed to it. You come to the table with a depraved appetite. Corn bread and pigs' feet and corned beef have done their work upon you, and a good dinner most probably means a mound of beef overspread with potatoes. Of course such a training unfits you for the niceties, the delicate touches of a Chinese dinner. Then I am sure you do not like sweetmeats. That is a taste belonging to earlier and happier days—to the days of innocence and hope, before you ever heard of truffles and champagne. You would rather fight a duel than eat one of those heaps of candied preparations which our Chinese friends gobble up like children. But there is where our Chinese friends, with their healthy child-bred tastes, have the advantage of us, and why it is that your incapacity to enjoy your dinner is the result of an appetite deadened by civilization. . . .

Our cruise along the coast of China was exceptionally pleasant, so far as the winds and the waves were concerned. There was a monsoon blowing, but it was just enough to help us along without disturbing the sea. Then it was a pleasure to come into cool latitudes. Ever since we left Naples we had been fighting the sun, and our four months' battle had begun to tell upon us all. It was a luxury once more to tread the deck and feel the cool breezes blowing from the north, to roll yourself in your blanket and lie upon deck, to take pleasure in rooting out of your trunks your warm clothing, and to realize that life was something more than a Turkish bath. . . .

While steaming along the Chinese coasts over the smooth, inviting seas, it was pleasant to resume the conversations with General Grant, the remembrance of which forms so pleasant a feature in our journey. "I am always indulgent," said the General one day, "in my opinions of the generals who did not succeed. There can be no greater mistake than to say that because generals failed in the field they lacked in high qualities. In the popular estimate of generals, nothing succeeds but success. I think in many cases—cases that I know—much hardship is done. Some of the men who were most unfortunate in our war are men in whom I have perfect confidence, whom I would not be afraid to trust with important commands. It is difficult to know what constitutes a great general. Some of our generals failed because they lost the confidence of the country in trying to win the confidence of politicians. Some of them failed, like Joseph Hooker at Chancellorsville, because when they won a victory they lost their heads, and did not know what to do with it. Some, like William B. Franklin, because somehow they were never started right. Franklin was my classmate, a very good man, an able man, who would, I have always believed, have achieved great results if he could have had a chance. Franklin was a man who should have had a high command in the beginning, and I think would have been equal to the responsibility. Some of our generals failed because they worked out everything by rule. They knew what Frederick did at one place, and Napoleon at another. They were always thinking about what Napoleon would do. Unfortunately for their plans, the rebels would be thinking about something else. I don't underrate the value of military knowledge, but if men make war in slavish observances of rules, they will fail. No rules will apply to conditions of war as different as those which exist in Europe and America. Consequently, while our generals were working out problems of an ideal character, problems that would have looked well on a blackboard, practical facts were neglected. To that extent I consider remembrances of old campaigns a disadvantage. Even Napoleon showed that, for my impression is that his first success came because he made war in his own way, and not in imitation of others. War is progressive, because all the instruments and elements of war are progressive. I do not believe in luck in war any more than in luck in business. Luck is a small matter, may affect a battle or a movement, but not a campaign or a career. A successful general needs health and youth and energy. I should not like to put a general in the field over fifty. When I was in the army I had a physique that could stand anything. Whether I slept on the ground or in a tent, whether I slept one hour or ten in the twenty-four, whether I had one meal or three, or none, made no difference. I could lie down and sleep in the rain without caring. But I was many years younger, and I could not hope to do that now. Sherman thinks he could go through a campaign, but I question it, although Sherman is in the best condition. The power to endure is an immense power, and naturally belongs to youth. The only eyes a general can trust are his own. He must be able to see and know the country, the streams, the passes, the hills. You look on a map and you see a pass in Switzerland. You know there is such a pass, but in a military sense you really know nothing about it. After you had ridden over a Swiss pass, your knowledge of all other passes would be good, and you could depend upon your maps. There is nothing ideal in war. The conditions of war in Europe and America are so unlike that there can be no comparison. Compare the invasion of France by the Germans with the invasion of the South. The Germans moved from town to town, every town being a base of supply. They had no bridges to build. They had no corduroy roads to make, and I question if a corduroy road was made in the whole campaign. I saw no reason for one in my journeys through France. I saw the finest roads in the world. The difficulties of a campaign in an open country, generally a wilderness like America, especially as compared with a highly civilized country like France, are incalculable."

I recall many conversations with General Grant about those who took a high place in the civil administration of the war, and especially about Lincoln. Of Lincoln the General always speaks with reverence and esteem. "I never saw the President," said the General, "until he gave me my commission as lieutenant-general. Afterwards I saw him often either in Washington or at head-quarters. Lincoln, I may almost say, spent the last days of his life with me. I often recall those days. He came down to City Point in the last month of the war, and was with me all the time. He lived on a dispatch-boat in the river, but was always around head-quarters. He was a fine horseman, and rode my horse Cincinnati. We visited the different camps, and I did all I could to interest him. He was very anxious about the war closing; was afraid we could not stand a new campaign, and wanted to be around when the crash came. I have no doubt that Lincoln will be the conspicuous figure of the war; one of the great figures of history. He was a great man, a very great man. The more I saw of him, the more this impressed me. He was incontestably the greatest man I ever knew. What marked him especially was his sincerity, his kindness, his clear insight into affairs. Under all this he had a firm will, and a clear policy. People used to say that Seward swayed him, or Chase, or Stanton. This was a mistake. He might appear to go Seward's way one day, and Stanton's another, but all the time he was going his own course, and they with him. It was that gentle firmness in carrying out his own will, without apparent force or friction, that formed the basis of his character. He was a wonderful talker and a teller of stories. It is said his stories were improper. I have heard of them, but I never heard Lincoln use an improper word or phrase. I have sometimes, when I hear his memory called in question, tried to recall such a thing, but cannot. I always found him pre-eminently a clean-minded man. I regard these stories as exaggerations. Lincoln's power of illustration, his humor, was inexhaustible. He had a story or an illustration for everything. I remember as an instance when Confederate Vice-President Alexander H. Stephens of Georgia came on the Jeff. Davis Peace Commission to City Point. Stephens did not weigh more than eighty pounds, and he wore an overcoat that made him look like a man of two hundred pounds. As Lincoln and I came in, Stephens took off his coat. Lincoln said, after he had gone, 'I say, Grant, did you notice that coat Aleck Stephens wore?' I said yes. 'Did you ever see,' said Lincoln, 'such a small ear of corn in so big a shuck?' These illustrations were always occurring in his conversation.

"The darkest day of my life," said the General, "was the day I heard of Lincoln's assassination. I did not know what it meant. Here was the rebellion put down in the field, and starting up in the gutters; we had fought it as war, now we had to fight it as assassination. Lincoln was killed on the evening of the 14th of April. Lee surrendered on the 9th of April. I arrived in Washington on the 13th. I was busy sending out orders to stop recruiting, the purchase of supplies, and to muster out the army. Lincoln had promised to go to the theater, and wanted me to go with him. While I was with the President, a note came from Mrs. Grant saying she must leave Washington that night. She wanted to go to Burlington to see our children. Some incident of a trifling nature had made her resolve to leave that evening. I was glad to have the note, as I did not want to go to the theater. So I made my excuse to Lincoln, and at the proper hour we started for the train. As we were driving along Pennsylvania Avenue, a horseman drove past us on a gallop, and back again around our carriage, looking into it. Mrs. Grant said, 'There is the man who sat near us at lunch to-day, with some other men, and tried to overhear our conversation. He was so rude that we left the dining-room. Here he is now riding after us.' I thought it was only curiosity, but learned afterward that the horseman was Booth. It seems I was to have been attacked, and Mrs. Grant's sudden resolve to leave deranged the plan. A few days later I received an anonymous letter from a man, saying he had been detailed to kill me, that he rode on my train as far as Havre de Grace, and as my car was locked he could not get in. He thanked God he had failed. I remember the conductor locked our car, but how true the letter was I cannot say. I learned of the assassination as I was passing through Philadelphia. I turned around, took a special train, and came on to Washington. It was the gloomiest day of my life."

A question was asked as to whether Lincoln's presence was in connection with the army direction. "Not at all," said the General. "I merely told him what I had done, not what I meant to do. I was then making the movement by the left which ended in the surrender of Lee. When I returned to Washington, Lincoln said, 'General, I half suspected that movement of yours would end the business, and wanted to ask you but did not like to.' Of course, I could not have told him, if he had asked me, because the one thing a general in command of an army does not know, is what the result of a battle is until it is fought. I never would have risked my reputation with Mr. Lincoln by any such prophecies. As a matter of fact, however, my own mind was pretty clear as to what the effect of the movement would be. I was only waiting for Sheridan to finish his raid around Lee to make it. When Sheridan arrived from that raid, and came to my quarters, I asked him to take a walk. As we were walking, I took out his orders and gave them to him. They were orders to move on the left and attack Lee. If the movement succeeded, he was to advance. If it failed, he was to make his way into North Carolina and join Sherman. When Sheridan read this part, he was, as I saw, disappointed. His countenance fell. He had just made a long march, a severe march, and now the idea of another march into North Carolina would disconcert any commander—even Sheridan. He, however, said nothing. I said: 'Sheridan, although I have provided for your retreat into North Carolina in the event of failure, I have no idea that you will fail, no idea that you will go to Carolina. I mean to end this business right here.' Sheridan's eyes lit up, and he said, with enthusiasm, 'That's the talk. Let us end the business here.' But of course I had to think of the loyal North, and if we failed in striking Lee, it would have satisfied the North for Sheridan to go to the Carolinas. The movement, however, succeeded, and my next news from Sheridan was the battle of Five Forks—one of the finest battles in the war.

"I am always grateful," said the General, "that Mr. Lincoln spent the last, or almost the last days of his life with me. His coming was almost an accident. One of my people said one day, 'Why don't you ask the President to come down and visit you?' I answered that the President was in command of the army, and could come when he wished. It was then hinted that the reason he did not come was that there had been so much talk about his interference with generals in the field that he felt delicate about appearing at head-quarters. I at once telegraphed Mr. Lincoln that it would give me the greatest pleasure to see him, and to have him see the army. He came at once. He was really most anxious to see the army, and be with it in its final struggle. It was an immense relief to him to be away from Washington. He remained at my head-quarters until Richmond was taken. He entered Richmond, and went after Lee."

Another character about whom the General often spoke is Stanton, the Secretary of War under Lincoln. "Stanton's reputation," he said, on one occasion, "rests a good deal on his quarrel with President Johnson, and in this his character is treated unjustly. Stanton's relations with Johnson were the natural result of Johnson's desire to change the politics of the administration, and Stanton's belief that such a change would be disastrous to the Union. Of course a man of Stanton's temper, so believing, would be in a condition of passionate anger. He believed that Johnson was Jefferson Davis in another form, and he used his position in the Cabinet like a picket holding his position on the line; but if Johnson had desired to move Stanton he would have done so. So far as the difference of opinion between the President and the Secretary of War is concerned, the responsibility is placed on the President. The Constitution is such that Johnson was right and Stanton was wrong; and this clinging to office by Stanton has injured him in the eyes of the country. We were all under deep feeling at that time.

It tried the patience of the most patient man to see all the results of the war deliberately laid at the feet of the South by the man we trusted. Stanton was not a patient man, but one whose temper had been tried by severe labor, and whose love for the Union was volcanic in its fierceness. If people would only remember the privation under which Stanton acted they would do him more justice. I confess, however, I should not have liked to have been in Johnson's place. Stanton required a man like Lincoln to manage him. I should not have liked to have had that responsibility. At the same time Stanton is one of the great men of the Republic. He was as much a martyr to the Union as Sedgwick or McPherson. I held him in great personal esteem, and his character in high honor. We never became very intimate; but looking back on our intercourse I am gratified to think that every day that Stanton lived we grew better and better friends. After my election to the Presidency, one of Stanton's friends came to see me, and said the Secretary was in bad health, his fortune was limited, and he thought the Republican party of the country owed him a debt of gratitude. I asked him what he thought would be gratifying to Stanton. I was told a small mission to Italy, Belgium, or somewhere where the climate would be agreeable would be grateful to his friends. I said I thought I could do for him much more than that, and that I had already resolved to make him Justice of the Supreme Court. A few days later the appointment was made. It was a great surprise to Stanton. His letter to me acknowledging it was beautiful and affectionate. He died within a few days of his appointment. I have always thought that the country could not do too much for Stanton and his family; and after the father's death I did all I could for the son. I made him my personal attorney. The promising young man died, to my great regret, not long since. If I were asked to name the greatest men of the Republic, I certainly should include Stanton among them."

Frequently our conversation would turn to home affairs and politics. On these questions the General always speaks without reserve. "I have never," he said, "shared the resentment felt by so many Republicans toward Mr. Hayes on the ground of his policy of conciliation. At the same time I never thought it would last, because it was all on one side. There is nothing more natural than that a President, new to his office, should enter upon a policy of conciliation. He wants to make everybody friendly, to have all the world happy, to be the central figure of a contented and prosperous commonwealth. That is what occurs to every President, it is an emotion natural to the office. I can understand how a kindly, patriotic man like Hayes would be charmed by the prospect. I was as anxious for such a policy as Mr. Hayes. There has never been a moment since Lee surrendered that I would not have gone more than halfway to meet the Southern people in a spirit of conciliation. But they have never responded to it. They have not forgotten the war. A few shrewd leaders like Mr. Lucins Q. C. Lamar and others have talked conciliation; but any one who knows Mr. Lamar knows that he meant this for effect, and that at least he was as much in favor of the old *régime* as Jefferson Davis. The pacification of the South rests entirely with the South. I do not see what the North can do that has not been done, unless we surrender the results of the war. I am afraid there is a large party in the North who would do that now. I have feared even that our soldiers would begin to apologize for their part in the war. On that point what a grand speech General Sherman made in New York on a recent Decoration Day. I felt proud of Sherman for that speech. It was what a soldier and the general of an army should say. The radical trouble with the Southern leaders is, that instead of frankly acting with the Republicans in the North, they have held together, hoping by an alliance with the Democrats to control the government. I think Republicans should go as far as possible in conciliation, but not far enough to lose self-respect. Nor can any one who values the freedom of suffrage be satisfied with election results like those in the last canvass for the presidency. I have no doubt, for instance, that Mr. Hayes carried North Carolina, and that it was taken from him. No one old enough to read and write can doubt that the Republican party with anything like a fair vote would have carried, and perhaps did carry, Arkansas, Alabama, and Mississippi. I never doubted that they carried Louisiana, South Carolina, and Florida. Whether it was wise or unwise to have given the negro suffrage, we have done so, and no one can look on satisfied and see it taken from him. The root of the whole difference lies in that.

"The South," continued the General, "has been in many ways a disappointment to me. I hoped a great deal from the South, but these hopes have been wrecked. I hoped that Northern capital would pour into the South, that Northern influence and Northern energy would soon repair all that war had wasted. But that never came. Northern capitalists saw that they could not go South without leaving self-respect at home, and they remained home. The very terms of the invitations you see in all the Southern papers show that. The editors say they are glad to have Northern men provided they do not take part in politics. Why shouldn't they take part in politics? They are made citizens for that. So long as this spirit prevails there will be no general emigration of Northern men to the South. I was disappointed, very much so. It would have been a great thing for the South if some of the streams of emigration from New England and the Middle States toward Iowa and Kansas had been diverted into the South. I hoped much from the poor white class. The war, I thought, would free them from a bondage in some respects even lower than slavery; it would revive their ambition; they would learn, what we in the North know so well, that labor is a dignity, not a degradation, and assert themselves and become an active Union element. But they have been as much under the thumb of the slave-holder as before the war. Andrew Johnson, one of the ablest of the poor white class, tried to assert some independence; but as soon as the slave-holders put their thumb upon him, even in the Presidency, he became their slave. It is very curious and very strange. I hoped for different results, and did all I could to bring them around, but it could not be done.

"Looking back," said the General, "over the whole policy of reconstruction, it seems to me that the wisest thing would have been to have continued for some time the military rule. Sensible Southern men see now that there was no government so frugal, so just, and fair as what they had under our generals. That would have enabled the Southern people to pull themselves together and repair material losses. As to depriving them, even for a time, of suffrage, that was our right as a conqueror, and it was a mild penalty for the stupendous crime of treason. Military rule would have been just to all, to the negro who wanted freedom, the white man who wanted protection, the Northern man who wanted Union. As State after State showed a willingness to come into the Union, not on their own terms but upon ours, I would have admitted them. This would have made universal suffrage unnecessary, and I think a mistake was made about suffrage. It was unjust to the negro to throw upon him the responsibilities of citizenship, and expect him to be on even terms with his white neighbor. It was unjust to the North. In giving the South negro suffrage, we have given the old slave-holders forty votes in the electoral college. They keep those votes, but disfranchise the negroes. That is one of the gravest mistakes in the policy of reconstruction. It looks like a political triumph for the South, but it is not. The Southern people have nothing to dread more than the political triumph of the men who led them into secession. That triumph was fatal to them in 1860. It would be no less now. The trouble about military rule in the South was that our people did not like it. It was not in accordance with our institutions. I am clear now that it would have been better for the North to have postponed suffrage, reconstruction, State governments, for ten years, and held the South in a territorial condition. It was due to the North that the men who had made war upon us should be powerless in a political sense forever. It would have avoided the scandals of the State governments, saved money, and enabled the Northern merchants, farmers, and laboring men to reorganize society in the South. But we made our scheme, and must do what we can with it. Suffrage once given can never be taken away, and all that remains for us now is to make good that gift by protecting those who have received it.

"And yet," said the General, "if the Southern people would only put aside the madness of their leaders, they would see that they are richer now than before the war. We hear a constant wail from the oppressed South, but the wail comes only from politicians. The South is richer now than before the war. There has been a fall in the value of lands, but the whole country has felt that. I do not count the value of the slaves, although I would not be surprised if the figures showed that the Southern people had earned more than the value of the slaves they lost. Money is not held in as few hands as before the war, but the people, *per capita*, are richer. And that, after all, is what we want to see in a republic. Take cotton alone. Before the war a crop of two and a half million or three million bales at six cents a pound was an immense result. Now we have crops of five millions of bales at ten cents a pound! What a commentary that is upon the old story that the negro could only work under the lash! Before the war the North sent the South pork, corn, iron, cloth—now the Southerners blast their own iron, raise their own pork, and make their own cloth. Many of these things they learned to do during the war, and now they feel the advantage of that stern education. British Prime Minister William E. Gladstone, in his remarkable article on 'Kin beyond the Sea,' spoke with wonder of the recuperative powers of the country. What would he have said if he had known the full statistics? Before the war the South sent its cotton to the North and to England. Now there are mills flourishing in the South, flourishing even under the depression which affects the cotton industry in the North. When I talk with New England cotton-spinners, they tell me of hard times and closing mills. When I talk to ex-Confederate General Roger A. Toombs of Georgia, he tells me that his money invested in cotton-mills in the South returns him twenty-five per cent. All of this is natural, because labor is cheap in the South, the cotton grows there, and there is an unlimited supply of waterpower. The growth of this cotton industry in the South must have an important effect on the commerce of the world. So with iron. The South is doing splendidly with iron, and I would not be surprised to see it compete with the established industries in older States.

In rice and sugar I do not see any advance upon what was done before the war. But these crops are as large, I think, as before. In this you see the success of the negro as a laborer. He has steadily worked during all this time of excitement. While his old masters have been declaiming upon their misfortunes, their ruin, their oppression, he has given the South a material prosperity that it never knew before the war. What a comment you find in these facts upon the cant of the demagogues who keep the South in an endless broil over its miseries, bringing disgrace on our country by repudiation schemes, while all the time it grows richer and richer. Since the war all this profit has been income, for during this time the people have not paid their State or local debts, and that has been to their gain. That is only temporary, however. In the end that will be a great loss. There is nothing that costs so much in the end as repudiation.

"The most troublesome men in public life," said the General, "are those over-righteous people who see no motives in other people's actions but evil motives, who believe all public life is corrupt, and nothing is well done unless they do it themselves. They are narrow-headed men, their two eyes so close together that they can look out of the same gimlet-hole without winking."

On the morning of the 17th of May the "Ashuelot," under Commander Johnson—who had relieved Commander Perkins at Hong-Kong—came in sight of the Woosung forts, which fired twenty-one guns as a welcome. The Chinese gun-boats joined in the chorus, and the "Ashuelot" returned the salutes. There was so much cannonading and so much smoke that it seemed as if a naval battle were raging. As the smoke lifted, the American man-of-war "Monocacy" was seen steaming toward us, dressed from stem to stern. As she approached a salute was fired. We were a little bit ahead of the time appointed for our reception in Shanghai, and when the "Monocacy" came within a cable's length both vessels came to an anchor. A boat came from the "Monocacy," carrying the committee of citizens who were to meet the General. Messrs. R. W. Little, F. B. Forbes, Helland, Purden, and Hübbe. The committee was accompanied by Mr. D. W. Bailey, the American Consul-General for China, who presented the members to General Grant, and by Mrs. Little and Mrs. Holcombe, who came to meet Mrs. Grant. The committee lunched with the General, and about half-past one the "Ashuelot" slowly steamed up to the city. As we came in sight of the shipping the sight was very beautiful. The different men-of-war all fired salutes and manned yards, the merchantmen at anchor were dressed, and as the "Ashuelot" passed the crews cheered. The General stood on the quarter-deck and bowed his thanks. As we came to the spot selected for landing, the banks of the river were thronged with Chinamen. It is estimated that at least one hundred thousand lined the banks; but figures are, after all, guesses, and fail to give you an idea of the vast, far-extending, patient, and silent multitude. It was Saturday afternoon, the holiday, and consequently every one could come, and every one did, in holiday attire. One of the committee said to me, as we stood on the deck of the "Ashuelot" looking out upon the wonderful panorama of life and movement that he supposed that every man, woman, and child in Shanghai who could come was on the river bank. The landing was in the French concession. A large "go down," or storehouse, had been decorated with flags, flowers, and greenery. This building was large enough to hold all the foreign residents in Shanghai, and long before the hour of landing every seat was occupied. At three o'clock the barge of the "Ashuelot" was manned, and the General and his party embarking, slowly pulled toward the shore, while the guns of the American man-of-war fired another salute. In a few minutes we reached the landing, which was covered with scarlet cloth. Mr. Little, Chairman of the Municipal Council, received the General and escorted him into the building, the audience rising and cheering. The Chinese Governor, accompanied by a retinue of mandarins, was present. The band played "Hail Columbia," and when the music and the cheering ceased, Mr. Little read the address welcoming General Grant to Shanghai on behalf of the foreign community. The General, speaking in a conversational tone, said:

"LADIES AND GENTLEMEN: I am very much obliged to you for the hearty welcome which you have paid me, and I must say that I have been a little surprised, and agreeably surprised. I have now been a short time in the country of which Shanghai forms so important a part in a commercial way, and I have seen much to interest me and much to instruct me. I wish I had known ten years ago what I have lately learned. I hope to carry back to my country a report of all I have seen in this part of the world, for it will be of interest and possibly of great use. I thank you again for the hearty welcome you have given me."

At the close of the speech the General was escorted to his carriage. There was a guard of honor composed of sailors and marines from the American and French men-of-war, and a company of volunteer rifles. Horses are not plentiful in Shanghai, and General Grant's carriage was

A Chinese Inn

drawn by a pair of Australian horses, which, not having had a military experience, grew so impatient with the guns, the music, and the cheering that they became unmanageable, and the procession came to a halt. Lieutenant Cowles of the "Monocacy," who was in command of the escort, suggested a remedy. The horses were taken out, and the volunteer guard, taking hold of the carriage, drew it along the embankment to the Consulate, a distance of more than a mile. On arriving at the Consulate the General reviewed the escort. The evening was spent quietly, the General dining with Mr. Bailey and a few of the leading citizens of the settlement. On Sunday General Grant attended service in the cathedral. On Monday morning he visited a dairy farm and afterward made a few calls. In the evening he dined with Mr. Little, and after dinner went to the house of Mr. Cameron, the manager of the Hong-Kong and Shanghai Bank, to witness the torchlight procession and the illumination. The whole town had been agog all day preparing for the illumination, and as we strolled along the parade every house was in the hands of workmen and Chinese artists. There was a threat of bad weather, but as the sun went down the ominous winds went with it, and the evening was perfect for all the purposes of the display. The two occasions when Shanghai had exerted herself to welcome and honor a guest, were on the visits of the Duke of Edinburgh and the Grand Duke Alexis. The display in honor of General Grant far surpassed these, and what made it so agreeable was the heartiness with which English, Americans, French, Germans, and Chinese all united. I had heard a good deal during the day of what Shanghai would do. But with the memory of many *fêtes* in many lands, fresh from the stupendous demonstration in Canton, I felt skeptical as to what a little European colony clinging to the fringe of the Chinese empire could really do in the way of a display. The dinner at Mr. Little's was over at half-past nine, and in company with Mr. Little and the General I drove along the whole river front. The scene as we drove out into the open street was bewildering in its beauty. Wherever you looked was a blaze of light and fire, of rockets careering in the air, of Roman lights and every variety of fire. The ships in the harbor were a blaze of color, and looked as if they were pieces of fireworks. The lines of the masts, the rigging, and the hulls were traced in flames. The "Monocacy" was very beautiful, every line from the bow to the topmast and anchor chain hung with Japanese lanterns. This graceful, blending mass of color thrown upon the black evening sky was majestic, and gave you an idea of a beauty in fire hitherto unknown to us. "Never before," says the morning journal—for I prefer to take other authority than my own in recording this dazzling scene—"never before has there been such a blaze of gas and candles seen in Shanghai." The trees in full foliage gave a richer hue to the scenes, and they seemed, under the softening influence of the night and the fire, to be a part of the fireworks. On the front of the club house was a ten-foot star in gas jets with the word "Welcome." There was the United States coat-of-arms, with the initials "U. S. G." flanked with the words "Soldier" and "Statesman." Russell & Co. had a ten-foot star, "Welcome to Grant," and in addition there were two thousand Chinese lanterns crossing the whole building. At the Central Hotel was a six-foot St. George's star, with "U. S. G." At the French a St. George's star, with a sunburst on either side. The American Consulate was covered with lanterns arranged to form sentences: "Washington, Lincoln, Grant—three immortal Americans;" "Grant will win on this line if it takes all summer;" "The fame of Grant encircles the world;" "Grant—of the people, with the people, for the people." There was also a mammoth device in gas jets, fifty feet high, "Welcome, Grant—soldier, hero, statesman." The Japanese Consulate and the offices of the shipping company were covered with lanterns—four thousand—arranged in the most effective manner. The Astor House had this quotation from the General's speech in Hong-Kong, "The perpetual alliance of the two great English-speaking nations of the world." The English Consulate had a multitude of lanterns and the word

"Welcome" in a blazing gas jet. The Masonic Hall was a mass of light. At ten the General returned to the house of Mr. Cameron, and from there reviewed the firemen's procession. Each engine was preceded by a band, which played American airs; and it gave one a feeling of homesickness, and recalled the great days of trial and sacrifice, to hear the strains of "John Brown" and "Sherman's March through Georgia." . . .

Tientsin and Pekin

Some of John Russell Young's most compelling travel writing concerned the boat trip up the Yangtze River from Tientsin to Pekin (today's Beijing), the last leg accomplished by bearers carrying the Grant party in sedan chairs—by eight men in the case of the general, a signal honor. Young commented, with wonder and admiration as well as with a chill of horror, on the Chinese multitudes of servants and on what seemed to him to be the cheapness of life. He found the Chinese both haughty and childlike—with the rod ever at hand when it came to disciplining the lower orders. None of the Americans made note of the terrible famine in northern China, from which hundreds of thousands were dying even as the esteemed visitors were eating up a storm.

Grant was feted by the two most powerful men in the China of 1879, Viceroy Li Hung Chang, the strongman who had put down the anti-European and anti-Manchu dynasty Taiping Rebellion with enormous cost in human lives, and the regent, Prince Kung, the effective head of state, as the emperor was but a seven-year-old boy. For their part, the Chinese regarded the Americans as useful barbarians, as potential white counterweights to the more aggressive European powers that were then in the process of wedging their way into China by violent incursions. More specifically, Li Hung Chang prevailed on Grant to carry a message to Japan in hope of settling a territorial dispute over Loochoo—the Ryukyu Islands. Political considerations dictated that the Grants be treated as near-royalty; the magnificent banquets even included one for the Western and Chinese ladies, a hitherto unthinkable exercise in diplomatic cuisine.

At Tientsin we met the famous Viceroy, Li Hung Chang, the most eminent man in China, whom some admirers call the Bismarck of the East. Li Hung Chang, because of his services as commander of the army that suppressed the Taeping rebellion, has been advanced to the highest positions in the empire. He is a nobleman of the rank of earl, Grand Secretary of State, guardian of the heir apparent, head of the War Office and of the Chinese armies, director of the coast defenses. He is in command of the province which guards the road to Pekin, the most honorable viceroyalty in the empire. It shows the genius of the man that he, a Chinaman, should receive such honors from a Tartar dynasty, and even be the guardian of a Tartar emperor. It shows the wisdom and conciliatory spirit of the dynasty that they should raise a Chinaman to a position in which he is practically custodian of the throne.

The great Viceroy took an interest almost romantic in the coming of General Grant. He was of the same age as the General. They won their victories at the same time—the Southern rebellion ending in April, the Taeping rebellion in July, 1865. As the Viceroy said to a friend of mine, "General Grant and I have suppressed the two greatest rebellions known in history." Those who have studied the Taeping rebellion will not think that Li Hung Chang coupled himself with General Grant in a spirit of boasting. "How funny it is," he also said, "that I should be named Li, and General Grant's opponent should be called Lee." While General Grant was making his progress in India the Viceroy followed his movements and had all the narratives of the journey translated. As soon as the General reached Hong-Kong, Judge Denny, our able and popular consul at Tientsin, conveyed a welcome from the Viceroy. When questions were raised as to the reception of the General in Tientsin the Viceroy ended the matter by declaring that no honor should be wanting to the General, and that he himself should be the first Chinaman to greet him in Tientsin and welcome him to the chief province of the empire.

As the "Ashuelot" came into the Peiho River the forts fired twenty-one guns, and all the troops were paraded. A Chinese gun-boat was awaiting, bearing Judge Denny, our consul, and Mr. Dillon, French consul and Dean of the Consular Corps. As we came near Tientsin the scene was imposing. Wherever we passed a fort twenty-one guns were fired. All the junks and vessels were dressed in bunting. A fleet of Chinese gun-boats formed in line, and each vessel manned yards. The booming of the cannon, the waving of the flags, the manned yards, the multitude that lined the banks, the fleet of junks massed together and covered with curious lookers-on, the stately "Ashuelot," carrying the American flag at the fore, towering high above the slender Chinese vessels and answering salutes gun for gun, the noise, the smoke, the glitter of arms, the blending and waving of banners and flags which lined the forts and the rigging like a fringe—all combined to form one of the most vivid and imposing pageants of our journey. As we came near the landing the yacht of the Viceroy, carrying his flag, steamed toward us, and as soon as our anchor found its place, hauled alongside. First came two mandarins carrying the Viceroy's card. General Grant stood at the gangway, accompanied by the officers of the ship, and as the Viceroy stepped over the side of the "Ashuelot" the yards were manned and a salute was fired. Judge Denny, advancing, met the Viceroy and presented him to General Grant as the great soldier and statesman of China. The Viceroy presented the members of his suite, and the General, taking his arm, led him to the upper deck, where the two generals sat in conversation for some time, while tea and cigars and wine were passed around in approved Chinese fashion.

Li Hung Chang strikes you at first by his stature, which would be unusual in a European, and was especially notable among his Chinese attendants, over whom he towered. He has a keen eye, a large head, and wide forehead, and speaks with a quick, decisive manner. When he met the General he studied his face curiously, and seemed to show great pleasure, not merely the pleasure expressed in mere courtesy, but sincere gratification. Between the General and the Viceroy friendly relations grew up, and while we were in Tientsin they saw a great deal of each other. The Viceroy said at the first meeting that he did not care merely to look at General Grant and make his formal acquaintance, but to know him well and talk with him. As the Viceroy is known to be among the advanced school of Chinese statesmen, not afraid of railways and telegraphs, and anxious to strengthen and develop China by all the agencies of outside civilization, the General found a ground upon which they could meet and talk. The subject so near to the Viceroy's heart is one about which few men living are better informed than General Grant. During his stay in China, wherever the General has met Chinese statesmen he has impressed upon them the necessity of developing their country, and of doing it themselves. No man has ever visited China who has had the opportunities of seeing Chinese statesmen accorded to the General, and he has used these opportunities to urge China to throw open her barriers, and be one in commerce and trade with the outer world.

The General formed a high opinion of the Viceroy as a statesman of resolute and far-seeing character. This opinion was formed after many conversations—official, ceremonial, and personal. The visit of the Viceroy to the General was returned next day in great pomp. There was a marine

Our Journey Up the Peiho

guard from the "Ashuelot." We went to the viceregal palace in the Viceroy's yacht, and as we steamed up the river every foot of ground, every spot on the junks, was crowded with people. At the landing troops were drawn up. A chair lined with yellow silk, such a chair as is only used by the Emperor, was awaiting the General. As far as the eye could reach, the multitude stood expectant and gazing, and we went to the palace through a line of troops, who stood with arms at "Present." Amid the firing of guns and the beating of gongs our procession slowly marched to the palace door. The Viceroy, surrounded by his mandarins and attendants, welcomed the General. . . .

Our journey from Tientsin to Pekin was an experience in Chinese civilization. The direct distance from Tientsin to Pekin, as the crow flies, is eighty miles. By river it is one hundred and fifty miles. I have seen some curious rivers, but none so curious as the Peiho. It is a narrow, muddy stream, running through a low, alluvial country, bordered with crumbling clay banks that break and fall into the water like the banks of the upper Missouri. Colonel Grant, who has had army experience on the upper Missouri, notes the resemblance between the two rivers. The Peiho runs in all directions, varying in width from twenty to a hundred feet, in depth from six feet to ten inches. The soil is rich, and our journey was through green and smiling fields of rice and wheat. We were in home latitudes, and although the sun was warmer than we had found it at any point since leaving Saigon, it was a relief to look over green meadows and swaying fields of corn; to see apple trees and be able in the morning and evening to step ashore and stride away over the meadows. Now and then familiar orchards, or clumps of trees that are called orchards, came upon the landscape to give it dignity, and near the trees clusters of small houses built of mud, baked and burned like the houses in Egypt, with this difference, that while the Egyptian houses are unroofed mud walls, with only room enough for the stones on which the corn is ground, and for the holes in which the family burrowed, these Chinese homes had pretensions to comfort. There are severe winters on the Peiho, when the snow falls and the frost binds the earth, and cold, searching winds come all the way from Siberia. From December to March the ice locks up the river, and at no time of the year have you the gentle, gracious climate of the Nile. The absence of stone makes clay a necessary element in building. If there were roads in China stone could be brought from quarries. The absence of roads prevents one section, like the Peiho, from enjoying advantages which nature has bestowed upon other sections, like those, for instance, which border on Mongolia. The Chinaman has no world to draw from but the world immediately around him, and all the resources of his empire beyond the reach of a day's journey are as far away as the resources of India or Japan.

Steam has never disturbed the waters of the upper Peiho. The barbarian brings his huge engines as far as Tientsin, but even this is a serious effort and there are few things a mariner would rather not do than make his way from the Taku forts at the mouth of the river to the Tientsin wharves. Our good and well-handled vessel, the "Ashuelot," made the trip, and it seemed to me that the only seamanship required was patience tempered with resignation. The "Ashuelot" was built for Chinese waters, and is kept on the Chinese coast because she can run in and out of awkward corners like a living, useful creature. She reminds you of the web-footed gun-boats, of which Lincoln spoke in one of his homely war documents, amphibious craft, almost as useful on land as on water, and to be trusted in everything but a high sea. But the Peiho was too eccentric even for the "Ashuelot," and she came up the river caroming from bank to bank, bulging into the mud, scraping over bars, sometimes lying across the river from bank to bank like a bridge or a boom. Navigation under these circumstances is teasing. In this venerable land where people live and labor as their ancestors did before the Christian era, where the boats go up and down the river as in the days of Confucius, where man in his own person accepts the lowest and severest forms of labor, taking the place of the steam-engine in your boats and of the horse in your wagons, you need no qualities so much as patience and resignation. Everything is primitive. You see nothing that does not speak of the experience and repose of centuries. A skilled Chinaman could build a shallow boat, drawing a few inches of water, with a propelling wheel in the stern, and skurry up and down the river under steam. But when you think of the labor that would thus be extinguished, the thousands who live on the river, whose home is on the boats, who labor on the water from infancy to old age, who have tracked and splashed and waded through the shallow Peiho, as their fathers did before them, we see what a serious economical problem is involved in steam navigation. As I remarked in Canton, there can be no successful labor-saving machinery in a country where man is so cheap.

The question of how we should go to Pekin had been discussed. You can go on horseback, or in carts, or in boats. It is only a question of degree in discomfort, for there is no comfort in China—none at least in travel. The quickest way of reaching Pekin from Tientsin is by horse. Horseback riding is the principal amusement in Tientsin, and you can find good horses with Chinese attendants at a reasonable rate. Mr. Holcombe went ahead in a cart, so as to prepare the legation for the reception of the General and party. The cart in China is the accustomed method of travel, although an attempt at luxury has been made in arranging a mule cart or litter. The litter seems to be a recollection of the Indian litter or palanquin. You creep into an oblong box, with a rest for the head should you care to lie down. This box is mounted on shafts, and you have a mule leading and another bringing up the rear. While reviewing our arrangements for the journey, Mr. Holcombe, who has seen nearly every form of adventure and travel in China, gave his preference to the mule litter. The horse was impossible for the ladies of the expedition. The carts embodied so many forms of discomfort that we were not brave enough to venture. They have no springs, and the roads worn and torn and gashed make travel a misery. There was no available method but the boats, and all day Judge Denny and other friends were busy in arranging the boats for the comfort of the General. In this labor the Judge was assisted by Mr. Hill, an old American resident of China, who knew the language, and who was so anxious to do honor to General Grant that he volunteered as quartermaster and admiral of the expedition. It would have been difficult to find a better quartermaster. There was no trouble, no care that he did not take to insure us a safe and easy road to Pekin.

When our boats assembled they formed quite a fleet. They were moored near the "Ashuelot," and all the morning Chinamen were running backward and forward, carrying furniture and food. The party who visited Pekin were General Grant and Mrs. Grant; Mrs. Holcombe, wife of the Acting American Minister; Colonel Grant; Lieutenant Belknap, Mr. Deering, and Mr. Case, officers of the "Ashuelot." Mr. Hill, as I have said, went along as quartermaster. Mr. Pethick, the accomplished vice-consul of Tientsin, and one of the best Chinese scholars in our service, and the secretary of the Viceroy, an amiable young mandarin, who knew English enough to say "Good morning," were among our escorts. There were two small, shallow gun-boats, which seemed to have no guns, except muskets, who brought up our rear. The General's boat was what is called a mandarin's boat, a large, clumsy contrivance that looked, as it towered over the remainder of the fleet, like Noah's ark. It had been cleaned up and freshened, and was roomy. There were two bedrooms, a small dining-room, and in the stern what seemed to be a Chinese laundry house three stories high. It seemed alive with women and children, who were always peeping out of windows and portholes to see what new prank the barbarians were performing, and scampering away if gazed at. These were the families of the boatmen, who have no other home but the river. The other boats were small, plain shells, divided into two rooms and covered over. The rear of the boat was given to the boatmen, the front to the passengers. In this front room was a raised platform of plain pine boards, wide enough for two to sleep. There was room for a chair and a couple of tables. If the weather was pleasant we could open the sides by taking out the slats, and as we reclined on the bed look out on the scenery. But during the day it was too warm, and in addition to the sun there were streaming clouds of dust that covered everything. During the night it was cold enough for blankets, so that our boats were rarely or never open, and we burrowed away most of the time as though in a kennel or a cage. Each of the small boats had room for two persons. In the rear the cooking was done. The General had a special cooking boat, which brought up the rear, and when the hour for meals came was hauled alongside.

We should have been under way at daybreak, and the General was up at an early hour and anxious to be away. But the Chinese mind works slowly, and a visit to the General's boat—the flagship as we called it—showed that it would be noon before we could go. Judge Denny had taken off his coat, and was trying to stimulate the Chinese mind by an example of western energy. But it was of no use. The Chinaman has his pace for every function and was not to be hurried. The day was oppressively warm and the knowledge of the General's departure had brought a multitude of Chinamen to the water side. About noon the last biscuit had been stored, all the sails were hoisted, and the fleet moved away under the command of our quartermaster and admiral, Hill. The purpose was to pull through the wilderness of junks that crowd the river for miles, and wait the General above. An hour later the General went on board the Viceroy's private yacht and pushed up the river. A small steam launch from the "Ashuelot" led the way. The result of this was advantageous. If the General had gone in his own boat it would have taken him some time to thread his way through the junks. But a boat carrying the viceroyal flag has terror for the boatmen, who, as soon as they saw it coming, hastened to make room. A Chinese officer stood in the bow and encouraged them to this by loud cries and imprecations. Whenever there was any apathy, he would reach over with his bamboo pole and beat the sluggard over the shoulders. It was woe to any boatman who crossed our path, and only one or two ventured to do so, to their sore discomfort. We pushed through the wilderness of junks at full speed. We passed the bridge of boats and under the walls of the ruined cathedral destroyed in the Tientsin massacre of the Sisters of Charity. Here there was a pause, as we were passing the house of the Viceroy, and etiquette demands that when one great mandarin passes the home of another he shall stop and send his card and make kind inquiries. So we stopped until Mr. Pethick carried the General's card to the viceregal house, and returned with the card and the compliments of the Viceroy.

After taking our leave of the Viceroy we came into the open country, and found our fleet waiting under the immediate and vociferous command of Admiral Hill. The admiral was on the bank, wearing a straw hat and carrying a heavy stick, which he waved over the coolies and boatmen as he admonished them of their duties. The admiral had learned the great lesson of diplomacy in the East—terror—and it was difficult to imagine anything more improving to the Chinese mind than his aspect as he moved about with his stick. Boating on the Peiho is an original experience. Sometimes you depend upon the sail. When the sail is useless a rope is taken ashore and three or four coolies pull you along. If you get aground, as you are apt to do every few minutes, the coolies splash into the water and push you off the mud by sheer force of loins and shoulders, like carters lifting their carts out of the mud. What one needs in boating like this is, I have remarked, resignation and patience. The men who pull your boats have done so all their lives. They are a sturdy, well-knit race, and seem to thrive under their exertions. Ordinary travelers generally tie up for the night and go on during the day. There are three or four villages on the river where the boats and junks rendezvous, and as we passed them we saw fleets at anchor, mainly rice-boats. The admiral however had organized his expedition so that we should move day and night. The boatmen do not like night service, but with double relays it is not arduous. The responsibility, however, of the undertaking was serious, for if the admiral ventured to go on board the boat and sleep the boatmen would tie up and sleep likewise. As it was impossible even for the most willing admiral to walk all night as well as all day, we discovered on the second morning of our journey that instead of moving along we were quietly at rest. The coolies were asleep, the boatmen had thrown down their oars and fallen asleep, disregarding the menaces of the admiral, who had admonished them to vigilance before he turned in. Human nature has its limitations, and once the eye of the admiral was closed the boatmen lay down on the banks and slept. We might have remained all night at rest, but Lieutenant Belknap discovered the situation and gave the alarm. The admiral turned out with his stick, and after a few minutes of vigorous and effective maneuvering we got under way. But there was no more sleep for the admiral that night. He had lost confidence in his boatmen, and as they tugged along the river bank with their ropes over their shoulders he tramped on behind with his cudgel, telling them in forcible Chinese what he thought of men who would basely go to sleep after promising to remain awake and pull. You can imagine that boating under these circumstances is not an exciting experience. Here we are fresh from the feverish West, where nothing that is worth doing is done at less than a pace of fifty miles an hour. Here we are journeying from a seaport to the capital of the oldest and most populous empire in the world—an empire before some of whose achievements even the proudest of us must bow. At home we could run the distance in two or three hours—in a morning train while we looked over the columns of the newspaper and smoked the breakfast cigar. Here your journey is a matter of days, and although you may chafe under the consciousness of so much time wasted there is no help for it. You must accept it, and you will be wise if you do as Mrs. Grant did, and take a cheerful view and look on the trip as a picnic, and see the pleasant side of a journey in which you are hauled along a muddy, shallow river at the pace of a mile or two an hour. We all of us seemed to be cheerful. Our expedition had grown into quite a fleet, and we named our boats after the English navy. We had a "Vixen" and a "Growler," a "Spitfire" and a "Terror;" the General's hulk was called "Téméraire," and the cooking boat the "Chow Chow." We exchanged visits from boat to boat. There was reading and sleeping, drawing sketches and writing. When the sun was in his strength we sheltered ourselves and dozed. In the cool of the evening, or as the sun went down, we went ashore and strode over the fields, crossing the bends of the river and meeting our boats further up. When we went ashore we were always followed by a policeman from the gun-boat, whose duty it was to see that we did not go astray or fall into unfriendly hands. When we came to a village the magistrates and head men came out and saluted us and offered us welcome and protection. Then we learned that the Viceroy had sent word of our coming, and had commanded the officials of every degree to hasten and offer their homage.

Even such a trip has its bits of adventure. In this country there are squalls, spits of wind that scud over the fields, and fill your sails and send you booming along. Then the coolie's heart rejoices, and he stays on board and gorges himself with rice and crawls into his corner and sleeps. Then the admiral comes on board and unbends himself, and tells stories of Chinese life and character: how he was chased by Chinamen near Shanghai when building the Woosung Railroad, how he knew Ward and Burgevine in the Taeping rebellion days. These squalls, however, have to be closely watched, for the sails are large, the boats wide and shallow, and a sudden whiff of wind will career them over. The boatmen, however, are alert, and as the wind comes over the wheat fields and the orchards down falls the sail. One morning some of the party went on board the mandarin's boat to show our Chinese friend as much attention as we could through an interpreter. These attentions never proceed far. You cannot say many things to a Chinese mandarin, no matter how civil you mean to be, when your medium is an interpreter, and where there is really no common theme of conversation. You see that you are objects of wonder, of curiosity to each other. You cannot help regarding your Chinese friend as something to be studied, something you have come a long way to see, whose dress, manners, appearance amuse you. To him you are quite as curious. He looks down upon you. You are a barbarian. You belong to a lower grade in the social system. You have strength, rude energy, prowess; you have navies and fleets; you have battered down his forts and put your heel on his breast. You can do so again. But he has no respect for this power; for it is the teaching of all the sages that the military quality is the last to be honored, that war is not in any sense to be commended, and that the great nations whose power is in their armaments are none the less barbarous. To stand before a mandarin and feel that you are being studied as a type of rude and barbarous civilization is not conducive to talk, to such talk, at least, as you seek with men of your own race. You are so far apart in all things that there is no common theme upon which talk becomes useful. You tell him wonderful things, he tells you polite things, for nothing can surpass his politeness, his careless politeness which runs along like the score of an opera, never missing a note. You tell him marvels, and as he hears each marvel he thanks you, very much as if you had given him a present. You tell him that the world is round; that our year begins in January; that our country is almost as large as the Chinese empire, fourth in size and sixth in population among the nations of the world; that we do not smoke opium; that our women do pretty much as they please; that we have steamboats and telegraphs; that we have no emperor; that we are on the other side of the globe; that if you bored through from where you stand you would come out in the United States; you tell him stories of this kind, and he sits in wonder and thanks you, and hopes happiness will follow you for long years, and that all the winds of heaven will blow blessings upon you. I half suspect that he regards most of your narrative as a kind of highly-colored rhetoric, marvelous and flowery, because you want to be polite to him, as he is to you.

As I was saying, some of our party had gone on the mandarin's boat, to be polite to him and tell him about the world being round. The mandarin was very civil, and, the admiral acting as interpreter, a great deal of information, mainly geographical, was imparted. Then one of the party stepped over to another boat for the purpose of calling on the General. The way you make calls while boating on the Peiho is to hop from boat to boat, for they all remain within easy distance of one another, and there is no trouble in going through the whole fleet when you are in a visiting humor. One of our party stepped on another boat. Before he had gone fifty paces a spitting squall came over the fields and caught the sail. The boat began to reel and bilge over against the bank. The boatman rushed toward his ropes, but too late. The boat was on its beam ends, and the best that could be done was to hold on to the sides of the deck and keep your feet out of the water. There was nothing calamitous in the situation. If the worst came to the worst you had only to walk ashore in water up to your knees. But the boat righted again, and not even that harm was done. Our Chinese mandarin pulled up in great excitement. Nothing could exceed his concern—his polite expressions of concern. The idea that one the Viceroy was honoring should be almost tossed into the water! Terrible! And by Chinamen, too! Horrible! He would make an example of that boatman. The only proper punishment would be to take his head off. At the very least he must have two hundred lashes. We interfered as well as we could. No harm had been done, and accidents will happen to the best-managed boats, and who can tell when a squall of wind may come spitting and hissing over the fields? The captain of the careening boat was already on his knees—abject and imploring. If Mrs. Grant's boat had been within reach, influence of a decisive nature might have been invoked in favor of mercy. But her boat was half a mile away, and justice to be effective must be summary, and the best that could be done was to reduce the blows from two hundred to twenty. So the unlucky captain was seized by two of his own crew, and laid down on his face on his own deck. One held his head down, another his feet, and a third kneeling gave him twenty blows with a thick bamboo cane. The blows did not seem to be severe, and would not have brought a whimper out of an average New England boy. At the close of the punishment the whipped man knelt before the mandarin, pressed his forehead to the ground, expressed his gratitude for the mercy he had received, and his contrition for his fault. Then with crestfallen looks he went to his boat and took command. About half an hour later I saw him gorging himself with rice and chattering away with his comrades as though he had never known a lash. The more you see of the Orientals the more you are struck with the fact that many of their ways are as the ways of children.

In the evening we would gather in the General's boat and talk. I recall no remarkable incident in the conversations except the discovery that one of the naval men knew some words of the song about Sherman's march through Georgia. He only knew one verse, and that inaccurately. But the fragmentary lines were constructed into a verse in some such fashion as scientific men take a bone and construct an animal, and the result was a Union war song, sung as badly perhaps as any song could be, but full of music to us in the memories it brought of home and of the great days in

American history. This snatch of song led to other snatches, all of them inaccurate and badly chanted, but homelike and familiar, and given with the usual gusto, so that when we went from the General's boat, and picked our way from boat to boat until we found our own, we were surprised to find it midnight, and that the long evening hours, which one would suppose to drag wearily along on this tedious, muddy river, had swept past us like a dream. So gentle are the memories of home. And some of us sat on the deck and smoked a last cigar—just one last cigar before turning in—to see the moon, and watch the night shadows, and think of home. . . . You see I am writing about it in rather a fanciful, poetic mood, talking about the moon and the voices of nature just as if I were describing the Wissahickon or the blue Juniata. That is, however, a privilege that writers have—the privilege of looking at subjects by any light they please, moonlight or sunlight or a red, glaring flame. Then everybody had told us that the trip to Pekin would be dreadful and would not pay for the trouble, and that we had much better stay in Shanghai or Tientsin, where there were clubs, and dancing, and newspapers, and every one dying to give us dinners and balls and princely welcome. And we had come on the journey in something like a spirit of defiance of all good advice, flying in the face of the Providence which one's friends are always carrying around in their carpet-bags and leveling at you, in highwayman fashion. . . .

On the morning of the third day of our departure from Tientsin we awoke and found ourselves tied up to the bank. . . .

. . . The sun was rising, and it was important to reach Pekin if possible before he was on us in all his power. There were chairs from Prince Kung for some of the party, and horses for others. There were mule litters for the luggage and donkeys for the servants, and at eight o'clock we were under way. The General rode ahead in a chair carried by eight bearers. This is an honor paid only to the highest persons in China. The other chairs were carried by four bearers. Mrs. Grant and Mrs. Holcombe rode some distance behind the General, two other chairs were occupied by two other members of the party, and the rest mounted. By the time we formed in procession it was really a little army. Our own party, with the servants, was large enough, and to this was added the Chinese troops who were to escort us to Pekin. So we scrambled up the dusty bank, and into the gates of the town, and through the narrow streets. The whole town was out, and as our chairs passed the people stared at the occupants with curious eyes. . . . Invaders and prisoners had been seen before, but never a barbarian in an imperial chair and escorted by Tartar troops. Those familiar with the history of China, and who remembered the days not long since gone, when an army marched over this very road to menace Pekin, burn the summer palace of the Emperor, and dictate a humiliating peace to China; those who remember the earnestness, the supplicating earnestness, with which the government resisted the efforts of the European Powers to introduce ministers into Pekin, could not but note the contrast in the reception of General Grant, and the changes in Chinese thought which that contrast implied.* It confirmed the remark made to me in Tientsin by one of the clearest-headed men I have seen in China, that General Grant's visit had done more than anything else to break down the great wall between China and the outer world.

Our journey from Tung Chow to Pekin lasted five hours. The horsemen could have gone ahead in two hours, but the chairs moved slowly. . . .

Shortly after midday we saw in the distance the walls and towers of Pekin. We passed near a bridge where there had been a contest between the French and Chinese during the Anglo-French expedition, and one of the results of which was that the officer who commanded the French should be made a nobleman, under the name of the Count Palikao, and had later adventures in French history. As we neared the city the walls loomed up, and seemed harsh and forbidding, built with care and strength as if to defend the city. We came to a gate and were carried through a stone-arched way, and halted, so that a new escort could join the General's party. The people of Pekin, after we passed the bazaars, did not seem to note our presence. Our escort rode on over the wide, dusty lanes called streets, and all that we saw of the city was the dust which arose from the hoofs of the horses that straggled on ahead. We were so hot, so weary with riding in our chairs, so stifled with the dust, that it was an unspeakable relief to see at last the American flag floating over the gateway of the Legation, and have a grateful and gracious welcome from our hosts.

The Legation in Pekin is shut off from the main street by a wall. As you enter you pass a small lodge, from which Chinese servants look out with inquiring eyes. The American flag floats over the archway, an indication that General Grant has made his home here. It is the habit for the Legation ordinarily to display their colors only on Sundays and holidays. On

---

* To compel the Chinese government to accept the unfavorable Treaty of Tianjin of 1858, the British, with the aid of the Americans and the French, ordered their troops to march into Beijing (Pekin), the capital, on October 18, 1860. They burnt to the ground the summer palace on the outskirts of Beijing and forced the emperor to flee the city. Prince Kung, the emperor's younger brother, was left behind to reaffirm the humiliating treaty.

the right side of the walk is a series of low, one-storied buildings, which is the home of the American Minister. They are of brick, painted drab, and covered with tiles. Nothing could be plainer and at the same time more commodious and comfortable. On the left side is another series, where the Chargé d'Affaires, Mr. Holcombe, the acting Minister, resides. In the rear is a smaller building, for the archives of the Legation. Standing a little way off is a building called the Pavilion, set apart for guests. In the arrangement of the grounds and the buildings you note American simplicity and American energy. The energy seems to be devoted to making flowers and trees grow. There are flowers and trees in abundance, and coming out of the hot, dusty town, as I did an hour ago, it was grateful to be welcomed by them. They have a forlorn time in this hard soil, and I have no doubt if the secrets of the Legation were unfolded it would be found that the preservation of the roses and the cedar was among the high cares of office. Under my window is a rosebush, a couple of roses depending from one stem being all that remain of its beauty. It seems to gasp for rain. Dr. Elmore, the Peruvian Minister, lives in Mr. Seward's section, and, as he gives a dinner to General Grant this evening, he has a small army of coolies watering his plants and trying to induce them to smile upon his guests. General Grant lives in Mr. Holcombe's apartments: the Colonel and I are in the Pavilion. Our naval friends are in Mr. Seward's house, under Dr. Elmore's hospitality, which is thoughtful and untiring. The Legation offices are plain but neatly kept. You have a library with the laws of the United States, Congressional archives, newspapers, and the latest mails. In a side room is an English clerk and a Chinese clerk. Behind this office is a row of other buildings, where the servants live and where the horses are kept.

On the evening of our arrival the American residents in Pekin called in a body on the General to welcome him and read an address. Dinner over our party entered the Legation parlors, and were presented to the small colony of the favored people who have pitched their tents in Pekin. The members of this colony are missionaries, members of the customs staff, diplomatists, and one or two who have claims or schemes for the consideration of the Chinese Government. After being introduced to the General and his party, Dr. Martin, the president of the Chinese-English University, stepped forward and read an address, to which General Grant responded, thanking his fellow citizens for their kindness, wished them all prosperity in their labors in China and a happy return to their homes, where he hoped some day to meet them. . . .

Within an hour or two after General Grant's arrival in Pekin he was

The Audience with the Emperor (from a Chinese drawing)

waited upon by the members of the Cabinet, who came in a body, accompanied by the military and civil governors of Pekin. These are the highest officials in China, men of stately demeanor. They were received in Chinese fashion, seated around a table covered with sweetmeats, and served with tea. The first Secretary brought with him the card of Prince Kung, the Prince Regent of the empire, and said that his Imperial Highness had charged him to present all kind wishes to General Grant, and to express the hope that the trip in China had been pleasant. The Secretary also said that as soon as the Prince Regent heard from the Chinese Minister in Paris that General Grant was coming to China he sent orders to the officials to receive him with due honor. The General replied that he had received nothing but honor and courtesy from China. This answer pleased the Secretary, who said he would be happy to carry it to the Prince Regent.

General Grant did not ask an audience of the Emperor. The Emperor is a child seven years of age, at his books, not in good health, and under the care of two old ladies called the empresses. When the Chinese Minister in Paris spoke to the General about audience, and his regret that the sovereign of China was not of age, that he might personally entertain an ex-President, the General said he hoped no question of audience would be raised. He had no personal curiosity to see the Emperor, and there could be no useful object in conversing with a child. This question of seeing the Emperor is one of the sensitive points in Chinese diplomacy. The Chinese idea is that the Emperor is the Son of Heaven, the titular if not the accepted king of the world, king of kings, a sacred being, not to be seen by profane, barbarian eyes. Foreign powers have steadily fought this claim, and have insisted by every means upon the Emperor standing on the same level as other sovereigns and heads of States, receiving and sending ministers, and taking an active personal interest in international affairs. These arguments went so far as to induce the last Emperor to receive the foreign ministers in the palace. This was a great triumph. It made a sensation at the time. I have seen a picture of the audience, drawn from memory by one of the interpreters. There are ministers standing in a row, the Emperor on his throne, mandarins in the background, Prince Kung on his knees handing the credentials of the ministers to the pale, thin, puny sovereign. The audience lasted some minutes, and was confined to the utterance of a few words in Tartar language to the effect that the credentials would be considered. That is the only time in recent years when barbarian eyes have looked on sacred majesty. The emperor who then reigned has, to use courtly speech, ascended on the great dragon to be a guest on high. The youth of the present sovereign has prevented any audience, for, of course, an audience would be a comedy, with the sovereign a timid unhealthy boy, who had never seen a foreigner, and who would probably run off crying. The Chinese, therefore, have postponed the audience question until the Emperor comes of age. At the same time the foreign ministers have always made a point of their right to demand it. The fact that General Grant had been the head of a nation, and had corresponded directly with the Emperor, gave him the right to request an audience. There was no reason, even in Chinese logic, why such a request should be refused. Many of those well informed on Eastern questions were anxious that this request should be made; that it would render things easier in dealing with the Chinese; that, in fact, the only way of dealing with the government was to hammer and hammer, and always to hammer, until these prejudices were broken down. But the General had not come to China in a hammering mood, and had no curiosity to see a boy seven years old, and the question dropped.

The day after his arrival in Pekin General Grant saw Prince Kung. The General and party left the Legation at half-past two, the party embracing Mr. Holcombe, the acting Minister; Colonel Grant, Lieutenant Charles

The Audience with Prince Kung

Belknap, C. W. Deering, and A. Ludlow Case, Jr., of the "Ashuelot." The way to the Yamen was over dirty roads, and through a disagreeable part of the town, the day being unusually warm, the thermometer marking 101 degrees in the shade. This is a trying temperature under the best circumstances, but in Pekin there was every possible condition of discomfort in addition. When we came to the courtyard of the Yamen the secretaries and a group of mandarins received the General and his party, and escorted them into the inner court. Prince Kung, who was standing at the door, advanced and saluted the General, and said a few words of welcome, which were translated by Mr. Holcombe. The sun was beating down, and the party passed into a large, plainly-furnished room, where was a table laden with Chinese food. The Prince, sitting down at the center, gave General Grant the seat at his left, the post of honor in China. He then took up the cards, one by one, which had been written in Chinese characters, on red paper, and asked Mr. Holcombe for the name and station of each member of the General's suite. He spoke to Colonel Grant, and asked him the meaning of the uniform he wore, his rank, and his age. He asked whether the Colonel was married and had children. When told that the Colonel had one child, a daughter, the Prince condoled with him, saying, "What a pity." In China, you must remember that female children do not count in the sum of human happiness, and when the Prince expressed his regret at the existence of the General's granddaughter, he was saying the most polite thing he knew. The Prince earnestly perused the face of the General, as though it were an unlearned lesson. He expected a uniformed person, a man of the dragon or lion species, who could make a great noise. What he saw was a quiet, middle-aged gentleman, in evening dress, who had ridden a long way in the dust and sun, and who was looking in subdued dismay at servants who swarmed around him with dishes of soups and sweetmeats, dishes of bird's-nest soup, sharks' fins, roast ducks, bamboo sprouts, and a teapot with a hot, insipid tipple made of rice, tasting like a remembrance of sherry, which was poured into small silver cups. We were none of us hungry. We had just left luncheon, and were on the programme for a special banquet in the evening. Here was a profuse and sumptuous entertainment. The dinner differed from those in Tientsin, Canton, and Shanghai, in the fact that it was more quiet; there was no display or parade, no crowd of dusky servants and retainers hanging around and looking on as though at a comedy. I didn't think the Prince himself cared much about eating, because he merely dawdled over the bird's-nest soup and did not touch the sharks' fins. Nor, in fact, did any of the ministers, except one, who, in default of our remembering his Chinese name and rank, one of the party called Ben Butler. The dinner, as far as the General was concerned, soon merged into a cigar, and the Prince toyed with the dishes as they came and went, and smoked his pipe. . . .

[After a few days in Beijing, it was back down the river.] Pleasant were our days in Tientsin, pleasant even with the severe and baking weather. Our host had the happy tact not to make his hospitality oppressive, and there was time to walk in the lanes, to go down on the ships, to sit on the piazza, and study out the wealth of flowers and shrubbery with which the Judge had decorated his gardens at the expense of all the other gardens in Tientsin. And the pleasant men and women you met in Tientsin, whose names you wish it were graceful to recall, but whose kindness you cannot fail to bear on and on in your memory! Pleasant, notably, were our relations with the great Viceroy, whose kindness seemed to grow with every hour, and to tax itself for new forms of expression. If it had been the kindness of a mere citizen, a merchant with tea to sell, it would have been pleasant, as showing good feeling; but coming from the greatest of Chinese statesmen, one of the first noblemen in the empire, ruler over an empire itself in the extent and population of his province, with power of life and death, with armies to follow him and ships to carry his will, it passed out of the range of hospitality and became a question of international politics. Li Hung Chang's reception of General Grant was as notable an event in the utter setting aside of precedents and traditions as can be found in the recent history of China. It required a great man, who could afford to be progressive and independent, to do it. I know that this appears to be trivial and is the record of small things; but in the East, and especially in China, it is only in trivial things that you can see the great progress which has been made in the opinions of the country. Whatever shows an advance on the part of Chinese rulers and statesmen toward America is so much an improvement on the cruel bayonet and broadside policy which has borne sway that I am glad to note it. There was probably nothing more notable than the entertainment given to Mrs. Grant by the wife of the Viceroy.

You must remember the position in which woman is held in China— her seclusion, her withdrawal from affairs, from social life, her relation to a society which acknowledges polygamy and the widest freedom of divorce—to understand how radical a thing it was for the Viceroy to throw open the doors of his house and bring the foreign barbarian to his hearthstone. This dinner was arranged for our last night in Tientsin, and in honor of Mrs. Grant. The principal European ladies in the colony were invited. Some of these ladies had lived in Tientsin for years and had never seen the wife of the Viceroy—had never seen him except through the blinds of the window of his chair. The announcement that the Viceroy had really invited Mrs. Grant to meet his wife, and European ladies to be in the company, was even a more extraordinary event than the presence of General Grant or the arrival of the band. Society rang with a discussion of the question which, since Mother Eve introduced it to the attention of her husband, has been the absorbing theme of civilization—what shall we wear? I have heard many expositions on this theme, but in Tientsin it was new and important. Should the ladies go in simple, Spartan style—in muslin and dimity, severely plain and colorless, trusting alone to their graces and charms, and thus show their Chinese sister the beauty that exists in beauty unadorned—or should they go in all their glory, with gems and silks and satins and the latest development of French genius in the arrangement of their hair? It was really an important question, and not without a bearing, some of us thought, on the future domestic peace of the Viceroy. The arguments on either side were conducted with ability, and I lament my inability to do them justice, and hand them over to the consideration of American ladies at home. The discussion passed beyond me and entered into the sphere of metaphysics, and became a moral, spiritual—almost a theological theme, and was decided finally in favor of the resources of civilization. The ladies went in all the glory of French fashion and taste.

No gentlemen were invited to the Viceroy's dinner, and the Viceroy himself did not entertain his guests. It was arranged that the ladies should go in chairs. Of ladies there were in all, Mrs. Grant, Mrs. Detring, Mrs. Denny, Mrs. Dillon, Mrs. Forrest, Miss Dorian, and Miss Denny. It was a distance of two miles to the Yamen, and the streets were filled with a curious multitude watching the procession of chairs, and having their own thoughts, we can well fancy, at this spectacle of the viceregal home invaded by the wives of foreign barbarians. It was quite dark when the ladies reached the Yamen. They alighted in a courtyard illuminated with lanterns, and crowded with officials in their quaint costumes. The band of the "Richmond" had been sent ahead by Captain Johnson, and as our ladies arrived they were welcomed with the familiar notes of home music. The Viceroy also had a band, and the musical effect of the two styles of music—the Chinese running largely to gongs, and the American with trumpet and drum—was unique, and added to the strangeness of the ceremony. As Mrs. Grant, who was in the first chair, descended, she was met by the wife of the Viceroy, who took her hand and escorted her into the house. The other ladies were shown in by one of the missionary ladies who came to act as interpreter. They passed through a sort of hall into a small library. The walls of this library were cut up into pigeon-holes filled with Chinese books made of soft, tough paper. The Viceroy's wife took her seat at the head of the table, and as each lady entered she was introduced by the interpreter. The hostess arose and shook hands with each in cordial European fashion, with perfect grace, and as though it had been her custom all her life to use this form of salutation. The wife of the Viceroy was found by our lady friends to be, if I may quote what one of them said to me, "the personification of well-bred ease and affability, a fine, intelligent-looking lady of middle age, her features showing marked beauty and character. When she smiled, two charming dimples played around her cheeks." The hostess wore a very long jacket and trousers of rich dark silk. Her ornaments were a long necklace of jade stone, with beads and bracelets of the same material, an immense butterfly-shaped ornament of pearls, and bits of green jade stone covering the whole back of the head. There were two other ladies of the viceregal family present, the daughter of the Viceroy, a maiden of sixteen, and his daughter-in-law, a lady of twenty-three. They sat at the opposite end of the table from the hostess, looking on with curious interest at the company of foreign ladies, the first they had ever seen. Still they restrained their curiosity, showing no wonder, no surprise, and received their European friends with as much ease as if they had been accustomed to a London drawing-room. The daughter-in-law of the Viceroy was dressed in subdued colors, much the same as the hostess, but the maiden was brilliantly costumed in a bright pink satin jacket, and green satin trousers, the whole embroidered with gold thread, and silk of a variety of colors. At every movement she tinkled with her abundant ornaments of pearl and jade, which hung in long pendants from her ears, wrists, fingers, and the cord of her fan. She wore two long gold finger-nail shields on the third and fourth fingers of her left hand, a curious ornament made necessary by the custom of high-bred persons in China of allowing the finger-nails to grow. Both of the young ladies wore their hair ornamented in the same manner as the wife of the Viceroy.

The company sat in the library about ten minutes. During this time they were served with strong pale tea, without sugar or milk, in tiny porcelain cups. Then, at a gesture from the hostess, the ladies arose and walked into another room, a larger one, the hostess conducting Mrs. Grant. Crowds of servants swarmed about, and other crowds of curious persons looked in at the windows and doors at the unusual spectacle. The dining-room was furnished in European fashion, with divans and chairs. A chandelier of four gas jets hung over the center of the table, and was an object of curiosity to all, as Tientsin has not yet attained to the blessing of gas. The dinner table was set in European style, with silver and French china, and decorated with a profusion of flowers. The ladies took seats according to the rank of their husbands, Mrs. Grant sitting on the right and Mrs. Denny on the left of the hostess. Each of the ladies had her own servant, who waited on her. The dinner was a blending of Chinese and European cookery. First came a European course. Then came a Chinese course, served in silver cups with small silver ladles and ivory chopsticks. Smaller silver cups in saucers sat at each plate, filled with the warm Chinese wine which you find at every dinner. The ladies tasted their Chinese food with fortitude, and made heroic efforts to utilize the chopsticks. The Chinese ladies partook only of their own food. The hostess kept up a conversation with all the ladies. First she asked each one her age, which in China is the polite thing to do. I have no information as to the responses elicited by this inquiry, the sources of my knowledge failing at this point. Then questions were asked as to the number of children in the families of the married ladies, and the age of each child. The younger Chinese ladies of the party sat at the other end of the table, and having no interpreter made themselves understood by signs—by graceful little gestures of the hand, nods, questioning eyes. It is wonderful how much talk can be done by pantomime, and the Chinese ladies with their quick intelligence soon found themselves in earnest conversation with their European friends. During the dinner there was a Chinese Punch and Judy show, and the noise of this entertainment, with the chatter of the servants, and the curious gazing crowd who never left the doors and windows, made an unceasing din. China has democratic customs and privileges which are never invaded. Whenever General Grant and party dined as the guest of a Chinaman, in Canton, or Shanghai, or Tientsin, it was always in presence of a multitude. If the people were to have the doors closed upon them, even the doors of the Viceroy, it would make trouble. And now, of all days in the calendar of China, this day when female barbarians are welcomed to a nobleman's house, it is important that all the world should stand by and see the wonder.

The hostess, with a gesture and smile of welcome, drank from her cup of warm wine a toast to her friends. The ladies sipped their wine in response. This astonished the hostess, who had been told that it was the custom of barbarian ladies to drink their glasses dry. But it was explained that while some ambitious gentlemen in foreign society ventured upon such experiments the ladies never did. The hostess wondered at this, and seemed to think that somehow it would be more like what she had heard if the ladies drank more champagne, if they drained their glasses and turned them upside down. Then the jewels were passed from hand to hand to be examined by the Chinese ladies. This study of jewelry, of diamond and emerald, of ruby and turquoise, occupied most of the time that remained to the dinner. Once or twice the tall form of the Viceroy could be observed looking over the heads of the crowd to see how his wife and her foreign friends were enjoying themselves. When observed his Excellency withdrew. Although not appearing during the dinner, nor at the reception before, the Viceroy was now and then seen moving about among the curious gazers, evidently anxious about his feast, anxious that nothing should be wanting in honor of his guests.

The Dance at the Viceroy's

After the dinner the party went into another room. Here was a piano which had been brought from the foreign settlement. This was a new delight to the hostess, who had never seen a piano, and she expressed her pleasure and surprise. One of the pieces was a waltz, a merry German waltz, and two of the ladies went through the measures, giving variety to the dance by balancing separately with one arm akimbo, the other holding up the skirt, then twirling away to different parts of the room and coming together again. This revelation of barbarian customs created great astonishment, and when the dance stopped there was a chorus of approbation from the Chinese, as if they had discovered a new pleasure in the world, the hostess nodding and smiling with more energy of manner than she had shown during the evening. This performance was witnessed by the Viceroy, who perhaps had his own thoughts as a far-seeing statesman as to what China would become if German music ever found its way into Chinese households, and mothers and maidens gave way to the temptations of the waltz. There were snatches of singing, one of the ladies who had an expressive voice warbling some roundelay from the Tyrol. This created another sensation, and was so new, and strange, and overwhelming that the Chinese maiden in the dazzling pink jacket lost her Oriental composure and gave a faint start and laughed, and fearing she had committed some breach of propriety, suddenly recovered herself and coyly looked about to see if she had in any way given offense to her barbarian guests. The hostess, however, sat by the side of Mrs. Grant during the whole performance, and looked on as calmly at these strange phenomena of an unknown civilization as if she had known the waltz and heard Tyrolean ditties all her days. The hostess, with high-bred courtesy, always arose when her guests did, and never sat down until they were seated. The feet of the Chinese ladies were extremely small—scarcely more than two or three inches long—and when they walked it was with difficulty, and only by the aid of the waiting-women who walked behind. A Chinese lady of rank does nothing without the aid of servants. If she wishes to take a handkerchief out of her pockets a servant performs the office. But during the whole evening, at every phase of the reception and the entertainment, the hostess showed a self-possession and courtesy that might have been learned in the drawing-rooms of Saint Germain. She took pains to show attention to every one. When the time came to leave she went with Mrs. Grant to her chair. When the others left she took her leave of them at the door, and they parted with good wishes and polite little speeches of thanks and welcome. A little rain began to fall as the guests went away. And as the country was suffering for rain, and priests had been to the temples to invoke divine propitiation in behalf of the harvests, the rain came as an omen and a blessing, and the hostess rubbed her hands with glee and laughed joyously as though heaven had sent the rain as a benediction upon her feast. Amid the hum of voices, the obeisance of courtiers, the din of the Punch and Judy show, and the fragrant sandal-wood incense, the party went out into the open courtyard, where the "Richmond's" band played "Hail Columbia." From thence into the dark street and homeward the procession of chairs kept its way. When the ladies reached home they found that the hostess had marked her appreciation of her guests by giving each one a roll of Chinese silk. The gentlemen were waiting, and it was near midnight when the line of chairs turned into the Consulate.

When the ladies returned from the dinner, General Grant and party came immediately on board the "Ashuelot." There we said farewell to our kind friends, and said our good-by, as lovers are supposed to prefer, under the stars. Our visit had been so pleasant, there had been so much grace and courtesy and consideration in our reception, that it was with sincere regret that we said farewell. The Viceroy had sent word that he would not take his leave of General Grant until we were on the border of his dominions and out at sea. He had gone ahead on his yacht, and with a fleet of gun-boats, and would await us at the mouth of the river and accompany the General on board of the "Richmond." We left our moorings at three in the morning, and were awakened by the thunder of the guns from the forts. Orders had been given that the forts should fire salutes as the General passed, that the troops should parade, and the vessels dress with flags. The day was warm and clear, and there was Oriental splendor in the scene as we slowly moved along the narrow stream and saw the people hurrying from the villages to the river side, and the smoke that came from the embrasures, and the clumsy, stolid junks teeming with sight-seers, the lines of soldiery, and the many-colored pennants fluttering in the air. The river widened as we came to the sea, and about eleven o'clock we came to the viceregal fleet at anchor under the guns of the Waku forts. As we passed, every vessel manned yards, and all their guns and all the guns from the forts thundered a farewell. Two or three miles out we saw the tapering masts of the "Richmond," which, after so long a chase, had at last found General Grant. The "Ashuelot" answered the salute and steamed over the bar at half speed, so as to allow the Viceroy's fleet to join us. The bar was crossed and the blue sea welcomed us, and we kept on direct toward the "Richmond." In a short time the white smoke was seen leaping from her deck, the sailors rushed up to the rigging, and we swung around amid the thunder of her guns. Then Captain Benham came on board and was presented to General Grant. The Chinese fleet came to an anchor, and at noon precisely General Grant passed over the side of the "Ashuelot." On reaching the "Richmond" the General was received by another salute, all the officers being on deck in full uniform. The American ensign was run up at the fore and another salute was fired, the Chinese vessels joining.

After the General had been received the barge was sent to the Viceroy's boat, and in a few minutes was seen returning with Li Hung Chang, followed by other boats carrying the high officers of his government. General Grant received the Viceroy, and again the yards were manned and a salute of nineteen guns was fired. The Viceroy and his suite were shown into the cabin. Tea was served, and Li Hung Chang having expressed a desire to see the vessel, he was taken into every part, and gave its whole arrangement, and especially the guns, a minute inspection. The working of the large guns especially interested him, and Captain Bonham ordered a special drill, so as to show his Excellency the manner in which Americans worked these engines of our sinister civilization. The crew's quarters, the store-rooms, the sick bay, the engines, all the machinery were examined, and not with the curiosity of an idle sightseer, but with the interest of intelligence, as one anxious to know, and know thoroughly. The inspection lasted for an hour, and the Viceroy returned to the cabin to take his leave. He seemed loath to go, and remained in conversation for some time. General Grant expressed his deep sense of the honor which had been done him, and his pleasure at having met the Viceroy. He urged the Viceroy to make a visit to the United States, and in a few earnest phrases repeated his hope that the statesmen of China would persevere in a policy which brought them nearer to our civilization—a policy that would give new greatness to China, enable them to control the fearful famines that devastated China, and secure the nation's independence. He repeated his belief that there could be no true independence unless China availed herself of the agencies which gave prestige to other nations, and with which she had been so largely endowed by Providence. The Viceroy was friendly, almost affectionate. He hoped that General Grant would not forget him; said that he would like to meet the General now and then, and prayed that if China needed the General's counsel he would give it. He feared he could not visit foreign lands, and regretted that he had not done so in earlier years. He spoke of the friendship of the United States as dear to China, and again commended to the General and the American people the Chinese who had gone to America. It made his heart sore to hear of their ill usage, and he depended upon the justice and honor of our government for their protection. He again alluded to the Loochoo question with Japan, and begged that General Grant would speak to the Japanese Emperor, and in securing justice remove a cloud from Asia, which threw an ominous shadow over the East. The General bade the Viceroy farewell, and said he would not forget what had been said, and that he would always think of the Viceroy with friendship and esteem. So we parted, Li Hung Chang departing amid the roar of our cannon and the manning of the yards, while the "Richmond" slowly pushed her prow into the rippling waves and steamed along to Japan.

CHAPTER SEVENTEEN

Leaving China

With a sense of symbolic completion, the Grant party visited the Great Wall as its farewell to the ancient kingdom. Then, as they sailed over the Yellow Sea and up the Sea of Japan, Grant shrewdly analyzed for Young his impressions of current Chinese political weakness and her immense promise. And then Grant went into a long rumination about his own inner passivity. He had never liked the military and had detested the Mexican War but had served in it out of loyalty to the flag. He had never sought military promotions, or power, or the presidency, but all had been thrust upon him. Grant may have half believed this fey stance, but he did protest far too much. It was at the core of his being for him to deny the ambitions he certainly felt in considerable measure. In part, this was an expression of the gentleman's code, and in part it came from a certain self-effacement, from an ever-present sense of imminent failure that Grant carried with him throughout his extraordinary career. Whether because of guilt or because of self-doubt, he never could believe that he had merited such good fortune.

As soon as the Viceroy took his leave, the "Richmond" steamed slowly up the coast, for the purpose of visiting the Great Wall of China. It had been proposed to make this journey overland, and see also the tombs of the Ming dynasty. But we were under the cruel stress of unusually warm weather, and our journeys to the Temple of Heaven, the city walls, and other temples, had been attended with unusual discomfort. It was our good fortune to have a smooth sea, and when the morning came we found ourselves steaming slowly along the shores of Northern China. Navigation in the China seas is always a problem, and the coast along which we were sailing is badly surveyed. As a general thing, so carefully has science mapped and tracked the ocean that you have only to seek counsel from a vagrant, wandering star, and you will be able to tell to the minute when some hill or promontory will rise out of the waves. There was no such comfort on the China coast, and the "Richmond" had to feel her way, to grope along the coast and find the Great Wall as best we could. Fortunately the day was mild and clear, and we could steam close to shore. All the morning we sailed watching the shore, the brown, receding hills, the leaping, jutting masses of rock, the bits of greenery that seemed to rejoice in the sun, the fishing villages in houses of clay that run toward the shore. It was a lonely sea. Heretofore, in our cruise on the China coast, we had been burdened with company. The coasting track is so large that junks were always in sight, junks and fishing-boats and all manner of strange, clumsy craft. If you are used to travel on the vast seas, where a sail a week is a rapture, this presence of many ships is a consolation. It takes away the selfishness of sea life and makes you think that you are a part of the real world. But it is at the same time a trial to the sailor. The junk is an awkward, stupid trap, and always crossing your bows or edging up against you. The Chinaman thinks it good luck to cross your bows, and if he can do so with a narrow shave, just giving you a clip with his rudder as he passes, he has had a joyous adventure. While creeping up the China coast we were always on the watch for junks, but never ran one down. It was trying, however, to naval patience, and we found it so much better to be alone on the sea and look for our Great Wall as well as we could, undisturbed by the heedlessness of Chinese mariners.

About two o'clock in the afternoon Lieutenant Sperry, the navigator, had an experience that must have reminded him of Columbus discovering America. He had found the Great Wall. By careful looking through the glasses, in time we saw it—a thick, brown, irregular line that crumbled into the sea. The "Richmond" steamed toward the beach, and so gracious was the weather that we were able to anchor within a mile of shore. All the boats were let down, and as many as could be spared from the vessel went ashore—the captain, the officers, sailors in their blue tidy uniforms, and an especial sailor with a pot of white paint to inscribe the fact that the "Richmond" had visited the Great Wall. . . .

As a mere wall there is nothing imposing about the Great Wall of China. There are a hundred thousand walls, the world over, better built and more useful. What impressed us was the infinite patience which could have compassed so vast a labor. Wonderful are the Pyramids, and wonderful as a dream the ruins of Thebes. There you see mechanical results which you cannot follow or solve, engineering achievements we could not even now

The Great Wall of China

repeat. The Great Wall is a marvel of patience. I had been reading the late Mr. Seward's calculation that the labor which had built the Great Wall would have built the Pacific Railways. General Grant thought that Mr. Seward had underrated its extent. "I believe," he said, "that the labor expended on this wall could have built every railroad in the United States, every canal and highway, and most if not all of our cities." The story is that millions were employed on the wall; that the work lasted for ten years. I have ceased to wonder at a story like this. In the ancient days—the days which our good people are always lamenting, and a return to which is the prayer of so many virtuous and pious souls—in the ancient days, when an emperor had a wall or a pyramid to build, he sent out to the fields and hills and gathered in the people and made them build on peril of their heads. It required an emperor to build the Great Wall. No people would ever have done such a thing. When you see the expression of a people's power it is in the achievements of the Roman, the Greek, and the Englishman—in the achievements of Chinamen when they have been allowed their own way. The Great Wall is a monument of the patience of the people and the prerogative of a king. It never could have been of much use in the most primitive days, and now it is only a curiosity. We walked about on the top and studied its simple, massive workmanship, and looked upon the plains of Mongolia, over which the dreaded Tartar came. On one side of the wall was China, on the other Mongolia. We were at the furthest end of our journey, and every step now would be toward home. There was something like a farewell in the feeling with which we looked upon the cold land of mystery which swept on toward the north—cold and barren even under the warm sunshine. There was something like a welcome in the waves as we again greeted them, and knew that the sea upon which we are again venturing with the confidence that comes from long and friendly association, would carry us home to America, and brighten even that journey with a glimpse of the land of the rising sun. . . .

We have had many talks about China among the members of our party—many discussions of this Chinese question. General Grant, during one of these talks, made one or two observations worthy, perhaps, of remembrance. "To those who travel for the love of travel," said the General, "there is little to attract in China or to induce a second visit. My own visit has, however, been under the most favorable circumstances for seeing the people and studying their institutions. My impression is a very favorable one. The Chinese are enduring, patient to the last degree, industrious, and have brought living down to a minimum. By their shrewdness and economy they have monopolized nearly all the carrying trade, coastwise, of the East, and are driving out all the other merchants. Through India, Malacca, Siam, and the islands from the shores of Africa to Japan, they are the mechanics, market gardeners, stevedores, small traders, servants, and in all callings that contribute to material progress. The Chinese are not a military power, and could not defend themselves against even a small European power. But they have the elements of a strong, great, and independent empire, and may, before many years roll around, assert their power. The leading men thoroughly appreciate their weakness, but understand the history of Turkey, Egypt, and other powers that have made rapid strides toward the new civilization on borrowed capital and under foreign management and control. They know what the result of all that interference has been so far as national independence is concerned. The idea of those leading men of China with whom I have conversed—and I have seen most of those in the government of the empire—is to gradually educate a sufficient number of their own people to fill all places in the development of railroads, manufactories, telegraphs, and all those elements of civilization so new to them but common and even old with us. Then the Chinese, with their own people to do the work, and with their own capital, will commence a serious advance. I should not be surprised to hear within the next twenty years, if I should live so long, more complaints of Chinese absorption of the trade and commerce of the world than we hear now of their backward position. But before this change there must be a marked political change in China. It may even affect the dynasty, although that will depend upon the dynasty. The present form gives no State powers whatever. It may take off the heads of weak offenders or of a few obnoxious persons, but it is as weak against outside persons as America would be if States rights, as interpreted by Southern Democrats, prevailed. There are too many powers within the government to prevent the whole from exercising its full strength against a common enemy."

During our trip over the China seas it was pleasant to resume our conversations on home subjects and home memories. I remember a conversation with General Grant on war mementos, and the theory of some public men in the North that no memory of the war—no monument—should be preserved. "I never saw a war picture," said the General, "that was pleasant. I tried to enjoy some of those in Versailles, but they were disgusting. At the same time, there was nothing in our war to be ashamed of, and I believe in cherishing the memories of the war so far as they recall the sacrifices of our people for the Union. Personally, I have reason to be more than satisfied with the estimate the American people have placed upon my services. I see no reason for dissatisfaction on the part of any of the chiefs of the army. But the South has been kinder to her soldiers than the North to those who composed her armies. In the South there is no surer way to public esteem than to have served in the army. In the North it is different. If you look at the roll of Congress, you will find that the list of Confederate officers has been steadily increasing, while the list of Federal officers has decreased. I can only recall two senators who had any rank in our army, Burnside and Logan. In the House there are very few—Banks, Butler, and Garfield are all that occur to me. It makes one melancholy to see this diminishing roll. While I would do nothing to revive unhappy memories in the South, I do not like to see our soldiers apologize for the war. Apart from the triumph of the Union, and the emancipation of the slaves, one of the great results of the war was the position it gave us as a nation among the nations of the world. That I have seen every day during my residence abroad, and to me it is one of the most gratifying results of the war. That alone was worth making a great sacrifice for."

"When I took command of the army," said General Grant on one occasion, "I had a dream that I tried to realize—to reunite and recreate the whole army. I talked it over with Sherman. Sherman and I knew so many fine, brave officers. We knew them in West Point and the army. We had the sympathy of former comradeship. Neither Sherman nor I had been in any way concerned in Eastern troubles, and we knew that there were no better soldiers in the army than some of those who were under a cloud with Mr. Stanton. Then I wanted to make the war as national as possible, to bring in all parties. I was anxious especially to conciliate and recognize the Democratic element. The country belonged as well to the Democrats as to us, and I did not believe in a Republican war. I felt that we needed every musket and every sword to put down the rebellion. So when I came East I came prepared and anxious to assign McClellan, Buell, and others to command. I had confidence in their ability and loyalty, confidence which, notwithstanding our differences in politics, has never faltered. But I was disappointed."

The question was asked as to whether Lincoln's administration prevented General Grant from carrying out this purpose. "Not at all," said the General, "the difficulties were not with the administration. The generals were not in a humor to be conciliated. I soon saw my plan was not feasible, and gave it up. I was very sorry, as I should have liked to have had McClellan and Buell, and others I could name, in important commands.

"In looking back at the war," said the General, "it seems most unfortunate both for themselves and the country that these officers should not have made the place in the war which their abilities would have commanded, and that they should not have rendered their country the service which every soldier is proud to do. I have always regretted that. We had work for everybody during the war, for those especially who knew the business. What interfered with our officers more than anything else was allowing themselves a political bias. That is fatal to a soldier. War and politics are so different. I remember my own feelings about the war when it commenced. I could not endure the thought of the Union separating. When I was in St. Louis the year before Lincoln's election, it made my blood run cold to hear friends of mine, Southern men as many of my friends were—deliberately discuss the dissolution of the Union as though it were a tariff bill. I could not endure it. The very thought of it was a pain. I wanted to leave the country if disunion was accomplished. I could not have lived in the country. It was this feeling that impelled me to volunteer. I was a poor man, with a family. I never thought of commands or battles. I only wanted to fight for the Union. That feeling carried me through the war. I never felt any special pleasure in my promotions. I was naturally glad when they came. But I never thought of it. The only promotion that I ever rejoiced in was when I was made major-general in the regular army. I was happy over that, because it made me the junior major-general, and I hoped when the war was over, that I could live in California. I had been yearning for the opportunity to return to California, and I saw it in that promotion. When I was given a higher command, I was sorry, because it involved a residence in Washington, which, at that time, of all places in the country I disliked, and it dissolved my hopes of a return to the Pacific coast. I came to like Washington, however, when I knew it. My only feeling in the war was a desire to see it over and the rebellion suppressed. I do not remember ever to have considered the possibility of a dissolution. It never entered into my head, for instance, to consider the terms we should take from the South if beaten. I never heard Mr. Lincoln allude to such a thing, and I do not think he ever considered it. When the [Confederate] commissioners came to Hampton Roads to talk peace [on February 3, 1865], he said peace could only be talked about on the basis of the restoration of the Union and the abolition of slavery. That was my only platform, and whenever generals went beyond that to talk of conciliation, and hurting brethren, and States rights, and so on, they made a fatal blunder. A soldier has no right to consider these things. His duty is to destroy his enemy as quickly as possible. I never knew a case of an officer who went into the war with political ideas who succeeded. I do not mean Democratic ideas alone, but Republican as well. The generals who insisted upon writing emancipation proclamations, and creating new theories of State governments, and invading Canada, all came to grief as surely as those who believed that the main object of the war was to protect rebel property, and keep the negroes at work on the plantations while their masters were off in the rebellion. I had my views on all of these subjects, as decided as any man, but I never allowed them to influence me.

"With a soldier the flag is paramount," said the General. "I know the struggle with my conscience during the Mexican War. I have never altogether forgiven myself for going into that. I had very strong opinions on the subject. I do not think there was ever a more wicked war than that waged by the United States on Mexico. I thought so at the time, when I was a youngster, only I had not moral courage enough to resign. I had taken an oath to serve eight years, unless sooner discharged, and I considered my supreme duty was to my flag. I had a horror of the Mexican War, and I have always believed that it was on our part most unjust. The wickedness was not in the way our soldiers conducted it, but in the conduct of our government in declaring war. The troops behaved well in Mexico, and the government acted handsomely about the peace. We had no claim on Mexico. Texas had no claim beyond the Nueces River, and yet we pushed on to the Rio Grande and crossed it. I am always ashamed of my country when I think of that invasion. Once in Mexico, however, and the people, those who had property, were our friends. We could have held Mexico, and made it a permanent section of the Union with the consent of all classes whose consent was worth having. Overtures were made to Scott and Worth to remain in the country with their armies. The Mexicans are a good people. They live on little and work hard. They suffer from the influence of the Church, which, while I was in Mexico at least, was as bad as could be. The Mexicans were good soldiers, but badly commanded. The country is rich, and if the people could be assured a good government, they would prosper. See what we have made of Texas and California—empires. There are the same materials for new empires in Mexico. I have always had a deep interest in Mexico and her people, and have always wished them well. I suppose the fact that I served there as a young man, and the impressions the country made upon my young mind, have a good deal to do with this. When I was in London, talking with Lord Beaconsfield, he spoke of Mexico. He said he wished to heaven we had taken the country, that England would not like anything better than to see the United States annex it. I suppose that will be the future of the country. Now that slavery is out of the way there could be no better future for Mexico than absorption in the United States. But it would have to come, as San Domingo tried to come, by the free will of the people.* I would not fire a gun to annex territory. I consider it too great a privilege to belong to the United States for us to go around gunning for new territories. Then the question of annexation means the question of suffrage, and that becomes more and more serious every day with us. That is one of the grave problems of our future.

"When the Mexican War broke out," said the General, "my ambition was to become an assistant professor of mathematics in West Point. I think I would have been appointed. But so many officers from my regiment had been assigned to other duties that it was nearly stripped, and although I should have been glad to have found an honorable release from serving in a war which I detested and deplored as much as I did our war with Mexico, I had not the heart to press the matter. But in that day conduct

---

* In 1869–71, Grant had pushed very hard to annex Santo Domingo (now the Dominican Republic), but the Republicans in the cabinet and Senate split, and the Senate finally rejected the treaty, a bitter and politically costly event for Grant.

counted against a cadet to such a degree that any special excellence in study would be affected by the manner in which he tied his shoes. 'Conduct' did not mean necessarily bad, immoral conduct, but late rising, negligence in dress, and so on. Schofield is one of the best mathematicians in the country, and in other respects a very superior man. Yet his marks in conduct kept him down. The same with Sheridan. Poor Sheridan was put back a year in his course for a row with one of his cadets, and was so low in conduct that in the end he only squeezed through. This conduct rule was an injustice in its old operation; and one reason why I assigned Schofield to command West Point was, that knowing how the rule worked in his day, and against so able a man as himself, he might amend it. I think West Point is the best school in the world. I do not mean the highest grade, but the most thorough in its discipline. A boy to go through four years in West Point, must have the essential elements of a strong, manly character. Lacking any of these he must fail. I hear army men say their happiest days were at West Point. I never had that experience. The most trying days in my life were those I spent there, and I never recall them with pleasure.

"I was never more delighted at anything," said the General, "than the close of the war. I never liked service in the army—not as a young officer. I did not want to go to West Point. My appointment was an accident, and my father had to use his authority to make me go. If I could have escaped West Point without bringing myself into disgrace at home, I would have done so. I remember about the time I entered the academy there were debates in Congress over a proposal to abolish West Point. I used to look over the papers, and read the Congress reports with eagerness, to see the progress the bill made, and hoping to hear that the school had been abolished, and that I could go home to my father without being in disgrace. I never went into a battle willingly or with enthusiasm. I was always glad when a battle was over. I never want to command another army. I take no interest in armies. When the Duke of Cambridge asked me to review his troops at Aldershott I told his Royal Highness that the one thing I never wanted to see again was a military parade. When I resigned from the army and went to a farm I was happy. When the rebellion came I returned to the service because it was a duty. I had no thought of rank; all I did was to try and make myself useful. My first commission as brigadier came in the unanimous indorsement of the delegation from Illinois. I do not think I knew any of the members but Washburne, and I did not know him very well. It was only after Donelson that I began to see how important was the work that Providence devolved upon me. And yet after Donelson I was in disgrace and under arrest, and practically without a command, because of some misunderstanding on the part of Halleck. It all came right in time. I never bore Halleck ill will for it, and we remained friendly. He was in command, and it was his duty to command as he pleased. But I hardly know what would have come of it, as far as I was concerned, had not the country interfered. You see Donelson was our first clear victory, and you will remember the enthusiasm that came with it. The country saved me from Halleck's displeasure. When other commands came I always regretted them. When the bill creating the grade of Lieutenant-General was proposed, with my name as the Lieutenant-General, I wrote Mr. Washburne opposing it. I did not want it. I found that the bill was right and I was wrong, when I came to command the Army of the Potomac—that a head was needed to the army. I did not want the Presidency, and have never quite forgiven myself for resigning the command of the army to accept it; but it could not be helped. I owed my honors and opportunities to the Republican party, and if my name could aid it I was bound to accept. The second nomination was almost due to me—if I may use the phrase—because of the bitterness of political and personal opponents. My re-election was a great gratification, because it showed me how the country felt. Then came all the discussions about the third term. I gave my views on that in my letters to State Senator Harry White of Pennsylvania. It is not known, however, how strongly I was pressed to enter the canvass as a candidate. I was waited upon formally by a distinguished man, representing the influences that would have controlled the Republicans in the South, and asked to allow my name to be used. This request was supported by men in the Northern States whose position and character are unquestioned. I said then that under no circumstances would I become a candidate. Even if a nomination and an election were assured I would not run. The nomination, if I ran, would be after a struggle, and before it had been unanimous. The election, if I should win, would be after a struggle, and the result would be far different from what it was before. If I succeeded, and tried to do my best, my very best, I should still have a crippled administration. This was the public view. I never had any illusions on the subject, never allowed myself to be swayed for an instant from my purpose. The pressure was great. But personally I was weary of office. I never wanted to get out of a place as much as I did to get out of the Presidency. For sixteen years, from the opening of the war, it had been a constant strain upon me. So when the third term was seriously presented to me I peremptorily declined it."

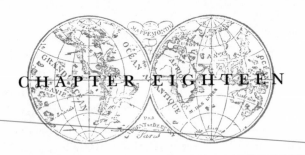

CHAPTER EIGHTEEN

To Japan

After narrowly avoiding a hurricane, Grant's ship steamed on to Japan. On deck during this leg of the trip, he and Young again discussed the war. In an extended analysis, Grant damned Robert E. Lee with faint praise, in part out of his resentment that the myth of Lee and the Lost Cause was gaining so much politically potent capital both in the United States and abroad. Grant also disliked what he considered to be the haughty and privileged aristocratic social forms that underlay the Lee legend. By contrast, Grant defended the reputations of Jefferson Davis and the Confederate secretary of war, John C. Breckinridge.

Grant went on to give an astute analysis of the men and events in Missouri at the onset of the war and of the battles of Fort Donalson and Shiloh. Seventeen years after Shiloh, Grant remained defensive of his performance and that of Sherman, denying once again, through selective memory, that he had failed to prepare his army for the Confederate attack, thus leading to enormous Union casualties. Grant portrayed this equivocal and bloody battle as a clear Union victory, which it had not been.

Landing in Nagasaki, Young and Grant were immediately struck by the rapid modernization that had swept Japan since 1868, which they mistakenly assumed was completely destroying all of the older mentality and social structure of that land. Feudalism had been abolished in 1871 and universal education introduced the next year. A series of rebellions in 1873–77 had permitted the military and militarists to gain the upper hand in newly centralized Japanese politics. Grant and Young unconsciously reflected American pride in their nation having played the leading role since the 1850s in forcing Japan to open to international trade and influence. Young was especially charmed by a traditional banquet, though the food was of less interest to him than was the service.

There was no special incident on our journey from Chefoo, except on the morning of June 18th, when the sea rose and the wind became a gale. We had had so much good weather since we left Marseilles, that when we came on deck and saw a white, frothing sea, the thermometer going down, and Captain Benham leaning over the rail and looking anxiously at the clouds, we were not in a critical but a grateful mood, for has it not been written that into all lives some rain must fall—some days be dark and dreary? At dinner in the ward-room one of my naval friends had expressed a disgust at the condition of the weather, saying that if these calm seas continued, our grandparents would take to a seafaring life, as the most comfortable way of spending their declining years. Captain Benham watched the storm for an hour, and then sent word to the "Ashuelot," which was in our rear, to run for a harbor. Our storm was a circular cyclone, a species of tempest that sometimes prevails in these seas. We were on the edge of it, and by moderating our pace, and keeping out of its way, we avoided its fury. By seven o'clock Lieutenant Patch came in from the watch with the cheerful news that the thermometer was going up and the sea was going down. In the morning all was clear and calm again, and we rejoiced in the sunshine and looked for the green shores of Japan.

I again take advantage of the pleasant hours of sailing over a calm sea to recall my memories of the conversations with General Grant.

Here before me is the narrative of Lee's surrender: "On the night before Lee's surrender," said General Grant, "I had a wretched headache—headaches to which I have been subject—nervous prostration, intense personal suffering. But, suffer or not, I had to keep moving. I saw clearly, especially after Sheridan had cut off the escape to Danville, that Lee must surrender or break and run into the mountains—break in all directions and leave us a dozen guerilla bands to fight The object of my campaign was not Richmond, not the defeat of Lee in actual fight, but to remove him and his army out of the contest, and, if possible, to have him use his influence in inducing the surrender of Johnston and the other isolated armies. You see the war was an enormous strain upon the country. Rich as we were I do not now see how we could have endured it another year, even from a financial point of view. So with these views I wrote Lee, and opened the correspondence with which the world is familiar. Lee does not appear well in that correspondence, not nearly so well as he did in our subsequent interviews, where his whole bearing was that of a patriotic and gallant soldier, concerned alone for the welfare of his army and his state. I received word that Lee would meet me at a point within our lines near

The Story of Lee's Surrender

Sheridan's head-quarters. I had to ride quite a distance through a muddy country. I remember now that I was concerned about my personal appearance. I had an old suit on, without my sword, and without any distinguishing mark of rank except the shoulder-straps of a lieutenant-general on a woolen blouse. I was splashed with mud in my long ride. I was afraid Lee might think I meant to show him studied discourtesy by so coming— at least I thought so. But I had no other clothes within reach, as Lee's letter found me away from my base of supplies. I kept on riding until I met Sheridan. The general, who was one of the heroes of the campaign, and whose pursuit of Lee was perfect in its generalship and energy, told me where to find Lee. I remember that Sheridan was impatient when I met him, anxious and suspicious about the whole business, feared there might be a plan to escape, that he had Lee at his feet, and wanted to end the business by going in and forcing an absolute surrender by capture. In fact, he had his troops ready for such an assault when Lee's white flag came within his lines. I went up to the house where Lee was waiting. I found him in a fine, new, splendid uniform, which only recalled my anxiety as to my own clothes while on my way to meet him. I expressed my regret that I was compelled to meet him in so unceremonious a manner, and he replied that the only suit he had available was one which had been sent him by some admirers in Baltimore, and which he then wore for the first time. We spoke of old friends in the army. I remembered having seen Lee in Mexico. He was so much higher in rank than myself at the time that I supposed he had no recollection of me. But he said he remembered me very well. We talked of old times and exchanged inquiries about friends. Lee then broached the subject of our meeting. I told him my terms, and Lee, listening attentively, asked me to write them down. I took out my 'manifold' order-book and pencil and wrote them down. General Lee put on his glasses and read them over. The conditions gave the officers their side-arms, private horses, and personal baggage. I said to Lee that I hoped and believed this would be the close of the war; that it was most important that the men should go home and go to work, and the government would not throw any obstacles in the way. Lee answered that it would have a most happy effect, and accepted the terms. I handed over my penciled memorandum to an aide to put into ink, and we resumed our conversation about old times and friends in the armies. Various officers came in—Longstreet, Gordon, Pickett, from the South; Sheridan, Ord, and others from our side. Some were old friends—Longstreet and myself, for instance, and we had a general talk. Lee no doubt expected me to ask for his sword, but I did not want his sword. It would only," said the General, smiling, "have gone to the Patent Office to be worshiped by the Washington rebels. There was a pause, when General Lee said that most of the animals in his cavalry and artillery were owned by the privates, and he would like to know, under the terms, whether they would be regarded as private property or the property of the government. I said that under the terms of surrender they belonged to the government. General Lee read over the letter and said that was so. I then said to the general that I believed and hoped this was the last battle of the war; that I saw the wisdom of these men getting home and to work as soon as possible, and that I would give orders to allow any soldier or officer claiming a horse or a mule to take it. General Lee showed some emotion at this—a feeling which I also shared—and said it would have a most happy effect. The interview ended, and I gave orders for rationing his troops. The next day I met Lee on horseback and we had a long talk. In that conversation I urged upon Lee the wisdom of ending the war by the surrender of the other armies. I asked him to use his influence with the people of the South—an influence that was supreme—to bring the war to an end. General Lee said that his campaign in Virginia was the last organized resistance which the South was capable of making—that I might have to march a good deal and encounter isolated commands here and there; but there was no longer any army which could make a stand. I told Lee that this fact only made his responsibility greater, and any further war would be a crime. I asked him to go among the Southern people and use his influence to have all men under arms surrender on the same terms given to the army of Northern Virginia. He replied he could not do so without consultation with President Davis. I was sorry. I saw that the Confederacy had gone beyond the reach of President Davis, and that there was nothing that could be done except what Lee could do to benefit the Southern people. I was anxious to get them home and have our armies go to their homes and fields. But Lee would not move without Davis, and as a matter of fact at that time, or soon after, Davis was a fugitive in the woods."

This led to a remark as to the great and universal fame of Lee—especially in Europe—a reputation which seemed to grow every day.

"I never ranked Lee as high as some others of the army," said the General, "that is to say, I never had as much anxiety when he was in my front as when Joe Johnston was in front. Lee was a good man, a fair commander, who had everything in his favor. He was a man who needed sunshine. He was supported by the unanimous voice of the South; he was supported by a large party in the North; he had the support and sympathy of the outside world. All this is of an immense advantage to a general. Lee had this in a remarkable degree. Everything he did was right. He was treated like a demi-god. Our generals had a hostile press, lukewarm friends, and a public opinion outside. The cry was in the air that the North only won by brute force; that the generalship and valor were with the South. This has gone into history, with so many other illusions that are historical. Lee was of a slow, conservative, cautious nature, without imagination or humor, always the same, with grave dignity. I never could see in his achievements what justifies his reputation. The illusion that nothing but heavy odds beat him will not stand the ultimate light of history. I know it is not true. Lee was a good deal of a head-quarters general; a desk general, from what I can hear, and from what his officers say. He was almost too old for active service—the best service in the field. At the time of the surrender he was fifty-eight or fifty-nine and I was forty-three. His officers used to say that he posed himself, that he was retiring and exclusive, and that his head-quarters were difficult of access. I remember when the commissioners came through our lines to treat, just before the surrender, that one of them remarked on the great difference between our head-quarters and Lee's. I always kept open house at head-quarters, so far as the army was concerned.

"My anxiety," said the General, "for some time before Richmond fell was lest Lee should abandon it. My pursuit of Lee was hazardous. I was in a position of extreme difficulty. You see I was marching away from my supplies, while Lee was falling back on his supplies. If Lee had continued his flight another day I should have had to abandon the pursuit, fall back to Danville, build the railroad, and feed my army. So far as supplies were concerned, I was almost at my last gasp when surrender took place."

The writer recalled a rumor, current at the time, about the intention of President Johnson to arrest Lee. "Yes," said the General, "Mr. Johnson had made up his mind to arrest Lee and the leading Southern officers. It was in the beginning of his administration, when he was making speeches saying he had resolved to make all treason odious. He was addressing delegations on the subject, and offering rewards for Jefferson Davis and others. Upon Lee's arrest he had decided. I protested again and again. It finally came up in Cabinet, and the only Minister who supported my views openly was Seward. I always said the parole of Lee protected him as long as he observed it. On one occasion Mr. Johnson spoke of Lee, and wanted to know why any military commander had a right to protect an arch-traitor from the laws. I was angry at this, and I spoke earnestly and plainly to the President. I said, that as General, it was none of my business what he or Congress did with General Lee or his other commanders. He might do as he pleased about civil rights, confiscation of property, and so on. That did not come in my province. But a general commanding troops has certain responsibilities and duties and power, which are supreme. He must deal with the enemy in front of him so as to destroy him. He may either kill him, capture him, or parole him. His engagements are sacred so far as they lead to the destruction of the foe. I had made certain terms with Lee—the best and only terms. If I had told him and his army that their liberty would be invaded, that they would be open to arrest, trial, and execution for treason, Lee would never have surrendered, and we should have lost many lives in destroying him. Now my terms of surrender were according to military law, and so long as Lee was observing his parole I would never consent to his arrest. Mr. Seward nodded approval. I remember feeling very strongly on the subject. The matter was allowed to die out. I should have resigned the command of the army rather than have carried out any order directing me to arrest Lee or any of his commanders who obeyed the laws. By the way, one reason why Mosby became such a friend of mine was because as General I gave him a safe-conduct to allow him to practice law and earn a living. Our officers in Virginia used to arrest leading Confederates whenever they moved out of their homes. Mrs. Mosby went to Mr. Johnson and asked that her husband might be allowed to earn his living. But the President was in a furious mood, and told her treason must be made odious, and so on. She came to me in distress, and I gave the order to allow Mosby to pass and repass freely. I had no recollection of this until Mosby called it to my attention. Mosby deserves great credit for his sacrifices in the cause of the Union. He is an honest, brave, conscientious man, and has suffered severely for daring to vote as he pleased among people who hailed him as a hero and in whose behalf he risked his life.

"I was anxious to pardon John C. Breckenridge,"* said the General, "during my administration, but when I mentioned the matter to some of my colleagues of the Senate, I found it could not be done. Breckenridge was most anxious to restore the Union to good relations. He was among the last to go over to the South, and was rather dragged into the position. I believe the influence of a man like Breckenridge in Kentucky would have been most beneficial. I talked with my father a good deal about it—he knew a good deal about Kentucky politics. I thought if we pardoned Breckenridge, he could become a candidate for governor, not on the Republican but on the Anti-Bourbon ticket. The influence of a man like Breckenridge, at the time, would have been most useful, but our Republican friends would not let me do it. That was one of the cases where the President had little influence in the administration."

An allusion was made to the feeling in the South that Jefferson Davis was an injury to the Confederacy, and did not do his best. "I never thought so," said the General. Davis did his best, did all that any man could do, to save the Confederacy. This argument is like some of the arguments current in history—that the war was a war against windmills; that if one man or another had been in authority the result would have been different; that some more placable man than Davis could have made a better fight. This is not true. The war was a tremendous war, as no one knows better than

---

* John C. Breckinridge was a prewar congressman from Kentucky, the presidential nominee of the Southern Democrats in 1860, a Confederate general, and the Confederate secretary of war.

those who were in it. Davis did all he could, and all any man could, for the South. The South was beaten from the beginning. There was no victory possible for any government resting upon the platform of the Southern Confederacy. Just as soon as the war united and aroused the young men of the North, and called out the national feeling, there was no end but the end that came. Davis did all he could for his side, and how much he did no one knows better than those who were in the field. I do not see any evidence of great military ability in the executive conduct of the war on the part of the South. How far Davis interfered I don't know. I am told he directed Hood's movements in the West. If he did so, he could not have done us a greater service. But that was an error of judgment. As President, I see nothing in his administration to show that he was false to his side, or feeble in defending it. Davis is entitled to every honor bestowed on the South for gallantry and persistence. The attacks upon him from his old followers are ignoble. The South fell because it was defeated. Lincoln destroyed it, not Davis.

"Speaking of McClellan," said the General, "I should say that the two disadvantages under which he labored were his receiving a high command before he was ready for it, and the political sympathies which he allowed himself to champion. It is a severe blow to any one to begin so high. I always dreaded going to the army of the Potomac. After the battle of Gettysburg I was told I could have the command; but I managed to keep out of it. I had seen so many generals fall, one after another, like bricks in a row, that I shrank from it. After the battle of Mission Ridge, and my appointment as Lieutenant-General, and I was allowed to choose my place, it could not be avoided. Then it seemed as if the time was ripe, and I had no hesitation.

"My first feeling with regard to the Potomac army," said the General, "when I undertook the command was, that it had never been thoroughly fought. There was distrust in the army, distrust on both sides, I have no doubt. I confess I was afraid of the spirit that had pervaded that army, so far as I understood it in the West; and I feared also that some of the generals might treat me as they treated Pope. But this distrust died away. I went among the generals, saw what they really felt and believed, and saw, especially, that they obeyed orders. I did not want to go to the army of the Potomac. The command was about to be offered to me after the fall of Vicksburg. I feared that I should be as unsuccessful as the others and should go down like the others. I suppose I should have been ordered to the command but for the interference of the Under-Secretary of War Charles A.

Dana. I am indebted to him for not having been disturbed in the West. After I became Lieutenant-General, and could select my place of service, I saw that the time had come for me to take the army of the Potomac. The success of that army depended a good deal on the manner in which the commissariat and quartermaster departments were arranged. It is an unfortunate position for a man to hold so far as fame is concerned, and Rufus Ingalls always suffered from that fact. I think it is greatly to the credit of General Ingalls that he spent hundreds of millions of dollars in the handling of the army under the various generals, and yet has never been accused of squandering a cent. But the fact is that Ingalls has wonderful executive ability. As a merchant he would have made a fortune. Nothing ever disturbed or excited him. He was ready for every emergency. He could move and feed a hundred thousand men without ruffling his temper. He was of the greatest service to me, and indeed to every general he served. I knew Ingalls at West Point and out on the Pacific coast. We were young officers together, and nothing but his holding a staff place kept him from rising to a high command. Still, men in his position have the satisfaction of having served their country, and perhaps that is the highest reward after all.

"In the early part of the war," said the General, "Halleck did very good service in a manner for which he has never received sufficient credit—I mean in his civil administration. Some of his orders were in anticipation, I think, of those of Butler's, which gave him so much fame in New Orleans. There was one about making the rebels support the families of those whose heads had gone to the war. This was a severe order, but a just one. When our troops occupied St. Louis, the secession ladies resolved to show their contempt by ostentatiously parading a white and red rosette. Instead of suppressing this by an order, as Butler did, Halleck quietly bought a lot of these rosettes. Then he sent his detectives and had them distributed among improper characters, who were instructed or employed to wear them. Then in a short newspaper article attention was called to the singular fact that all the loose characters were coming out in white and red rosettes. In a flash that rosette disappeared from the persons of all respectable St. Louis ladies who were anxious to show their secession sympathies.

"By the way," said the General, "there was some splendid work done in Missouri, and especially in St. Louis, in the earliest days of the war, which people have now almost forgotten. If St. Louis had been captured by the rebels it would have made a vast difference in our war. It would have been a terrible task to have recaptured St. Louis—one of the most difficult that could be given to any military man. Instead of a campaign before Vicksburg, it would have been a campaign before St. Louis. Then its resources would have been of material value to the rebels. They had arranged for its capture, to hold it as a military post, and had even gone so far as to arrange about the division of the Union property. I have heard this from sources that leave no doubt in my mind of its truth. We owe the safety of St. Louis to Frank Blair and General Nathaniel Lyon—mainly to Blair. That one service alone entitles Blair's memory to the lasting respect of all Union men. The rebels, under pretext of having a camp of instruction, sent their militia regiments into a camp called Camp Jackson. The governor did it, as was his right. But the governor, Claiborne Jackson, was in sympathy with the rebellion, and he had never done such a thing before. The purpose, of course, was evident. Under pretext of a militia camp, he would quietly accumulate a large force, and suddenly proclaim the Confederacy. At this very time the rebel flag was hanging out from recruiting stations, and companies were enrolled for the South. The best families, the best young men in the city, leaned that way. There were, no doubt, many Union men in the ranks of Camp Jackson; but when the time came they would have been taken into the rebellion at the point of the bayonet, just as so many of their brethren were carried in East Tennessee. It was necessary to strike a decisive blow, and this Blair resolved to do. There were some regular troops there under the command of Lyon. Blair called out his German regiments, put himself under the command of Lyon, went out to the camp, threatened to fire if it did not surrender, and brought the whole crowd in as prisoners. That was the end of any rebel camps in St. Louis, and next day the rebel flags all came down.

"I happened to be in St. Louis," said the General, "as mustering officer of an Illinois regiment at the time. I remember the effect it produced. I was anxious about this camp, and the morning of the movement I went up to the arsenal. I knew Lyon; but, although I had no acquaintance with Blair, I knew him by sight. This was the first time I ever spoke to him. The breaking up of Camp Jackson had a good effect and a bad effect. It offended many Union Democrats, who saw in it an invasion of State rights, which," said the General, with a smile, "it certainly was. It was used as a means of exciting discontent among these well-disposed citizens, as an argument that the government was high-handed. Then the fact that Germans were used to coerce Americans—free Americans in their own camp, called out by the governor of the State—gave offense. I knew many good people, with the North, at the outset, whose opinions were set Southward by this incident. But no really loyal man, to whom the Union was paramount, ever questioned the act. Those who went off on this would soon have gone on something else—emancipation or the use of troops. The taking of the camp saved St. Louis to us, saved our side a long, terrible siege, and was one of the best things in the whole war. I remember how rejoiced I was as I saw Blair and Lyon bring their prisoners into town."

An expression of regret that Lyon, who did so well then, was so soon to fall, led the General to speak of him. "I knew Lyon well," he said, "at West Point and during Mexico. He was a peculiar man, a fanatic on religious questions, like Stonewall Jackson; except that while Jackson was orthodox, Lyon was the reverse. He had more of Stonewall Jackson's peculiar traits than any one I knew. In fact I call him Stonewall Jackson reversed. He was a furious Union man, hated slavery, was extreme in all his views, and intolerant in his expressions of dissent. He went into the war with the most angry feelings toward the South. If he had lived, he might have reached a high command. He had ability enough, and his intense feeling would have carried him along, as it carried Jackson. Still you cannot tell how that may have been. Jackson's fame always seemed to be greater because he fell before his skill had been fully tested.

"No battle," said General Grant on one occasion, "has been more discussed than Shiloh—none in my career. The correspondents and papers at the time all said that Shiloh was a surprise—that our men were killed over their coffee, and so on. There was no surprise about it, except," said the General, with a smile, "perhaps to the newspaper correspondents. We had been skirmishing for two days before we were attacked. At night, when but a small portion of Buell's army had crossed to the west bank of the Tennessee River, I was so well satisfied with the result, and so certain that I would beat Beauregard, even without Buell's aid, that I went in person to each division commander and ordered an advance along the line at four in the morning. Shiloh was one of the most important battles in the war. It was there that our Western soldiers first met the enemy in a pitched battle. From that day they never feared to fight the enemy, and never went into action without feeling sure they would win. Shiloh broke the prestige of the Southern Confederacy so far as our Western army was concerned. Sherman was the hero of Shiloh. He really commanded two divisions—his own and McClernand's—and proved himself to be a consummate soldier. Nothing could be finer than his work at Shiloh, and yet Shiloh was belittled by our Northern people so that many people look at it as a defeat. The same may be said of Fort Donelson. People think that Donelson was captured by pouring men into it ten to one, or some such odds. The truth is, our army, a new army, invested a fortified place and compelled a surrender of a force much larger than our own. A large number of the rebels escaped under Floyd and Pillow, but, as it was, I took more prisoners than I had men under my command for the first two days of my investment. After the investment we were reinforced, so that at the surrender there were 26,000 Union troops, about 4,000 of which were sent back to guard the road to where the steamers lay with our supplies. There were 22,000 effective men in Donelson at the beginning of the siege. Of course there was a risk in attacking Donelson as I did, but," said the General, smiling, "I knew the men who commanded it. I knew some of them in Mexico. Knowledge of that kind goes far toward determining a movement like this."

"Suppose Longstreet or Jackson had been in command at Donelson," said the writer.

"If Longstreet or Jackson," said the General, "or even if Buckner had been in command, I would have made a different campaign. In the beginning we all did things more rashly than later, just as Jackson did in his earlier campaigns. The Mexican War made the officers of the old regular armies more or less acquainted, and when we knew the name of the general opposing we knew enough about him to make our plans accordingly. What determined my attack on Donelson," said the General, "was as much the knowledge I had gained of its commanders in Mexico as anything else. But as the war progressed, and each side kept improving its army, these experiments were not possible. Then it became hard, earnest war, and neither side could depend upon any chance with the other. Neither side dared to make a mistake. It was steady, hard pounding, and the result could only be ruin to the defeated party. It was a peculiarity in our war that we were not fighting for a peace, but to destroy our adversary. That made it so hard for both sides, and especially for the South.

"Speaking of Shiloh," continued the General, "notwithstanding the criticisms made on that battle by my military friends in the press, if I were to name the two battles during the war with which I myself have reason to be satisfied, I would say Shiloh and Mission Ridge. Mission Ridge was a tactical battle, and the results obtained were overwhelming when we consider the loss sustained. Shiloh was a pitched battle fought in the open field. And when people wonder why we did not defeat the Southern army as rapidly and effectively as was done at other places, they forget that the Southern army was commanded by Sydney Johnson, and that to fight a general as great as Sydney Johnson was a different thing from fighting John Floyd. I have every reason to be fully satisfied with the battle of Shiloh. In its results it was one of our greatest victories. To that battle, I repeat, we owe the spirit of confidence which pervaded the Western army. So far were we from being surprised, that one night—certainly two nights before the battle—firing was heard at the front, and it was reported that my army was making a night attack. On one of these evenings I mounted my horse and started for the front. I met McPherson and W. H. L. Wallace coming from the front. They reported all quiet and I returned. It was raining very hard, and on the way my horse stumbled in a hollow and sprained my ankle, so that during the battle I was in the greatest physical pain from this wound. If Buell had reached us in time we would have attacked Sydney Johnson; but, of course, Johnson knew Buell was coming, and was too good a general to allow the junction to take place without an attack. Another criticism on that battle is the statement that I did not happen to be present in person at the point of our line where the attack was made. The reason for this was that I did not happen to be in possession of Sydney Johnson's order of battle. The trouble with a good many of our critical friends in the press is that they look upon a battle in the field as they would do a battle upon the stage, where you see both armies as the scenes shift, and consequently know just what is going to be done. It was my misfortune that I did not know what was going to be done; but at the point of the line where the attack was delivered Sherman's command was thoroughly ready to receive it, and nothing could be finer during the whole day than Sherman's conduct. I visited him two or three times during the action, for the purpose of making suggestions, and seeing how things were going on; but it was not necessary. Sherman was doing much better than I could have done under the circumstances, and required no advice from me."

The question was asked of General Grant, whether the death of Johnson, during the battle, affected the result. General Grant said: "I never could see that it did. On the contrary, I should think that the circumstances attending the death of General Johnson, as reported by his friends, show that the battle was against him when wounded, that he was rallying his troops at the time he was struck in the leg by a ball, and that he lost his life because he would not abandon his troops in order to have his wound properly dressed. If he had gone to the rear and had the wound attended to, he might have lived. If he had had no anxiety about his army, to see if it was victorious, there could be no reason why he should not go to the rear; but the battle was so pressing that he would not leave his command, and so he bled to death. This, at least, is my judgment from reading the statement. I never could see that the course of the battle was affected, one way or another, by the event. The death of so great a man as Johnson was a great loss to the South, and would have been to any cause in which he might have been engaged. But all he could do for the battle of Shiloh was done before he was killed. The battle was out of his hands, and out of that of his army. What won the battle of Shiloh was the courage and endurance of our own soldiers. It was the staying power and pluck of the North as against the short-lived power of the South; and whenever these qualities came into collision the North always won. I used to find that the first day, or the first period of a battle, was most successful to the South; but if we held on to the second or third day, we were sure to beat them, and we always did."

On the 21st of June we found our ship threading its way through beautiful islands and rocks covered with green, looming up out of the sea; and standing like sentinels on the coast—hills on which were trees, and gardens terraced to their summits, and high, commanding cliffs. Through green and smooth tranquil waters we steamed into the bay of Nagasaki, and had our first glimpse of Japan. Nagasaki is said to be among the most beautiful harbors in the world. But the beauty that welcomed us had the endearing quality that it reminded us of home. For so many weeks we had been in the land of the palm, and we were now again in the land of the pine. We had seen nature in luxuriant moods, running into riotous forms, strange and rank. We were weary of the cocoa-nut and the brown, parched soil, of the skies of fire and forests with wild and creeping things. It had become so oppressive that when our course turned toward the north there was great joy. The Providence who gave us our share of the world no doubt considered this, and made it happen that some of us should rejoice under the tropical and others under the temperate zone. I have come to the conclusion that a longing for green is among our primitive and innocent impulses, and I sometimes think that if Adam had only had a good supply of grass—of timothy and clover—in the Garden of Eden, and less of the enticing and treacherous fruits, there would have been no trouble in his family, and all would have gone well. There is temptation in sunshine. One has a feeling of strengthened virtue as the landscape draws near and unfolds itself, and you have glimpses of Scotland and the Adirondacks and the inland lakes; and the green is an honest, frank, chaste green, running from hilltop to waterside, and throwing upon the waters long, refreshing shadows. It was this schoolboy sense of pleasure that came with my first view of Japan. All the romance, all the legends, the dreams I had dreamed and the pictures I had seen; all the anticipations I had formed of Japan were immersed in this joyful welcome to the green that I had not seen since leaving England—our own old-fashioned green of the temperate zone. This is not a heroic confession, and I should have thought of some fitting emotion with which to welcome this land of romance and sunshine. But I can never get into a heroic vein, and my actual impressions, as I go around the world, are often of so homely a character that I ought not to confess them. How much grander it would be to intimate that my feelings overcame me and I was too much affected for speech. This would sound as a more appropriate welcome to Japan. All that I saw of the coast was the beauty of the green, which came like a memory of childhood, as a memory of America, and in which I rejoiced as in a mere physical sensation, like bathing, or swinging on the gate, or dozing under the apple-trees in the drowsy days of June. . . .

The "Richmond" steamed between the hills and came to an anchorage. It was the early morning, and over the water were shadows of cool, inviting green. Nagasaki, nestling on her hill-sides, looked cosy and beautiful; and it being our first glimpse of a Japanese town, we studied it through our glasses, studied every feature—the scenery, the picturesque attributes of the city, the terraced hills that rose beyond, every rood under cultivation; the quaint, curious houses; the multitudes of flags, which showed that the town knew of our coming and was preparing to do us honor. We noted also that the wharves were lined with a multitude, and that the available population were waiting to see the guest whom their nation honors, and who is known in common speech as the American Mikado. Then the "Richmond" ran up the Japanese standard and fired twenty-one guns in honor of Japan. The forts answered the salute. Then the Japanese gun-boats and the forts displayed the American ensign, and fired a salute of twenty-one guns in honor of General Grant. Mr. W. P. Mangum, our consul, and his wife came on board. In a short time the Japanese barge was seen coming, with Prince Dati and Mr. Yoshida and the Governor, all in the splendor of court uniforms. These officials were received with due honors, and escorted to the cabin. Prince Dati said that he had been commanded by the Emperor to meet General Grant on his landing, to welcome him in the name of his Majesty, and to attend upon him as the Emperor's personal representative, so long as the General remained in Japan. The value of this compliment can be understood when you know that Prince Dati is one of the highest noblemen in Japan. He was one of the leading daimios, one of the old feudal barons who, before the revolution, ruled Japan, and had power of life and death in his own dominions. The old daimios were not only barons but heads of clans, like the clans of Scotland; and in the feudal days he could march an army into the field. When the revolution came Dati accepted it, not sullenly and seeking retirement, like Satsuma and other princes, but as the best thing for the country. He gave his adhesion to the Emperor, and is now one of the great noblemen around the throne. The sending of a man of the rank of the Prince was the highest compliment that the Emperor could pay any guest. Mr. Yoshida is well known as the present Japanese Minister to the United States, a discreet and accomplished man, and among the rising statesmen in the empire. Having been accredited to America during the General's administration, and knowing the General, the government called him home so that he might attend General Grant and look after the reception. So when General Grant arrived he had the pleasure of meeting not only a distinguished representative of the Emperor, but an old personal friend.

At one o'clock on the 21st of June, General Grant, accompanied by Prince Dati, Mr. Yoshida, and the Governor, landed in Nagasaki. The Japanese man-of-war "Kango," commanded by Captain Ito, had been sent down to Nagasaki to welcome the General. The landing took place in the Japanese barge. From the time that General Grant came into the waters of Japan it was the intention of the government that he should be the nation's guest. As soon as the General stepped into the barge the Japanese vessels and the batteries on shore thundered out their welcome, the yards of the vessels were manned, and as the barge moved slowly along the crews of the ships in the harbor cheered. It was over a mile from the "Richmond" to the shore. The landing-place had been arranged not in the foreign section nor the Dutch Concession, carrying out the intention of having the reception entirely Japanese. Lines of troops were formed, the steps were covered with red cloth, and every space and standing spot and coigne of vantage was covered with people. The General's boat touched the shore, and with Mrs. Grant on his arm, and followed by the Colonel, the Japanese officials, and the members of his party, he slowly walked up the platform, bowing to the multitude who made their obeisance in his honor. There is something strange in the grave decorum of an Oriental crowd—strange to us who remember the ringing cheer and the electric hurrah of Saxon lands. The principal citizens of Nagasaki came forward and were presented, and after a few minutes' pause our party stepped into jinrickshaws and were taken to our quarters.

The jinrickshaw is the common vehicle of Japan. It is built on the principle of a child's perambulator or an invalid's chair, except that it is much lighter. Two men go ahead and pull, and one behind pushes. But this is only on occasions of ceremony. One man is quite able to manage a jin-rickshaw. Those used by the General had been sent down from Tokio from the palace. Our quarters in Nagasaki had been prepared in the Japanese town. A building used for a female normal school had been prepared. It was a half mile from the landing, and the whole road had been decorated with flags, American and Japanese entwined, with arches of green boughs and flowers. Both sides of the road were lined with people who bowed low to the General as he passed. On reaching our residence the Japanese officials of the town were all presented. Then came the foreign consuls in a body, who were presented by the American Consul, Mr. Mangum. After this came the officers of the Japanese vessels, all in uniform. Then came a delegation representing the foreign residents of all nationalities in Nagasaki, who presented an address. Mr. John A. Bingham, the American Minister, came as far as Nagasaki to meet General Grant and go with him to Yokohama. He brought us sad news of the pestilence ravaging the empire, which would limit our journey. Mr. Bingham was fresh from America, and it was pleasant not only to meet an old friend, but one who could tell us of the tides and currents of home affairs. . . .

There was a visit to the government schools and an address to the scholars, a short conversational speech on the value of education. There was a visit to the Nagasaki Fair, which had been in progress during the summer, but was then closed. The Governor opened it for our inspection, and it was certainly a most creditable display of what Japan could do in art, industry, and science. The fair buildings were erected in the town park, a pleasure ground with unique old temples gray and mossy with age, and tea-houses where tea was brought in the tiniest of cups by demure wee maidens from six to seven, dressed in the ancient costumes of Japan, who came and knelt as they offered their tea. The town people were out in holiday attire to take the air and look out on the bay and stare at the General. After we had made our tour of the fair grounds the Governor asked the General and Mrs. Grant to plant memorial trees. The species planted by the General was the *Ficus religiosa*, while to Mrs. Grant was given the *Saurus camphora*. The Governor then said that Nagasaki had resolved to erect a monument in honor of General Grant's visit, that this memorial would be near the trees, and that if the General would only write an inscription it would be engraved on the stone in English and Japanese characters. The General wrote the inscription as follows:

"NAGASAKI, JAPAN, June 22, 1879.

"At the request of Governor Utsumi Togatsu, Mrs. Grant and I have each
planted a tree in the Nagasaki Park. I hope that both trees may prosper, grow
large, live long, and in their growth, prosperity, and long life be emblematic of
the future of Japan.

U. S. GRANT." . . .

During our visit to Nagasaki we took part in a famous dinner given in
honor of General Grant, about which I propose to write at some length,
because it is interesting as a picture of ancient life in Japan.

In my wanderings round the world I am more interested in what reminds me of the old times, of the men and the days that are gone, than
of customs reminding me of what I saw in France. All that reminds you of
the old times is passing away from Japan. Here and there you can find a
bit that recalls the days when the daimios ruled, when the two-sworded war-
riors were on every highway, when the rivalry of clans was as fierce as was
ever known in the highlands of Scotland or the plains of North America,
when every gentleman was as ready to commit suicide in defense of his
honor as a Texas swashbuckler to fight a duel. All of this is crumbling
under the growth of modern ideas. The aim of Japanese statesmen is now
to do things as they are done in London and Washington, and this impulse
sweeps on in a resistless and swelling current. It is best that it should be so.
God forbid that Japan should ever try to arrest or turn back the hands of
her destiny. What was picturesque and quaint in the old time can be preserved in plays and romances. This century belongs to the real world, and
Japan's incessant pressing forward, even if she crushes the old monuments, is in the interest of civilization.

It seemed good to the citizens of Nagasaki to give General Grant a dinner that was to be in itself a romance and a play. Instead of doing what is
done every day, and rivaling the taste of Paris, it was resolved to entertain
him in the style of the daimios, the feudal lords of Japan. The place selected for the fête was an old temple in the heart of the city, from whose
doors you could look over the bay. Moreover, it was to be the work of the
citizens of Nagasaki. The merchants would do it, and this in itself was a delicate thought; for in the East it is not often that we have any recognition
of men as men and citizens. The awakening of the people of Japan to a
perception of the truth that the men who form the groundwork of the
State, and upon whose genius and industry it rests, are as important as
heaven-born rulers, is one of the thought-provoking incidents of the later

A Japanese Family at Dinner

amusements in Japan. That is a voice it is not easy to still. It may speak with the wavering tones of childhood, but will gather strength and in time be heard. It was peculiarly gratifying to General Grant to meet the citizens of Japan, and they left nothing undone to do him honor. The company was not more than twenty, including General Grant and party, our Japanese hosts, Consul Mangum and family, and Consul Denny and family. The dinner was served on small tables, each guest having a table to himself. The merchants themselves waited on us, and with the merchants a swarm of attendants wearing the costumes of old Japan.

The bill of fare was almost a volume, and embraced over fifty courses. The wine was served in unglazed porcelain wine cups, on white wooden stands. The appetite was pampered in the beginning with dried fish, edible sea-weeds, and isinglass, in something of the Scandinavian style, except that the attempt did not take the form of brandy and raw fish. The first serious dish was composed of crane, sea-weed, moss, rice bread and potatoes, which we picked over in a curious way, as though we were at an auction sale of remnants, anxious to rummage out a bargain. The soup, when it first came—for it came many times—was an honest soup of fish, like a delicate fish chowder. Then came strange dishes, as ragout, and as soup, in bewildering confusion. The first was called namasu, and embodied fish, clams, chestnuts, rock mushrooms, and ginger. Then, in various combinations, the following:—duck, truffles, turnips, dried bonito, melons, pressed salt, aromatic shrubs, snipe, egg-plant, jelly, boiled rice, snapper, shrimp, potatoes, mushroom, cabbage, lassfish, orange flowers, powdered fish flavored with plum juice and walnuts, raw carp sliced, mashed fish, baked fish, isinglass, fish boiled with pickled beans, wine and rice again. This all came in the first course, and as a finale to the course there was a sweetmeat composed of white and red bean jelly-cake, and boiled black mushroom. With this came powdered tea, which had a green, monitory look, and suggested your earliest experiences in medicine. When the first pause came in the dinner a merchant advanced and read an address to General Grant. This was at the end of the first course—the ominous course that came to an end amid powdered tea and sweetmeats composed of white and red bean jelly-cake and boiled black mushrooms. . . .

[Later] the music is in full flow, and the lights of the town grow brighter with the shades of darkening night, and some of the company have long since taken refuge from the dinner in cigars, and over the low brick wall and in the recesses of the temple grounds crowds begin to cluster and form; and below, at the foot of the steps, the crowd grows larger and larger, and you hear the buzz of the throng, and the clinking of the lanterns of the chair-bearers—for the whole town was in festive mood—and high up in our open temple on our hillside we have become a show for the town. Well, that is only a small return for the measureless hospitality we have enjoyed, and if we can gratify an innocent curiosity, let us think of so much pleasure given in our way through the world. It is such a relief to know that we have passed beyond any comprehension of our dinner, which we look at as so many conceptions and preparations—curious contrivances, which we study out as though they were riddles or problems adjusted for our entertainment. The dining quality vanished with that eccentric soup of bass-fish and orange flowers. With the General it went much earlier. It must be said that for the General the table has few charms, and long before we began upon the skylarks and buckwheat degraded by the egg-plant, he for whom this feast is given had taken refuge in a cigar, and contented himself with looking upon the beauty of the town and bay and cliff, allowing the dinner to flow along. You will observe, if you have followed the narrative of our feast, that meat plays a small and fish a large part in a daimio's dinner—fish and the products of the forest and field. The red snapper has the place of honor, and although we have had the snapper in five different shapes, as a soup, as a ragout flavored with cabbage, broiled with pickled beans, and hashed, here he comes again, baked, decorated with ribbons, with every scale in place, folded in a bamboo basket. . . .

CHAPTER NINETEEN

Tokyo and the Emperor of Japan

In addition to the naval cannonades and the endless dinners and sightseeing excursions—the normal, everyday lives of these wandering Americans—while in Japan, Grant played a diplomatic role. He brought the position paper of the Chinese on their dispute over the Ryukyu Islands and presented it with some force to the young emperor of Japan and his cabinet. At the same time Grant made it clear that he detested the bigoted European bullying of the Chinese and the Japanese and underlined the American policy of free, or relatively free, trade in contrast to European force. The Japanese, who had the advantage over the militarily weak Chinese, listened politely, as they did when Grant urged representative government upon them, because the United States had both diplomatic leverage and trading possibilities on offer. Soon, their brutal military incursions into China would more than match those made by the European powers, beginning with their invasion of the Ryukyus in 1879, shortly after Grant's visit.

In addition to being moved by the elegance of Japanese customs and design, Grant was impressed with the potential for economic development, despite what he considered Japanese inefficiency in the use of labor. In sum, Grant showed considerable knowledge, insight, and tact in his dealings with the Japanese authorities. Yet he failed to discern that the emperor and his cabinet were window dressing and that the military high command was in the process of consolidating dictatorial power. After a long stay of more than two months, the Grants finally sailed for home on September 3, 1879.

General Grant's landing in Yokohama, which took place on the 3d of July, as a mere pageant, was in itself a glorious sight. Yokohama has a beautiful harbor, and the lines of the city can be traced along the green background. The day was clear and warm—a home July day tempered with ocean winds. There were men-of-war of various nations in the harbor, and as the exact hour of the General's coming was known, everybody was on the lookout. At ten o'clock our Japanese convoy passed ahead and entered the harbor. At half-past ten the "Richmond" steamed slowly in, followed by the "Ashuelot." As soon as the "Monongahela" made out our flag, and especially the flag at the fore, which denoted the General's presence, her guns rolled out a salute. For a half hour the bay rang with the roar of cannon and was clouded with smoke. The "Richmond" fired a salute to the flag of Japan. The Japanese and the French and Russian vessels fired gun after gun. Then came official visits—Admiral Patterson and staff, the admirals and commanding officers of other fleets, Consul-general Van Buren, and officers of the Japanese navy, blazing in uniform. The officers of the "Richmond" were all in full uniform, and for an hour the deck of the flagship was a blaze of color and decoration. General Grant received the various dignitaries on the deck as they arrived. It was arranged that General Grant's landing was to take place precisely at noon. The foreign residents were anxious that the ceremony should be on what is called the foreign concession, but the Japanese authorities preferred that it should be on their own territory. At noon the imperial barge and the steam launch came alongside the "Richmond." General Grant, accompanied by Mrs. Grant, his son, Prince Dati, Judge Bingham, Mr. Yoshida, and the naval officers specially detailed to accompany him, passed over the side and went on the barge. As soon as General Grant entered the barge, the "Richmond" manned yards and fired a salute. In an instant, as if by magic, the Japanese, the French, and the Russians manned yards and fired salutes. The German ship hoisted the imperial standard, and the English vessel dressed ship. Amid the roar of cannon and the waving of flags the General's boat slowly moved to the shore. As he passed each of the saluting ships the General took off his hat and bowed, while the guards presented arms and the bands played the American national air. The scene was wonderfully grand—the roar of the cannon, the clouds of smoke wandering off over the waters; the stately, noble vessels streaming with flags; the yards manned with seamen; the guards on deck; the officers in full uniform gathered on the quarter-deck to salute the General as he passed; the music and the cheers which came from the Japanese and the merchant ships; the crowds that clustered on the wharves; the city; and over all a clear, mild, July day, with grateful breezes ruffling the sea.

As the General's barge slowly came to the Admiralty wharf, there in waiting were the princes, ministers, and the high officials of the empire of

The Arrival at Yokohama

Japan. As the General stepped out of the boat the Japanese band played the American national air, and Mr. Iwakura, Second Prime Minister, advanced and shook hands with him. General Grant had known Mr. Iwakura in America, when he visited our country at the head of the Japanese embassy. The greeting, therefore, was that of old friends. There were also Ito, Inomoto, and Tereshima, also members of the Cabinet, two princes of the imperial family, and a retinue of officials. Mr. Yoshida presented the General and party to the Japanese, and a few moments were spent in conversation. Day fireworks were set off at the moment of the landing—representations of the American and Japanese flags entwined. That, however, is the legend that greets you at every door-sill—the two flags entwined. The General and party, accompanied by the ministers and officials and the naval officers, drove to the railway station. There was a special train in waiting, and at a quarter past one the party started for Tokio.

Our ride to Tokio was a little less than an hour, over a smooth road, and through a pleasant, well-cultivated, and apparently prosperous country. Our train being special made no stoppage; but I observed as we passed the stations that they were clean and neat, and that the people had assembled to wave flags and bow as we whirled past. About two o'clock our train entered the station at Tokio. A large crowd was in waiting, mainly the merchants and principal citizens. As the General descended from the train a committee of the citizens advanced and asked to read an address. At the close of the address General Grant was led to the private carriage of the Emperor. Among those who greeted him was his Excellency J. Pope Hennessy, British Governor of Hong-Kong, who said that he came as a British subject, to be among those who welcomed General Grant to Japan.

The General's carriage drove slowly, surrounded by cavalry, through lines of infantry presenting arms, through a dense mass of people, under an arch of flowers and evergreens, until, amid the flourish of trumpets and the beating of drums, he descended at the house that had been prepared for his reception—the Emperor's summer palace of Enriokwan. The Japanese, with almost a French refinement of courtesy, were anxious that General Grant should not have any special honors paid to him in Japan until he had seen the Emperor. They were also desirous that the meeting with the Emperor should take place on the Fourth of July. Their imaginations had been impressed with the poetry of the idea of the reception of one who had been the head of the American nation on the anniversary of American Independence. Accordingly it was arranged that at two o'clock on the afternoon of the Fourth of July the audience with the Emperor should take place. The day was very warm, although in our palace on the sea we had whatever breeze might have been wandering over the Pacific. General Grant invited some of his naval friends to accompany him, and in answer to this invitation we had Rear Admiral Patterson, attended by Pay Inspector Thornton and Lieutenant Davenport of his staff; Captain Benham commanding the "Richmond;" Captain Fitzhugh, commanding the "Monongahela;" Commander Johnson, commanding the "Ashuelot;" Lieutenant Springer, and Lieutenant Kellogg. At half-past one Mr. Bingham, our Minister, arrived, and our party immediately drove to the palace. The home of the Emperor was a long distance from the home of the General. The old palace was destroyed by fire, and Japan has had so many things to do that she has not built a new one. The road to the palace was through the section of Tokio where the old daimios lived when they ruled Japan as feudal lords, and made their occasional visits to the capital. There seems to have been a good deal of Highland freedom in the manners of the old princes. Their town-houses were really fortifications. A space was inclosed with walls, and against these walls chambers were built—rude chambers, like winter quarters for an army. In these winter quarters lived the retainers, the swordsmen and soldiers. In the center of the inclosure was the home of the lord himself, who lived in the midst of his people, like a general in camp, anxious to fight somebody, and disappointed if he returned to his home without a fight. A lord with hot-tempered followers, who had come from the restraints and amenities of home to have a good time at the capital and give the boys a chance to distinguish themselves and see the world, would not be a welcome neighbor. And as there were a great many such lords, and each had his army and his town fortress, the daimio quarter became an important part of the capital. Some of the houses were more imposing than the palace—notably the house of the Prince of Satsuma. There was an imposing gate, elaborately buttressed and strengthened, that looked quite Gothic in its rude splendor. These daimio houses have been taken by the government for schools, for public offices, for various useful purposes. The daimios no longer come with armies and build camps and terrorize over their neighbors and rivals.

We drove through the daimios' quarter and through the gates of the city. The first impression of Tokio is that it is a city of walls and canals. The walls are crude and solid, protected by moats. In the days of pikemen and sword-bearers there could not have been a more effective defense. Even now it would require an effort for even a German army to enter through these walls. They go back many generations; I do not know how many. In these lands nothing is worth recording that is not a thousand years old, and my impression is that the walls of Tokio have grown up with the growth of the city, the necessities of defense, and the knowledge of the people in attack and defense. We passed under the walls of an inclosure which was called the castle. Here we are told the Emperor will build his new palace. We crossed another bridge—I think there were a dozen altogether in the course of the drive—and came to a modest arched gateway, which did not look nearly as imposing as the entrance to the palace formerly occupied by the great Prince Satsuma. Soldiers were drawn up, and the band played "Hail Columbia." Our carriages drove on past one or two modest buildings and drew up in front of another modest building, on the steps of which the Minister Iwakura was standing. The General and party descended, and were cordially welcomed and escorted up a narrow stairway into an anteroom. When you have seen most of the available palaces in the world, from the glorious home of Aurungzebe to the depressing, mighty cloister of the Escurial, you are sure to have preconceived notions of what a palace should be, and to expect something unique and grand in the home of the long-hidden and sacred Majesty of Japan. The home of the Emperor was as simple as that of a country gentleman at home. We have many country gentlemen with felicitous investments in petroleum and silver who would disdain the home of a prince who claims direct descent from heaven, and whose line extends far beyond the Christian era. What marked the house was its simplicity and taste; qualities for which my palace education had not prepared me. You look for splendor, for the grand— at least the grandiose—for some royal whim like the holy palace near the Escurial, which cost millions, or like Versailles, whose cost is among the eternal mysteries. Here we are in a suite of plain rooms, the ceilings of wood, the walls decorated with natural scenery—the furniture sufficient but not crowded—and exquisite in style and finish. There is no pretense of architectural emotion. The rooms are large, airy, with a sense of summer about them which grows stronger as you look out of the window and down the avenues of trees. We are told that the grounds are spacious and fine, even for Japan, and that his Majesty, who rarely goes outside of his palace grounds, takes what recreation he needs within the walls.

The palace is a low building, one story in height. They do not build high walls in Japan, especially in Tokio, on account of the earthquakes. We enter a room where all the Ministers are assembled. The Japanese Cabinet is a famous body, and tested by the laws of physiognomy would compare with that of any Cabinet I have seen. The Prime Minister is a striking character. He is small, slender, with an almost girl-like figure, delicate, clean-cut, winning features, a face that might be that of a boy of twenty or a man of fifty. The Prime Minister reminded me of Alexander H. Stephens in his frail, slender frame, but it bloomed with health and lacked the sad, pathetic lines which tell of the years of suffering which Stephens has endured. The other Ministers looked like strong, able men. Iwakura has a striking face, with lines showing firmness and decision, and you saw the scar which marked the attempt of the assassin to cut him down and slay him, as Okubo, the greatest of Japanese statesmen, was slain not many months ago. That assassination made as deep an impression in Japan as the killing of Lincoln did in America. We saw the spot where the murder was done on our way to the palace, and my Japanese friend who pointed it out spoke in low tones of sorrow and affection, and said the crime there committed had been an irreparable loss to Japan. A lord in waiting, with a heavily-braided uniform, comes softly in, and, making a signal, leads the way. The General and Mrs. Grant, escorted by General Bingham, and followed by the remainder of our party, entered. The General and the Minister were in evening dress. The naval officers were in full uniform, Colonel Grant wearing the uniform of lieutenant-colonel. We walked along a short passage and entered another room, at the farther end of

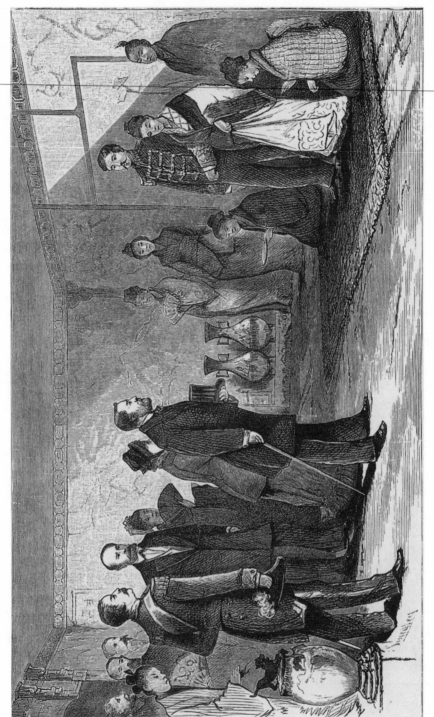

The Audience with the Emperor of Japan

which were standing the Emperor and the Empress.* Two ladies in waiting were near them, in a sitting, what appeared to be a crouching, attitude. Two other princesses were standing. These were the only occupants of the room. Our party slowly advanced, the Japanese making a profound obeisance, bending the head almost to a right angle with the body. The royal princes formed in line near the Emperor, along with the princesses. The Emperor stood quite motionless, apparently unobservant or unconscious of the homage that was paid him. He is a young man, with a slender figure, taller than the average Japanese, and of about the middle height according to our ideas. He has a striking face, with a mouth and lips that remind you something of the traditional mouth of the Hapsburg family. The forehead is full and narrow, the hair and the light mustache and beard intensely black. The color of the hair darkens what otherwise might pass for a swarthy countenance at home. The face expressed no feeling whatever, and but for the dark, glowing eye, which was bent full upon the General, you might have taken the imperial group for statues. The Empress, at his side, wore the Japanese costume, rich and plain. Her face was very white, and her form slender and almost childlike. Her hair was combed plainly and braided with a gold arrow. The Emperor and Empress have agreeable faces, the Emperor especially showing firmness and kindness. The solemn etiquette that pervaded the audience chamber was peculiar, and might appear strange to those familiar with the stately but cordial manners of a European court. But one must remember that the Emperor holds so high and so sacred a place in the traditions, the religion, and the political system of Japan that even the ceremony of to-day is so far in advance of anything of the kind ever known in Japan that it might be called a revolution.

His Imperial Majesty, for instance, as our group was formed, advanced and shook hands with General Grant. This seems a trivial thing to write down, but such a thing was never before known in the history of Japanese majesty. Many of these details may appear small, but we are in the presence of an old and romantic civilization, slowly giving way to the fierce, feverish pressure of European ideas, and you can only note the change in those incidents which would be unnoticed in other lands. The incident of the Emperor of Japan advancing toward General Grant and shaking hands becomes an historic event of consequence, and as such I note it. The manner

---

* Mutsuhito (1852–1912), who came to the throne in 1867, was known as the Meiji Emperor; his consort was Empress Shoken.

of the Emperor was constrained, almost awkward, the manner of a man doing a thing for the first time, and trying to do it as well as possible. After he had shaken hands with the General, he returned to his place, and stood with his hand resting on his sword, looking on at the brilliant, embroidered, gilded company as though unconscious of their presence. Mr. Bingham advanced and bowed, and received just the faintest nod in recognition. The other members of the party were each presented by the minister, and each one, standing about a dozen feet from the Emperor, stood and bowed. Then the General and Mrs. Grant were presented to the princesses, each party bowing to the other in silence. The Emperor then made a signal to one of the attendants, Mr. Ishibashi, who advanced. The Emperor spoke to him for a few moments in a low tone, Mr. Ishibashi standing with bowed head. When the Emperor had finished, Mr. Ishibashi advanced to the General, and said he was commanded by his Majesty to read him the following address:

"Your name has been known to us for a long time, and we are highly gratified to see you. While holding the high office of President of the United States you extended toward our countrymen especial kindness and courtesy. When our ambassador, Iwakura, visited the United States, he received the greatest kindness from you. The kindness thus shown by you has always been remembered by us. In your travels around the world you have reached this country, and our people of all classes feel gratified and happy to receive you. We trust that during your sojourn in our country you may find much to enjoy. It gives me sincere pleasure to receive you, and we are especially gratified that we have been able to do so on the anniversary of American independence. We congratulate you, also, on the occasion."

This address was read in English. At its close General Grant said:

"YOUR MAJESTY: I am very grateful for the welcome you accord me here today, and for the great kindness with which I have been received, ever since I came to Japan, by your government and your people. I recognize in this a feeling of friendship toward my country. I can assure you that this feeling is reciprocated by the United States; that our people, without regard to party, take the deepest interest in all that concerns Japan, and have the warmest wishes for her welfare. I am happy to be able to express that sentiment. America is your next neighbor, and will always give Japan sympathy and support in her efforts to advance. I again thank your Majesty for your hospitality, and wish you a long and happy reign, and for your people prosperity and independence."

At the conclusion of this address, which was *extempore,* Mr. Ishibashi translated it to his Majesty. Then the Empress made a sign and said a few words. Mr. Ishibashi came to the side of Mrs. Grant and said the Empress had commanded him to translate the following address:

> "I congratulate you upon your safe arrival after your long journey. I presume you have seen very many interesting places. I fear you will find many things uncomfortable here, because the customs of the country are so different from other countries. I hope you will prolong your stay in Japan, and that the present warm days may occasion you no inconvenience."

Mrs. Grant, pausing a moment, said in a low, conversational tone of voice, with animation and feeling:

> "I thank you very much. I have visited many countries and have seen many beautiful places, but I have seen none so beautiful or so charming as Japan."

All day, during the Fourth of July, visitors poured in on the General. The reception of so many distinguished statesmen and officials reminded one of state occasions at the White House. Princes of the imperial family, princesses, the members of the cabinet and citizens and high officials, naval officers, ministers and consuls, all came; and carriages were constantly coming and going. In the evening there was a party at one of the summer gardens, given by the American residents in honor of the Fourth of July. The General arrived at half-past eight, and was presented to the American residents by Mr. Bingham, the minister. At the close of the presentation, Mr. Bingham made a brief but singularly eloquent address. Judge Thomas B. Van Buren made a patriotic and ringing speech, after which there were fireworks and feasting, and, after the General and Mrs. Grant retired, there was dancing. It was far on toward morning before the members of the American colony in Tokio grew weary of celebrating the anniversary. . . .

You wonder at the number of servants about you—servants for everything. There, for instance, is a gardener working over a tree. The tree is one of the dwarf species that you see in Japan—one of the eccentricities of landscape gardening—and this gardener files and clips and adorns his tree as carefully as a lapidary burnishing a gem. "There has been work enough done on that tree," said the General, "since I have been here, to raise all the food a small family would require during the winter." Labor, the General thinks, is too good a thing to be misapplied, and when the result of the labor is a plum-tree that you could put on your dinner-table,

A Japanese Village

he is apt to regard it as misapplied. Here are a dozen men in blue cotton dress working at a lawn. I suppose in a week they would do as much as a handy Yankee boy could achieve in a morning with a lawn-mower. Your Japanese workman sits down over his meadow, or his flower-bed, or his bit of road, as though it were a web of silk that he was embroidering. Other men in blue are fishing. The waters of the lake come in with the tide, and the fish that come do not return, and much of our food is found here.

The sprinkling of the lawns and of the roads is always a serious task, and employs quite an army of servants for the best part of the afternoon. One of the necessities of palace life is that you have ten times as many servants about you as you want, and work must be found to keep them busy. The summer-houses by the lake in the grounds at Enriokwan are worthy of study. Japan has taught the world the beauty of clean, fine-grained natural wood, and the fallacy of glass and paint. I am writing these lines in one of these houses—the first you meet as you come to the lake. Nothing could be more simple and at the same time more tasteful. It is one room, with grooves for a partition should you wish to make it two rooms. The floor is covered with a fine, closely-woven mat of bamboo strips. Over the mat is thrown a rug, in which black and brown predominate. The walls looking out to the lake are a series of frames that can be taken out—lattice-work of small squares, covered with paper. The ceiling is plain un-varnished wood. There are a few shelves, with vases, blue and white pottery, containing grow-ing plants and flowers. There are two tables, and their only furniture a large box of gilded lacquer for stationery, and a smaller one containing cigars. These boxes are of exquisite workmanship, and the gold chrysanthemum indicates the imperial ownership. I have described this house in detail be-cause it is a type of all the houses that I have seen in the palace grounds, not only at Enriokwan but elsewhere in Japan. It shows taste and economy. Everything about it is wholesome and clean, the workmanship true and minute, with no tawdry appliances to distract or offend the eye.

The weather was such that going out during the day was a discomfort—warm, torrid, baking weather. During the day there are ceremonies, calls from Japanese and foreign officials, papers to read, visits to make. If the evening is free the General has a dinner party—sometimes small, some-times large. To-night it will be the royal princes, tomorrow the Prime Min-isters, on other evenings other Japanese of rank and station. Sometimes we have Admiral Patterson or officers from the fleet. Sometimes Mr. Bing-ham and his family. Governor Hennessy, the British Governor of Hong-Kong, has been a frequent visitor, and no man was more welcome to the General. General Grant was the guest of the Governor during his resi-dence in Hong-Kong, and formed a high opinion of his genius and char-acter. Prince Dati, Mr. Yoshida, and some other Japanese officials live at Enriokwan and form a part of our family. They represent the Emperor, and remain with the General to serve him and make his stay as pleasant as pos-sible. Nothing could be more considerate or courteous than the kindness of our Japanese friends. Sometimes we have merchants from the bazaars with all kinds of curious and useful things to sell. Sometimes a fancy for curiosities takes possession of some of the party, and the result is an after-noon's prowl about the shops in Tokio, and the purchase of a sword or a spear or a bow and arrows. The bazaars of Tokio teem with beautiful works of art, and the temptation to go back laden with achievements in porce-lain and lacquer is too great to be resisted, unless your will is under the control of material influences too sordid to be dwelt upon. Sometimes we have special and unique excitements, such as was vouchsafed to us a few evenings since. Our party was at dinner—an informal dinner—with no guests except our Japanese friends and Governor Hennessy. While dining there was a slight thunder-storm, which gave some life to the baked and burning atmosphere. Suddenly we heard an unusual noise—a noise like the rattling of plates in a pantry. The lanterns vibrated, and there was a tremulous movement of the water and wine in our glasses. I do not think we should have regarded it as anything else than an effect of the thunderstorm, but for Governor Hennessy. "That," he said, "is an earthquake." While he spoke the phenomenon was repeated, and we plainly distinguished the shock. So, altogether, nothing could be more quiet than our days in Enriokwan. We read and wrote and walked about the grounds, and sat up very late at night on the veranda, talking about home, about the East, and our travels in Japan. Japan itself grew upon us more and more. The opportunities for studying the country, its policy, the aims of its rulers, its government, and its diplomacy, have been very great. . . .

The Emperor had sent word to General Grant that he desired to see him informally, and the General answered that he was entirely at the pleasure of his Majesty. Many little courtesies had been exchanged between the Empress and Mrs. Grant, and the Emperor and his ministers kept a constant watch over the General's comfort. The day fixed for the imperial interview was unusually warm. At half-past two in the afternoon, as we were sitting on the veranda, a messenger came to say that his Majesty had arrived, and was awaiting the General in the little summer-house on the banks of the lake, which I have described. The General, accompanied by Colonel Grant, Prince Dati, Mr. Yoshida, and the writer, left the palace and proceeded to the summer-house. We passed under the trees and toward the bridge. The imperial carriage had been hauled up under the shade of the trees and the horses taken out. The guards, attendants, and cavalrymen who had accompanied the sovereign were all seeking the shelter of the grove. We crossed the bridge and entered the summer-house. Preparations had been made for the Emperor, but they were very simple. Porcelain flower-pots, with flowers and ferns and shrubbery, were scattered about the room. One or two screens had been introduced. In the center of the room was a table, with chairs around it. Behind one of the screens was another table, near the window, which looked into the lake. As the General entered, the Prime Minister and the Minister of the Imperial Household advanced and welcomed him. Then, after a pause, we passed behind the screen and were in the presence of the Emperor. His Majesty was standing before the table in undress uniform, wearing only the ribbon of a Japanese order. General Grant advanced, and the Emperor shook hands with him. To the rest of the party he simply bowed. Mr. Yoshida acted as interpreter. The Emperor said:

> "I have heard of many of the things you have said to my ministers in reference to Japan. You have seen the country and the people. I am anxious to speak with you on these subjects, and am sorry I have not had an opportunity earlier."

General Grant said he was entirely at the service of the Emperor, and was glad indeed to see him and thank his Majesty for all the kindness he had received in Japan. He might say that no one outside of Japan had a higher interest in the country or a more sincere friendship for its people.

A question was asked which brought up the subject now paramount in political discussions in Japan—the granting of an assembly and legislative functions to the people.

General Grant said that this question seemed to be the only one about which there was much feeling in Japan, the only one he had observed. It was a question to be considered with great care. No one could doubt that governments became stronger and nations more prosperous as they became representative of the people. This was also true of monarchies, and no monarchs were as strong as those who depended upon a parliament. No one could doubt that a legislative system would be an advantage to Japan, but the question of when and how to grant it would require careful consideration. That needed a clearer knowledge of the country than he had time to acquire. It should be remembered that rights of this kind— rights of suffrage and representation—once given could not be withdrawn. They should be given gradually. An elective assembly, to meet in Tokio, and discuss all questions with the Ministry might be an advantage. Such an assembly should not have legislative power at the outset. This seemed to the General to be the first step. The rest would come as a result of the admirable system of education which he saw in Japan.

An expression of gratification at the treaty between Japan and the United States, which gave Japan the right to manage her own commerce, led to a conversation about foreign policy in Asia.* "Nothing," said the

---

* The American-Japanese trade treaty was signed on July 29, 1858. It followed the famous 1854 American naval incursion into Japanese waters, led by Commodore Matthew C. Perry, that had forced Japan to open to the world. Although the 1858 treaty contained a reopener clause, the 1872 Iwakura mission to the United States, during the Grant administration, failed to secure alterations desired by the Japanese.

General, "has been of more interest to me than the study of the growth of European and foreign influence in Asia. When I was in India I saw what England had done with that empire. I think the British rule is for the advantage of the Indian people. I do not see what could take the place of British power but anarchy. There were some things to regret, perhaps, but a great deal to admire in the manner in which India was governed. But since I left India I have seen things that made my blood boil, in the way the European powers attempt to degrade the Asiatic nations. I would not believe such a policy possible. It seems to have no other aim than the extinction of the independence of the Asiatic nations. On that subject I feel strongly, and in all that I have written to friends at home I have spoken strongly. I feel so about Japan and China. It seems incredible that rights which at home we regard as essential to our independence and to our national existence, which no European nation, no matter how small, would surrender, are denied to China and Japan. Among these rights there is none so important as the right to control commerce. A nation's life may often depend upon her commerce, and she is entitled to all the profit that can come out of it. Japan especially seems to me in a position where the control of her commerce would enable her statesmen to relieve the people of one great burden—the land-tax. The effect of so great a tax is to impoverish the people and limit agriculture. When the farmer must give a half of his crop for taxes he is not apt to raise more than will keep him alive. If the land-tax could be lessened, we have no doubt that agriculture would increase in Japan, and the increase would make the people richer, make them buy and consume more, and thus in the end benefit commerce as well. It seems to me that if the commerce of Japan were made to yield its proportion of the revenue, as the commerce of England and France and the United States, this tax could be lessened. I am glad the American government made the treaty. I hope other powers will assent to it. But whether or not, I think I know the American people well enough to say that they have, without distinction of party, the warmest wishes for the independence of Japan. We have great interests in the Pacific, but we have none that are inconsistent with the independence of these nations."

Another subject which arose in the course of the conversation was national indebtedness. General Grant said that there was nothing which Japan should avoid more strenuously than incurring debts to European nations. So long as the government borrowed from its own people it was well. But loans from foreign powers were always attended with danger and humiliation. Japan could not go into a European money market and make a loan that would be of an advantage to her. The experience of Egypt was a lesson. Egypt was allowed to borrow right and left, to incur an enormous debt. The result is that Egypt has been made a dependency of her creditors. Turkey owed much of her trouble to the same cause. A country like Japan has all the money she wants for her own affairs, and any attempt to bring her into indebtedness to foreign powers would only be to lead her into the abyss into which Egypt has fallen.

The General spoke to the Emperor on this question with great earnestness. When he had concluded he said there was another matter about which he had an equal concern. When he was in China he had been requested by the Prince Regent and the Viceroy of Tientsin to use his good offices with the Japanese government on the question of Loochoo. The matter was one about which he would rather not have troubled himself, as it belonged to diplomacy and governments, and he was not a diplomatist and not in government. At the same time he could not ignore a request made in the interest of peace. The General said he had read with great care and had heard with attention all the arguments on the Loochoo question from the Chinese and Japanese sides. As to the merits of the controversy, it would be hardly becoming in him to express an opinion. He recognized the difficulties that surrounded Japan. But China evidently felt hurt and sore. She felt that she had not received the consideration due to her. It seemed to the General that his Majesty should strive to remove that feeling, even if in doing so it was necessary to make sacrifices. The General was thoroughly satisfied that China and Japan should make such sacrifices as would settle all questions between them, and become friends and allies, without consultation with foreign powers. He had urged this upon the Chinese government, and he was glad to have the opportunity of saying the same to the Emperor. China and Japan are now the only two countries left in the East capable, through their resources, of becoming great, that are even partially independent of European dictation and laws. The General wished to see them both advance to entire independence, with the power to maintain it. Japan is rapidly approaching such a position, and China had the ability and the intelligence to do the same thing.

The Prime Minister said that Japan felt the most friendly feelings toward China, and valued the friendship of that nation very highly, and would do what she could, without yielding her dignity, to preserve the best relations.

General Grant said he could not speak too earnestly to the Emperor on this subject, because he felt earnestly. He knew of nothing that would give him greater pleasure than to be able to leave Japan, as he would in a very short time, feeling that between China and Japan there was entire friendship. Other counsels would be given to his Majesty, because there were powerful influences in the East fanning trouble between China and Japan. One could not fail to see these influences, and the General said he was profoundly convinced that any concession to them that would bring about war would bring unspeakable calamities to China and Japan. Such a war would bring in foreign nations, who would end it to suit themselves. The history of European diplomacy in the East was unmistakable on that point. What China and Japan should do is to come together without foreign intervention, talk over Loochoo and other subjects, and come to a complete and friendly understanding. They should do it between themselves, as no foreign power can do them any good.

General Grant spoke to his Majesty about the pleasure he had received from studying the educational institutions in Japan. He was surprised and pleased at the standing of these schools. He did not think there was a better school in the world than the Tokio school of engineering. He was glad to see the interest given to the study of English. He approved of bringing forward the young Japanese as teachers. In time Japan would be able to do without foreign teachers; but changes should not be made too rapidly. It would be a pity to lose the services of the men who had created these schools. The men in the service of the Japanese government seemed to be, as far as he could learn, able and efficient.

I have given you the essential points of a conversation that lasted for two hours. General Grant said he would leave Japan with the warmest feelings of friendship toward the Emperor and the people. He would never cease to feel a deep interest in their fortunes. He thanked the Emperor for his princely hospitality. Taking his leave, the General and party strolled back to the palace, and his Majesty drove away to his own home in a distant part of the city. . . .

Life at Nikko was a pleasant episode in General Grant's visit to Japan, because it took him out of the rush and roar of Tokio life and ceremony and parade. It was at Nikko that General Grant met the representatives of the Japanese government who came to speak to him officially of the difficulty between China and Japan on the Loochoo question. This conference, which may some day have historical value, took place on the 22d of July. General Grant had intimated to the Japanese government, on his arrival in Tokio, that he had received a communication from the Chinese government which he would like to present officially to the Japanese cabinet, if he could do so without appearing to interfere in their concerns.

The Emperor sent Mr. Ito, Minister of the Interior, and General Saigo, the Minister of War, to receive the statement. Mr. Ito presented the case of Japan at length, contending that Japan's rights of sovereignty over Loochoo were immemorial, and going over the whole question. When Ito had finished, General Grant said that he had been anxious to have this conversation with the Japanese government, because it enabled him to fulfill a promise he had made to Prince Kung and the Viceroy, Li Hung Chang. He had read the Chinese case and studied it. He had heard with great interest the case of Japan. As to the merits of the controversy he had no opinion to express. There were many points, the General said, in both cases, which were historical and could only be determined by research. His entire interest arose from his kind feeling toward both Japan and China, in whose continued prosperity America and the entire world were interested. Japan, the General said, had done wonders in the past few years. She was, in point of war materials, army and navy, stronger than China. Against Japan, China, he might say, was defenseless, and it was impossible for China to injure Japan. Consequently, Japan could look at the question from a high point of view. At the same time, China was a country of wonderful resources, and although he had seen nothing there to equal the progress of Japan, there had nevertheless been great progress.

General Grant continued by saying that there were other reasons why Japan should, if possible, have a complete and amicable understanding with China. The only powers who would derive any benefit from a war would be foreign powers. The policy of some of the European powers was to reduce Japan and China into the dependence which had been forced upon other nations. He had seen indications of this policy during his travels in the East which made his blood boil. He saw it in Siam and China and Japan. In Siam the king was unable, as he had told the General, to protect his people from opium. In China opium had been forced upon the people. That was as great a crime against civilization as slavery. In Japan, only the other day, he saw Germans deliberately violate a Japanese quarantine by sending down a German gun-boat and taking a German merchantman out of quarantine. No European power would dare to do such a thing in the United States. But it illustrates European policy in the East. If war should ensue between China and Japan, European powers would end it in their own way and to their own advantage, and to the disadvantage of the two nations. "Your weakness and your quarrels are their opportunity," said the General. "Such a question as Loochoo offers a tempting opportunity for the interference of unfriendly diplomacy." Minister

Ito said that these were all grave considerations; but Japan, standing on her immemorial rights, had simply carried out an act of sovereign power over her own dominions. General Grant answered that he could not see how Japan, having gone so far, could recede. But there might be a way to meet the susceptibilities of China, and at the same time not infringe on any of the rights of Japan. The conversation then took a range that I do not feel at liberty to embrace, as propositions and suggestions were made which it would be premature to disclose, and which, in fact, would have no value until they were considered and adopted by the cabinets of Japan and China. The Japanese ministers showed the most conciliatory spirit. General Saigo did not speak English, but Mr. Ito and Mr. Yoshida both conversed fluently in that tongue. The subject of the Formosan expedition, which General Saigo commanded, came up, and was discussed for some time.

The afternoon was warm and the clouds swept over the mountains, and it was pleasant to watch the sun's rays toying around the stately cedars that clothed the mountain sides, lighting up the green summits, and losing themselves in the clouds and the mist. But this land of the mountains is also a land of rain, and suddenly the black clouds came over the ridges and we had a rattling summer thunder-storm. When the talk ran out and the rain ceased, Minister Ito said that what had been communicated by General Grant would be submitted to the cabinet and be considered very carefully. He had no idea what the cabinet would decide. He would probably have occasion to speak with General Grant again on the subject. But on behalf of the government of Japan he desired to express their thanks and their gratitude to General Grant for having presented this question, and for his efforts to continue between Japan and China relations of peace, based upon the honor and independence of both nations. Japan had no desire but peace, and no feeling toward China but a desire to preserve the friendship which had existed so long. . . .

On Saturday General Grant took his leave of the Emperor. An audience of leave is always a solemn ceremony, and the court of Japan pays due respect to splendor and state. A farewell to the Mikado meant more in the eyes of General Grant than if it had been the ordinary leave-taking of a monarch who had shown him hospitality. He had received attentions from the sovereign and people such as had never before been given. He had been honored not alone in his own person, but as the representative of his country. His visit had this political significance, that the Japanese government intended by the honors they paid him to show the value they gave to

The Falls near Hakone

American friendship. In many ways the visit of the General had taken a wide range, and what he would say to the Emperor would have great importance, because every word he uttered would be weighed in every Japanese household. General Grant's habit in answering speeches and addresses is to speak at the moment, without previous thought or preparation. On several occasions, when bodies of people made addresses to him, they sent copies in advance, so that he might read them and prepare a response. But he always declined these courtesies, saying that he would wait until he heard the addresses in public, and his best response would be what came to him on the instant. This was so particularly at Penang, when the Chinese came to him with an address which opened up the most delicate issue of American politics, the Chinese question. A copy of this address had been sent to the Government House for him to look over, but he declined, and his first knowledge of the address which propounded the whole Chinese problem was when the blue-buttoned mandarin stood before him reading it. The response was one of the General's longest and most important speeches, and was made at once, in a quiet, conversational tone. The farewell to the Emperor was so important, however, that the General did what he had not done before during our journey. He wrote out in advance the speech he proposed making to his Majesty. I mention this circumstance simply because the incident was an exceptional one, and because it showed General Grant's anxiety to say to the Emperor and the people of Japan what would be most becoming, in return for their kindness, and what would best conduce to good relations between the two nations. . . .

. . . The Emperor is not what you would call a graceful man, and his manners are those of an anxious person not precisely at his ease—wishing to please and make no mistake. But on this farewell audience he seemed more easy and natural than when we had seen him before. After the salute of the Emperor there was a moment's pause. General Grant then took out of his pocket the manuscript of his speech, and read it as follows:

"YOUR MAJESTY: I come to take my leave, and to thank you, the officers of your government, and the people of Japan, for the great hospitality and kindness I have received at the hands of all during my most pleasant visit to this country. I have now been two months in Tokio and the surrounding neighborhood, and two previous weeks in the more southerly part of the country. It affords me great satisfaction to say that during all this stay and all my visiting I have not witnessed one discourtesy toward myself, nor a single unpleasant sight. Everywhere there seems to be the greatest contentment among the people; and while no signs of great individual wealth exist, no absolute poverty is visible. This is in striking and pleasing contrast with almost every other country I have visited. I leave Japan greatly impressed with the possibilities and probabilities of her future. She has a fertile soil, one half of it not yet cultivated to man's use, great undeveloped mineral resources, numerous and fine harbors, an extensive seacoast abounding in fish of an almost endless variety, and, above all, an industrious, ingenious, contented, and frugal population. With all these nothing is wanted to insure great progress except wise direction by the government, peace at home and abroad, and noninterference in the internal and domestic affairs of the country by the outside nations. It is the sincere desire of your guests to see Japan realize all possible strength and greatness, to see her as independent

The Dinner at Mr. Yoshida's

of foreign rule or dictation as any Western nation now is, and to see affairs
so directed by her as to command the respect of the civilized world. In saying this I believe I reflect the sentiments of the great majority of my countrymen. I now take my leave without expectation of ever again having the
opportunity of visiting Japan, but with the assurance that pleasant recollections of my present visit will not vanish while my life lasts. That your Majesty
may long reign over a prosperous and contented people and enjoy every
blessing is my sincere prayer." . . .

The audience with the Emperor was the end of all festivities; for, after
taking leave of the head of the nation, it would not have been becoming
in others to offer entertainments. Sunday passed quietly, friends coming
and going all day. Monday was spent in Yokohama making ready for embarking. The steamer, which was to sail on Tuesday, was compelled to wait

another day. On Tuesday the General invited Admiral Patterson, Captain Benham, Commander Boyd, and Commander Johnson, commanding respectively the American men-of-war "Richmond," "Ranger," and "Ashuelot," Mr. Bingham, General Van Buren, and several members of the Japanese cabinet, with the ladies of their families, to dinner, our last dinner in Japan. In the evening was a reception, or rather what grew into a reception, the coming of all our friends—Japanese, American, and European—to say good-by. The trees in the park were hung with lanterns, and fireworks were displayed, furnished by the committee of the citizens of Tokio. There was the band from the War Department. The night was one of rare beauty, and during the whole evening the parlors of the palace were thronged. There were the princes and princesses of the imperial family, the members of the cabinet, the high officers of the army and navy, Japanese citizens, ministers, and consuls. The American naval officers from four ships, the "Monongahela" having come in from Hakodadi, were in full force, and their uniforms gave color to what was in other respects a brilliant and glittering throng. . . .

. . . We had been strangely won by Japan, and our last view of it was a scene of beauty, Yokohama nestled on her shore, against which the waters of the sea were idly rolling. Her hills were dowered with foliage, and here and there were houses and groves and flagstaffs, sentinels of the outside world which had made this city their encampment. In the far distance, breaking through the clouds, so faint at first that you had to look closely to make sure that you were not deceived by the mists, Fusiyama towered into the blue and bending skies. Around us were men-of-war shimmering in the sunshine, so it seemed, with their multitudinous flags. There was the hurry, the nervous bustle and excitement, the glow of energy and feeling which always marks the last moments of a steamer about to sail. Our naval friends went back to their ships. Our Yokohama friends went off in their tugs, and the last we saw of General Van Buren was a distant and vanishing figure in a state of pantomime, as though he were delivering a Fourth of July oration. I presume he was cheering. Then our Japanese friends took leave, and went on board their steam-launch to accompany us a part of our journey. The Japanese man-of-war has her anchor up, slowly steaming, ready to convoy us out to sea. The last line that binds us to our anchorage is thrown off, and the huge steamer moves slowly through the shipping. We pass the "Richmond" near enough to recognize our friends on the quarter-deck—the Admiral and his officers. You hear a shrill word of command, and seamen go scampering up the rigging to man the yards. The guns roll out a salute. We pass the "Ashuelot," and her guns take up the iron chorus. We pass the "Monongahela," so close almost that we could converse with Captain Fitzhugh and the gentlemen who are waving us farewell. Her guns thunder good-by, and over the bay the smoke floats in waves—floats on toward Fusiyama. We hear the cheers from the "Ranger." Very soon all that we see of our vessels are faint and distant phantoms, and all that we see of Yokohama are lines of gray and green. We are fast speeding on toward California. For an hour or so the Japanese man-of-war, the same which met us at Nagasaki and came with us through the Inland Sea, keeps us company. The Japanese cabinet are on board. We see the smoke break from her ports and we hurry to the side of our vessel to wave farewell—farewell to so many friends, so many friends kind and true. This is farewell at last, our final token of good will from Japan. The man-of-war fires twenty-one guns. The Japanese sailors swarm up on the rigging and give hearty cheers. Our steamer answers by blowing her steam-whistle. The man-of-war turns slowly around and steams back to Yokohama. Very soon she also becomes a phantom, vanishing over the horizon. Then, gathering herself like one who knows of a long and stern task to do, our steamer breasts the sea with an earnest will—for California and for home.

Across the Pacific to California

It was perhaps fitting that, during his last conversations on the way home, Grant should discuss at length the Vicksburg campaign, his masterpiece. Grant took considerable pride in the skill he had shown then.

On September 20, 1879, the Grants reached San Francisco, slightly more than two years and four months after their departure from Philadelphia. Surely, this had been one of the very grandest of grand tours—regal all the way and incalculably expensive.

And still Grant was not done. After touring the bay area, the Grant party was off to Yosemite for some hiking, after which, in early October, Young took a train for his home in New York. But the Grants persisted on their long voyage, taking the train up to Portland, Oregon, and then wending their way eastward, through Nevada and Wyoming to Omaha, and then through the Midwest—Chicago, Indianapolis, Louisville, Cincinnati, Harrisburg—and on to Christmas 1879 in Philadelphia. On December 16, the mayor of Philadelphia declared a special holiday, and Grant stood on the reviewing stand as 350,000 people watched an endless parade that greeted his return to the city from which he had departed. It certainly looked like the start of a presidential campaign, whether or not that was clear in Grant's mind. Then it was on to Washington, Savannah, and Florida before the return home to Galena, Illinois, in the spring of 1880.

Long as it was, this grand tour was too short, for Grant arrived back in the United States six months before the 1880 Republican Convention, at which at least part of him hoped to secure the nomination for a third term. Being abroad had made him scarce and desirable; by dragging through the United States, he had made himself all too available—the procession, grand as it was, went on far too long. And so the voyage around the world, a detour from the public eye made to heighten esteem for the grand old man, was undermined by one magnificent banquet and public reception too many, or perhaps a couple of dozen. The nomination would go to the dark horse, James A. Garfield.

In private life, Grant would go on to New York and stock speculation and be swindled and ruined by Ferdinand Ward, his shark of a partner—one more Gilded Age crook of the sort who surrounded this gullible man. Finally, dying of cancer in 1885, he would write his memoirs in an attempt to provide for his family after he was gone. That celebrated book, if clearly written, was penned with Grant's feelings held close to the vest. It was the loose verbal memoir he gave to John Russell Young that revealed far more of this ambitious, diffident, sensitive, distant, bright, obtuse, successful, and somehow lonely and yearning man, surely the oddest member of the American pantheon.

We steamed across the Pacific over a gentle, easy sea. There was a hope that we might bend the "Tokio" from her course so far as to allow us to visit the Sandwich Islands. But commercial reasons were paramount, and so we kept our way direct to San Francisco. We had pleasant idle days on the "Tokio," General Grant spending most of his time in reading. But we talked of home subjects, and the General was easily led to speak again of the great rebellion.

"War has responsibilities," said he one day, "that are either fatal to a commander's position or very successful. I often go over our war campaigns and criticise what I did, and see where I made mistakes. Information now and then coming to light for the first time shows me frequently where I could have done better. I don't think there is one of my campaigns with which I have not some fault to find, and which, as I see now, I could not have improved, except perhaps Vicksburg. I do not see how I could have improved that. When General Sherman fell under the censure of Mr. Stanton, because of his convention with Johnston, and there arose that inexplicable and cruel storm of defamation, even going to the extent of impugning Sherman's loyalty—one of the charges against him was that he had been unfaithful to me in the Vicksburg campaign.* It was said, with circumstantial detail, that, not believing in that movement, he had written a protest against it; so that if I failed he would have the merit of having prophesied failure and profited by my blunder. Nothing could be more cowardly than such a charge. Sherman's behavior in that whole business

---

* After Appomattox, on April 18, 1865, Sherman had been gulled into signing a peace treaty with Joseph Johnston that would have allowed Confederate legislatures to remain in power, therefore blocking any reconstruction policy. The treaty was rejected in Washington, with Stanton taking the occasion to impugn Sherman's loyalty.

showed the generosity and manliness of his high character. When I determined on that campaign I knew, as well as I knew anything, that it would not meet with the approval of the authorities in Washington. I knew this because I knew Halleck, and that he was too learned a soldier to consent to a campaign in violation of all the principles of the art of war. But I felt that every war I knew anything about had made laws for itself, and early in our contest I was impressed with the idea that success with us would depend upon our taking advantage of new conditions. No two wars are alike, because they are generally fought at different periods, under different phases of civilization. To take Vicksburg, according to the rules of war as laid down in the books, would have involved a new campaign, a withdrawal of my forces to Memphis, and the opening of a new line of attack. The North needed a victory. We had been unfortunate in Virginia, and we had not gained our success at Gettysburg. Such a withdrawal as would have been necessary—say to Memphis, would have had all the effects, in the North, of a defeat. This was an ever-present consideration with me; for, although I took no open part in politics, and was supposed to be as much of a Democrat as a Republican, I felt that the Union depended upon the administration, and the administration upon victory. I talked it over with Sherman. I told him it was necessary to gain a success in the southwest, that the country was weary and impatient, that the disasters in Virginia were weakening the government, and that unless we did something there was no knowing what, in its despair, the country might not do. Lee was preparing to invade Maryland and Pennsylvania, as he did. Sherman said that the sound campaign was to return to Memphis, establish that as a base of supplies, and move from there on Vicksburg, building up the road as we advanced and never uncovering that base. My reply was that the move backward would further discourage the loyal North and make it difficult to get men or supplies. Already the elections had shown discouragement. I felt that what was wanted was a forward movement to a victory that would be decisive. In a popular war we had to consider political exigencies. You see there was no general in our army who had won that public confidence which came to many of them afterward. We were all of us, more or less, on probation. Sherman contended that the risk of disaster in the proposed movement was so great that even for my own fame I should not undertake it; that if I failed no credit would be given me for my intentions; that the administration, about which I was worrying so much, would root me up and throw me away as a useless weed; that the politicians in Washington should take care of their affairs and we would take care of ours. I thought that war anyhow was a risk; that it made little difference to the country what was done with me. I might be killed or die from fever. The more I thought of it the more I felt that my duty was plain. The story then is that Sherman went to his tent and wrote out that formal protest which might arise in evidence against me should I fall on evil days. This is not true; what Sherman did was to write a letter to Rawlins—a hurried, friendly letter—asking Rawlins to use his influence with me not to incur the risk of ruin, which a rash move would insure; anyhow to consult with my principal generals, and if they approved to at least have a divided responsibility; but assuring him that he would give an earnest support to whatever plan was adopted. Rawlins was in the same mood as Sherman, shared his anxieties, and although not learned in the art of war, was so entirely devoted to me that he trembled at anything that might do me harm. The letter to Rawlins, so far as it referred to me, was no more than what one brother might have written to another. Rawlins brought it to me. I read it over and said nothing. The fact even that such a letter had been written never came from me. Sherman first told about it himself. I felt, however, that to carry out my move fully I must have it developed before it could be stopped from Washington, before orders could come—as they did in fact come—that would have rendered it impossible. I gave Sherman his orders. Nothing could exceed his energy and enthusiasm in carrying out his part of the campaign. I moved my troops down the river to Port Hudson.

"The gun-boats and six or seven steamers ran the batteries at Vicksburg, while I marched the troops from Young's Point to opposite Grand Gulf, expecting to silence the batteries at Grand Gulf and land my troops there, as the first point of high land, on the east bank of the Mississippi, from which I could operate. But the water-batteries proved about as strong as at Vicksburg, and after the gun-boats had fired upon them nearly all day they failed to silence their guns. I had, in the middle of the river, on board my transports, about ten thousand men ready to land at any moment, as soon as the batteries should be silenced. Admiral Porter was there as the flag officer commanding the fleet of gun-boats. So toward evening, finding that we would not be able to effect a landing there, I took a tug and went on board Porter's flag-ship. We were under fire at the time, and Porter's vessel, I found, had been considerably battered, shots having passed through the sides of the ship, killing and wounding a great many men. I told Porter that I saw that the idea of landing there was hopeless; but that, as soon as it was dark, I should take my transports and land the whole of the troops and march there across the point to a point below Grand Gulf; if he would

On the Pacific

run the batteries as he had done at Vicksburg, that I would run the transports too, and that at daylight in the morning the enemy would find we were crossing the river. The important object I had in seeing Porter was to find out if he would consent to the use of his gun-boats as ferry-boats, as they would be so much better than the steamers we had, and would reinforce and supplement them. Besides, the engines of some of my transports had been disabled and they would require to be towed, and Porter's gun-boats would answer admirably for this purpose. But Porter was not under my command, and I could not order him.

"I was naturally anxious. If he had been a touchy admiral, jealous of his rank, in a severe state of discipline, he would have objected to his boats doing ferry duty—certainly would have resented the suggestion, even, from an army officer. He might have told me, as he would have had the right to do, to command my troops and he would command his boats. So I was very anxious to know how Porter would take it. But as soon as the matter was suggested to him he relieved my anxiety by saying that all his gun-boats were at my disposal to be used as transports and ferry-boats for getting the troops over the river. He saw at once what I needed, and himself pointed out in what way his boats could be of service. This is a fine trait in Porter. He sees in an instant the best way of doing a thing, and does it with energy and ability. I was delighted with Porter's co-operation. I never can be too grateful to him for his promptitude. He turned his gun-boats into ferry-boats, and men, cannon, horses, and all, were ferried over next morning at Bruensburg.

"Instead of making a report to Washington of what had been done thus far, I hurried into the interior and developed my movement. You know the theory of the campaign was to throw myself between Johnston and Pemberton, prevent their union, beat each army separately if I could, and take Vicksburg. It was important to have this movement so far advanced before even the knowledge of it reached Washington that it could not be recalled.

"After landing at Bruensburg, below Grand Gulf, I moved out to secure the high land before the enemy could get down from Grand Gulf and confront me, dispatching the troops as fast as they were landed, without waiting for the whole force to move in a body. We had no transportation for the troops on shore after we crossed the river. Three days' rations had been issued, with orders that they must last five, and we also had rations in abundance on board the transports, but no transportation for them to the interior. I directed the officers to gather all the wagons and teams they could from the plantations as we moved on. We met the enemy and fought what is called in history the battle of Port Gibson, although, as a matter of fact, the battle was fought at Thompson's Hill, some five miles before we arrived at Port Gibson. After driving the enemy from that position we followed him toward Port Gibson until night overtook us. Then we lay upon our arms, not in any regular camp, but just where night had overtaken us. We marched on to Port Gibson the following morning, to find that the enemy had crossed Bayou Pierre, burning the bridges, of which there were two. This forced a halt to enable us to build a bridge to carry the army over. Before night we had a bridge built, the army had crossed, and the advance had marched eight miles, to the North Fork of the Bayou Pierre, where the enemy had also burned the bridge. This bridge we repaired during the night, so as to be able to cross on the morning of the third day. From there we pushed on toward the Big Black River, at Hankerson's Ferry, fighting and driving the enemy from all the high points which they had occupied, more to delay us and enable them to get back to Vicksburg than from any hope of stopping us altogether. By the night of the third day our advance was across Hankerson's Ferry, on the Big Black, and within six or seven miles of Vicksburg. There I halted the troops. Then I rode back at once that night to Grand Gulf, where our gun-boats were lying. It was seventeen miles away, and I had to get there, write my dispatches for Washington, and return by morning. I had been in the saddle since we crossed the river, three days before, and had not had a regular meal or any sleep in that time. I wrote my dispatches and sent them by courier to Young's Point, to go by dispatch-boat to Cairo, the nearest point from which they could be telegraphed to Washington. It would take these dispatches some time to reach Cairo by boat, and some time for the response—eight days, I think. I remember how anxiously I counted the time I had to spare before that response could come. You can do a great deal in eight days. Sherman, McPherson, and all of us worked and marched and moved, sleeping on the ground, our army in the lightest marching order. From Hankerson's Ferry, withdrawing the troops that had crossed the Big Black, I marched, keeping my left flank on the Big Black and my right extending out so as to occupy all the roads we could leading toward the north, so that when I arrived near to the railroad connecting Vicksburg and Jackson, my left was on the Big Black and my right at Raymond, within twelve or fifteen miles of Jackson. There McPherson encountered the enemy, fought a sharp battle, and gained a victory. Then I determined to move rapidly upon Jackson, and capture and destroy that place and the railroads leading to and from it before turning toward Vicksburg. I gave my orders in the evening after the battle of Raymond for a rapid move by the right flank upon Jackson, leaving the Thirteenth Army Corps, under McClernand, where they were—in the neighborhood of Raymond—as a sufficient force between my moving column and the rebel troops in Vicksburg, in case they should come out to attack us. Jackson was taken by storm that afternoon in a heavy rain. McPherson captured an order from Johnston to Pemberton to come out from Vicksburg and force the attack there. I was rejoiced when I learned Johnston's plans, and turned about to meet Pemberton. I did meet him half way, at Champion Hill.

"At a point some miles before reaching Champion Hill—feeling that I had troops enough without Sherman's command, and knowing that it would be impossible to cross the Big Black, which was then much swollen, in presence of an enemy—I detached Sherman with his corps, and all the pontoons we had, and turned him upon a road to strike the Big Black some six or seven miles above where the railroad leading into Vicksburg crosses it, expecting that by having his force on the Vicksburg side of the Big Black, he would be able to turn the enemy's position, force them back, and leave a free crossing for us on the main straight road. With the troops left with me we fought the battle of Champion Hill, captured some 3,000 prisoners, besides a considerable amount of artillery, cut off one division, and forced back toward Vicksburg the remainder of Pemberton's army, following them until night overtook us. On the morning following the battle of Champion Hill we pursued the enemy to the Big Black, where we found them in a fortified position in the flats on the east side of the river, with a portion of their army occupying the heights on the west bank. I disposed my troops so as to surround the enemy on the side of the river where I was, not intending to make any attack then, but to await the result of Sherman's move to turn the enemy and drive them back. It was while in this position—there being then some little firing of artillery and musketry on both sides—that I received the orders directing me to go back to the Mississippi, move down and co-operate with Banks in the reduction of Port Hudson, and when that was secured to move, with Banks's and my forces combined, back on to Vicksburg, having then New Orleans for a base of supplies. An officer came into my lines from Banks's army, then investing Port Hudson. This officer was a brigadier-general, in a high state of excitement, a small and impressive man, so overcome with the sense of his tremendous responsibility that he seemed to stand on his toes to give it emphasis. He had the order from Halleck for me to withdraw at once with my force and join Banks. This order was so important that he, a general officer, had come all the way to bring it and to escort me, if necessary, to Port Hudson. I acknowledged the order, but said I was there in front of the enemy and engaged, and could not withdraw; that even General Halleck, under the circumstances, would not expect me to do so. The little brigadier, standing on his toes, became more and more emphatic. I pointed out that we were not only engaged with the enemy, but winning a victory, and that General Halleck never intended his order to destroy a victory. While explaining to this officer the impossibility of my retreating after I had progressed so far, one of my brigade commanders, without orders from me, had given the command "Charge!" This commander was a brave but impulsive man, and seeing an opportunity he had taken advantage of it. A bayou filled with fallen trees and debris lay between his command and the enemy, and if they had shown a resistance to the attack our men might have been slaughtered. But the enemy were tired out with fighting the day before, and so, when they saw our troops charging them, after a show of resistance they just pulled out wads of cotton from the cotton-bales, stuck them on their bayonets and muskets, and held them up as a sign of surrender. The charge, of course, was successful, and we captured the whole batch—over 2,000 prisoners—and all the artillery on that side of the river. The enemy on the west bank immediately commenced their retreat on Vicksburg, without waiting to be turned by our troops, who had successfully crossed above them, burning their bridges, however, as they left. I immediately set my command to building temporary bridges over the river, which was then very deep and with a swift, strong current. We built three of them. One I gave McPherson the direction of, one to Lieutenant Haynes, a young engineer who was just out of the Military Academy, and one to General Thomas E. G. Ransome, a brave volunteer officer. They each adopted different plans of building, but all three bridges were completed by daylight the following morning, giving us three bridges to cross on at the same time. After we had crossed the Big Black River I moved upon Vicksburg, aiming to get possession of the Yazoo above Vicksburg before accomplishing any other object, so as to give us a base of supplies.

"I remember when I came to the point which would give us a base for our supplies. That is, having this point, it gave us a safe place to bring our supplies from the right flank of the army. You see, our army was acting as a movable column, without a base. We were nearing what is called Walnut Hills, which overlook the Yazoo, at the point where Sherman had made his attack the December before. I felt very anxious, and so did Sherman—so anxious that we became impatient. We were together at the time, riding in advance of our column. We increased our pace and rode ahead, sometimes beyond our skirmish lines. When we ascended the hill we saw that our movement was a success. I remember Sherman's exclamations of joy at my side on that hill, his rapture over the success of the movement, his compliments to me especially. He could not have been more pleased if the plan had been his own. We were standing at the point which had been occupied by the enemy when Sherman made his attack the fall before. The enemy held this hill, and Sherman had reached the swamps and flats below, but without the possibility then, owing to the high water, of deploying his column so as to make a successful attack.

"Of course when Vicksburg fell Port Hudson went with it. I made all the explanations necessary to Halleck, who treated me handsomely, approved my campaign to the letter, comparing the move to Napoleon's movements on Ulm. Mr. Lincoln also wrote me letters, which he published at the time, saying that he had not approved the campaign when he heard of it, but the result showed that I was right and he was wrong. So far, in fact, from Sherman trying to belittle that campaign, as is the charge against him, he was most enthusiastic in his commendations. Citizens, and particularly the State officers of Illinois, began to come to our head-quarters after the fall of Vicksburg—Governor Yates and others—and Sherman would tell them, in his eager way, how he had opposed the movement, and that the credit was all mine. Nothing could be more generous than his treatment of me. But that is Sherman's way. He is generous to everybody, and while at West Point, he was one of the most popular boys at the Academy.

"If the Vicksburg campaign," continued General Grant, "meant anything, in a military point of view, it was that there are no fixed laws of war which are not subject to the conditions of the country, the climate, and the habits of the people. The laws of successful war in one generation would insure defeat in another. I was well served in the Vicksburg campaign."

Allusion was made in our conversation to the statement of the Confederate General, Dick Taylor, that Pemberton in surrendering Vicksburg betrayed the South. "That," said General Grant, "is one of Taylor's romances. Pemberton could not have held Vicksburg a day longer than he did. But desperate as his condition was, he did not want to surrender it. He knew that, as a Northern man by birth, he was under suspicion; that a surrender would be treated as disloyalty, and rather than incur that reproach he was willing to stand my assault. But as I learned afterward his officers, and even his men, saw how mad would have been such a course, and he reluctantly accepted the inevitable. I could have carried Vicksburg by assault, and was ready when the surrender took place. But if Pemberton had forced this, had compelled me to throw away lives uselessly, I should have dealt severely with him. It would have been little less than murder, not only of my men but his own. I would severely punish any officer who, under such circumstances, compelled a wanton loss of life. War is war, and murder is murder, and Vicksburg was so far reduced, and its condition so hopeless when it surrendered, that the loss of another life in defending it would have been criminal.

"Taking it all in all," said General Grant, "I see fewer mistakes in the Vicksburg campaign than in any other. Others, no doubt, see many; but I am speaking now as a critic of myself. Mission Ridge, although a great victory, would have ended in the destruction of Bragg but for our mistake in not knowing the ground. If I had known the ground as well before the battle as I did after, I think Bragg would have been destroyed. I saw this as soon as the battle was over, and was greatly disappointed. Sheridan showed his genius in that battle, and to him I owe the capture of most of the prisoners that were taken. Although commanding a division only, he saw in the crisis of the engagement that it was necessary to advance beyond the point indicated in his orders. He saw what I could not know, on account of my ignorance of the ground, and with the instinct of military genius pushed ahead. If the others had followed his example we should have had Bragg's army. The victory satisfied the country, but it might have been more fruitful. There were mistakes enough in our Virginia campaign, but fortunately we did not make as many as the enemy. So far as battles are concerned I always deplored Cold Harbor. That was a serious mistake. Lee's great blunder was in holding Richmond. He must have been controlled by Davis, who, taking the gambler's desperate view of the situation, staked the Confederacy on one card. It must have been that Davis felt that the moral effect of the fall of Richmond would have been equal to the fall of the South. Or it may be, as I have sometimes thought, that Lee felt that the war was over; that the South was fought out; that any prolongation of the war would be misery to both the North and the South. After I crossed the James, the holding of Richmond was a mistake. Nor have I ever felt that the surrender at Appomattox was an absolute military necessity. I think that in holding Richmond, and even in consenting to that surrender, Lee sacrificed his judgment as a soldier to his duty as a citizen and the leader of the South. I think Lee deserves honor for that, for if he had left Richmond when Sherman invaded Georgia, it would have given us another year of war."

On Saturday, September 20th, that being the eighteenth day of our homeward journey from Japan, we came to the coast of California. Our first news from home came with the pilot-boat, when we learned from the newspapers which it brought of the reception awaiting the General. The details of this proposed honor were a great surprise to the General, who had no idea of the magnitude and enthusiasm of the compliment in store for him.

The sun was setting behind the hills as we steamed into the Golden Gate. But the story of General Grant's reception in California has been told so fully that I despair of being able to add to it. On the whole, the scene was wondrously beautiful. The lines of brown hills, the puffs of smoke that told of salutes fired so far off that the sound of the cannon could scarcely be heard, the welcoming of the fog-horns, the trim and bending yachts bright with flags, the huge steamers covered with people coming out to meet us and cheering again and again, the deep thunder of the batteries of Angel Island, Black Point, and Alcatraz, the cheers from the thousands who swarmed on Telegraph Hill, as our vessel slowly steamed past; and, finally, the brilliant, blazing city, which burst upon us as we turned into our anchorage—all of this formed a picture which could not be forgotten, even by those who had seen the pageantry of Europe and the splendor of the East. But it had a quality which neither Europe nor the East could give, for it was a welcome home! Coming from the silent multitudes of Japan and China, it was a thrilling sound to hear once again the Anglo-Saxon cheer ringing out from thousands of voices.

At eleven o'clock in the evening General Grant reached his hotel, and dined quietly with Senator John P. Jones and Senator William Sharon, of Nevada. A. J. Bryant, Mayor of San Francisco, took the utmost pains to make General Grant's welcome a hearty one; and this courtesy was the more gracious from him, because Mayor Bryant is known to belong to a different political party. The General's time in California was spent in seeing the sights. The visit was to him one of peculiar interest. Twenty-five years before he had been, as a young officer, stationed in California; and, as he said to the writer, it had always been the dream of his life to live in California. What surprised him were the changes that had taken place. The San Francisco that he had known in the early days had vanished, and even the aspect of nature had changed; for the resolute men who are building the metropolis of the Pacific have absorbed the waters and torn down the hills to make their way. Many were the old friends the General met in San Francisco—companions of other days. There were visits to the City Hall, where the General reviewed the veterans of our war, representatives from the various armies of the Union who had made their homes in California. There was a visit from the Methodist Conference, who called in a body. Bishop Gilbert Haven made an address, and the General and Mrs. Grant spent an hour in conversation with the members of the Conference. There were visits to the stock exchanges, the banks, and the various centers of business. General McDowell, commanding the Military De-

The Arrival at San Francisco

partment of the Pacific, gave General Grant a reception, and this was one of the pleasantest features of our stay. It was while at the house of General McDowell that the delicate question, whether or not General Grant should receive a delegation from the Chinese of San Francisco, was decided. The Chinese are not loved in California, and so, when it was proposed to present him with an address from the Chinese merchants, there were strong objections from some quarters, for fear that it would give offense to the people of California. When the matter was submitted to General Grant he said that the kindness he had received from the statesmen and rulers of China was so marked that he would be only too happy to return it by any courtesy he could show to Chinamen in America. As the home of General McDowell is a government property, it was thought better that the Chinese delegation should there present their address. So, on the afternoon of the reception, the delegation came, headed by Colonel Bee. An address was read, and a scroll of worked silk presented to the General. On this scroll were the following words in Chinese: "To General Grant. We join our voices to swell the pean which has girdled the earth, wafted over seas and continents. Praises to the warrior and statesman. Most graciously presented by the Chinese of California." General Grant, in return, acknowledged the great kindness and hospitality shown to him by the people and authorities of China, and expressed the hope that China, by breaking down the seclusion in which she has been shrouded for ages, would continue to draw nearer to her the trade and sympathy of the civilized world. At the close of the speech Colonel Bee said that Mrs. Grant had done much to break down the spirit of domestic exclusiveness that reigns in China, and asked her to accept, on behalf of the delegation, a small casket of ivory. There were visits to the theaters, and a very pleasant day at Oakland. Oakland is a suburb of San Francisco, and is certainly one of the most beautiful cities I have seen in my journey around the world. Here were processions, banners and flags; but especially worthy of note was the gathering of five thousand school children, who formed in line, and as General Grant walked up and down threw roses at his feet.

There was a dinner at the house of D. O. Mills, a banquet at his beautiful home, Millbrae. There was a reception at the house of Senator Sharon, Belmont, a famous house, famous in the social annals of California. Here Senator Sharon entertained General Grant with princely and splendid hospitality. There was a visit to the house of J. C. Flood, Menlo Park, and a pleasant day at San José, the General accompanied on this occasion by Colonel J. P. Jackson, M. D. Boruck, Mayor Bryant, and others.

Life in California was a round of hospitalities so continuous as almost to be distressing. A pleasant episode was our trip to the Yosemite. The party who made this little journey was composed of the General and Mrs. Grant, U. S. Grant, jr., General John F. Miller and wife, their daughter, Miss Eudora Miller, Geo. W. Dent, Miss Florence Sharon, daughter of the Senator, Miss Jennie Flood, daughter of J. C. Flood, Esq., and the writer. Mr. Washburne accompanied us on behalf of the company who own the stage lines and are building the road through the Yosemite. It was a vivid and graphic experience—these long drives through the sierras, the nights we spent in the lonely out-of-the-way taverns, the glimpse of the primitive but hearty kindness shown in the little towns by the wayside, whose inhabitants all came out to welcome General Grant. A few days were spent in the Yosemite, every point of interest in the valley being visited. The General climbed the rocks, rode over the peaks, and seemed to enjoy once more the freedom and the motion of outdoor life. There was a visit to the Big Trees, and we spent an hour or two wandering about, clambering over fallen trunks, and endeavoring to form some idea of the real magnitude of these gigantic phenomena of nature. So much has been written about the Yosemite that I venture but one remark: that having seen most of the sights that attract travelers in India, Asia, and Europe, it stands unparalleled as a rapturous vision of beauty and splendor. The view from Inspiration Point—as suddenly turning from the wooded road that brings you down the mountain you have before you the whole of the Yosemite Valley, every feature of its daring and mighty scenery blended as it were into a picture sweeping beneath you as you look down from your giddy height—is the most beautiful that I have seen in the world.

My journey with General Grant ended with the visit to the Yosemite. His ways led to Oregon, mine to the Atlantic coast.

So came to an end an experience that one can never hope to see again.

INDEX

MICHAEL FELLMAN is professor of history and director of the Graduate Liberal Studies Program at Simon Fraser University in Vancouver, British Columbia. His books include *Inside War: The Guerrilla Conflict in Missouri during the American Civil War* (1989), *Citizen Sherman: A Biography of William T. Sherman* (1995), and *The Making of Robert E. Lee* (2000). He also serves as advisory editor of the War/Culture/Society series for Johns Hopkins University Press.